WITHDRAWN

To Understand and To Help

Susan Isaacs. Reprinted from *Susan Isaacs: The First Biography*, by Dorothy E. M. Gardner (London: Methuen Educational Ltd., 1969).

To Understand and To Help

The Life and Work of Susan Isaacs (1885–1948)

Lydia A. H. Smith

Rutherford • Madison • Teaneck
Fairleigh Dickinson University Press
London and Toronto • Associated University Presses

© 1985 by Associated University Presses, Inc.

Associated University Presses
440 Forsgate Drive
Cranbury, NJ 08512

Associated University Presses
25 Sicilian Avenue
London WC1A 2QH, England

Associated University Presses
2133 Royal Windsor Drive
Unit 1
Mississauga, Ontario
Canada L5J 1K5

The paper used in this publication meets the minimum requirements of the American National Standard for Permanence of Paper for Printed Library Materials Z39.48-1984.

Library of Congress Cataloging in Publication Data

Smith, Lydia Averell Hurd.
   To understand and to help.

   Bibliography: p.
   Includes index.
   1. Isaacs, Susan Sutherland Fairhurst, 1885–1948.
2. Educators—England—Biography. 3. Psychoanalysts—England—Biography. 4. Child development. 5. Child rearing—England. I. Title.
LB775.I82S63   1985   370'.92'4 [B]   83-48187
ISBN 0-8386-3211-4 (alk. paper)

Printed in the United States of America

Contents

Preface		9

Part One *Susan Isaacs's Work*

1	Introduction and Biographical Sketch	17
2	The Contemporary Setting	24
	Child-Rearing Practices	24
	Systems of Psychology	29
	Studies of Childhood	35
	Mental Testing	38
	Psychoanalysis	44
	The "New Education"	48
	Government Support	56
	Summary	59
3	The Malting House School Study	62
	The Malting House School (1924–27)	62
	Intellectual Growth In Young Children (1930)	76
	Social Development in Young Children (1933)	87
	Psychoanalytic Interpretation	102
	Implications for Educators	108
4	Two Books for Lay Audiences	114
	The Nursery Years (1929)	114
	The Children We Teach (1932)	120
5	Further Practical Work	130
	The Department of Child Development, University of London (1933–43)	130
	The Educational Guidance of the School Child (1936)	134
	The Cambridge Evacuation Survey (1942)	140
6	Susan Isaacs and Others	154

Reviews of Susan Isaacs's Books 154

Contemporaries 161

John Dewey 161
Nathan Isaacs 169
Jean Piaget 182
Melanie Klein and Anna Freud 190
Cyril Burt 197
Maria Montessori 203

7 In Conclusion 210

Part Two   *Selected Documents*

1 "Ursula Wise" Columns—for *The Nursery World*, 1929–36. 225

LEADER *or* FOLLOWER? 225
YOU *MUST* OBEY! 226
THE PUNISHMENT 228
CHILDHOOD PROBLEMS 229
CHILDHOOD PROBLEMS, cont. 231
NERVOUS CHILDREN 232
OLD-FASHIONED *or* MODERN METHODS? 234
The MOTHER'S ATTITUDE *to the* CHILD 236
THE VALUE OF COMPANIONSHIP 238
TRAINING IN INDEPENDENCE 239
A CHILD'S WONDER *of* LIFE 241
A CHILD'S POINT OF VIEW 245
FIRST OCCUPATIONS 247
NERVOUS HABITS 248
CONCENTRATION: IS IT A HABIT THAT CAN BE ACQUIRED? 250
LEARNING TO READ AND WRITE: SOME MODERN METHODS 253
THE NEED FOR CONSISTENCY 256
NERVOUS HABITS AND MASTURBATION 257
CAN SELF-CONTROL BE TAUGHT? 258
"I SMACKED HER" 260

2 Articles and Talks, 1929–46 263

THE TRIALS OF THE CHILD 263
CORPORAL PUNISHMENT 266
THE CHILD AS SCIENTIST 271
THE HUMANE EDUCATION OF YOUNG CHILDREN 273
A CONTRIBUTION TO THE SOCIAL PSYCHOLOGY OF YOUNG CHILDREN 276

ORIGINAL SIN	287
PERSONAL FREEDOM AND FAMILY LIFE	291
"SAFETY FIRST" EXAMINED	298
THE ESSENTIAL NEEDS OF CHILDREN	303

3 What Active Enquiry Means for the Child, by Nathan Isaacs
   (1960)   313

Notes   322

Bibliography   334

  1. Works by Susan Isaacs   334
  2. Works by Nathan Isaacs   336
  3. Other Original Sources   338
  4. Periodicals Consulted   345
  5. Secondary Sources   345

Index   349

Preface

It has always seemed to me that effective research into educational theory and practice is too often either ignored or forgotten in a rather short time, even when it results in real progress in the way we understand and teach children. Instead of building on the work done earlier and moving ahead, we tend to reinvent the wheel, for when we do not know the history of our craft, we are condemned (as Toynbee warned us) to repeat it. I think this is particularly true of England and the United States: these countries, after all, share so much in terms of a common language and cultural heritage, but educational work done in one is sometimes little known in the other. It seems like the educational version of American industry's suspicion of anything "Not Invented Here."

Over the past ten years, thanks to sabbaticals and grants, I have lived, traveled, and studied in England, and my research has put me in touch with a body of truly remarkable educational and psychological ideas and practices, of very long standing, and much too good to ignore or lose. Influenced by the success of Pestalozzian methods, Robert Owen established in 1816, at his mill in New Lanark, the first "infant school" where small children could "play and be happy." By the middle of the nineteenth century, the followers of Friedrich Froebel found themselves welcome in England; the first kindergarten was established and Froebelian teacher training colleges were founded. The traditional English "pastoral" concern for small children was thereby strengthened by a pedagogy based on thorough understanding of the value of play and direct experience.

This early combination of theory and practice, centering on the activity and experience of children, continues to this day, I soon found. Experienced English teachers had long been working with children in quite informal, nontraditional ways, developing their interests and guiding them to deepen interest into solid knowledge by active engagement with a wide variety of materials and experiences. The work produced by these children was frequently beautiful, quite mature, and at a very high standard.

During the sixties and early seventies, many Americans made their pilgrimages to Leicestershire, to Oxfordshire, or to the West Riding of Yorkshire to see the wonders there. Books and articles about what these visitors had seen soon appeared, and in 1972, inspired and curious, I too made my journey. I had introductions to many older teachers, heads of schools, and school inspectors, all of whom were now retired but had been working along child-centered lines for many years. I found that they, in turn, had been taught their way of teaching by an earlier generation of teachers, and so on. I had had a hunch that the classrooms and schools so enthusiastically and glowingly described by American observers in the late sixties could not have sprung up overnight in that very traditional and slowly changing country, and my interviews with these retired educators proved my hunch to be correct. The result was my first book, *Activity and Experience: Sources of English Informal Education* (N.Y.: Agathon Press, 1976).

As I visited the remote corners of the lovely English countryside to which my contacts had retired, and as I talked with them over cups and cups of tea, the name Susan Isaacs came up very often. Her work, both in theory and practice, had provided an explicit rationale for the teaching methods that my friends had already been using to good effect, often simply out of concern for the quality of children's lives in school. Now they were confirmed in their practice.

Perhaps the most exciting findings of my study of teaching that is based on the activity and experience of children are (1) that it is absolutely consonant with everything we know now about cognitive and psychosocial growth and development, and (2) that it is closely allied to democratic, egalitarian ideas about citizenship in a free society. Traditional, authoritarian methods can make neither claim. These are, of course, the reasons that I say that such ideas and practices are too good to forget or lose.

By 1979, American interest in the informal teaching methods used in English schools had waned. "Back to basics" was (and is) the key slogan, often for the reason that child-centered methods had been poorly understood and therefore badly used. The serious intellectual and organizational challenge that they posed to teachers was not grasped, and in the antiauthoritarian sixties, baby and bathwater alike went out the window. Little wonder that the phrase "open classroom" has come to mean chaos and drift—in fact, the very abdication of any attempt to teach children anything they don't fancy, or to exert any sort of appropriate adult authority or control over the teaching/learning environment.

However, I continued to be interested in teaching methods that are organically and deliberately linked to children's cognitive and psychosocial development. And having begun in 1972 to hear about the work of Susan Isaacs in explicating the psychological grounds of such teaching, in 1979 I went back again to look in more detail at her work, as well as that of her husband, Nathan, in linguistic and epistemological matters. This volume is the result.

In the interests of modernization, certain usages have been changed from those of Susan Isaacs and her contemporaries. While her use of the masculine pronoun ("the child . . . he") has been maintained throughout, Dr. Isaacs's spelling of "phantasy" has been changed to the more up-to-date "fantasy." Also, titles used with women's surnames only ("Miss Low") have been removed to balance usage for men's ("Piaget").

Like any author embarked on such a study, I have more debts of gratitude than I can ever number, much less repay. But first among those who gave me so much help is surely Dr. Evelyn Lawrence Isaacs, who was a teacher at the Malting House School, a longtime associate and close friend of the Isaacses at the National Froebel Foundation, and who, when Susan Isaacs died in 1948, became the second Mrs. Nathan Isaacs. Her generous hospitality, friendly patience with my questions, and kindly interest in my work were, of course, absolutely essential to its success.

Second in line must be the people at the Froebel Educational Institute (F.E.I), especially Chris Athey, who extended her friendship and her study to me—both sources of much-appreciated support. Michael Morgan, Principal of F.E.I., extended the courtesy of the Institute to me, and its librarians were marvels of patience and resourcefulness. I was also allowed to use the excellent library of the University of London Institute of Education, with the skillful help of Miss M. Couch at every turn, and the even more extensive Senate House Library at the University of London itself.

I also visited with a number of people whom I had met during my earlier study, and with others to whom I was recommended. I was again gratified by the friendly way in which I was handed around, from one educator or psychologist to another, in a most collegial and helpful way. These people were, of course, absolutely critical to the work I was doing, since they had either known Susan and Nathan Isaacs, or had been involved in the whole educational and psychoanalytic scene to which they made such an important contribution. In listing them, I have resorted to simple alphabetical order, and I can only hope that I have left no one out: Frances Batstone, Dr. John Bowlby, Molly Brearley, S. Clement Brown, Joan Cass, Sir Alec Clegg, Emilie Davies, Alice Eden, Abigail Eliot (in the U.S.), Anna Freud, Dorothy Glynn, Dr. Ilse Hellman, Margaret Metcalfe-Smith, Rae Milne, Marion Milner, Alice Murton, Edna Oakshott, Lady Plowden, David Pyke, Margaret Roberts, Dr. Rosalie Taylor, Willem van der Eyken, Grace Wacey, M. Waddington, and Dr. Elsa Walters.

The greatest debt of gratitude, of a different kind, I owe to my family. My husband, Alan, is not only an excellent editor: he also knows what to do with a dishbrush. And our children, Andy, Bonnie, Emilie, and Ken, have taught me much about the complex and fascinating process of human maturation. Therefore, this book is dedicated to them, my husband and children, with love and thanks.

To Understand and To Help

Part One

Susan Isaacs's Work

From
SUSAN ISAACS, M.A., D.Sc.   16c, PRIMROSE HILL ROAD,

Tel.: Primrose 4753.   LONDON, N.W.3.

11.5.33

Sir Percy Nunn,
The Institute of Education,
Southampton Row,
W.C.1.

Dear Sir Percy,

         I have much pleasure in accepting the appointment of Head of the Department of Child Development, subject to the conditions stated in your letter of today.

                 Yours sincerely,

                    Susan Isaacs

The letter Susan Isaacs wrote to Sir Percy Nunn in 1933 to accept the position as head of the Department of Child Development at the University of London.

1
Introduction and Biographical Sketch

Few people have done significant, pioneering work that still matters fifty years later. Susan Isaacs, an English psychologist and educator, was one of those people. She made contributions to child development studies, psychoanalysis, and education, on both theoretical and practical levels. She founded a school for little children that was unique in concept and pedagogy; she wrote books and articles concerning her findings about intellectual and social growth; she established a training program at the first university-level department of child development at the University of London; she was a practicing psychoanalyst, a training analyst, and a recorder of important analytic discoveries; she was involved in studies of practical problems, such as school record keeping and the wartime evacuation scheme, bringing to each her psychological understanding of children and making specific recommendations for solutions; she gave lectures and workshops for teachers all over the country about children and their social and cognitive growth; she understood the new mental tests and knew how to make best use of them; she answered hundreds of letters from mothers and nurses and helped them to deal wisely with their children.

She probably did more than anyone else to integrate the increasing theoretical knowledge of child psychology with practical methodology in both education and in child-rearing practices. Her professional purpose was, in her husband's words, "to understand to help": to understand more and more about children and their needs, and to help others to do so as well, especially adults with responsibility for children.

Today, reading her many books and articles, one is struck by the contemporaneity of their message. Although she was very much a part of her times in the fields of child psychology, mental testing, psychoanalysis, and progressive education, what she said about children's development and the role played by the adults in their lives has a considerable claim on contemporary attention.

Susan Isaacs was born Susan Fairhurst, in 1885 in Bromley Cross, near Bolton in Lancashire.[1] She was the ninth child of her parents in this north of England cotton mill town, where her father was both a journalist and a

Methodist lay preacher. He was a man of intellect and scholarship, severe in his standards of conduct, but capable of inspiring affection nonetheless. Her childhood was not easy, and in later life, Susan remembered meals of bread and water as punishment for infractions like a grammatical error or failure to apologize. The family was hardly rich and had to observe a careful economy in order to maintain itself. Much of this burden fell on the daughters, who had to help extensively with the housework, make their own clothes, and do without outings and other opportunities that money could have bought.

More important than these problems, however, were the deaths and other separations in the family, from which Susan suffered very much as a child. Before she was eight months old, a brother only a little older than she developed pneumonia and died. During his illness, her mother was preoccupied with him and left Susan much to herself, though she was still an infant. Before Susan was three, another much older brother left, against the family's wishes, to join the merchant marines; she had loved him very much, and felt his departure deeply. When Susan was four, her mother, always an energetic and careful wife, fell seriously ill and lived only two more years. "The household which had been so perfectly cared for gradually fell into disorder and discomfort, and Susan remembered sometimes playing not as a happy child plays, but as a desperate one trying to find comfort or at least distraction."[2] Her father soon remarried, to the nurse who had cared for Susan's mother, but Susan and her stepmother never established a warm relationship.

When Susan went to school, she hoped to find there an orderly place where she could learn new things. Instead, she found a teacher whom she badly wanted to please, but who insisted on a strict conformity in all matters. Despite this poor experience in her first school, Susan's enthusiasm for learning was not dimmed. She held all her life a "deep conviction that learning is one of the ways in which we achieve stability and happiness, and that young children need to be taught in ways which they can understand."[3]

With her older brother, Enoch, Susan began to read philosophy, and this influence led to another sad separation, though a temporary one. She became an agnostic, and her father, shocked and unable to tolerate this repudiation of what he stood for, would not speak to her for two years. She was removed from school, although she was not quite fifteen, since education had apparently made her godless. Two other sisters continued in school and even went to teacher-training colleges, while Susan helped her stepmother and older sister, Bessie, with housework.

Nonetheless, Susan continued her own education, reading voraciously, listening to the conversations of her father and his guests, rambling the nearby hills, and talking with friends about virtually all varieties of subjects. The home was full of books and ideas, despite its severity, and both Bessie and Susan were avid students. They discussed everything from Darwin to women's suffrage, vegetarianism to music, labor relations to biology. In all these areas, Susan demonstrated her wish not only to understand new ideas but also to make use of them in some service to others.

Still, Susan Fairhurst had not yet found a focus for her brilliance or her energy. She next held a series of three teaching positions, both as a private governess and in a school; feeling her lack of formal training, she begged her father to let her qualify at Manchester University as an infant-school teacher. She was by then about twenty-two, older than most students, and she soon distinguished herself among them for her ability to grasp theories and ideas, compare and weigh them, and come to a sensible estimate of their soundness in practice. At Manchester she came into contact with the ideas of Friedrich Froebel, long influential in English educational thinking, and with those of the American philosopher John Dewey. Throughout her life, she felt that the concern for children that the Froebelians exemplified and the progressive educational ideas of Dewey were major influences on her thinking.

At Manchester, too, she attracted the notice of the head of her training course, who talked about her to a university professor. The upshot was that she was invited to try for a full university degree (beyond that of a teacher-training course). The professor's kindly interest helped persuade her father to let her continue her studies, but a greater difficulty was completing the required academic qualifications to enter the university. It was, however, typical of her intelligence and concentration that in three months she mastered enough Greek and German to qualify in the necessary two languages.

When she finally entered the university, Susan was twenty-four, and at that age she lost her father, who succumbed to a perforated ulcer. This was another serious loss for her, since they had become fully reconciled and she had been much involved in caring for him toward the end of his life.

Fortunately, however, he left her a legacy that permitted her to go on with her work at Manchester, where she finally took a first-class honors degree in philosophy. Her major professor had become interested in her work and its future; he brought her to the notice of a colleague at Cambridge, who in turn got her a scholarship at that university for further work. Her mind had been turning from philosophy to biology and especially to psychology, and at Cambridge she found full opportunity to study the latter, moving her "more and more away from the generalities and abstractions of philosophy to the concrete and living field of psychology and the possibilities of knowledge-increasing research."[4]

Although she spent only a year at Cambridge, Susan learned much there of general psychology and the basics of research, and distinguished herself to all who knew her. She also found herself increasingly interested in children and child development, and she was next appointed a lecturer at Darlington Training College, which trained infant-school teachers. Here she began to demonstrate her ability to explain complex ideas clearly, to teach beginners in ways that brought out the best in them, and to help them relate theory to practice in real situations. She was remembered for her constant search for "true methods of teaching" based on her growing understanding of children's real needs and interests.

Susan then lectured for a year at Manchester University in logic, but moved to London after marrying her former instructor in biology and botany, William Brierley. There she was invited to give lectures in psychology for the London University tutorial classes, and also at the Workers' Educational Association (W.E.A.). Her first approach to psychology was biological, as is clear in the book she wrote in 1921, *An Introduction to Psychology*. At the same time, however, she was interested in the ideas of Freudian psychoanalysis and began her own first long analysis, with J. C. Flügel, so as to grasp this new discipline at first hand. It was typical of her not only to reach out for new ideas in the abstract, but also to involve herself personally with them and let them change her life, if that followed as she had, earlier, been unable to read metaphysical and logical writings without making them part of her life by becoming an agnostic. Later on, in Europe, she underwent a brief analysis with Otto Rank in order to understand his ideas thoroughly and later still, when she learned of Melanie Klein's interpretation and development of Freud's views about the analysis of very young children, she entered still another extended analysis, this time with Joan Rivière.

While lecturing in London, Susan Brierley began to realize that her marriage was not satisfactory, either to herself or to her husband. It was subsequently dissolved, although this was an unusual occurrence at that time, but again she had to act upon her convictions. In 1922 she married Nathan Isaacs, whose intellectual acumen she had much respected ever since they had met at one of her lectures at the W.E.A. Although he was ten years her junior, there was no mistake about this marriage, for it became a rich and fulfilling partnership, both intellectual and emotional, that sustained them both for twenty-six years. By 1922, also, she was qualified to take patients in psychoanalysis, and continued to treat both adults and children for the rest of her professional life.

In 1924, when Susan Isaacs was thirty-nine and had had years of biological and psychological work, the opportunity arose for her to design and direct a school for young children along definitely scientific lines. Geoffrey Pyke had put an advertisement in *The New Statesman* for a woman of exactly her qualifications and, after much discussion, she and Nathan went to Cambridge to found the Malting House School. For the next three and a half years, she worked closely with a group of little children, studied their intellectual and social development, and developed a method of teaching that promoted that growth.

In 1927, the Isaacses left the Malting House School, and in 1929 it was closed for lack of money. Susan then plunged into the work of writing up her data from the observations she had made at the school; in 1930 she published *Intellectual Growth in Young Children,* and in 1933 *Social Development in Young Children* followed. A third volume of case studies had been planned, to round out the work, but it was never completed.

In these years also, she continued receiving patients daily for psychoanalysis, wrote numerous technical and nontechnical journal articles, served on a variety of editorial boards, reviewed Piaget's first five books, lectured all over the country to teachers who wanted to learn more about children, began her second analysis, became a training analyst at the Institute of Psycho-Analysis, and even found time to write an important weekly column for mothers and nurses, answering their questions in the pages of *The Nursery World* as "Ursula Wise." Two other important books were published at this period in her life; *The Nursery Years* (1929), dealing with the growth of children from birth to age six, and *The Children We Teach* (1932), which continued her account through years seven to eleven.

One of her many friends in the educational and psychological world was Sir Percy Nunn, then director of the University of London Institute of Education. In 1932, he came to her with a proposal to set up at the university a new center to advance the study of child growth and development and to train experienced teachers and other educators to take up leading positions in the field. Susan's interest in the growing field of psychoanalysis was great, however, and she was concerned that she would lose her daily, close contact with patients if she undertook to implement Sir Percy's plan at the University of London. Nonetheless, she decided to do so, and from 1933 to 1943, she was the head of the Department of Child Development. Her appointment was never officially more than half-time, although she invested far more time and energy in the work of the department and her students than that might imply.

Still, she had time to continue her lectures and articles, to sit on a variety of editorial boards of professional journals, to tutor advanced students in psychology at the University of London, to take patients in analysis, and to correspond personally with the many people who sought her advice and help. In 1935, she wrote *Psychological Aspects of Child Development,* which provided a careful summary of the progress to date in child development studies, including work on cognitive growth, mental tests and their results, and the psychoanalytic treatment of very young children.

In 1936, with Sir Fred Clark of the University of London Institute of Education, Susan was asked by the educational authorities in Wiltshire to develop a sound, usable record-keeping scheme for teachers. The result was *The Educational Guidance of the School Child,* containing general background material about child psychology, and practical recommendations for making regular observations of children and using them appropriately in planning for their needs and interests.

In 1937 she was a member of an international team of distinguished educators, organized by the New Education Fellowship (N.E.F.) and the Australian Council for Educational Research, sent out to a conference in Australia and New Zealand on new ideas in education. There they gave lectures to large audiences and made many contacts with colleagues, including some who were en route to the United States and Canada.

When the Second World War threatened, many city children and whole schools were evacuated to the countryside of England, to avoid German bombing. With her friend, Sybil Clement Brown (and later Melanie Klein), Susan Isaacs moved to Cambridge, continuing to take patients in analysis, completing the training of students for whom she was still responsible, and commuting to be with Nathan on weekends, since he was working in the war effort elsewhere.

At this time, authorities in charge of evacuation plans became puzzled as to why evacuees sometimes had problems settling down, and in particular why many returned to their city homes, even under the known threat of bombardment. Some of the children had come to Cambridge, and with the help of colleagues like Clement Brown, Melanie Klein, R. H. Thouless, John Bowlby, and others, Susan Isaacs put together a team of investigators. They hoped to analyze the situation in detail, and to shed some light on the psychological problems encountered.

In 1941, under Susan's editorship, the group published *The Cambridge Evacuation Survey,* describing the results of the interviews and written statements that they had collected from the many sorts of people involved in the whole evacuation program: officials, social workers, teachers, foster parents, and even the children themselves. On the basis of this study, and a thorough knowledge of psychological and developmental processes, the investigators established that the scheme to evacuate people to protect them from physical harm had been poorly planned with regard to emotional needs, so that problems arose which might have been avoided with more understanding and forethought. Susan Isaacs also published other articles important to an understanding of the dislocations caused by the war situation, including "Fatherless Children" and "Children in Institutions." Part of the latter piece was later republished and widely circulated as "The Essential Needs of Children." And for an American audience, she wrote "Children of Great Britain in Wartime."

By 1945, the war was over, but Isaacs did not return to the Department of Child Development. She had been engaged in a long battle with cancer, and now she knew she was losing it. In the next two years, she underwent a number of unsuccessful treatments, as well as surgery for a duodenal ulcer. Her own professional background made it impossible for her not to know exactly what was happening; she spent her last years producing as much work as she could in the time that remained, chiefly bringing together papers and lectures that she had prepared earlier, and now collected into

Childhood and After (1948), *Troubles of Children and Parents* (1948), and two chapters (one in collaboration with Paula Heimann) of Melanie Klein's book, *Developments in Psycho-Analysis* (1948).

When Susan Isaacs died in 1948, tributes from people who had known and benefited from her work poured in from all over the world. She had had an unusually active and varied career that had managed to combine successfully the theory of human development with its practical application in real situations with children.

2
The Contemporary Setting

"The history of childhood," writes a modern author, "is a nightmare from which we have only recently begun to awaken."[1] Susan Isaacs's whole career was devoted to awakening parents and educators to the real needs and characteristics of children, and to the great importance of studying their development in order to provide most wisely for their "optimal growth."[2] The environment in which she carried on her work was increasingly conducive to this effort. Childhood had taken on new signifiance and child care had been improved; child-labor laws were passed and educational opportunities more widely extended; the social sciences produced useful studies of human intelligence and of childhood, educational practices were becoming more child-centered, child guidance clinics and mental testing were established, and the government's committee reports, debates, and Acts of Parliament increasingly supported the public care and protection of children.

Child-Rearing Practices

The idea that childhood was a separate period worthy of special attention was not new, however, Philosophers and theologians had long known that childhood experiences powerfully affect adult character, and had set about explaining their views of the nature of the child and the appropriate methods of training him for adulthood. And as their views of the relationship between the individual and society varied, so did their ideas about child rearing and character development. Plato's *Republic* is only the first in this long series of statements about education for the young.

The major views that influenced European thought, in more modern times, fall into three categories. For John Locke, the child's nature is receptive and malleable; in order to develop in him the disciplined, rational character that the Enlightenment period valued, the child should be habituated early to approved manners; adults (especially fathers) should never do anything in front of the child that they would not wish him to imitate, and growing boys should be given wide experience and contacts:

"the best fence against the world is a thorough knowledge of it." The authority of the father should be felt by the child, while at the same time the child should also realize that the father only insists on what is best for him.

Rousseau's views of childhood and child rearing were as much a reaction and protest against the social mores of his time as a fresh step ahead for children. Locke had accepted the order of society as he found it; Rousseau saw society as a corrupt and distorting influence on the child, whose pure nature was closest to God's. His cry, "Retournez à la Nature," was truly revolutionary in his day.[3] For him, the child is all good, and since contact with society can only damage him, he should be kept from it as long as possible. If possible, he should contract no habits at all, but rather follow the dictates of his nature, shaped only by the sensations that come to him and the natural consequences of his responses. A natural, expressive man, capable of the fullest living and untainted by mere conventions will result.

Both these views were countered by the long-standing belief that children are born in the grip of evil and that their wills must be broken and brought into submission. This essentially Calvinistic idea was spelled out in great detail in Puritan domestic catechisms like Cotton Mather's *A Family Well-Ordered*, a strict code of family discipline under the father's dictation, governing every minute of the day. If young children could not learn to obey their earthly fathers, how could they obey God when they were older? And since children were born evil, being the offspring of the flesh, they would surely be damned if, by conformity and submission, they did not show some early "evidences of election." "Break their wills that you may save their souls," preached John Wesley; "If they are not too little to die, they are not too little to go to Hell," growled John Cotton.

This harsh view of childhood was not only characteristic of the Puritans, but runs parallel with gentler ideas to this day.

> These two attitudes run in counterpoint . . . those who like children against those who do not; those who trust nature versus those who fear God; those who discipline lightly opposed to those who believe that pain is good for the young; the Age of Reason confronting the Puritan Ethic.[4]

Whether adults are child-haters or child-lovers, in any period of history, the real question is how far their treatment of the young is dictated by their own or the child's needs. Human childhood is exceptionally long, as compared to any other animal's, a lengthy period of dependency. It can be a time of successful adaptation and growth, but it is also a vulnerable time, when adults can exploit children's weakness and their natural desire for relatedness with their caretakers. Modes of child rearing differ enormously, and they depend more on the intimate attitudes and feelings that govern in the homes where children and parents meet than on philosophers' formulations.

One contemporary historian, Lloyd DeMause,[5] has developed a "psychogenic" description of child-care modes that he believes have evolved over the centuries. Whether or not his historical account is accurate, his description of types of family interactions, especially under stress, is useful.

Disturbing problems arise when an adult is confronted with a child who is demanding, disobedient, unruly, or needy in some way. This generational conflict sets up a variety of reactions in the adult, reactions that DeMause believes can be traced in sequence from the earliest periods of civilization to today. Faced with an upsetting scene with his child, the adult, in fantasy,* regresses to his own childhood and faces his own childish needs and anxieties again. Sometimes the disturbance is simply the presence of an unwanted child; sometimes it is a child acting in ways natural to his immaturity, but too disturbing to an adult who may have only just grown beyond them and won some measure of control over the fears he felt as a child.

In responding to the child who needs something from him, the adult does so appropriately or not, depending on how he reexperiences his own needs from years ago, and the anxieties they aroused at the time. He may then react to the child by *reversal,* to use DeMause's psychoanalytic term: the adult sees the child not as he is, but as a person who can meet his (the adult's) own needs in some way. If he responds by *projection,* he assumes that his own feelings of distress are felt by the child also, and responds to them as such. But if his reaction is *empathic,* he identifies the child's needs and satisfies them realistically and appropriately. The adult's ability to put aside his own unconscious, earlier needs and see the child as a separate person governs his response. Each of the three reactions described is more mature and realistic than the preceding one, and DeMause believes that they, in turn, characterize child-parent interactions over the course of time, and are in fact the cause of the evolution of civilization:

> [They are] a continuous sequence of closer approaches between parent and child as generation after generation of parents slowly overcame their anxieties and began to develop the capacity to identify and satisfy the needs of their children.
> ... Psychogenic theory can, I think, provide a genuinely new paradigm for the study of history. It reverses the usual "mind as tabula rasa," and instead considers the "world as tabula rasa," with each generation born into a world of meaningless objects which are invested with meaning only if the child receives a certain kind of care.[6]

The meaning that children are able to make of the world heavily depends on how their early needs are met by the adults closest to them, and to what extent they fear being punished or deprived, especially when conflicts arise. All three types of adult reactions have undoubtedly existed in all

---

*Susan Isaacs's spelling of the word was "phantasy." See also below, chap. 6, n.124.

societies, among adults who care for children, past and present, but DeMause believes that not until the nineteenth and early twentieth centuries was it possible to consider that:

> the raising of a child became less a process of conquering its will than of training it, guiding it into proper paths, teaching it to conform, socializing it. The socializing mode is still thought of by most people as the only model within which discussion of child care can proceed, and it has been the source of all twentieth-century models, from Freud's ... to Skinner's.[7]

Yet this "socializing mode" did not necessarily proceed from an understanding of the real needs of children. It was more kindly than earlier, brutal forms of child care, yet adult needs to use children for their own purposes were still only too possible.

Novelists who depict families of the nineteenth century, for example, testified that the effect on the child of this closer approach between parents and children could be disastrous as well as satisfying, and could produce emotional cripples. Samuel Butler's *The Way of All Flesh* shows an authoritarian, depriving father who demanded great deference from his son, who actively hated him all the time that he was conforming to the older man's strict views. D. H. Lawrence's *Sons and Lovers* shows a mother so starved for love from her husband that she turns to her son for satisfaction and companionship, preventing him from living separately from her. In both, parents' needs governed their child rearing, to the detriment of the offspring under their care.

Still, the idea grew that the middle-class Victorian home could be a nest, a safe haven from the world. Socializing the child was not cruelly done, but certain expectations were made clear, so that, in form if not in substance, the serene home atmosphere was kept. Particular forms of unacceptable behavior were rigorously stamped out, especially those that aroused Victorian anxiety: early sexual interests and/or masturbation, which was thought to lead directly to insanity. Indeed, mechanical instruments of great ingenuity were devised to make sure the child could never "touch himself."

In England more than on the Continent, children were typically toilet trained from the earliest months onward; they were kept separate from adults in nurseries where the nanny held undisputed sway; they were often given food that was different and less interesting than that of the adults; and while they often had long hours of playtime, their contact with their parents was strictly "on their best behavior."[8]

All this is not to say that parents in the past did not love their children, for parents have always loved them, especially when they are not troublesome. And in the nineteenth century, just because child rearing *was* seen to be an important matter, with all the pressure for respectability, self-control, and good manners typical of the day, both socialization into approved patterns of behavior and the extinction of disapproved actions took on increased significance. When successful, this mode of child rearing produced adults (especially men) who were self-disciplined, well-mannered, able to get along with their superiors—just what was needed for an industrialized, expanding, capitalistic society. Women, for their part, were to maintain the homes as "the happiest place on earth," a retreat from the harsh business world for their men and filled with pleasantly behaved children. A possible result of such relationships could have been certain "explosive" equality born of the mixed signals being sent and received: good manners and a serene atmosphere may have been created only by massive repression of natural feelings, love purchased at the price of surrender.[9]

Beginning in the mid-twentieth century, DeMause thinks, a still more appropriate mode of child rearing has become possible, the "helping mode."

> The helping mode involved the proposition that the child knows better than the parent what it needs at each stage of life . . . there is no attempt at all to discipline or form "habits." Children are neither struck nor scolded, and are apologized to if yelled at under stress. . . . helping a young child reach its daily goals means continually responding to it, playing with it, tolerating its regressions, being its servant rather than the other way around, interpreting its emotional conflicts, and providing the objects specific to its evolving interests.[10]

There seems to have been an important transition in child-rearing beliefs and practices: interest in children and improvements in their care and the conditions of their life did grow substantially, as scholars in the field of the history of the family agree.[11] Susan Isaacs's work was carried on at precisely that time, as she tried to help parents and educators move away from the "socialization" mode toward the more "helping" mode of child rearing and education. In summary:

> Childhood had become both interesting and serious, and the standardized indifference or brutality of earlier centuries were mitigated in the nineteenth by greater understanding.
> . . . at the end of the century came a new movement toward freedom, when [it was] predicted that the twentieth century would be "The Century of the Child."
> Solicitude for infants seemed like a virtue of the modern period, it is true, but it could not, at first, be truly enlightened. At the very least, however, the nineteenth century was the time when public bodies began to think of children as children, with special needs because of their helplessness and vulnerability, rather than as small adults with the right to hire themselves out for sixteen hours a day, or as the chattels of their parents. The change in sentiment that began within the family had, before the century was over, grown to work great changes in society as a whole.[12]

Systems of Psychology

In the scholarly world, this period also saw the rapid expansion of psychology as a recognized field of study, with investigations into the nature of man's intelligence and consciousness, and studies of child growth and development. Research took two main directions: structuralists focused on "primary forms of experience and the interrelations of sense experience"; functionalists "stressed adjustment and adaptation."[13]

The earlier work of Darwin had, of course, been a great watershed. No longer could human nature be the sole province of speculation, whether philosophical or theological. As his evolutionary theory came to be accepted, human nature was seen from a biological, developmental point of view, to be observed and studied like that of any other living organism.

British psychology, or mental philosophy, had for a long time been primarily associationist, deriving from the empirical view of mind. Knowledge and ideas were seen as the results of combining or associating sensations received from outer experience, so that mind was essentially a mechanism, automatically processing the data sent in by the senses. It was built up of sensory elements that, together, defined its contents and powers. This mechanistic view of mind was radically altered by the evolutionary one, which emphasized the human mind as active, adaptive, and purposive; consciousness and intelligence had evolved over time as a unique tool of adaptation to environmental conditions.

The evolutionary idea did not originate with Darwin, however, although his immense collection of data and careful analysis gave it its most complete and convincing expression. For years, geologists had been disputing the biblical description of the origin of the earth, the special creation of man, the effects of the Flood on the world, and so on, trying to establish that the earth was a product of millions of years of slow change and that the appearance of life on the planet was part of this gradual development. So too with man, whose origins were seen to be biological, not divine.

Before Darwin, Lamarck had been working out his theory of the inheritance of acquired human characteristics, over many eons, as mankind slowly developed into an ever more complex and adaptive creature. Herbert Spencer published his great *Principles of Psychology* in 1855, and the *System of Synthetic Philosophy* between 1860 and 1893, and in these massive works he attempted to demonstrate that everything in the universe is fundamentally related to everything else in a unified, lawful way. Development had always proceeded in the same way, in stages, toward increased differentiation or complexity of structure or function, to periods of integration at the newer level of adaptation. Evolution, in Spencer's words, is "change from incoherent, indefinite homogeneity to coherent, definite heterogeneity," by means of the constant adjustment and adaptation of inner capacities to outer conditions. This process, for him, was as true of plants and fishes as of mankind and human societies. Man's mind, then, has come to be what it is as a result of successfully coping with environment over time, achieving higher and more varied levels of behavior and intelligence, and passing on traits acquired by adaptation from generation to generation. Mind and body were no longer seen as separate entities, but rather as intimately and organically connected: "both sprang from the same soil."[14] And in this gradual process of evolving ever more adaptive, complex modes of functioning, acquired human characteristics became the "innate possessions of the race."[15]

The evolutionary theory, thus applied to humanity, explained how heredity controlled both the general characteristics of human mental structure as well as individual differences among people, as the laws of natural selection and variation of species had operated in different environments over uncounted millions of generations.

> No one before Darwin [was] able to treat the total personality as the product of complex developmental processes beginning at birth and going on throughout life.[16]
>
> All post-Darwinian psychologies have had to deal in one way or another with the unity of the living system, with the profound internal motivating forces which appear in behavior, and with the basic problem of adaptation to the environment.[17]

Darwin's method of arriving at his theory was as influential as the theory itself. He based his conclusions on direct observation of the characteristics and behavior of a great variety of organisms, whose likenesses and differences he was trying to understand. The collection of data systematically observed in natural settings came to be the more scientific method of psychologists (and others) who came after him, whether they set out to study lower animals, primitive societies, the growth of children, the nature of cognition, or individual differences among human beings.

It remained for Francis Galton, Darwin's half-cousin, to make use of quantitative measures in studying how human beings vary one from another. Like Darwin, he was interested in the effects of heredity as opposed to those of environment, but rather than look at the entire human race and its slow, adaptive development over time, he was fascinated by the variations within the race in individual people or families. It was his view that hererdity governed each person's intelligence far more powerfully than the environment into which he might be born.

> Man's natural abilities are derived by inheritance, under exactly the same limitations as are the form and physical features of the whole organic world.[18]

In his *Hereditary Genius,* published in the same year as Darwin's *Descent of Man,* he compiled statistics to show that certain families in England had produced more than their share of great men, and that their extraordinary talents could not be a product of environmental influences but rather of inherited traits of genius. If this were true, then by selective breeding *(eugenics)* human beings could improve and increase the overall intelligence of the race, and at the same time reduce the incidence of mental defectiveness.

> I conclude that each generation has enormous power over the natural gifts of those that follow, and maintain that it is a duty we owe to humanity to investigate the range of that power, and to exercise it in a way that, without being unwise to ourselves, shall be most advantageous to future inhabitants of the earth.
> ... The processes of evolution are in constant and spontaneous activity, some pushing towards the bad, some towards the good. Our part is to watch for opportunities to intervene by checking the former and giving free play to the latter ... with the view of estimating the possible effects of reasonable political action in the future, in gradually raising the present miserably low standard of the human race to one in which the Utopias in the dreamland of philanthropists may become practical possibilities.[19]

It actually seemed as if man's scientific knowledge could change the development of civilization for the better—indeed, that it was a duty that human intelligence had been evolved to undertake.

Galton's use of numerical measurement of human traits and his belief in the heritability of intelligence made him the father of statistics and mental testing; he also left £45,000. to University College, London, to establish a Chair of Eugenics. The Eugenics Society soon followed, whose purpose was

> to spread a knowledge of the laws of heredity so far as they are surely known, and so far as that knowledge may affect the improvement of the race.[20]

At the same time that statistical methods were being worked out to measure, describe, and control human traits, there were also several systematic descriptions of human nature from the new, evolutionary perspective. Ward's famous entry in the *Encyclopedia Britannica* on "Psychology" created a stir when it was published in the edition of 1886. It was the first time that the topic had been treated separately in the encyclopedia, and not under "Metaphysics." As opposed to the associationist view of consciousness, Ward wrote that sensory "presentations" in the mind occur in an ongoing, complex, shifting continuum, and therefore cannot be analyzed or separated into units. Mind is active and functional; "attention" is its major conscious activity; the self or ego is the basic factor in awareness; and it is the self that integrates and unifies the flow of sensory and motor data as they appear before it in experience. This more dynamic view of mental activity was clearly more in accord with evolutionary thinking about the develoment of mind, consciousness, and mental functioning.

Sully's *Outline of Psychology* appeared in 1884, and *The Human Mind* in 1893; for years they were the basic texts in the field. Soon after Sully's publications appeared, G. F. Stout wrote *A Manual of Psychology* (1899). Using introspection rather than measurement, as well as observation of others' behavior and inferences about their states of mind, he sought to understand the general, fundamental "laws of mental process," in the belief that

> we must assume that as with physical occurrences, so in the sphere of the mind, events occur in an orderly way.[21]

Psychology, for Stout, is the study of the processes of knowing, feeling, and striving or willing (a classification first suggested by Kant), as they appear in consciousness, which itself is the relationship between mental and bodily states and the outside world. These processes work together in a unified, functional way to harmonize individual needs with environmental conditions and achieve satisfaction.

Two American manuals of psychology appeared in this period: one by John Dewey in 1887, and the more influential work, *Principles of Psychology* by William James, in 1890. James's work was a similarly dynamic, functionalist view of man's mind. However, instead of analyzing human mental life into its cognitive, affective, and conative aspects, he emphasized the unity and flow of conscious experience. The "stream of consciousness" was dynamic, fluctuating, at every moment a combination of individually acquired experiences and memories with innate dispositions and instincts. Its functions are two: consciousness leads to knowledge (or "knowing") and to action, and these two are closely related, for the purpose of knowledge is appropriate action, and the result of action is further practical knowledge. Man is

> primarily a practical being, whose mind is given to him to aid in adapting him to this world's life. . . . We cannot escape our destiny, which is practical; and even our most theoretic faculties contribute to its working out.[22]

McDougall took a somewhat similar tack. In his popular *Introduction to Social Psychology* (1908) and in later books, he tried to move psychology away from a merely descriptive and analytic study of consciousness, toward a more active, functional, vigorous view of man as a purposive, goal-seeking, striving organism.

> The manifestation of purpose and the striving to achieve an end is, then, the mark of behaviour; and behaviour is the characteristic of living things. . . . the mind of any organism is the sum of the enduring conditions of its purposive activities. . . . that sum is not a mere aggregation, but rather an organised system of which each part is functionally related to the rest in definite fashion.[23]

The goals man sets for himself, reflecting his innate needs, provide motivation for his activities. "The essential nature of the mind is to govern present action by anticipation of the future in the light of past experiences."[24] Human motives or "instincts" are expressed by means of conscious purpose, and as the "purposive activities" accumulate, they develop into an "organised system" of sentiments. Of these, the "self-regarding sentiment" is, in a mature human being, the governing force behind any action or behavior.

Meanwhile, Spearman was studying the nature of cognition itself, using the statistical measurement techniques that Galton had pioneered and that Pearson had later refined. He analyzed its basic characteristics by correlating the experimental data from mental tests, and in 1904 he postulated his theory of general intelligence and specific abilities:

> The existence, on the one hand, of a general factor of ability (subsequently called g), varying in power from one individual to another, but operative to some extent in all performances; and, on the other hand, of a large number of specific abilities (collectively called s), some one of which at least is also operative in each performance, though the relative importance of g and s may vary greatly from one performance to another.[25]

Spearman developed a long series of experiments aimed at measuring intelligence objectively; using Pearson's correlational techniques, he then compared test performances and found what he described as a general, underlying function of mind: "the universal unity of the intellective function."[26] In his later books, *The Nature of Intelligence and the Principles of Cognition* (1923) and *The Abilities of Man* (1927), he reported fully on these research results.

Mind, for Spearman, was more than simply adaptive, however: it was also creative, capable of making new meaning. It apprehends experiences with the world of things, people, and events; it relates ideas to one another and to past experience; and it makes fresh meaning in so doing. Mind grows in a unified, gradual way, accumulating experiences and contributing to understanding them by *noetic synthesis* (using Stout's term). This process is governed by heredity and varies widely within human populations. The specific factor, s, influences the operation of g and causes it to vary in adpativeness becauses of individual differences in, for instance, sensosry acuity, muscular power, or mental retentiveness. Spearman's view was, then, a theory of cognition that was at once functional and unified, and that comprehended both the common human ability to adapt to and act upon the world, and also the specific ways in which one person is different from another.

In 1921 Susan Isaacs (then still Susan Brierley) brought out her own *Introduction to Psychology,* which derived from her lectures in psychology for the Workers' Educational Association, and was addressed to a nonprofessional audience. Although she spoke from her own point of view about psychology, she presented no new system of thought, but instead a careful review of the main fields of inquiry at the time, and the methods by which psychologists were doing their work.

> My aim has been to present a consistent point of view with regard to some of the outstanding controversies which tend to bewilder the beginning student—a point of view in harmony with a biological outlook.[27]

She emphasized the necessity of looking at human behavior from a biological point of view:

> The theory of evolution laid the foundations of the scientific approach to the study of human nature. Any serious interpretation of psychology must be in harmony with this fundamental attitude; . . . advantages of this view are that it starts from simple facts of immediate observation, and that it leads us to look upon the data of our science as the dynamic processes of life, continually changing and developing, rather than as separable and fixed mental "states" or "faculties."[28]

In the first part of her book, Brierley goes over the "scope and method" of psychology, and in the second she deals with progress made to date in studying some of psychology's major problems, namely, the "wish," the relationship of the human organism to its environment, instinct and the origins of intelligence, and the conscious and unconscious aspects of human nature.

In 1928, she revised her book and added an appendix that was written to bring the original account up to date, with regard to the "five main directions in which the general theory of psychology had developed in the interim." These were presented in a series of brief summaries of progress made. The "Gestalt" school of thought, including work by Köhler, Koffka, and Wertheimer, laid emphasis on the "structure," "shape," or "form" in an act of perception, as being distinct from and unifying the basic elements of any sensation or mental image. An insight into the total pattern of an experience provided meaning that went beyond its separate parts, and was crucial in learning. Spearman's experimental and statistical work

[has] led not only to a firmer belief in the existence of *g*, a general factor in intelligence, and various specific factors, *s*, in abilities operating in specified directions, but also to the development of theories of the cognitive processes which, it is claimed, lay the first foundations of a genuine science of cognition.[29]

She then discussed the work of Piaget, recognizing very early how important it was, although at the time only one volume had been translated; she was to deal extensively with his first five volumes, as they appeared in succession (see chapter 6). She felt that the behaviorist school led by Watson

is making many very useful experimental studies of the behaviour of young infants in the nursery, by methods exactly comparable to those familiar in the study of the young of other animals.[30]

She considered these studies important but

the refusal of the behaviourists to consider facts of consciousness remains a severe limitation on their final contribution.[31]

Finally, she described the further development of psychoanalytic theory, and its deeper understanding of major mental illnesses, the structure of the ego, the use of "play" techniques with very young children, and primitive customs and societies. True to her biological point of view, she concludes, "the approach of psycho-analysis is, of course, genetic through and through."[32] And, while recognizing that McDougall's "self-regarding sentiment" is a useful concept and not unlike Freud's superego in its effect on human behavior, because of her own deepening knowledge of psychoanalysis she dismissed McDougall's view as "superficial and trivial" by comparison.

However, she, like many others in the field, was increasingly turning her attention to the study of childhood: one result of evolutionary theory was that human traits were increasingly explained in developmental terms, that is, by tracing their origins not only in the earliest development of the race, but also in any one child.

Studies of Childhood

Studies of childhood, in fact, began with Darwin himself. In 1877, he published in *Mind* his article, "Biographical Sketch of an Infant," the result of the minute, day-by-day observation of his own child. Typically, he noted down every change in behavior as it occurred in exact detail. In 1888, Wilhelm Preyer published *The Mind of a Child*, a similarly detailed set of observations of his son. Preyer focused on the growth of the senses, on the child's ability to express his wishes or desires, and evidences of the growth of intellect, especially as embodied in language. In his preface, he puts forward his point of view about the relative influence of heredity and environment on development:

> The fundamental activities of mind, which are manifested after birth, do not originate after birth. . . . each one, by means of experience, [must] fill out and animate anew his inherited endowments, the remains of the experiences and activities of his ancestors.[33]

In his account of development, Preyer laid particular stress on the importance of language in the young child, both the language of gesture and movement, and speech itself. For him, language is the result of the evolution of intellect over the ages, and is man's primary means of achieving his purposes. It grows in adaptive capacity as children grow from the expressive movements that infants make to gain attention and the satisfaction of their needs, to the verbal expression of their ideas and desires.

In 1895 James Sully published his *Studies of Childhood,* long a classic in the field, and also a result of minute observation of the infancy and early childhood of his own children. For Sully, the child is a little primitive; the development of reasoning powers recapitulates that of the race. Mental life begins with imagination, freely operating within the mind, but gradually moving toward observing and responding to the outside world. Then come ideas of similarity and difference between things, moving to generalizing, classifying and naming, and thus thought itself appears. In all this, mind's "essential characteristic [is] an impulse to comprehend things, to reduce the confusing multiplicity to order and system."[34] He, too, saw mind as adaptive, always trying to make sense out of experience and doing so with increasing precision as the child develops.

William Stern's *Psychology of Early Childhood Up to the Sixth Year of Age,* first published in Germany in 1914 and revised and enlarged in 1924, included lengthy extracts from his wife's diary as well as his own observations of their own three children over many years. Like Preyer, Stern's view of heredity and environment was interactionist: psychic development is a matter of "convergence between inner qualities and outer conditions,"[35] that influence each other in varying degrees in different children. He also took a holistic and lawful view of the essential nature of man and its development.

> Psychic development is no haphazard succession of events, but the regular unfolding of the periods of a unified growth . . .[36]

> All the divisions inside the personality are relative only, mere abstractions—which however are requisite for purposes of consideration and treatment—in all development of single functions . . . the unity of personality is the compelling force.[37]

Children are born with undifferentiated aptitudes or dispositions, which environment can bring out and cultivate into definite qualities or skills as they grow. Thus from simple beginnings in infancy, development proceeds to ever more complex levels as children grow and interact with the environment in more adaptive and sophisticated ways.

By the time Stern was writing, studies of childhood had been going on for some time, so he included a section on method: how best to conduct such a study, based on his own experience. An observer should distinguish between a child's observed action or utterances, and the inferences one might draw about them; all conclusions should be in accord with the simplicity of child nature, not reading adult characteristics into them; no general assertions or explanations of behavior should be made without considerable observational support; everything should be recorded that is observed, but spontaneous action is a better source of information than a response to a planned set of events; the child's home, status, and family setting should be carefully noted; he should be kept as unaware as possible of one's observation; the observer should also take pains to be in a good, friendly relationship with the child; observations should be written down as soon as possible to avoid forgetting or distortion, even if a kind of shorthand has to be used.

In this type of study, Stern felt, there was no substitute for careful and exact observation. Mental tests, especially of infants, were of not much use to him, nor childhood reminiscences, which are always altered to some extent over time, nor large-scale collections of data about children, since they tended to focus on just one or two aspects of development. Although these methods might produce some interesting information, only exact, long-term, deteached observation of real children in natural contexts could result in a sound picture of the nature of human growth.

Charlotte Bühler's *The First Year of Life,* first published in German in 1927 and translated in 1930, followed similar lines, although covering only one year. By uninterrupted, systematic observation of one child, twenty-four hours a day, for the whole first year, she arrived at "a very exhaustive inventory of every item of observable behavior."[38] This inventory she used to develop age norms, standards to assess average behavior and its normal development through the first year. Her famous "baby tests," which she brought from Germany to England, were used to determine the developmental level of children by watching their performance on certain assignments or tasks that had been planned for each month of the first year. In each set of ten tests, the child responds to something the tester does, and thus shows his level of growth in social reactions, bodily control, mental abilities, and the manipulation of objects. For example, children of five months, when given one rattle, should be able to hold it easily and then to hold another and move both independently. Children of eight months, when something is rattled behind a screen, should try to find or look for it.

On the basis of such performances, children's developmental profiles, which describe how closely they approximate the norms for their age and stage of development, can be plotted.

Developmental schedules were also produced by Arnold Gesell in the United States, although he went far beyond the first year of life. His method of observing children broke new ground, for he used one-way glass to watch and photograph his subjects while remaining invisible to them. Like William James, his work was soon known in England, and prompted many further studies aimed at laying out generally valid developmental schedules that could be used to assess the progress or deficiency of any particular child.

Beginning in 1926, Jean Piaget's studies of the development of children's thinking were translated into English. Trained in evolutionary biology and interested in epistemology, Piaget began his work with children by using mental tests. But it was the mistakes the children made that interested him, and he began to unravel the mystery of the differences between adult and child thought. Egocentrism is the first and most prominent characteristic of infantile thinking: the objective world beyond the self is perceived only slowly, and at first the child does not recognize the subjectivity of his point of view, since he cannot yet distinguish between what is himself and what is not himself. Gradually, a child is freed from the egocentric mode of thought, through interacting with the environment, assimilating new objective experiences and accommodating his mind to them. The mind takes its shape, then, through continuous and reciprocal action with the world, and moves through definable stages in its ability to make meaning of it.

Piaget was recognized at once as a very important student of human thought, although not without some criticism (see chapter 6, "Susan Isaacs and Others" for a detailed study of her and her husband's critique of his work), and his "genetic epistemology" is today probably the best-known and most influential theory.

Mental Testing

In the first quarter of this century, then, psychology had made great strides in several directions: there were studies of the general laws or psychological principles that characterized the development of the human race; there were studies of individual variations within the broad range of human capacities; and there were specific studies of the stages of infant and child growth. Methods of studying psychological phenomena were also developed with greater precision and appropriateness to the subject: descriptive studies used systematic observation as well as introspection; more experimental investigations arranged planned situations and noted the responses; and increasingly these later studies were analyzed and reported statistically.

Galton's early experiments, moving beyond his investigation into hereditary genius, were published in his *Inquiries into Human Faculty* (1883). Here he dealt with a variety of different traits or abilities among human beings. He was the first to use the questionnaire: in studying the power of mental imagery, first among scientific professionals and then among younger people, he was able to establish that the ability to call a clear image before the mind's eye varies greatly, yet bears no direct relationship to intellect. In fact, it tends to lessen precisely among people who devote a great deal of time to abstract thinking, like scientists. Another experimental innovation was his use of "free association." He drew up a list of words, presented them to himself one at a time, and noted what word was associated with each and the exact time it took to appear in his mind in response. From this study, he was surprised to find how large a proportion of the associated words seemed to arise from his own boyhood and early adolescence, and in this type of experiment he clearly foreshadowed psychoanalytical methods. Some of Galton's other wide-ranging investigations measured differences in people's sensitivity to high-pitched sounds, vision and touch, memory and fatigue. He also studied identical twins and man's sociability or gregariousness. In all of his work, Galton was thinking quantitatively. He developed the correlative technique, which allowed him to state statistically the degree to which phenomena varied similarly or separately. His work on individual psychology and his experimentation and statistical analysis of the data led directly to the development of tests to investigate such practical problems as mental deficiency and vocational aptitudes. And with Pearson's further development of the mathematical formulation of the "coefficient of correlation," and Spearman's systematic application of that formulation to psychological data, appropriate tools were at hand for analyzing the results of mental tests.

Mental tests themselves were first devised in France by Binet, when in 1904 he was asked to sit on a committee appointed to study ways of dealing with the "backward" child in school. This group wished to distinguish between a child's innate ability and those environmental factors that might make him appear to lack interest in his school work or seem lazy. In 1905, Binet published his first tests, which consisted of a series of tasks or problems in increasing order of difficulty, and which dealt with real-life situations or information that most children would have grasped. The tests were revised, modified, standardized for age, and reissued in 1908 and 1911, and in their later form they aimed to report on intelligence in terms of "mental age." The unusual approach that Binet (and his colleague, Simon) took was to consider intelligence as a problem-solving activity, as evidenced primarily in verbal responses to questions. As Susan Isaacs put it,

The practical psychologist has gone rapidly ahead devising ways and means to do this [mental measurement], and he has demonstrated the feasibility of measuring the mind *as it is expressed in behavior.*[39]

Binet's test items moved from simple motor, sensory, or perceptual responses toward the "higher" conceptual mental processes, for he believed that these reached increasing levels of complexity and abstraction as growing children interacted with their everyday environment, and as their language matured as well.

The Simon-Binet tests were rapidly translated into English. In the United States, Terman, Goddard, and Yerkes adapted them and devised new items, especially for use in the armed forces. In England, Cyril Burt[40] made his own translations and revisions, and was soon using them in his investigation of London schoolchildren.

In 1870, Britain had passed its first compulsory education act; in 1899, a board of education was set up to establish a national system of education; and in 1902, local education authorities (L.E.A.'s) were empowered to deal with the full range of education provision. In 1913, the Mental Deficiency Act was passed, following the report of a royal commission (appointed in 1904) that had come to the conclusion that there were many mentally deficient persons, both young and old, who were not being cared for appropriately in the community. The 1913 Act classified such people as idiots, imbeciles, feeble-minded, or moral defectives; it charged the L.E.A.'s with the responsibility for all mentally defective children between the ages of seven and sixteen. And as school populations rose, authorities were faced with the problem of classifying large numbers of children and providing appropriate education for them all. Of particular concern to educators was what seemed to be alarming evidence of mental and moral deficiency among working-class children.

In 1913 also, Burt was appointed by the London County Council to serve (part-time) as an educational psychologist, the first such appointment ever made. Looking back some years later, he described the reasons for his appointment in somewhat Galtonian terms:

> Like many writers at that date, I believed that, owing to recent changes in the birth-rate, the mentally defective and the mentally retarded were multiplying far more rapidly than the normal or super-normal; while other critics, particularly employers, had complained that, owing (it was supposed) to the introduction of less formal methods of instruction, attainments in the fundamental subjects of the curriculum, especially in reading, spelling, and arithmetic, had been steadily declining. Today [1947] these problems are no less urgent.[41]

In the first edition of his book, he had already written:

> [There is] a striking correlation between the intelligence of school children and the occupational class from which they are drawn. . . . it is difficult to withstand the inference that the average level of intelligence among the population as a whole must be slowly but steadily declining.[42]

He was clearly reflecting the educational authorities' concern that, while increased educational opportunity was being extended, new social problems were being uncovered that had to be investigated and solved. Therefore, he set up an extensive testing program both to detect those children who were deficient enough so that special arrangements should be made for them, and also to find "super-normals" who might be provided with scholarships for grammar schools.

Burt's first preliminary report was published in 1917,[43] with an extensive preface by Sir Robert Blair, then the chief education officer for London and a strong supporter of Burt's investigations. Blair says of Burt's work:

> He finds that children of the ordinary elementary schools in London are in intelligence slightly above the level of other children of similar social status tested elsewhere with similar scales: that delinquents differ from normals rather by backwardness and instability than by mental deficiency in the narrower sense: and that the defectives of the London special schools differ from normals far less in lack of intelligence than in lack of school ability: and concludes that: 'when the dull and backward are recognized as requiring definite educational provision, a larger proportion of the special school cases will doubtless be accommodated in the special classes in the ordinary school rather than associated with those whose future lies forever in an institution'.[44]

Here Burt was distinguishing between school achievement on the one hand and innate intelligence on the other, and he was also noticing that, among delinquent or "morally defective" children, other factors than intelligence could have caused their poor performance on tests or in school: "In the street he plays the precocious urchin; in the school he is put down as a mental deficient."[45] Discrepancies between ability and attainment caught his attention continually, and he understood well what environmental influences might be at work, despite his earlier, somewhat eugenic comments:

> Attainment is a poor measure of capacity and ignorance no proof of defect. Merely from school work, neither normal ability nor abnormal, neither high quality nor low, can conclusively be inferred. . . . Poor health, poor homes, irregular attendance, lack of interest, want of will—these are far commoner as causes of inability to spell or calculate than are inherent weakness of intellect or genuine defect of mind.[46]

The problem in discovering which children needed special classes lay with current methods of diagnosis. It was impossible to rely on the ordinary observation of classroom teachers alone, since they had many children to deal with and a set curriculum to convey. Therefore, following the Simon-Binet tests, but with certain alterations, Burt tested individually some two thousand children in London, either personally or using trained help.

In his *Mental and Scholastic Tests* (1921), long the standard work in the field, Burt explained at length just how his tests were to be given so as to promote each child's comfort and success; he specified the other kinds of information about any child under investigation that must be gathered before a diagnosis could be made—home conditions, health data, and the like—and then he listed sixty-five specific test items, used in ascending order of difficulty, grouped by the ages at which success would be expected, and with instructions as to how a child's responses should be interpreted and scored. As distinguished from the curriculum of the schools, his test items were chiefly based on experiences and information common to most children (and his instructions include advice as to varying items for different children), and on their ability to pay attention, remember, and reason.

For example, a child at age three should be able to point to his or her nose, repeat some numbers, name his or her sex, and name simple, familiar objects like a penny, knife or key. At older stages, children should be able to repeat longer and longer strings of syllables, and count backward starting with higher and higher numbers. Children are asked to describe pictures, and with increasing age they should improve in the complexity and interpretive qualities of their responses. Copying geometric figures similarly improves with age, as does sentence building, remembering a number of items shown and taken away, generating lists of words on request, and distinguishing between abstract terms like *kindness* and *justice*.

In his article, "The Development of Reasoning in School Children," Burt cites the kind of problem situations he set out for children to solve.[47] A child of seven years should be able to answer correctly the following: "Tom runs faster than Jim; Jack runs slower than Jim. Who is the slowest—Jim, Jack, or Tom?"[48] An eleven year old should be able to deal successfully with:

> A man was found nearly dead with his throat cut, and on the back of his left arm was a blood-stained mark of a left hand. The policeman says he tried to kill himself. Do you think the policeman was right?[49]

And by fourteen years, this problem should be solved:

> When you enter my house you will find a window on your right in the side wall of the passage. When the sun sets it shines straight through this window on to the wall opposite. What direction are you facing, when you stand in the doorway and look across the street?[50]

In analyzing his results, Burt had to face the question of how to define precisely which children should be considered "backward" and given additional educational help, and which should be diagnosed as truly defective, put into special classes or even institutions, and perhaps not allowed to reproduce. This was a serious problem, since it so deeply affected the lives of children, and clear guidelines were needed to decide between "freedom and segregation." He came to believe that 1½ percent of any age group may be called "mentally deficient" in varying degrees. Some who are "incapable of receiving proper benefit from the instruction in the ordinary public elementary schools" should be put into special classes.[51] The next lower type of child will be able to profit from only those basic educational and vocational skills that will permit him to undertake a simple work assignment. Next come the children who will always need constant help and can deal with only a minimum of freedom; and finally there are those who will need complete, protective institutional settings. But, again, Burt never believed that such diagnoses should be based on simple school backwardness, or on test results, but only on the fullest possible investigations of the child's whole life situation. In *Mental and Scholastic Tests,* he put the matter forcibly:

> Psychology is the science of the whole mind, not of its cognitive aspects only.... In my view the function of the school psychologist is to deal with every aspect of the child's personality and with all forms of training, moral and emotional, as well as intellectual.... The psychologist must never be content to look at nothing but the mind before him. It is his task to extend his survey to the surrounding influences that are making the mind what it is; he must ascertain the current situations and the crucial problems which that mind is called upon to meet. To study a mind without knowing its *milieu* is to study fishes without seeing water.[52]

Although he did believe in the heritability of intelligence, he assigned it about 60 percent of a child's ability, with 40 percent being the influence of environmental factors. Test results, therefore, while useful as objective measures, could never be considered definitive by themselves.

The effectiveness of mental tests was nonetheless established. The first American IQ test was the Stanford-Binet, introduced by Terman in 1916. In 1917, when the United States entered the war, Yerkes developed the famous Alpha (for literates) and Beta (for illiterates) tests, in order to find out which army recruits were mentally incompetent, which possessed sound general abilities, and which were superior and should be given officer training. In all, some 1,750,000 men were tested, the first such large-scale program.[53] From that time on, IQ tests were widely used, both in England and in the U.S.A., for choosing people to employ in certain types of work, whether in industry or civil service, or for entrance into institutions of higher education. To some extent, Burt's important warnings about environmental influences were ignored, as the tests seemed to provide a quick, efficient, "scientific" way to assess capacities and to differentiate among large numbers of people. And when analyzed by the increasingly sophisticated statistical techniques that were also being developed, these tests constituted a powerful tool in the hands of psychologists, as well as educators, employers, and government agencies. Born of a need to deal efficiently with large populations (children, soldiers, immigrants, industrial workers), and to classify and organize them in some reasonable way, mental tests had great appeal, although today they seem much more controversial.[54]

At the Malting House School, Susan Isaacs used IQ tests routinely, to ascertain the intelligence of her young children there; in her important work, *The Children We Teach,* which deals with children from ages seven to eleven, she included a section on the use and importance of mental testing; and while she was at the Department of Child Development of the University of London, part of the course work she provided for her students included methods of mental testing. In 1933 she collaborated with Cyril Burt in a long memorandum to the Hadow Committee, dealing with the emotional and intellectual growth of children up to the age of "seven-plus." And in her summary of psychological studies, *Psychological Aspects of Child Development* (1935), she speaks of mental tests as a useful way of assessing intelligence. Clearly, she accepted tests and testing, although, like Burt, she warned against using them without carefully considering other factors affecting the child, and against using them on very young children, whose store of information is slight and whose feelings are still too unstable to yield any reliable results.

An important reason for these caveats was the increasing progress of psychoanalytic studies, especially with young children, and her own deep involvement in this field.

Psychoanalysis

As with Darwin—and, indeed, Marx—Freud's work was a watershed: all three laid their axes to the roots of long-standing, deeply held beliefs about humanity's rational and social nature. After Darwin, human beings could no longer be thought of as special creations of God, given dominion over all the world; rather, they had descended, over eons of time, from the great apes, and were governed by the blind forces of evolutionary change over which they had no control. After Marx, the inventive mind that had produced industrialized capitalism had also let loose economic forces that could destroy the very society it had built. And after Freud, reason, humanity's most treasured possession, was known to be powerfully and uncontrollably affected, from birth onward, by the unconscious, instinctual aspect of the mind, the legacy of an evolutionary heritage. Earlier views of the unconscious had treated it as the repository of reflexes, habits, or old memories. For Freud, it was an active source of primitive energy, striving for expression and satisfaction, and fighting back if frustrated. This force meant that ideas, memories, purely mental products could in fact produce physical suffering and illness, and in ways that no one's conscious mind could control.

As Dr. John Rickman pointed out in 1937, the study of psychology before 1900 had dealt mostly with consciousness or aware experience, and with cognition.[55] Few investigations had been made dealing with mental suffering in normal life or with mental illness and pathology. Even the later studies of child development had focused primarily on the growth of intelligence and language. It seemed, for academic psychology, as if life were always guided by reason and experience was always happy or at least orderly.

On the other hand, Freud's epoch-making ideas about the unconscious, infantile sexuality, the content of dreams, psychic disorders, and the whole relationship between mind and body did have some predecessors, as did also his method of treatment. In England, specifically, W. B. Carpenter's classic, *Principles of Mental Physiology* (1874), had laid the foundation for a physiological approach to psychology, and described the brain as having three distinct levels of functioning. Carpenter's idea of "unconscious cerebration" linked the sensory apparatus of the body to the conscious mind, where the will operated. G. H. Lewes's *Problems of Life and Mind*, published between 1874 and 1879, emphasized the organic unity of mental and physical processes, rather than separate levels of function. Nonetheless

> important as sensation and ideation are, they are less important than the appetites, instincts, emotions, and sentiments.... The actions of men are determined by motives, but the motives are determined by motors lying deep down in the mental structure [which] play by far the greater part in mental life.[56]

In 1883, Galton's fertile mind produced *Inquiries into Human Faculty*, which included an introspective analysis of his own apparent acts of free will, and the actual motives that seemed to govern them. There were, he came to see, "whole strata of mental operations that had lapsed out of ordinary consciousness [which] admit of being dragged to light,"[57] especially the effects of childhood events. His method of free association, too, had showed him that from an unconscious region of the mind, ideas can arise that have much to do with current activities and that have roots deep in a person's early life.

Freud's contemporary, Havelock Ellis, wrote his monumental (seven-volume) *Studies in the Psychology of Sex* between 1897 and 1928, the most extensive and detailed study of the subject to date. Ellis brought a new, objective approach to sex, devoid of guilt or inhibition; he produced the first work on normal sexual development and mature sexuality; he made a thorough study of "auto-erotic" phenomena, coining the term that Freud used later; and he wrote an extended account of sexual "inversion" as well. Ellis's work aroused considerable opposition and even litigation, especially the volume on sexual deviance, so that until 1935 subsequent volumes were published in the United States. His clinical, detached approach was similar to Freud's, and most of later, enlightened opinion on the subject, including that of Susan Isaacs. Her book, *Social Development in Young Children*, explores just those areas of children's behavior that are so often dismissed or punished as shameful, naughty, or disgusting, but that are demonstrably important expressions of their inner fantasies.

Freud, as is well-known, began his career as a medical man and neurologist, so he had an essentially physiological attitude toward mental phenomena. Early interested in hysterical symptoms, he studied with Charcot in Paris, learning his method of hypnotism and posthypnotic suggestion for curing patients. With Janet, he felt that mental illness was caused by some kind of "dissociation" within the mind, causing the usual equilibrium to be disturbed. Later, collaborating with Breuer, he moved beyond hypnotism to the "talking-out" method, and, when he and Breuer parted company, he went on to use free association and dream analysis, within the context of the transference relationship between patient and therapist.

Gradually, on the basis of his work with many patients, Freud developed his theories and began to publish them. *Studies in Hysteria* appeared in 1895, followed by *The Interpretation of Dreams* in 1900, *The Psycho-Pathology of Everyday Life* in 1904, and *Three Essays on Sexuality* in 1905. Vienna at the turn of the century could not accept his ideas of infantile sexuality, but eventually he came to international attention. In 1908, the first psychoanalytic congress was held, and Ernest Jones came to Vienna from England, met Freud, and became convinced of the veracity and great importance of his work. Jones (and Brill) went to North America and carried word of Freud's epoch-making discoveries there; in 1909, G. Stanley Hall invited Freud to deliver the now-famous lectures at Clark University. In 1910, the International Psycho-Analytic Association was founded. In 1912, Jones, back in England, published *Papers on Psychoanalysis* and, in 1918, wrote a brief and lucid basic text, *Psycho-Analysis*. Until Freud's own works were translated, Jones's explications of Freud's ideas were the best accounts available in English.

When the First World War was over, psychoanalysis received additional impetus; the war itself caused much rethinking of conventional views of man's nature and the progress of society. In addition, large numbers of soldiers, reacting to the experiences they had undergone, were coming home with severe symptoms of shell-shock.

> The resistances to the acceptance of psychoanalytic doctrines, though not removed, were markedly lowered, and psychoanalysis was to become in the post-war period of the 1920's and 1930's a major intellectual movement, by no means confined to medical circles.[58]

Following the war, too, Freud's own thinking underwent some changes, especially as regards the basic instincts of human nature, sexuality and aggression, the stages of emotional development, and the formation of the superego. In 1921, Susan Isaacs's *An Introduction to Psychology* presented his views as they stood at that time. By then, she had already begun her own analysis with Flügel, and had discovered at first hand the illumination that it brought to the deepest, most obscure levels of the mind. For psychoanalysis, from the beginning, had always been a therapeutic method as well as a theory of normal and abnormal development, and a topography of the mature human mind as it had evolved from its primitive origins.

The method of psychoanalysis necessarily differed from the other psychological studies of the time, since it focused on precisely those areas of mental functioning that are not directly observable or measurable. The patient is encouraged to relax his conscious, directed thinking and to wander in thought and fantasy quite freely, without concern for decorum or consistency. Memories, desires, dream scenes, impulses all well up, as do resistances to the more disturbing ones. At just the points of resistance, the therapist urges the patient to move ahead, nonetheless, and gradually the source of anxiety and symptoms, events in early life that deflected normal development and fixated energy at an immature stage, is revealed. With the therapist at his side, uncritical and accepting, the patient then has a second chance to live through those early scenes that caused such pain, now with adult eyes and with an interpreter, and so to free up the clogged channels of his emotional growth. In all of this

> the analyst enables the patient to arrive at an understanding of himself. The work of the analyst is not to command, to suggest or to give judgment, but to assist in the process of self-understanding on the part of the patient, and this latter can only come about by the patient's own overcoming of his "resistances."[59]

In 1923 Freud published *The Ego and the Id*, in which for the first time he explicitly divided the mind into its three component parts: the ego, the consciousness; the id, the unconscious reservoir of instinctual and repressed desires; and the superego, the moral agent within the mind.

The libido is the basic, energy-giving force of all human life, consisting of the instinctual drives for erotic satisfaction centered around the different zones of the body at different stages, together with characteristic aggressive defenses if satisfaction is denied. The ego, the mediating, life-sustaining force, emerges slowly out of the primitive id, as the pressures of reality impinge on the immature child. It strives to maintain a balance between the demands of the id and its libidinal desires; the guilt-making strictures of the superego; and the facts of the outside world of people, events, and things. It defends itself against the demands of the id when satisfactory expression is not possible, by a variety of mechanisms that deal in a compromised way with conflict—projection, displacement, regression, inversion, and the like. Among these, only sublimation, Freud thought, contained any hope for civilization,[60] for it provides the libido with a channel or outlet for satisfaction that is at the same time socially acceptable:

> The forms of activity in which infantile tendencies find expression, are well adjusted to reality, and compatible with social purposes. Instances of this socialized expression of tendencies, which in their native form are unacceptable to adult standards, are fortunately to be found on every hand. . . . Sublimation is clearly the most desirable fate for the primitive tendencies, since it puts the greater part of their energy at the service of the social life.[61]

The other details of Freudian theory are too well-known to need further explication here, but for Susan Isaacs these aspects of the development of the mind and the dynamic, functional view that they implied were critical, especially for understanding children's growth through progressive stages of crisis and resolution. Psychoanalysis, in both strictly Freudian terms and in variations on his themes (such as Hart's popular *The Psychology of Insanity* of 1912) entered into society; "psycho-analysis became a craze as well as a serious study,"[62] and people began to use freely terms like *complex, symptom, projection,* and the like. And although the process of psychoanalysis was slow and expensive, its methods more inferential than strictly scientific, yet the insight it provided into the causes of human behavior was a permanent contribution:

> Humility at the unknown increases as the illusions born of ignorance are dispelled. . . . some day man will realise that he gains instead of loses by exchanging humility and confidence for arrogance and fear. . . . [psychoanalysis] advances the high claim of enabling man to deal finally with the dark fears that have hitherto so enslaved him. . . . it can only heighten man's real power, and in this instance where he is most in need of it, over himself.[63]

The "New Education"

> No one English educationalist, by reason of her teaching, writing and practice has had more influence on the treatment and understanding of young children than Susan Isaacs.[64]

Isaacs's influence on education and child-rearing practices was greatest between the world wars, but the ground had been well prepared. That childhood should be considered as a special period of life, with its own needs and quality, and that trained teachers and nurses should build their efforts on an understanding of children's natural interests and activities—these ideas were not new in her time.

Years earlier, Rousseau's disciple, Pestalozzi, conducted, at Yverdun,

Switzerland, a very successful and widely known school, to which Friedrich Froebel went to teach in 1808. There he saw at first hand how much children benefited from the social experience of being a member of a group, how interested they were in their natural surroundings, and how their earliest words could be vitally connected to concrete experience. And in their spontaneous play, he saw the "self-active representation" of their developing selves.

Over the years, Froebel developed a unified theory and practice of education. Its purpose was to enable children to grow in inner harmony and self-knowledge through understanding of the Divine unity behind the world of nature, as they moved through the stages of their growth in unhurried, unrestricted sequence. As a later Froebelian summed it up:

> The end of education is harmonious development. . . . Learn by doing. . . . Never, if you can help it, deprive the child of the sacred right of discovery.[65]

Educational practices, therefore, must attend closely to the inner, natural force of growth in children and respect its direction and pace, choosing toys, games, and other experiences for them that would heighten perception and deepen knowledge. Froebel devised a set of six "gifts" for little children, intended not only as pleasant toys but also to symbolize and teach the unity and diversity of the universe: soft balls of wool, cubes divided into smaller cubes, cylinders, rods, and the like would amuse the child and also demonstrate abstract attributes of shape, size, color, and material. For older children, he planned a series of "occupations," similarly using abstract geometric designs that they pricked into cards, folded out of paper, drew, embroidered, or cut out.

Froebel was aiming to match appropriate activities to each stage of the child's sensory and cognitive development, and this remained a basic precept of later Froebelian educational thinking. By the time he died in 1853, he had attracted many devoted disciples in Europe and America, had written important books on both theory and practice which were translated into other languages, and had founded the kindergarten both as a good early environment for little children, and for training future teachers. For although Froebel believed that women were the best teachers of young children, he also thought that maternal instinct alone was not enough. Soon these two ideas—child-centered education and thorough teacher training—had found root in England.

English infant schools date from 1816, when Robert Owen established one at his mill in New Lanark, where children were to "play and be happy." In 1837, the British Home and Colonial Society had been set up to train teachers to use and disseminate Pestalozzian methods, on which Froebel had based his own. However, monitorial schools were more the order of the day: they could, at small expense, deal with large numbers of children, and at least provide them with basic literacy and numeracy, although their methods were primarily rote learning and systematic drill. Yet when the first kindergarten was opened by the Ronges in London in 1851, the German influence from Froebelian disciples had begun to take hold, and to work against this mechanistic way of dealing with little children. And by 1854, one of His Majesty's inspectors of church schools was actually commending Froebelian methods of teaching. The Reverend Muirhead Mitchell wrote in his report for that year that the Froebelian kindergarten apparatus (the "gifts" and "occupations") were among the "few novelties" on the educational scene, and he continued:

> This system, though intellectual, is truly infantile; it treats the child as a child; encourages him to think for himself; teaches him, by childish toys and methods, gradually to develop in action or hieroglyphic writings his own idea, to tell his own story, and to listen to that of others; there is no use of hard names, no singing of "perpendicular" or "horizontal," but whatever is said and whatever is done is totally and altogether such as belongs to a child.[66]

England was therefore fertile soil in which Froebelian kindergartens and methods could flourish. Among the more well-to-do members of society, too, there was an increasing interest in the education of young children, between the days of the nursery and boarding school. Small groups were taught in private homes, or governesses were employed to teach them separately. Literature for children had taken on a more entertaining and less moralizing tone; literature about children and childhood drew attention to the special experiences of early life. Fairy tales were translated and published; Wordsworth and Coleridge looked back on childhood with nostalgia as a time when the innate self develops freely and spontaneously; Dickens and Eliot portrayed children's experiences and the effects of loneliness or deprivation.

When Froebel's most dedicated disciple, the Baroness von Marenholtz-Bülow visited England in 1854, lectured on Froebelian philosophy, and demonstrated his materials at the Ronges' kindergarten, she found an enthusiastic audience. Soon more kindergartens were formed in various places, chiefly Manchester, and training for teachers and governesses was carried on. By late Victorian times, parents who could pay the price could employ Froebel-trained nurses and governesses, or send their children to private Froebelian kindergartens.

> Through improved living conditions and medicine, children of the upper middle classes now had a much better chance of survival. Parents consequently considered early education more seriously and compassionately, as they became more emotionally involved with their young.[67]

It was no accident, then, that child-rearing practices underwent a considerable improvement at about the same time, becoming far less coercive and more encouraging.

Throughout these years Froebelians set up training colleges with demonstration schools attached, all charging fees. Yet they were also committed to free kindergartens for poorer children, and by philanthropic subscriptions managed to set up a number of them, beginning in 1872. The needs of these children were different from those of more middle-class status: they seemed more self-reliant, and yet at the same time needed baths, medical care, school meals, and regular rest. These nursery schools for children under five also provided for ample free play, active movement, informal instruction, and individual attention for the few fortunate slum children lucky enough to attend.

Rachel and Margaret McMillan were prominent in the work for slum children's nursery schools; in 1894, Margaret was elected to the Bradford School Board, and said, "I was elected to fight . . . the battle of the slum child."[68] She later wrote about the importance of early childhood in terms that are reminiscent of Froebel, Dewey, and Freud:

> Let it be stated once for all, that during the first years the child is getting materials together. Every day he amasses a certain amount of treasure, of dross, or of mingled ore, and this, with, of course, his hereditary tendencies, is the capital with which he starts his conscious life. Is a man brave, strong, refined, sympathetic? These fine qualities cannot be evolved from nothing. The man has something *good* to draw on in the subconscious. Is he an evil person? In that case in any case—there has been accumulation. Nothing comes out of Nothing. As a great Teacher puts it, "A good man out of the good treasure of his heart bringeth forth good things, and an evil man out of the evil treasure of his heart bringeth forth evil things." The quality of the treasure, and even its amount, is determined largely by the mother and the Infant Teacher.[69]

The Act of 1870 had extended schooling to children from five to ten, and therefore greatly increased the numbers in schools. Fixed, tiered galleries with seventy-five or more children sitting in them became the standard. Teacher-direction, passive learning, mass drill, and silence were necessary in order to deal with such numbers. Sometimes Froebel's "occupations" of card pricking or paper folding were carried on, but often in a mechanical way by untrained teachers. Members of the Froebel Society (founded in 1875) became concerned about the abuse of kindergarten methods and materials in elementary schools, and did their best to influence public policy through the sympathetic vice-president of the education department, M. Mundella. In his circular to His Majesty's inspectors of 1893, Mundella provided a long and careful document on the right instruction of infants along Froebelian lines, and a guide to what could be expected of children from three to five, and five to seven. The 1892 Code recognized the private Froebel Certificate as an acceptable qualification for infant teaching.[70]

Pressure to provide a more utilitarian type of education for children who would begin to work at ten was severe, however, and continued until the 1918 Act raised the school-leaving age to fourteen. Those responsible for public education of young children had to consider literacy, numeracy, and habits of attention and industry as higher priorities than the harmonious development of rational personalities. Thus although Froebel's ideas were applicable in theory to every class of child, the exigencies of mass infant education in industrial slum conditions were the harsh realities to be faced.

News about the revolutionary pedagogical methods developed by Dr. Maria Montessori in Roman slums came to England also, and between 1919 and 1938 a six-month training course for Montessori teachers was held every other year. A physician who had taught mentally retarded children, she adapted her methods for poor children in her Casa dei Bambini. Gradually, she developed a theory of consecutive periods of mental development, at each of which the child is particularly sensitive to or ready for certain learnings. Her emphasis on sense experience as leading to intellectual growth was worked out through her "didactic materials," which were graduated in difficulty, self-corrective, and individualized. In her "prepared environment," children learned in an orderly and self-directed way, without classroom instruction or repressive discipline. The furniture of the room was child-sized, the routines of school life were handled by the children themselves, and the "directress" moved quietly about, guiding the children unobtrusively as each engaged in "auto-education" using the Montessori apparatus. Another innovation was the separation of writing from reading: the more mechanical skill was developed by Montessori materials before children moved on to the more abstract one.

However, Froebelians reacted with some hostility to her ideas, especially her rejection of fantasy as mere escapism, and imaginative play as having no place in the schoolroom. Also, a complete set of her didactic materials, graded for the full age range between three and seven, was expensive and well beyond what public funds could manage. So, as was typical in English education, teachers took from Montessori what would benefit the children, like her small-sized furniture and domestic equipment, the idea of an individualized, prepared environment for children, self-directed learning, and her emphasis on concrete sensory experience; but Froebelians, as well as people like Susan Isaacs and Margaret McMillan, rejected what they felt was an extreme didacticism and a theory of development that did not do full justice to children. By that time

> the Froebelians were entrenched in the English educational world as the experts on the education of young children, acknowledged alike by gov-

ernment, training colleges and public opinion. . . . [Montessori's] apparent mistrust of teachers' ability to use their initiative aroused the suspicions of Froebelians who were themselves fighting against the mechanical use of kindergarten exercises in babies' and infants' classes.[71]

The Froebelians' training colleges and examining body, their society and its publication, with its articles on child psychology and pedagogy, and their willingness to move with new ideas as they seemed appropriate to the welfare of children, all contributed to their becoming "entrenched," first in the private sector and then gradually in the public elementary schools.

Further, when this writer investigated the sources of what in modern times have been called "open" or "informal" schools, most of the prominent nursery and infant-school teachers, head teachers, inspectors, and lecturers at training colleges had been "Froebel trained." Others, often in small villages with one- or two-room schools, had long been working informally with their children, finding and developing "centers of interest" as themes for individual work. Later, when courses for teachers or lecturers became available, they found that their practical intuition about good teaching was firmly supported by child psychology and Froebelian philosophy.[72]

An equally important movement that developed at the same time as the Froebelians' was the "New Education,"[73] an attempt by progressive thinkers to make education for children reflect the optimistic social ideals of evolving a better world. In 1911, Edmond Holmes wrote his famous *What Is and What Might Be*, the confession of an old-fashioned school inspector who had seen an extraordinary school working along child-centered lines in the south of England, and who became deeply convinced that the work of this teacher, "Egeria," was "the true gospel of education." Converted, he founded the New Ideals Group, which worked for educational reform, spread their ideas worldwide, and founded progressive schools with "messianic enthusiasm."[74]

The group included prominent people, like Bertrand Russell and Percy Nunn, and the books they wrote and the schools they founded embodied their faith that only a right education could reform society and bring about a better world. Holmes's book went through many printings; H. B. Smith (also a Froebelian) wrote *Education by Life* in 1912; Caldwell Cook brought out *The Play Way* in 1917; and Percy Nunn himself, in 1920, wrote the textbook of progressive education, *Education: Its Data and First Principles*, and in 1924 he wrote the preface to J. M. Mackinder's important *Individual Work in Infants' Schools*. Soon books of great variety that explained progressive philosophy (especially Dewey's) and worthwhile new programs or plans for good practice (like the Dalton Plan) were being published.

Abbotsholme had already been established in 1889, and Bedales had followed soon after, in 1893. Especially after the horrors of the first war and the progressives' increasing concern for fundamental social change, a variety of private schools that professed the New Education were founded.[75] Homer Lane's Little Commonwealth was open from 1913 to 1917; Dartington Hall, under Leonard and Dorothy Elmhirst, established their broad-scale attempt to regenerate country life, beginning in 1925; Bertrand and Dora Russell's Beacon Hill opened in 1927; A. S. Neill's famous Summerhill settled in Suffolk in the same year; Gordonstoun was founded in 1934; and there were others like St. Christopher's School in Letchworth, King Alfred's School in Hampstead, Rudolph Steiner's school at Streatham, and Tiptree Hall in Essex. These schools included older children as well as the younger age group, but proceeded along similar lines: informal approaches to social life, encouragement of individual interest and activity, an emphasis on creative arts, and, to the extent possible, self-government. Susan Isaacs's Malting House School was no strange phenomenon when it was founded in 1924.

In 1920 a conference was held in Calais, and there Miss Beatrice Ensor and Adolphe Ferrière founded the New Education Fellowship (N.E.F.). Its first annual report of 1921 was characteristically called *The Creative Self-Expression of the Child.* The N.E.F. grew in numbers and influence, published *The New Era* with articles of interest to members, held conferences around the world, ran summer courses, and was the body that sponsored the international lecture tour which took Susan Isaacs and other prominent educators out to New Zealand and Australia in 1937, where they lectured to thousands of interested people.

> Comprising administrators, teachers, educationalists and even governments, the New Education Fellowship rapidly increased its membership, becoming, as one of its members wrote, the "most highly vitalised body which exists in the world for the investigation of new methods of teaching and for the recording of experience gained in all lands in the fascinating and urgently needed task of adapting education to new social ideals."[76]

Percy Nunn's influential little book expresses some of the ideals of these progressives, as well as their fervor:

> That freedom for each to conduct life's adventure in his own way and to make the best he can of it is the one universal idea sanctioned by nature and approved by reason; and that the beckoning gleams of other ideals are but broken lights from this . . . that freedom is, in truth, the condition, if not the source, of all higher goods. Apart from it duty has no meaning, self-sacrifice no value, authority no sanction. It offers the one sure foundation for a brotherhood of nations, the only basis upon which men can join together to build the city of God. Dare we find a higher ideal to be our inspiration and guide in education? . . .
>
> Though our children cannot build a fairer world on any other foundation than our own, yet they are not bound, unless in our folly we will have it so, to repeat for ever our failures; . . . they have in them a creative

power which, if wisely encouraged and tolerantly guided, may so remould our best that, as the dark shadows pass, 'the life of the world may move forward into broad, sunny uplands' and become worthier than any we have yet seen.[77]

Not all the progressives were of exactly the same mind: Lane and Neill were frankly Freudian in their approach; King Alfred's School's founder was an adherent of William Blake; Rudolph Steiner's inspiration was theosophical; Dewey's Laboratory School in Chicago and his philosophy inspired several schools, including Susan Isaacs's; while still others proceeded either on the basis of intuitive understanding of children, like E. F. O'Neill, or their wide reading in rationalist and idealist philosophy, like Bertrand Russell. But in practice they shared a common concern for the wholesome growth of the child into a rational, expressive adult, and based their work both on psychological studies of childhood and on their own liberal, optimistic hopes for the progress of society.

They differed from the Froebelians somewhat, although they frequently shared both ideas and members, in that they were definitely international in outlook, their schools were most typically tuition-charging boarding schools for all ages of boys and girls, and their goals were as much social amelioration as individual development. Yet clearly they were complementary and in no sense opposed to one another, with one exception: the N.E.F. was much more enthusiastic about Montessori than the Froebelians. And although the adherents of the New Education began somewhat on the outside of educational debates and reforms, gradually their influence was felt in training colleges and university departments of psychology, and among leaders of opinion who were not specifically educators, like Sir Henry Hadow and R. H. Tawney—one was a musician, the other a historian. Hadow, who chaired the Consultative Committee for years, came to believe that

> Rousseau had shifted the centre of gravity in education, and instead of imposing it on the child as a scheme from above, began with the investigation of the child's mind and worked outwards from that. . . . the psychological method in education . . . begins by endeavouring to find out what the boy or girl is good for.[78]

Tawney's political convictions, liberal and progressive, brought to bear on education, made him see that, "to an educational system which takes as its point of departure, not the social conventions of adults but the needs of children, the conventional vulgarities of class and income are merely irrelevant."[79]

> Progressive ideas were sufficiently prominent in educational debate to be adopted by men who did not have time to forge their own educational vocabularies but who were not satisfied to mouth conventional pieties.[80]

Government Support

Educational legislation, from 1870 onward, gradually widened educational opportunity for English children, broadened the services that the schools provided, especially for poor children, abolished fees, raised the school-leaving age, and, by 1944, changed its somewhat elitist position by eliminating the 11+ examination except by parental choice. At the same time, the impact of progressive and enlightened educational ideas was steadily evident in the government's educational publications. For example, there was a series of remarkable *Handbooks of Suggestions for the Consideration of Teachers* (1905, 1918, 1937, 1944, and 1959); there were the Hadow Reports on educational problems beginning in 1927; and there was the publication in 1949 of a very remarkable experiment in education, begun in 1940 in wartime Birmingham, *Story of a School.*

The tone of the *Handbooks* was important: the books were to be considered only as "suggestions," not as dictating the work of teachers. English classroom teachers, as well as head teachers, have long had very considerable freedom as to how their work is conducted, and the *Handbooks* respected that. However, such freedom could mean a very poor as well as a very good school, so the *Handbooks* collected and expressed the best available knowledge and practices to help teachers who wished to use them. The *Handbook* of 1918 puts this succinctly:

> The only uniformity of practice that the Board of Education desires to see in the teaching of Public Elementary Schools is that each teacher shall think for himself, and work out for himself such methods of teaching as may use his powers to the best advantage and be best suited to the particular needs and conditions of the school. Uniformity in details of practice (except in the mere routine of school management) is not desirable even if it were attainable. But freedom implies a corresponding responsibility in its use. . . . the teacher need not let the sense of his responsibility depress him or make him afraid to be his natural self in schools. Children are instinctively attracted by sincerity and cheerfulness; and the greatest teachers have been thoroughly human in their weaknesses as well as in their strength.[81]

When the 1959 *Handbook, Primary Education,* was written, it took note of the historical development of primary education: "the ever deepening concern with children as children," and the gradual spread of this concern upward from the nursery and infant schools into the junior stage (age seven to eleven):

> This concern shows itself especially in the awareness of the child as a whole with inter-dependent spiritual, emotional, intellectual and physical needs, and in the appreciation of the wide range of aptitudes, abilities and temperaments which any class of children presents. . . . Equally important is the growing realisation that the capacities of all children,

dull and bright alike, must be exercised to the full, and that to achieve this end the work must be made interesting and a sense of standard must pervade.[82]

Good teachers, the *Handbooks* asserted, have always known that the "initiative for learning comes from the learner," especially when he is actively engaged in what is interesting to him. When a child's natural curiosity or his expressive wish to make something or do something is effectively at work, then learning is allied with the natural developmental forces. Yet the *Handbooks* were also concerned with standards and discipline; no one who had seen the chaotic attempts at "free" schools and laissez-faire methods could feel otherwise. The work they advocated produced, in fact, higher standards of achievement than older, grill-and-drill methods, and the discipline of such schools was based on democratic values of citizenship and social responsibility. Methodical teaching was not discarded, but found its place "to the extent that the children see it aiding their own efforts, . . . holds their attention, and helps them to achieve something they want to achieve or have a use for or a pride in doing."[83]

The Board of Education had a long-standing practice of using consultation with experts and interested parties in arriving at its decisions.

> The value of liberal consultation, and of the personal discussions to which it gives rise, is very great, and indeed is essential to the easy and effective working of the English system.[84]

The official Consultative Committee was established in 1902, and after the first war, Sir Henry Hadow was the chairman until 1934, when Sir Will Spens succeeded him. The committee inquired into a total of seven major problems in education between the wars, receiving evidence from those who were concerned and knowledgeable, and published its influential reports beginning in 1922. Enlightened educational thinking was increasingly influential in these Reports, such as *The Education of The Adolescent* (1927), *The Primary School* (1931), and most of all in *Infant and Nursery Schools* (1933).

The 1927 Report on postprimary education begins with a long, historical chapter, detailing the development of secondary education from Peel's Factory Act of 1802 down to the Fisher Education Act of 1918. Chapter 2 then moves on to the situation facing education, "The Nature of the Problem":

> Is it possible so to organise education that the first stage may lead naturally and generally to the second; to ensure that all normal children may pursue some kind of post-primary course for a period of not less than three and preferably four, years from the age of 11+; and to devise curricula calculated to develop more fully than is always the case at present the powers, not merely of children of exceptional capacity, but of the great mass of boys and girls, whose character and intelligence will

determine the quality of national life during the coming quarter of a century?[85]

The answer was to examine the children at the age of eleven (and up) to send some to grammar schools for advanced, academic work leading to university entrance, and to recommend the establishment of "secondary modern" schools for the other 90 percent of the school population who would not otherwise receive any education beyond the primary level. The committee had already studied and reported on the use of intelligence tests (1924), as devised by Burt and his colleagues, and now used them to plan what they hoped would be appropriate secondary educational settings for all children up to fourteen and fifteen.

Closer to the spirit of progressive education was the 1931 Report. In it appears a paragraph long quoted and requoted by educators concerned both with curriculum development and with stages of children's growth:

> The curriculum is to be thought of in terms of activity and experience rather than of knowledge to be acquired and facts to be stored. Its aims should be to develop in a child the fundamental interests of civilised life so far as these powers and interests lie within the compass of childhood, to encourage him to attain gradually to that control and orderly management of his energies, impulses, and emotions, which is the essence of moral and intellectual discipline, and to help him to discover the idea of duty and to ensue it, and to open out his imagination and his sympathies in such a way that he may be prepared to understand and to follow in later years the highest examples of excellence in life and conduct.[86]

To the *Report on Infant and Nursery Schools* (1933) Cyril Burt and Susan Isaacs jointly contributed a memorandum, "The Emotional Development of Children Up to the Age of Seven Plus," which became the basis for one of the chapters in the body of the *Report* itself. This memorandum gives a careful, sympathetic review of the developmental crises and achievements from birth to seven, and advice to those who are responsible for them:

> Quiet, positive encouragement, showing the child what to do and how to do it, is far more effective than scolding or punishment, or emphasis on what he should not do. Successes should be emphasized; failures should be minimised; and above all, any feeling of shame or hostility should be avoided.[87]

The whole memorandum shows the influence of Freud's theory of infantile sexuality and Melanie Klein's extension of it, although not explicitly so stated, of pschoanalytic studies of the family, and of other investigations into the nature of childhood. Although coauthored by Burt, there is little emphasis on inherited intelligence or IQ testing, and considerable explanation of little children's great need to be understood and wisely handled through all their intense and confusing early experiences.

Story of a School was an unusual publication for the government to issue, and it dealt with A. L. Stone's work with the children of the Steward Street Junior School in the Birmingham slums of 1940. Air raids had already begun; many houses had no glass in their windows; playing space was limited and often hazardous; long hours were spent in shelters. The children lived in dreary, back-to-back houses, often with no plumbing, in "stark ugliness" as Stone put it. Yet, "when they were allowed to express themselves freely, . . . they created something beautiful."[88]

This extraordinary school demonstrated that even slum children could be attracted by beauty and produce artwork at a high standard; that adults and children could work harmoniously to promote such expressive work; and that good academic levels were achievable, but only *after* the desire for artistic expression had been satisfied. What Stone was after was "that confidence, that interest, that concentration" from children that comes from total absorption in a task that they find meaningful. When "interest, concentration and imagination" were fully aroused, then the 3 R's and the rest of the academic curriculum fell into their natural place as means to the greater end of exploration and self-expression.

Summary

This brief, condensed account of the contemporary ideas and practices existing during Susan Isaacs's career may sound as if there were one great messianic push toward child-centered education, so that the "century of the child" had become reality and society was ready to move toward those "broad, sunny uplands." But there was always opposition, and from many quarters. There were and always will be both child-haters and child-lovers, and all shades of opinion in between. People will always differ as to whether education should shape children up, or help them grow; fit them for the slot in society for which their birth has destined them, or foster whatever gifts they have, wherever they are born; teach accepted habits, skills, and knowledge early, or hold back until children are developmentally ready to discover for themselves "the funded capital of civilization" (Dewey).

It is also true that, then as now, responsible authorities have to be concerned about financial support for educational endeavors and to expect results and clear standards of achievement in return for the investment of public money. Freer methods, especially in untrained hands, can look sometimes more like chaos than school, and experienced traditional teachers can in fact show demonstrable results from their work. In addition, working-class parents may realistically emphasize vocational training, not self-expression and harmonious development for their children, while middle-class parents, anxious for their children to rise, may push for examination-governed methods and curricula, so as to improve the chances of university acceptance. Freer methods may seem like a luxury or at least a waste of valuable time, to people with these practical or personal concerns.

Yet there was another kind of opposition. It was correct, if crude, to point out that compulsory education for children who might otherwise be earning wages meant that the poor would have less income, and that, at the same time, "if you make the cattle think, they will become dangerous,"[89] and possibly refuse to become cannon fodder for the Germans. Certainly the extension of compulsory schooling did work an economic hardship on the working classes for which no other adjustment was made. And there is always the chance that enlightenment will indeed make the masses unwilling to accept orders blindly and create social unrest for which the authorities may not be prepared. The Federation of British Industries was concerned about these possibilities, as well as about the loss they might sustain in the work force if youngsters of fourteen went to work half-time and to school half-time, as Fisher proposed. R. H. Tawney scornfully derided their opposition, as if

> British industry is suspended over an abyss by a slender thread of juvenile labour, which eight hours continued education will snap, . . . after a century of scientific discovery and economic progress it is still upon the bent backs of children of fourteen that our industrial organization and national prosperity, and that rare birth of time, the Federation of British Industries itself repose[90]

In still a different vein of opposition, Lord Eustace Percy reminisced in 1958 about the growth of progressive ideas in the preceding decades:

> Educational philosophy had become dangerously romantic since the (1914–18) war, the more dangerously so because it was being encouraged by, for instance, the American school of Dewey to clothe its romance in the trappings of science and to dignify it by the title of psychology. . . . It aimed at civilizing children rather than instructing them; and it assumed—o sancta simplicitas—that the social virtues need not be inculcated but would develop naturally. . . . Believing thus in free development it believed also that the individual's capacity for development was predetermined at birth and that its limits could be measured in advance. The individual's "intelligence quotient" could be ascertained at an early age, at any rate by the age of eleven; and it was unalterable. . . . Those who cannot believe in the daylight fact of original sin fall easy victims to the calvinistic nightmare of predestination[91]

Whatever one may think of Lord Percy's invective, he at least points to potential contradiction between the hereditarians' view that intelligence is largely inborn and cannot be changed, and the environmentalists' hopes for bringing out children's talents and interests by creating the appropriate educational setting.

One did not have to be a child-hater to be concerned about that paradox;

yet there certainly were some. At a conference in the 1920s, organized by progressive educators

> a hard-bitten schoolmaster by the look of him, sprang to his feet in the middle of the hall, and informed the assembled pundits, in a rather truculent tone, that the main cause of our failures had been overlooked by every one of the speakers. The main cause of failure in our educational system, he said—or rather shouted, for he seemed very angry—was
> "THE STUPIDITY OF THE PUPIL,"
> and with that he sat down.[92]

Nonetheless, the ideas that childhood was worthy of careful study, that children should be reared in ways that responded to their developmental needs, and that such treatment should be available to all children, not just the few—these ideas were widely influential and had taken solid root, forming the setting in which Susan Isaacs carried on her important work for children.

3
The Malting House School Study

In this liberal and progressive period, prospects for children brightened. Serious attempts were made to understand human growth and development much more fully than ever before, and ways were found to put this growing body of theory into practice. Susan Isaacs was very much part of this broad-scale attempt to improve the lives of children. Her contributions stemmed from her pioneering work at the Malting House School (1924–27), from her graduate program at the Department of Child Development (1933–43), and from the great variety of publications and lectures that she prepared over the years, explaining children to adults who were responsible for them.

The Malting House School (1924–27)

In the spring of 1924, a full-page advertisement appeared that caught Susan and Nathan Isaacs's attention:

> WANTED—an Educated Young Woman with honours degree—preferably first class—or the equivalent, to conduct education of a small group of children aged 2½–7, as a piece of scientific work and research.
>
> Previous educational experience is not considered a bar, but the advertisers hope to get in touch with a university graduate—or someone of equivalent intellectual standing—who has hitherto considered themselves too good for teaching and who has probably already engaged in another occupation.
>
> A LIBERAL SALARY—liberal as compared with research work or teaching—will be paid to a suitable applicant who will live out, have fixed hours, and opportunities for a pleasant independent existence. An assistant will be provided if the work increases.
>
> They wish to obtain the services of someone with certain personal qualifications for the work and a scientific attitude of mind towards it. Hence a training in any of the natural sciences is a distinct advantage.
>
> Preference will be given to those who do not hold any form of religious belief but this is not by itself considered to be a substitute for other qualifications.
>
> The applicant chosen would be required to undergo a course of pre-

liminary training, 6–8 months in London, in part at any rate the expenses of this being paid by the advertisers.
Communications are invited to Box No. 1.[1]

The qualifications set out in the advertisement corresponded surprisingly well to Susan Isaacs's background and interests. The author was Geoffrey Pyke, a remarkable man in his own right.

> Pyke had both critical penetration and vision of a high order. One of his particular gifts was to uncover in the social system around us some of the major stupidities, muddles, and inefficiencies which the rest of us take for granted, and to suggest practicable remedies. . . . One of the things Pyke wanted to change was the education of young children. He had some valuable general ideas about the matter, some practical schemes, and the means to finance them. He persuaded Susan Isaacs to plan and run a small school in Cambridge where new ideas would really be tried out.[2]

There were already progressive schools in abundance, in England and overseas. In 1926 *The New Era* listed fifty-three private and twenty public schools working along progressive lines in England alone. Special issues of the magazine chronicled the work of others in the United States, Europe, India, and South Africa. Alone among them, however, the Malting House School was planned with both scientific and pedagogical aims in mind. It was to be a laboratory for the detailed, long-range study of children's intellectual and social growth, while at the same time it was to provide a group of young children with an educational environment that was based on the best psychological thinking then available, and that avoided the worst features of traditional practice.

To this venture, Geoffrey Pyke brought his own dissatisfaction with current education, considerable insight into better methods, his only child, and enough money to support the whole project. Susan Isaacs brought her theoretical training in philosophy, logic, biology, and psychology, as well as her direct involvement in teaching itself; she had also acquainted herself with the most advanced educational thinking and with the theory and practice of psychoanalysis. Nathan Isaacs, who soon became an important partner in this project, brought years of philosophical and psychological interest in the meaning of knowledge and its development, and the acquisition and use of language.

Susan Isaacs was to be in charge of the school, and Margaret Pyke agreed to handle household and business matters. The school met, in October of 1924, in one of the large rooms of a house Pyke had just rented, Malting House, at the corner of a lane in Cambridge.[3] At one end of the room was a gallery for visitors who wished to observe the children. The large main room was used for general purposes, including make-believe and dressing up, dancing to Mrs. Isaacs's playing on the piano, and the like. Gradually, other rooms were used as well: there was a room for quiet occupations, one for carpentry and scientific pursuits, another for handicrafts, painting, modeling, and drawing. There were a cloakroom, a lavatory, and a kitchen for preparing the noon meal. Later, when the school included boarders, there was a separate residence for them, with a room for each child.

The equipment of the school was carefully planned and often had to be imported from America or the Continent. It included the first "jungle gym" in Britain, and real easels for the children to paint at. Their seesaw was specially designed by Pyke, with a set of hooks on the underside from which weights could be hung: the children would be learning the principle of the fulcrum while playing. They had double-handed woodsman's saws, so they would have to learn to cooperate with each other. A real typewriter was available for their use, to help with reading and writing. None of the equipment was chosen haphazardly, for it was all intended to stimulate the children's powers of inquiry and curiosity, and thus they would learn.

Cupboards and tables and chairs were of light construction, easy for children to move either indoors or outside in fair weather. Rugs and cushions were available for sitting on the floor or in a corner. In the garden there were a sandpit, with water coming through a handy spigot, a toolshed with real tools, a summerhouse open at the sides, ladders, and boards of various lengths. Inside, there were scissors, paper, and paint, plasticine and clay, crayons and chalks and blackboards, all kinds of construction supplies like raffia, beads, thread, cloth, cardboard pieces, and boxes, as well as hammers, saws, shovels and spades, wooden and glass containers in various sizes for measuring, shells and beans often arranged in different-sized groups, pins and needles and sewing equipment, tape measures and rulers and pulleys and scales, lengths of rope and string, a magnifying glass, maps of Cambridge and environs, a big box of old clothes and dressing-up materials—in short, all the kinds of manipulative materials that children love to use and explore. In the garden were kept the animals for whose care the children were responsible. Every child had his or her own plot in the garden, while the adults did more systematic gardening in a joint area set aside.

Nor did the school stop at the garden gate. When a need was expressed, trips to the town or nearby fields were taken, to buy material at a shop, paint for new chairs, or stamps for letters inquiring about deliveries of goods; to go on bus rides in the country, long walks to gather flowers and leaves, or pond-hunting for eggs and little fish; to investigate the railway station, firehouse, and telephone exchange; to visit the lumber shop to measure and buy wood for ladders and sheds—all these were fruitful ways to follow up interests in practical, constructive pursuits.

As for the 3 *R*'s:

> The technical processes of learning to read and write fell into their proper places as aids to recording and communicating. . . . every one of the children grew eager to use these tools. . . . Reading and writing were often used in their games, as when they were "mending the road," and put up notices saying, "Road up—repairs," and so on. Very often we had to help the younger ones with spelling and did so freely. We held that for the children to gain this practical sense of the value of reading and writing was at their ages more important than mere formal progress.[4]

Labels were put on a great variety of items; these were often written by the children, using the "word-whole and sentence-whole methods," as better fitted to their situation than the alphabetic system of teaching reading. And there were shells for counting, beads for stringing, rulers for measuring, geometrical shapes for comparing, and blocks for building, to encourage number interests.

With the older children, reading, writing, and arithmetic played a larger part. Their need to compare shapes, to measure, to balance weights, and so on grew with the increasing complexity of the projects they undertook. Gradually, "the usual school subjects began to crystallise out of the various directions of interest."[5] Historical information was needed to explain the origins of everyday matters, such as roads and bridges, cars and buses, industry, clothing, houses, and the like. Geography grew from their interest in modeling their own school premises and then their town. Country walks collecting plant- and wild-life moved into more systematic study of botany; the use of a variety of balancing and weighing instruments led into physics. Equally, there was increasing interest in imaginative literature and the creative arts, as the children's abilities in language and in more finely detailed work improved. As more formal information and teaching was needed, it was given.

The children who came, ten small boys at first, were not by any means an average group. The first group included boys between the ages of 2:8 (two years and eight months) and 4:10, and during the next year they ranged from 3:0 to 10:5. The first girl came in the third term of the first year, but although in the last term of her stay at the school there were twenty children, the ratio of girls to boys never rose above one in four. Also, these children were unusually intelligent. Using the mental tests of the day, the staff found that the children's IQ's ranged from 114 to 166, with a mean of 131. They came from professional families in this university town, some from parents of considerable distinction. And some of the children came with a history of quite severe behavior problems, one even judged by Susan Isaacs to be "on the border line of pathology."

It was not usual for parents to send such young children to school, and they did so for different reasons. On the one hand, there were parents who understood something of the purposes and methods of the school and who trusted those in charge, and they supported the work in every way. On the other hand, there were also parents who sent their young children to this school "only because they had already proved themselves difficult to manage at home."[6] It was sometimes said in the town that Susan Isaacs had the ten most difficult children in Cambridge. Some parents expected miracles to occur overnight, and withdrew their children when they did not. Yet when progress was clearly made, however slowly, the children were then proclaimed to be very easy to deal with, as they were unusually amiable. Thus, like all experimental schools, this one had its attendant myths and fables. Nonetheless, it is important to recall that the group of children there was never very large, it contained some quite difficult children, it fluctuated in membership somewhat, it included unusually intelligent children, and it was primarily made up of boys. Susan Isaacs was not blind to any of these factors, and she explicitly stated that her conclusions were only beginnings, and that she hoped that they would stimulate more extensive research along similar lines elsewhere.

The entire educational environment, both as to the materials provided and the adults' way of working with the children, was designed to stimulate the active inquiry of the children, rather than to "teach" them, and to provide ample opportunities for dramatic play and creative, imaginative experiences as well. These two aspects of children's development were equally important and deliberately fostered.

> Active pleasure in looking at these things and eager curiosity about them is one of the most striking features of the minds of intelligent children of two years and more. It has quite as large a place in their spontaneous behavior as their delight in stories and "make-believe", in song and dance, and in all forms of "self-expression." And yet it has been very largely shut out of the tradition of schools for young children, even of progressive schools. . . . The actual relation between the phantasy life and active intellectual interest in the real world of things and events is itself a profound psychological problem, and one which we had in mind throughout our work.[7]

The educational method used started quite simply, and was gradually refined during the life of the school:

> On the educational side, I took up the work with the deliberate hope that a greater degree of freedom in the children's relations with each other than is usually allowed, and especially a greater freedom of verbal expression of their feelings and interests, would prove a benefit to them both in their intellectual and in their social development.[8]

Although there was no formal staff training[9] as such, since there were never more than two or three staff members, there were extensive discussions among the adults involved at the school. Later, Susan Isaacs paid generous tribute to the founder of the school, Geoffrey Pyke, for his part in these discussions and in the gradual development of what became a "definite technique with clear positive aims."[10] She wrote in May of 1927,

> Much of the detailed technique that is being worked out there [at the school] was originally devised by Mr. Geoffrey Pyke, who initiated and brought together the school, and who was throughout contributed the most illuminating suggestions and criticisms, and collaborated closely in the work of the school.[11]

For her, a school ideally had two functions: first, to provide for a child's bodily, social, and expressive development; second, "to open the facts of the external world (the real external world, that is, not the school subjects) to him in such a way that he can seize and understand them."[12] The first goal is familiar to everyone in progressive education, from Froebel and Dewey to present-day educators. The second, in her view, had not yet been taken seriously enough in the education of young children.

> We have been content to apply our new psychological knowledge of *how* the child learns, to the ways of getting him to learn the old things. We have not used it to enrich our understanding of *what* he needs to learn, nor of what experience the school should bring to him. The school has on the whole remained a closed-in place, a screen between the child and his living interests.[13]

Rather than a screen closing off the real world from the child's active interest in exploring and making sense of it,

> the school is, on my view, simply a point of vantage for the child in his efforts to understand the real world, and to adapt himself to it. It should be a place of shelter for him; but not in the sense that it shuts the larger world away from him. Its task is to bring the world to him, in ways and at a pace fixed by his needs and interests. The school, the teacher and the teaching alike are simply a clarifying medium, through which the facts of human life and the physical world are brought within the measure of the child's mind at successive stages of growth and understanding.[14]

Thus it was the actual world around the child that she sought to make clear to him, the world of people and things, and of his own inner and outer responses. Again, the Malting House plan was unique among progressive schools of the time, in that "finding out about things" and feeling and fantasy were never separated, but equally provided for and enjoyed in ways that relied for direction primarily upon the children's own expressed needs and interests.

The children were very free, then, to engage in a great variety of activity and discussion, and the adults helped them to do so willingly. This was not, however, a laissez-faire situation, in which adults simply stood aside in the naive belief that the children would develop naturally and happily if only they were left alone. There were, on the contrary, what Susan Isaacs called definite "limits and negative conditions" to their freedom, and clear rules established for the benefit of all concerned. Such rules were kept simple and were always based on either practical or educational grounds. With regard to the midday meal, for example, the staff always gave the children a few minutes warning, and then went on laying the table with those children whose turn it was to help. The meal was served promptly and the latecomer might find a cold dinner, or be left behind to finish alone.

The children were also expected to plan the dinner menu each day, in good time for the cook to shop and prepare the meal. They were allowed to spend two shillings per child, and had to consider seasonal vegetables, nutrition, and the like. When all this was not done on time, one day, the children discovered their omission, and went to the cook to see if there were anything she could give them. She happened to have some extra eggs in stock; they helped to make toast while she scrambled the eggs, and all sat down to a rather frugal meal. They seldom forgot again.

Each child was also expected to wash up his own crockery after the meal. If this was not done, no one would serve the next day's meal onto a dirty plate, and a cup could get very nasty inside if left long enough. In such ways, the actual consequences of their actions served as ample sanction for the children, and there was no need for moralizing or reproach on the part of the adults. And at the same time, the children were learning to take responsibility for an important part of their life together, responsibility that might interfere with absolute freedom to do as they wished at any time, but of the kind that is part of real life.

There were also safety conditions laid down. The Bunsen burner had real gas coming from it, but only the adults had the key to turn it on. Real matches, spades, hammers, knives and saws were used, but with adult supervision. Only one child at a time was allowed on a ladder, on the roof of the summerhouse, or near another in a tree. If anyone threatened to hit another with a tool, it was immediately taken away without comment. Material had to be put away after use, so that it was available for others.

With regard to the children's play with each other, no bullying of the smaller, weaker children was allowed. Nor was any cruelty permitted to the many animals that they kept. And although the adults in general fostered the children's activities in every way and joined in with them, they did set some limits as to their own cooperation. Children could not tyrannize over them, using them indefinitely to push the swing or give piggyback rides. Turns had to be taken and the children had to manage without adults' help to the greatest extent possible.

All these limitations were based on clear, practical considerations. The rules were few; once made clear, they were adhered to without exception but also without moralizing. Denials and requests were made in a straightforward way, with the expectation that they would be adhered to. If that failed, often the comment, "Perhaps you will do it later on," was enough. If not, and if the rule was important, a definite command or physical enforcement was used, such as quietly lifting a child down from the ladder that another child was climbing.

> We saw, then, no particular virtue in obedience for obedience' sake. . . . [we fostered] the children's growth towards such desirable behaviour as gentle manners, positive consideration for others, and active social cooperation. These things refuse dictation, but they grow in response to the friendliness and reliability of the adults, and happy reciprocal relations with other children. . . . they must be spontaneous, and spring from a happy, free friendliness, which is in its turn the fruit of the child's experience of our behaviour to him. . . . Our aim was to lessen progressively the need for mere implicit obedience, just because it was to us an *instrument* of education not an absolute value.[15]

In talking with the children about some of these issues, the adults were careful not to mix them up by using "must" in any but a simple, causal sense. If a child puts a block too many on a tower, it "must" fall down. But "you must do thus and so" was not used, in the sense of moral obligation. "Must" then represented no more than a real condition in the physical world, not the will or whim of adults. "In other words, we wanted to help the children to realize and adjust to other people's wishes as every-day facts, rather than as mysterious absolutes."[16]

The adults at the school aimed to exert a mild, reasonable, but firm control over the children. After a period of careful observation and discussion, it was decided that, indeed, absolute freedom was really too frightening for little children, and that they needed the security of knowing that there were grown-ups nearby who would, in effect, protect them from themselves. In general, however, within a safe framework, it was assumed that the children's impulses were best conditioned most of the time by seeing their outcomes in the real world, not by commands or prohibitions.

In only two areas were there more definite demands made, again after careful thought. It became clear that children needed and would benefit from definite prohibitions with regard to their universal practice of spitting, and their often explicit interest in excrement. It was decided that these were too primitive, too close to their original oral and anal sources, that is, still too libidinized, for them to yield simply to gradual identification with adults who did not indulge in them. No one spanked the children or preached to them, but when spitting or excremental talk occurred, the adults withdrew from cooperating in joint activities more sharply and for a longer period of time, and explicitly requested that there be no more such talk, and only one child in the lavatory at a time. Susan Isaacs believed that thus the child's still immature superego was given the support it needed to stand firmly against his own aggressive and therefore feared impulses.

Aside from such sanctions as there were, the adults allied themselves very actively with the children's natural currents of inquiry and imagination. They provided "willing and unstinted sharing of the children's play, coupled with the complete absence of the more usual superiority and moralisation of the adults."[17] They knew that adults play an absolutely key role in children's lives. Children naturally identify with adults, especially friendly and encouraging adults, and come to feel that what they do is worthwhile doing.[18]

> The children are psychologically oriented towards him as an adult. Their world hangs upon him, and his slightest sign is full of meaning.... If any adults are with the children, it is the children-in-relation-to-the-grown-ups which form the matter of observation. And even if no grown-ups are with the children at the moment, yet the latter will still be deeply affected in their total behaviour by the parental images as crystallised in infantile phantasy; and by their previous experience of adults.[19]

Since, in Susan Isaacs's view, children use reality as a "canvas" on which to project their feelings, and since that reality included both people and things, the whole environment had to provide for successful projection; that is, a child had to find surroundings that were both safe and stimulating. Then he could grow toward making his own meaning of the world, and ultimately taking responsibility for his own actions in it.

> In general, we tried to use our parental powers in such a way as to reduce the children's need for them. We held one of our tasks as educators to be that of counteracting the dramatic tensions in the child's mind; and the only way to do that is to bring in the real world at every possible point. The way out from the world of phantasy is through constant appeal to objective reality, to physical and social facts, and to interests and activities directed upon these. In the external world, the dramatic inner tensions of the child's mind and the adult's are deflected and diffused. And in our school our constant aim was therefore to throw our weight always on the side of an appeal to the world of objective fact, and to stimulate intelligent observation and judgment on the part of the children.[20]

In general, the staff did establish successfully the friendly relationships with the children that allowed for the process of identification to be established. For instance, when a game had run a little wild, it was often enough for a nearby adult to sit down and begin modeling; soon the children became interested and joined in, so that peace and constructive activity were reestablished. Put another way,

> these then seem to be the main factors—the transference itself, the symbolic gratification through our sharing in the children's play, the resultant lessening pressure of the ego-ideal, and the consistency and intelligibility of the real environment.[21]

The materials and equipment of the school were positive forces in encouraging children's active thought and inquiry; the adults, in turn, took up their suggestions and helped to follow them out. A third ingredient in the school life was the very large amount of verbal freedom. Few bans were put on speech at any time, and there was much lively talk throughout the day.

The younger children (under about six) were given complete verbal liberty, even if their remarks were hostile or their wishes antisocial. It seemed wise for them to have the opportunity for free expression of such feelings in words: "There is good reason to think that the younger child needs this verbal freedom, while he is learning control of the cruder forms of behavior."[22] Especially during the period of development before latency, the child is still at the mercy of his inner fantasies and ambivalence toward adult figures. Free verbal expression is a testing, a formulation to which the adults can respond in turn, providing him with feedback. Language development, too, is fostered by the opportunity to speak what one feels. As the children grew older, however, it was expected that they would gradually learn more control of speech, especially that which expressed defiance or hostility. Such control is part of latency, when earlier conflicts have been overcome and repressed, and a greater interest in other children and in the world of facts is evident. To ask for greater control over antisocial speech, then, fosters this natural line of development.

However, expressions of opinion or disagreements or ideas were never discouraged at any age. The meal table often proved to be the scene of stimulating discussions of all kinds of questions and events. The adults' part in these was restrained deliberately. They responded when children asked them questions or made specific comments to them. But often a question was put back to a child, "How does it seem to you? What do you think will happen? Shall we find out and see?" Thus the children were helped to formulate their own hypotheses, rather than being given an adult version. The final appeal was always to facts and not dogma.

> Wherever possible we turned them back to the active search for the facts they wanted. We thus used speech chiefly to provoke active exploration of the world, and to make its results clear and precise. We did this because, after all, words are only tokens of experience, and are either empty or confusing to the children until they have had enough immediate experience to give the words content. . . . We avoided offering ready-made explanations to the children, not only because we did not want to foster verbalism, but also because we did not want to substitute ourselves as authority for the children's own discovery and verification. . . . It is the child's understanding that matters, not our pleasure in explaining.[23]

A final aspect of the school should be noted as well, namely, relationships with parents. Parents came to luncheon or on visits, children went to teachers' houses for tea or invited them to their own homes, fathers sometimes helped with construction projects, and mothers with sewing and domestic activities. Also, there were reports to the parents. Since these were quite young children, the reports were chiefly anecdotal, and evidently designed to help the parent understand the child better by seeing him or her through the teacher's sympathetic eyes. Here is one such, written by Susan Isaacs herself:

Dear Mrs. X,
You may perhaps like to have a word from me as to Anne's development in the school during this term. It followed a very interesting course, determined chiefly, I think, by the great event of the twins. At the beginning she was most sociable and friendly, full of fun and liveliness with the other children, joining in their games and sharing their various doings—digging, building, drawing, modelling, bead-threading, cutting out, and feeding the animals. (This last named has taken up more time than any other single thing throughout the term.) She ran and sang in the most care-free and delightful way. On her return after the three weeks' absence, however, when she announced to us "I have twins," she was very much subdued and clung to me or Miss Irvine far more exclusively than she had done, even during the summer term when she first came to school. Her mind was clearly occupied with the twins to the exclusion of almost everything else. She talked about them freely to the adults, and invited us to go see them, but showed no inclination to run or sing or to join in with what the other children did. She even showed a little fear of the other children, occasionally, for example, of Timmy. She said Timmy "teased" her, although in fact he had done so only to the slightest possible extent: he was really interested in the various toys she brought to school, but she felt this interest to be "teasing." However, during the last three weeks of the term this wore off, and she returned to her normal self, beginning again to join in with the other children and to run and sing and dance and to march with the others, even when the bigger children such as David and Dillon, were arranging the marching. She very quickly picked up the names of the different tunes that I played to the children to march and dance to, and came and asked me for them. Her one grief towards the end of the term was that on several mornings we took all the other children out to the Fens just at the time when she was leaving school at 11:30, and she felt very sad that she was not coming with us!

With kind regards.

Yours sincerely,

Susan Isaacs[24]

That rather thoughtful appraisal was written in December of 1927. Others for this child still exist for the spring, summer, and autumn terms of 1928, and the spring term of 1929, although Susan Isaacs was no longer at the school. Clearly such reports were an established practice and must have done much to link home and school effectively together, by explaining what the school was doing to the parents who supported it.

Despite the occasional gossip and unsympathetic attitude of a few parents, response to the school was very favorable. The first group of ten children became twenty, and, over the span of the school's existence, a total of thirty-one children attended, tangible evidence of parental approval. There came a time, however, when Geoffrey Pyke's financial ventures grew less and less successful, and when efforts had to be made to find the money to keep the school going. Such an endeavor was mounted, and a long appeal was drafted and sent to the Rockefeller Foundation in the United States, in the hope that they would contribute funds to continue the scientific and educational work. It was signed by a remarkable galaxy of notables, among them Professor Jean Piaget of the Institut Jean-Jacques Rousseau in Geneva; Sir Charles Sherrington, past president of the Royal Society; Cyril Burt, Professor of Psychology at the University of London and Educational Psychologist for the London County Council; G. E. Moore, Professor of Moral Philosophy at Cambridge; and Sir Percy Nunn, also a professor at the University of London.[25] The appeal was rejected, however, and financial problems continued.

Another kind of reaction to the school appeared in the pages of *The New Era* for April 1928, where a long and positive description of the school was given, detailing its "very valuable experimental work under definitely scientific conditions." Later, the young American science teacher, Richard Slavson, who had worked at the school for a short time, wrote in the same journal in 1932 an article entitled, "Integrated Science for Young Children." There he stated that the "technique for unhampered investigation of the environment with ample material and adequate adult guidance provided at the Malting House School, Cambridge, England, was superior" to any he knew of elsewhere.

A fuller reaction to the school is provided by Evelyn Lawrence, an experienced teacher and expert in mental testing, who came to teach at the school after it had been in operation for two years. She says, in part:

> The three most interesting contributions of the Malting House were the attention paid to the child's spontaneous urge towards finding out, to all the influence on his thought exercised by and through language, and to his emotional needs. . . . The best way to prepare a person for life is to safeguard his zest for life. . . . When I first came to the school I tried to decide what was the most striking difference between this school and any other I had known. I came to the conclusion that it is the happiness of the children. . . . I have never seen so much pleased concentration, so many shrieks and gurgles and jumpings for joy as here. . . . There are three main advantages of freedom of action and emotional expression. In the first place you can get to know your children. Second, the danger of driving strong emotions underground, to work havoc in the unconscious, is avoided. . . . [Third] with conventional discipline, the child is kept wriggling under a dead weight of adult disapproval and prohibition. Here his position is that of a fencer, continually adapting himself to

the shifting conditions of the group mood.... surely [it is] a mistake to make all his social adjustments for him until adolescence, then pitchfork him into the world to discover from the beginning how human relationships work.[26]

But this was not simply a school, nor was it planned only as such. From the first, Geoffrey Pyke had hoped that this would become a true laboratory, in which the growth and development of children under carefully planned circumstances could and would be studied, with a view to making a unique contribution to the field of genetic psychology. The "definitely scientific conditions" at the school consisted of the environment provided, the specific style of adult-child interaction developed, and the records kept. The staff had a "writing-down book," as the children called it, and they jotted down notes there as they were able to "snatch time" from their work with the children. Susan Isaacs dictated a full record of the events of each day, in the afternoon when the children had gone home. Even more complete records were possible when money was found for a trained stenographer to take down her observations. The aim was to note and record everything about "the spontaneous behavior of children in the real situations of their daily social life."[27] No censorship, selection, or judgment entered in. "The records themselves are direct and dispassionate observations, recorded as fully as possible under the conditions; and as free as possible from evaluations and interpretations."[28] Still there were obvious limitations to compiling a truly complete account of everything that went on: the education of the children had to come first and the collection of data second, whenever there was any choice to be made; also, there were, of course, no modern tape recorders, either audio or video, at that time.

> Naturally I cannot claim that it is in fact a total record, since neither I nor any of my staff was always free to write down these (or any other) instances at the moment they occurred, or as soon after as made memory reliable. But I am content that it is not far short of complete, and enough so to suffice, whether for judgment of the behavior of these particular children, or for theoretical purposes.[29]

When Susan Isaacs and her staff made these detailed observations, they had no particular question or theory in mind. Isaacs was interested in getting a fully rounded view of children's behavior, and in making that view available to others. It had been said that the Malting House School was a deliberate application of psychoanalytic principles, but Susan Isaacs was, after all, a trained teacher of young children and a student of Dewey and Froebel long before she knew anything about Freud.

The school could hardly be described as an "application of psychoanalytic theory to education". It was far more truly an application to the education of very young children of the educational philosophy of John Dewey. This was my active inspiration.[30]

Also, she had only been in analytic practice for two years when the school was founded, and that was chiefly with adults. She says of herself that during the time when she was collecting the data (1924–27) she was "still so much an elementary student of children's . . . development" that she simply took down everything for later analysis. It was at this same time that Melanie Klein's important investigations into the analysis of young children were being carried on.[31] Klein was Susan Isaacs's friend and colleague, and her work clearly influenced the interpretation made of the Malting House material, but that came later.

The records concerned a total of thirty-one children, over a period of three and a half years:[32]

Years 1924–25. Ages on 1.10.24

Benjie	4:0	Laurie	4:6
Cecil	3:10	Martin	2:7
Christopher	4:0	Paul	3:6
Dan	3:4	Penelope	3:1
Duncan	6:5	Priscilla	5:1
Frank	4:11	Robert	4:6
George	4:1	Theobald	4:7
Harold	4:8	Tommy	2:7
James	2:6		

Year 1925–26. Ages on 1.10.25 (in addition to above children)

Alfred	3:6	Jessica	3:0
Conrad	4:9	Lena	2:9
Dexter	4:0	Phineas	2:7
Herbert	2:3		

Year 1926–27. Ages on 1.10.26 (in addition to above children)

Alice	2:4	Gerry	4:9
Denis	2:10	Noel	7:11
Jane	10:5	Ivan	5:10
Joseph	3:6		

Looking at the ages of these children, it is clear that there were many quite young ones, and a few older, with one child over ten years of age. Chronologically, there was a total spread of some eight years, which meant a considerable developmental difference among the children.

A large amount of useful data, of a kind that no other student of child development was producing at that time, was accumulated. Gesell used one-way glass, Burt administered mental tests, Charlotte Bühler described the minute-by-minute behavior of infants, Piaget talked with and asked questions of children one by one, and Bridges devised a developmental rating scale. But only at the Malting House were extended observations made of children interacting within an environment specifically designed to stimulate their powers of inquiry and imagination, to provide considerable verbal freedom and the company of other children, and to include adults who dealt with them according to a deliberately planned technique.

Susan Isaacs felt that such complete, "qualitative" records were essential for any valid picture of children's development. Strictly quantitative studies were inevitably oversimplified and impersonal; psychological experiments and mental tests had to be carried on in artificial surroundings that made their results narrow in focus; developmental rating scales tended to list desirable behavior and then to watch children's growth in that direction. Only full descriptive accounts taken over a long period of time could be the basis of a sound analysis of growth. No claim was made that this was a large-scale, statistically controlled and significant study, since the children were few in number, and their ages ranged widely. The value of the data, however, resided in the complete picture of children at work and play that emerged.

Intellectual Growth in Young Children (1930)

The actual records from the Malting House School were given at length in both of Susan Isaacs's books about the work there, for not only did she want to arrive at a sound theoretical understanding of children's growth; she also wanted to give the reader every opportunity to see the evidence on which her conclusions were based, and even to make further studies based on the data, as appropriate. Since there were few such records in existence, she felt an obligation to make hers fully available. In *Intellectual Growth in Young Children,* she provided the day-by-day incidents illustrating cognitive growth; a special section about the children's biological interests; a complete narrative account of four sample weeks; and a summary of all the types of activities that the children had engaged in during her three and a half years at the school. In *Social Development in Young Children,* she even went beyond the data from the Malting House, bringing in illustrative material from other authors as well.

The arrangements and educational technique at the Malting House School, already described, appear in the first two chapters of *Intellectual Growth in Young Children.* Isaacs then moved to an analysis of her data, in particular, "discovery, reasoning and thought," while social and emotional growth were discussed in the second book. She classified her data on cognitive behavior on the basis of themes that seemed to emerge after a direct scrutiny of the records themselves, although she felt it was important to bear in mind constantly that children's thought is a unified and continuous *process:*

> It would not be possible for anyone who had lived with the children while these records were being made, and had felt the continuous impact of their minds upon things and events and each other, to rest content with any formal scheme of relations or relation finding, of types of judgment or reasoning. The children themselves compel us to look at the problem of cognition in terms of *process,* and of genetic history. Their thought is active and prehensile. It changes as their purposes change, and rests no longer in the static form of explicit judgment and inference than is momentarily needed for the momentary aim. It moves continuously on, developing and growing as their practical and social situations change and develop from moment to moment.[33]

Among the continuous activities of the children, there were three distinguishable types: practicing or perfecting bodily skills, make-believe play, and investigations of the physical surroundings. Intellectual processes could be seen in all of these, as the records show. Here is a small sampling, to show children thinking in different ways.

A. Sometimes the children took information they already had, and used it in new situations, either directly or by imaginative reconstruction:

> 19.1.27 (19 January, 1927) Using the blocks to build a bridge, Phineas (aged 3:10) took two triangular bricks and fitted them together, saying, "These go together, then they go the same as these"—pointing to a square one.

> 2.6.25 A lady visitor came to talk to the children about her journey from Australia. When they heard that she was several weeks on the boat, Dan (4:1) said, "Then you'd have to have beds on the boat," and one of the others, "Did you have breakfast and supper on the boat?" "Yes." Dan: "Then you'd have to have tables and chairs."

> 22.2.26 In the afternoon, Herbert and Alfred were coming down the stairs from the gallery, and H. slipped on A., so that they both fell heavily to the bottom. They were not hurt, but their cries brought the other children to ask what had happened. Dan begged them to show him "how it happened." Mrs. I.* made some remark about the steepness of the stairs, and Dan (5:1) replied, "Yes, because there's not enough room at the bottom. If there was more room, we could push the bottom of the stairs out, and they wouldn't be so steep."

> 11.12.26. A new carpenter's bench had come, and the children looked at it with great interest. They wondered what the big wooden screws were for. Conrad (5:11) said, "I know, perhaps they're to steady the wood against."

> June, 27. The children wanted to re-paint the seesaw, and Joseph was eager to do

---

*The children's name for Susan Isaacs.

it at once. James (5:2), however, said, "It would be a good thing to wait until the last day of the term, and then it would have all the holiday to dry in."

1.5.27. James (5:1) found a long pole, which led to a play of a butcher's shop, in which Mrs. I. bought "meat," and he hooked it down with the pole. When selling a small piece of meat, he asked her, "Will that be enough? How many children have you?" She replied, "Fourteen." He laughed and said promptly, "Well, then, *that* won't be enough meat."

17.10.24. The children had been carrying water out into the garden in cans and jugs, and as there were some damp feet, Mrs. I. said, "no more today." Tommy (2:8) was doleful when Mrs. I. would not let him take more, and passing back through the schoolroom, he saw the vases on the tables, full of flowers. Without saying anything, he put down his can on the floor, and took each of the four vases in turn, lifting the flowers out, pouring the water into his can, and putting the flowers back, and the vase back on the table. He then walked out into the garden smiling, and saying to the others, "Tommy has some water now!"

4.3.27. Dan (5:9) was sitting on his tricycle in the garden, backpedalling. Mrs. I said to him, "You're not going forward, are you?" "No, of course not, when I'm turning them the wrong way." She asked, "How does it go forward when it does? What makes it?" He replied, in a tone of great scorn for her ignorance, "Well, of course, your feet push the pedals round, and the pedals make that thing go round (pointing to the hub of the cranks), and that makes the chain go round, and the chain makes that go round (pointing to the hub of the wheel), and the wheels go round, and there you are!"

4.3.27. The kettle was on the stove boiling, a jet of steam coming out of the spout. Dan and Priscilla waved their hands at it, and Dan (5:9) spat at the kettle. When Mrs. I. asked him, "Please don't spit," he replied, "But I wanted to stop that coming out!"

1.10.27. At tea, Denis (3:10) said, "The bread's buttered already isn't it? So if we want it without butter we can't, can we?—unless we 'crape it off wiv a knife . . . and if we want it without butter and don't want to 'crape it off wiv a knife, we have to eat it wiv butter, don't we?"

B. Sometimes the children made experiments, in order to find out what would happen:

12.11.24. Some modelling wax having been dropped on a hot-water pipe, the children discovered that it melted, and tried some more. When they found that all the wax would melt, whatever colour it was, they went on to try other materials—plasticine, wood, chalk, and so on, talking about it together and telling Mrs. I., "Plasticine melts. Wood won't melt", and so on. The whole of this was entirely spontaneous. (Ages 4:0 to 5:0)

19.6.25. Frank (5:8) saw a stick floating on the water in a bowl, and put other things in to see if they would float—a penny, scissors, a piece of plasticine, a shell, a piece of chalk, paper, a pencil, a tin lid, etc. He said, "All the things made of wood will float," and took the lot out into the garden to show the others. They, however, were not interested at the time; but later on, Dan (4:0) put some paper on the water, and said, "If it's crumpled up, it floats, but a flat piece sinks."

21.10.25. The lights in the school room are on pulleys, and Frank (6:0) today pointed out "that white thing above the light" (the white china weight on the pulley), and asked, "What is it for?" Mrs. I. pulled the light down until it was within his reach, and he moved it up and down with great interest, calling the others to "come and see." The children then asked Mrs. I. to pull all the six lights down low, and they made "houses" under each of them. They all felt the bulbs, "Feel how warm it is."

30.11.25. Tommy (3:8) was using coloured chalk, and discovered that when he used yellow and blue on top of each other, "They make green." He then asked, "What do red and blue make when they're mixed?" Mrs. I., "Try and you'll see."

27.1.26. A Bunsen burner had been fitted in the school-room, and the children experimented with it a good deal today. They noticed the difference in the flame as they turned the nozzle round to control the supply of air. Frank (6:3) blew down the pipe, "to feel the air come out." A few days earlier that had been a long discussion as to "Whether glass would melt." One of the children had been told (elsewhere) that it would, and the others didn't believe it. Today Mrs. I. held a glass rod in the flame, and they watched it melt with great interest. "Oh, it does melt!"

29.1.26. Frank (6:3) and Christopher (5:4) used the Bunsen for sometime, altering the flame constantly with the air supply. Priscilla (6:5) joined them, and they held glass rods in the flame, watching them when they "went soft," and discovering accidentally that they could join two pieces together by fusion when soft.

22.6.26. The children having long been very interested in the problems of water supply, today Mrs. I. gave them a glass U tube. Dan on seeing it said, "That's a U." They poured water into one arm with a funnel. They remarked at once that the water came up into the other arm of the tube, and they took turns at pouring the water in and out, with delighted interest. They told Mrs. I. to write down (in the Writing-Down Book) "We found a U that is a bottle, and if you put water down into it, it goes up the other side of the U. The water weighs up and down when you've done it" (Dan 5:1); "like a scale" (Christopher 5:9).

14.7.26. The weather was extremely hot and dry, and today the children had a hose-pipe in the garden. Dan (5:2) and Christopher (5:10) spent a long time making various experiments with the stream of water. They found that they could make the see-saw swing up and down by directing the water against one end or the other, and washed out a hole in the gravel path with the water.

19.7.26. The children had a bonfire of rubbish in the garden, and they remarked on the volume of smoke coming from it, and called themselves "brave" when they ran through it. Dan (5:2) said, "It makes me choke when it goes down inside." He asked, "Is there any soot in the smoke?" Mrs. I. replied, "Let's hold something in it and see." They held a white plate in the smoke; a thin brown film was deposited, and the children said, "Yes, there *is* soot in it." Mrs. I. then took a candle, lit it, and held the plate in the smoke from it. The children said, on seeing the heavier deposit of soot, "There's *much* more soot in that." Dan said, "You've burnt the plate." Mrs. I. washed the plate, and he saw that the soot came off and that the plate itself was not burnt.

4.2.27. When Phineas (3:11) had eaten his orange, he went to wash his plate, and asked for something else to wash. He was given a mug to wash, and spent twenty minutes slowly pushing the mop in and out of the mug, watching the water come up around it, and saying, "Look at the bubbles!" The mop fitted fairly tightly, and he experimented with the suction as he pulled it, and noticed the way the water came up round as he pushed it in.

C. Sometimes the children asked questions of each other or of adults, or entered into discussions, which led to more exact knowledge.

1.7.26. The children had to wait twenty minutes for something, and asked, "Will it be long?" Mrs. I. replied, "It will be twenty minutes. I don't know how long that will seem to you." Dan said, "Will you show us on the clock?" Mrs. I. did so. He then said, "How many is twenty? Will you count?" She counted from one to twenty. This was done once or twice. Christopher (5:9) said, "What is counting? That's not twenty *minutes*." Mrs. I. replied, "Oh, no, I counted faster than the minutes go." They then said, "Will you show us how long one minute is?" They sat still for one minute.

19.1.25. The children had seen Mrs. I. opening the skylight and came to do it too, taking turns. One of them said, "Me after Tommy," and then Tommy (2:11) himself said, "Me after Tommy" He at once drew Mrs. I.'s attention to this, laughing and repeating it—"I said "Me after Tommy"

1.2.27. Lena (4:1) and Conrad (6:2) were looking at the fresh-water aquarium. Conrad said, "I can see the snail." Lena said, "I can see it, but I wonder why it's sinking at the top." Conrad, with great scorn, "It couldn't sink at the top (turning to Mrs. I.), could it? If it sinks, it goes to the bottom." Lena looked at Mrs. I. questioningly so Mrs. I. said, "Yes, if it sinks it goes to the bottom." What does it do if it stays at the top?" asked Lena. Conrad: "It's floating", and Lena said with a happy little laugh, "It's floating."

June, 1927. At lunch, the children talked about "the beginning of the world." Dan (6:1) insists, whatever may be suggested as "the beginning", that there must always have been "something before that." He said, "You see, you might say that first of all there was a stone and everything came from that—but (with great emphasis), *where did the stone come from?*" There were two or three variants on this theme. Then Jane (11:0) from her superior store of knowledge, said, "Well, I have read that the earth was a piece of the sun, and that the moon was a piece of the earth." Dan with an air of eagerly pouncing on a fallacy, "Ah! but where did *the sun* come from? Tommy (5:4), who had listened to all this very quietly, now said with a quiet smile, "I know where the sun came from!" The others said eagerly, "Do you, Tommy? Where? Tell us!" He smiled still more broadly, and said, "Shan't tell you!" to the vast delight of the others, who thoroughly appreciated this joke.

2.2.26. There was a discussion as to whether Priscilla should marry Dan or Frank. Frank said, "You can't marry Dan because daddy must be bigger than mammy." The children appealed to Mrs. I. as to whether this was so, and each child was asked in turn whether his daddy was bigger than his mammy. Conrad said quite accurately that his daddy was not. Dan said, "No, they're just the same." The others all agreed that "daddies *must* be bigger than mammies." Dan (4:8) at once said, "Yes, you see, I shall be bigger than she is."

17.11.25. The children had made a large "boat" with chairs, and were modelling while sitting in it. They talked about trains and boats "that went all night," and one of them said, "What about the driver? When would he go to sleep?" After discussion, they came to the conclusion that "you might have two drivers, one for the night and one for the day."

26.4.26. The children talked of "how the garden would look to the man in the aeroplane." Mrs. I. showed them an aerial photograph, and they identified trees, houses and the road. Christopher (5:8) said the man in the aeroplane would "see some little specks walking about", and the others agreed that he would see "only the tops of heads." When later they made a model of the garden in plasticine, some of them put in small oval lumps, "that's how we look to the man in the aeroplane."

16.2.26. The children were writing and posting letters to Christopher's father in Switzerland, and the word "two" came in. Priscilla (6:10) asked Mrs. I. to spell it, and when she wrote "two", she said, "That's not 2—you should put "to". Mrs. I. told her that there were three different meanings. The children then supplied instances of these different words, with much amusement. Christopher (5:9) then said, "Yes, and there is C, the letter C, and there is *sea*-bathing, and the see when I say 'I see' ".

All of these vignettes show the children busily at work, chatting and finding out and practicing their new-found grasp of the world,

> a complex dynamic series of adaptive reactions and reflections. These crystallise out here and there into clear judgments or definite hypotheses or inferences, which, however, gain all their meaning from their place in the whole movement of the child's mind in its attempt to grasp and organise its experience.[34]

Children think in different ways at the same time, then, and also they are not always in top form. Depending on their feelings at the moment, the social situation, or their previous information, children may be quite logical at one moment, as when Dan so clearly explained how the tricycle worked, and quite fanciful the next, as when he spat back at the kettle to stop the steam from coming out. These are not equally logical responses, yet in fact the same child made them on the same day.

Yet bearing all the complexities and difficulties in mind, Susan Isaacs believed that central features of children's thought do emerge from the records: little children do show a capacity for logical thinking; it is not fundamentally different from adults; and it is a continuous process from the simplest forms of adaptive behavior to the more complex. What is different is the amount of experience the children have had. Their reasoning improves in precision as their experience increases, and as they learn how to predict, observe, make discoveries, and refine their knowledge. Further, this process can be fostered but not dictated: it moves first in one direction and then in another, depending on the child's inner needs or interests, or the mood of the group. Children make their own meaning of the world, within the range of their native ability and their environment.

If this is true, then one comes to the age-old controversy of nature vs. nurture. If children's cognitive development is, in large part, a function of their increasing ability to deal with experience, what part does heredity play? For Susan Isaacs, heredity does determine the level of cognitive performance that any child can achieve. Here "nature" has the final word:

> Nature is all-powerful in fixing the level of intelligence or general mental ability to which any one of us attains. . . . nature not only gives the original measure of general ability, but has also the main voice in decreeing its form of expression in the successive periods of development.[35]

Thus, as children mature, their innate abilities do limit how well they can profit from their experience. But aside from determining ability level, maturation should be seen as no more than a "limiting" concept, and nothing should be attributed to it that can be seen to be a product of experience. Maturation, in other words, sets the ceiling on what children can grasp at any stage, but it does not produce thinking or understanding unaided. Interaction with the world calls for ever more mature forms of cognition; but without such experience, maturation alone does not produce development. No new adaptive forms of beavhior, unheralded by earlier, simpler forms, suddenly appear because of maturational timing. Nor are there innate ideas that appear without preparatory experience leading up to their formulation and paving the way. In general, mental development proceeds along a smooth and continuous line. "There is no break anywhere; no plateau, no steep ascent, no sudden change of direction."[36] There is flexible movement back and forth, and there is overlapping, but the general movement is that of unified progress.

> Development is very far from being an affair of the successive appearance of a number of isolated functions or faculties. The central factor remains dominant throughout the period of growth.[37]

There is, then, a fundamental unity of all mental processes. As Spearman had brought out, the essential act of cognition consists of seeing relationships or their correlates, on the basis of the "direct apprehension of experience."[38] The simplest recognition of similarities between shapes, sizes, and colors is no different from an adult's more abstract use of mathematical symbols. Both proceed according to the same "noetic" (unified) principles of mental processes. For instance, the boy who noticed the butter already on the bread and figured out what would happen if he "'craped it off wiv a knife" was expressing his understanding of how things operate in relation to one another. So too, the boy who understood that a ship would need tables and chairs and beds for a long voyage had grasped the relationship between his own daily experience and that of the traveler.

> In each case, the child's cognitive act is similar in its most essential character to his later acts of understanding, of reasoning, or of practical organization, as a historian, a scientist, or a man of affairs. Each proceeds, in so far as new knowledge on a new application of knowledge is achieved, by the eduction of relations or their correlates; and in each, taken in relation to the age of the thinker, his general ability will be revealed.[39]

From this point of view, maturation appears as a matter of increasing depth, breadth, and range of cognitive functioning, the growing power of abstract and symbolic thought, and the capacity to solve ever more complex problems, all within the limits of inborn intelligence.

This discussion of the characteristics of children's thought and of the relative influence of innate and environmental factors led Susan Isaacs to a lengthy critique of the work of Jean Piaget in the same field, as it was then available in his first five books. She and her husband both had grasped immediately the great importance of his work, yet the broader observations made at the Malting House caused her to disagree with some of his findings about cognitive development. The final selection in *Intellectual Growth in Young Children* was a long essay by Nathan Isaacs, "Children's Why Questions." Here he examined the different kinds of questions children asked at the Malting House School, and, like his wife, was led to differ with Piaget's views (see chapter 6 for a fuller discussion of this essay, and of the long dialogue between Piaget and the Isaacses).

After analyzing the nature of cognitive development, Susan Isaacs turned to the emotional side of growth as it affected the intellectual. One of the main types of activities among the children was make-believe, fantasy, and dramatic play, in great variety and vividness. What could be the relationship between fantasy and thought, especially since they so often appeared together? If thought proceeds by a noetic synthesis in such a way that all processes work together, what role does fantasy play as reasoning develops?

First, the fantasies, wishes, fears, and dreads of little children are very immediate to them, and they make use of the physical world to deal with them in a very specific way:

> Much of the child's earliest interest in physical objects is certainly derivative, and draws for its impetus from early infantile wishes and fears in relation to its parents. . . . the *first* value which the physical world has for the child is as a canvas upon which to project his personal wishes and anxieties, and his first form of interest in it is one of dramatic representation.[40]

By means of imaginative play, children symbolize and externalize their inner drama and conflicts, and work them through, achieving a measure of relief from their pressure and a diminution of anxiety and guilt. Conflicts are an inevitable part of growing up, and mental health is therefore dependent on the degree to which children have opportunities to deal with them in the objective world. Doing so successfully strengthens the ego's grasp on reality, and leads a child on ultimately to an interest in things for their own sake.

> Imaginative play builds a bridge by which a child can pass from the symbolic value of things to active inquiry into their real construction and real way of working.[41]

The uses that children may make of the opportunities provided for them cannot be planned or dictated ahead of time, because they depend on the individual child's psychic biography, and to exert such pressure might in fact do positive harm. The adult's role, rather, is to provide ample opportunities for imaginative play, for verbal expression, and for inquiry, and then to follow and support the children's interests as they appear.

Another way in which fantasy and thought are related is shown in the degree to which children's thinking is affected by current anxieties or fears, especially those stemming from the home. Susan Isaacs's report to Anne's mother demonstrates how the birth of twins so preoccupied her that she was unable to engage in activities as she had before. Another example is of Christopher, who had been playing with Dan at home and hurt Dan's finger badly with a hammer. Christopher, usually an active and lively child, spent the next whole day,

> quite unable to lose himself in any pursuit, and wandered about helplessly, asking, "What can I do, Mrs. I.? What is there to do?"

There are many examples in the records to show that general mental alertness and activity are very dependent on the absence of inner tensions or conflicts. Again, make-believe play can provide a chance to allay some anxieties by giving external form to feared objects or events, and thus achieve a measure of objective control.

A final relationship between fantasy and thought is that dramatic play provides children with the opportunity to create a make-believe situation, and to predict or hypothesize what might happen, and to play it out. They can act "as if" something were true, freed from the here-and-now of the concrete world. There seems to be

> this cognitive relation between thought and phantasy, and the way in which imaginative play fosters the development of thought and reasoning—particularly when, as in our special technique, the openings it offers for discussion or experiment are taken up sympathetically by interested adults.[42]

Yet for all that fantasy and thought intermingled in these ways, the children never confused fact and fancy. They could move easily from one to the other, and often an imaginative scene produced a statement of sound common sense, but the distinction was clear. James, for instance, could "sell" Mrs. I. a small piece of meat, but he also knew realistically that it would not feed all her children. Or, again:

October, 1927. Alfred was threatening James with hostile expressions of what he would do to James., "I'll go to a shop and I'll get all the guns and all the swords and all the knives there are in the shop, and I'll kill you." James (5:6) replied with a laugh, "They don't sell those things to children."

Gradually, as experience and accumulated knowledge increased, the use of fantasy or magical thinking decreased:

> Thus, through (1) the continuous growth of actual experience, both of physical fact and of other people's behaviour, and (2) the continuous development of intelligence itself, as noetic synthesis, the child becomes able to build the pattern of the objective world more and more securely into his modes of response. Ego-centric phantasy thus becomes more and more automatically tested against recognised experience, and more transformed by real situations. In later development, the direct expression of phantasy becomes more closely related to imaginative art and literature. Yet it leaves a permanent representative behind in the realm of thought itself, in the shape of the disciplined imagination of "as ifs" and of scientific hypothesis.[43]

There was one particular area of cognitive activity that the children engaged in, that Susan Isaacs singled out for special comment, namely, their "biological interests." She did so because she had a point to make. It was her view, made on the basis of her observations, that children show a vital interest in biological processes, especially in animals, and that it can and should be used for educational purposes. Their curiosity about digestion, reproduction, excretion, birth, and death are as natural as their interest in anything else, and closely allied to their understanding about themselves as human beings. Yet current opinion, she felt, was quite rigid and inhibitory about such interests, and just how far they should be followed up. The child is encouraged to tend animals and treat them kindly, but not to inquire or observe in detail how their bodies function as living creatures, or to look inside at their structure when they die.* Further, adults themselves make very contradictory uses of animals: they insist on kindness to animals, yet they eat them, kill them for sport, wear their skins, fear them, even experiment on them.

All this is further complicated by the fact that children also have contradictory impulses within themselves, impulses to cherish and to destroy, to be tender and to be cruel, to hurt and to make amends. When adults inhibit the expression of these impulses, or turn away from natural interests in matters like sex or death, the child is left confused and bereft of adults' guidance. The problem for Susan Isaacs was an educational one:

---

*See "The Humane Education of Young Children" in Part Two.

to make positive educational use of the child's impulses, so that they shall be fertile in skill and imaginative understanding, and lead out of themselves to the world of objective knowledge and common human purpose.[44]

The impulse to master or destroy, she felt, was an inner drive like any other, and could and should be expressed in the world of reality and thus objectified. When a child comes to know and recognize an animal as an independent entity, it becomes much less an object upon which to project these impulses, but rather a familiar creature to enjoy and learn about. The teachers welcomed and followed up any sign of interest in the children about life processes, whatever they were—heartbeats, running, digestion, illness, dying—and ways to find out more about them were provided. If an animal died, it was dissected to discover, if possible, what had caused the death. Questions about human processes were also taken seriously and appropriate means found to learn about them, without any inhibition of the child's curiosity on "sentimental or quasi-moral" grounds.[45]

The records showed the children's real and active interest in animals, as well as their varied responses of fantasy, cruelty, tenderness, and fear.

27.4.25. Mrs. I and the children had prepared a hutch for a hen, and this afternoon the hen and a sitting of eggs arrived. The children were very interested. Frank, having fowls at home, already understood that the hen would hatch chicks out of the egg, but the others did not. Dan asked whether they were "the same eggs as we eat?" They watch the man make a nest with straw in the coop, and arrange the eggs and put the hen on—and listened to his instructions about feeding, etc. In the following days, the children helped to put food and water for the hen, and often talked about the eggs.

8.5.25. The hen has deserted her eggs, and so the children each cracked one, to see what it was like inside. After talking about the blood-vessels which they could see, they stirred the egg up and said, "It's a scrambled egg."

23.3.26. Dan pretended to be a "crocodile", pulling his mouth out at the side with his fingers—a long ritualised play. Christopher and Priscilla made a bed for the crocodile and kept him in their house. Later Mrs. I. was "the keeper", and they bought him from her, but he would not stay with them as they did not give him enough to eat, nor food of the right kind, nor any water, and so on. Each time they went out for a walk he ran away and came back to his keeper, making a loud noise with his mouth as if he were hungry. He kept this play up, refusing to speak or behave as other than a crocodile, for a long time. At cocoa time, the crocodile was given cocoa to drink.

18.2.26. The children went into the garden. Priscilla wanted to pull a worm into halves, and said she would marry the boy who did. They all said they wanted to marry her, and Dan eventually did pull the worm in halves. Frank then pulled the rest of it apart; they were very excited about this.

29.6.25. Harold, Frank and Duncan threw a puppy into a bath of water, throwing it from some distance. They laughed when it looked wet and miserable.

15.7.25. Frank brought to the school a very small kitten—having talked for several days about the kittens at home. The children were delighted with it, and most charming to it. They all took turns at nursing it, carrying it to the house, and feeding it, all through the morning. They put it in a basket and fed it with milk.

20.7.26. Christopher, Dan, and Priscilla each dissected a mouse. While dissecting, Priscilla and Dan carried out a play of "mother" and "doctor", with the dead mice as children. They pretneded to telephone to each other about it, saying, "Your child is better now" and so on. Priscilla telephoned to Dan, "Your child is cut in two." Dan replied, "Well, the best thing to do would be to put the two halves together again." There were many inquiries and answers as to whether it was "better," and that it would "be better again soon," and so on. Presently Dan said, "Now I'm going to put some water on it, and make it come alive again." Priscilla joined in this. Priscilla gave Mrs. I. a dead mouse to hold, and said, "Now it is alive again" and pretended to make it walk. Mrs. I. said, "is it?" "Well, we are only pretending."

7.10.24. Robert found a spider in its web in a corner of a shed. Several of the children ran to look at it. Dan was also interested but refused to come nearer to it than several feet. He showed definite signs of fear, shivering as he looked at it. On several occasions, this mixture of interest and fear was shown; only gradually was the fear sufficiently overcome by suggestion and encouragement for him to come close and look at it.

Susan Isaacs found that the children benefited more from their contact with animals than with plants. Although the plants and their seasonal changes were observed, and the garden was a never-failing source of interest and enjoyment, the animals had a special appeal. Unlike plants, they move, respond, make noises, and have characteristics; their life cycle of birth, growth, reproduction, and death is more readily seen than the comparatively slow processes of plant life, as well as being more directly comparable to human beings. She found, in fact, that the wise use of animals was an important part of an educational environment for children, and helped them to understand and cherish all forms of life.

Social Development in Young Children (1933)

Intellectual Growth in Young Children had presented the reader with a full description of the Malting House School, the educational technique developed there, detailed observations of the children's spontaneous activities, and an analysis of their cognitive development arising from these records. *Social Development in Young Children* also provided extensive anecdotal accounts of the children, this time of their personal and social behavior, and a theoretical discussion and analysis. Isaacs was concerned, however, that readers understand this division, for it was made only to facilitate discussion, not because the children or the records showed any such division. She was emphatic that it would be unfair to the school and to the children if her two books were not seen as complementary accounts.[46]

While the emphasis in the second book was on social behavior, the observations made included much behavior that was not specifically interpersonal or reciprocal, but primarily egocentric. This was partly caused by the wide age range of the children. But Isaacs also believed that the stable social relationships that develop in the middle years of childhood have their beginnings in the earliest years of infancy, and must go through a definite pattern of gradual progress throughout childhood, although always with some movement backward as well as forward. And since later social skills crucially depend on earlier ones, a full consideration of even presocial behavior must be included.

Susan Isaacs was also well aware that much of the behavior in her records was upsetting and even shocking to adults. It was sometimes crude, aggressive, hostile, or sexual, although at other times the children enjoyed hours of friendly cooperation. Whatever behavior occurred was reported, even if it was of the kind that is usually "slurred over, hidden away, or altogether denied"[47] by ordinary people and even by psychologists studying children. Her motive in presenting a more complete picture was to persuade readers that less acceptable behavior is "neither abnormal nor very unusual,"[48] but is as much and as important a part of growing up as the more fully socialized actions that please adults. Here her point of view derived from her early biological training; she saw children essentially as creatures with survival needs, whose primitive, defensive behavior is gradually shaped by their interaction with the environment into more and more appropriate modes. There was nothing to be shocked or horrified about in this.

> I myself happen to be interested in everything that little children do and feel. I am unable to accept the idea that anything that is true of children can be too shocking for adults to know. If a thing is true, we should surely be able to bear knowing it.[49]

This was the spirit in which she and her staff made their observations, so that whatever patterns emerged would be based on records of the children's total behavior.

For children have "a great, a desperate need to be understood,"[50] and they need enlightened help to move beyond their primitive impulses toward social, stable relationships. The adults at the Malting House School did not simply ignore or sanction aggressive or sexual behavior, however. Their technique was rather to find ways to provide activities and adult support that would enable the children to make use of reality to deal with the inner conflicts and anxieties that caused antisocial behavior. This method proceeded on the basis of understanding what the children needed and providing it; there were no moralizings or inhibitions born of adult inconvenience or upset.

Susan Isaacs also wanted the reader to have a full picture of children's behavior because she had become convinced that the data clearly confirmed Freud's theory of infantile sexuality. Some psychologists and educators at the time were trying to dismiss it as mere "dogma," but she believed that others were beginning to see the scientific validity of this theory. She therefore added to the Malting House School data some additional accounts of little children written by nonanalytic observers. These consisted of observations sent to her by friends who knew she was interested, selections from the more than four hundred letters written to her as "Ursula Wise" by mothers and nurses who read her weekly column in *The Nursery World*, an extensive account of one child's behavior during a difficult phase of her life, and anecdotes reported by a total of five other authors in their books about child development. These additional data provided

> an indication that the eyes of non-analytic observers are gradually being opened to what, only a few years ago, would never have been seen, or, if seen, admitted, in the emotional life of little children. [This] marks a very great advance in the scientific accuracy and dispassionateness of the academic text-books. This most significant chapter in the child's psychological history is now beginning to gain admittance to the previously closed pages of academic teaching on mental development.[51]

The theory of infantile sexuality, she felt, threw profound light on the origins of children's behavior, and when used with neurotic children in play therapy, as Melanie Klein was then doing, it provided an effective tool for interpretation and treatment. Yet all children, at one time or another, show disturbances and difficulties that may seem neurotic or even bizarre, but that are normal and with sensible handling soon pass away.*

The general lines of classification of the social and personal data derived from Susan Isaacs's interest, as a psychoanalyst, in the "problems of love and hate, and of the relation between sexuality and guilt."[52] The more detailed groupings under these two broad headings were arrived at from a direct study of the records themselves.

The first heading is "Social Relations: Love and Hate in Action." Here, incidents were grouped that showed primitive egocentric attitudes, hostility, and aggression, both on the part of individuals and of groups of children, and also instances of unusual friendliness and cooperation. Naturally, there was a good deal of overlap among these accounts, since a friendly game may turn into teasing or bullying, or an agrument about a prized possession may, sometimes with adult help, become a shared game of make-believe.

A. Primary egocentric attitudes in social play: this type of behavior includes instances that show that

---

*See sample "Ursula Wise" columns in Part Two.

the child implicitly expects other people's behaviour to fall into the pattern of his own phantasies, and when it does not, he attempts to enforce his will upon them.[53]

In so doing, the child may arbitrarily assign another person to a part in a game whether or not the other person is willing or interested; he may claim to be leader and give everyone else inferior parts to play; he may then refuse to take a lower part once he has been on top; or he may threaten, bribe, or make appeals to his playmates in order to get his own way.

> 21.4.25. Harold found a toy revolver in the sand pit, and used it for some time. He said to Mrs. I., "I know a lovely game. You go along there and then I will say, 'A lady to shoot,' and then you must fall down." The others joined in too.
>
> 24.2.25. Tommy brought his mouth organ to school and Dan suggested, "Shall all the boys take turns to use it? Shall we be a band, and *I'll* go first?" He then tried to take the mouth organ from Tommy. "Oh, *give* it me," he said, "I'm going first, we're going to be a band!"
>
> 16.2.26. Priscilla suggested a game. All the children sat round on the platform, she bowed to each in turn, and then took them to a row of chairs which she had arranged, and told them to do certain things—to put their toes on the floor and their heads back, and clasp their hands. She washed them then, told them to open their mouths, and so on; put them to bed and "took their temperature." She is "the nurse" and Conrad is to be "the doctor." They have "a temperature of 103." Frank and Dan were the patients in bed. When they grew tired of the game and of having everything determined by her, Priscilla kept them in bed by the continual threat, "Well, then, I won't *marry* you!" Frank in the end said, "I don't care if you don't," and went to his own pursuits.
>
> March, 1927. Dan wanted to use the potter's wheel, and asked Gerry to turn the handle for him. He said to Gerry, "You turn this handle will you? and when *your* arm gets tired—I'll get someone else to turn it!"

B. Hostility and aggression: all the children, both individually and in small groups, showed hostility to other children and to adults at one time or another. The motives varied: sometimes the issue was a wish for power, sometimes for sole possession of a favorite toy, sometimes for ascendancy over a rival; sometimes, however, aggressive behavior arose from no evident cause, or was directed at a stranger, newcomer, or scapegoat.

> 17.10.24. The children plucked the withered hollyhock stalks and used them to march round the garden in "Follow my Leader." There was a good deal of squabbling amongst the children as to whose was the longest of the sticks, everyone wanting these. Conrad was standing in the sand-pit with his own stick in his hand, and saw another child with one exactly similar in shape and size. Immediately, quite unaware of the stick he was holding, he shouted out, "That's *mine*," and tried to take it—looking surprised when we pointed out that he already had his.
>
> 20.10.26. Laurie and Dexter had a struggle for the use of the bicycle, and Laurie said, "I *mentioned* for it first."

21.10.26. Laurie and Dexter had two or three struggles during the morning for the bicycle, trumpet, etc., Laurie being very determined and tenacious. She scratched Dexter.

26.10.26. Laurie and Joseph had several struggles for the tricycle, in which they seemed to be very evenly matched. The elder children kept an even justice, taking either of the two off when they thought she had had "her turn".

May 1927. Christopher constituted himself "the gramophone man," and bullied the younger children into letting him take charge of it, choose the records and decide everything!

5.3.25. When Phineas was resting in the afternoon he wanted to go downstairs, but Mrs. I. said, "No, will you rest a little longer, please." Phineas said angrily, "I don't think you are *really* kind, Mrs. I." and "I'll send you away, and cut you up and eat you."

27.10.25. Priscilla and Dan were making a "mulberry bush," and asked Mrs. I. not to look at it until it was finished. Presently Priscilla called Mrs. I. to look, but Dan said, "No, it's not enough," and when Priscilla persisted, he shrieked out, "No, it's *not* enough," and pushed her. She hit him, and he then bit her severely, leaving a deep mark. She cried bitterly and came to Mrs. I. for comfort. He stood beside her looking very miserable; and, looking at the mark, said, "That doesn't hurt."

20.1.25. Harold invented a game. He built a large tower with bricks, asked Mrs. I. to sit on the table at one end of the room, and all the children under his direction ran round the room, saying as they passed her, "We are going to blow it up," and she was instructed to say, "No, no," every time they passed.

12.11.24. Benjie and others had been melting modelling wax on the hot water pipes with much interest and excitement. Duncan ran to see it, but Benjie said to him, "No, *you* shan't see it," and pushed him down.

9.12.24. Speaking to Dan, Mrs. I. called him "darling." Benjie at once said, "Why don't you call *me* that?" Mrs. I. replied, "But I often do." Benjie then said to Conrad, "I don't like you, Conrad. I'll get a gun and shoot you dead."

29.4.27. Lena and Joseph (Joseph's first term) were playing in the sand-pit when Penelope arrived. As soon as Penelope approached, Joseph stiffened aggressively and clenched his fists. They both eyed each other up and down hostilely for several seconds, then Joseph relaxed, Penelope moved away—and each went on with his own pursuit. No word was spoken.

May 1927. Joseph was overheard to say in the fourth week, "I don't like Priscilla—she tries to take Dan away from me." Phineas often expressed dislike of the other children—very emphatically: "I *hate* Lena"—"I *hate* Joseph." One morning Lena had a quarrel with Dan, who pushed her down so that she got up sandy and muddy. She came running to Mrs. I. to tell her. "I don't like Dan. He pushed me down—I hate him." All this was said with a frowning face of anger. Then, suddenly, lifting her face up, with a most ingratiating smile, she said, "And I hope you do, too." She seemed very disappointed when Mrs. I. said, "No, I don't."

12.11.24. Frank came into school saying, "Kill Miss B., kill Miss B., kill Miss B." and kept saying it every now and then during the day. After one of these moments of unprovoked and moody hostility, Frank suddenly burst into tears, and when asked what was the matter, could only sob, "I don't know, I don't know." This was one of his specially unhappy days.

27.5.25. Towards the end of the morning, Theobald without saying a word to anyone, and with a very determined air, went round the room taking off all the labels which the others had written and pinned on the various things in the room, and crumpled them up and threw them out of the window.

28.10.26. Dan began the day in a quarrelsome mood, trying to intimidate the others, to break up Phineas' modelling, and so on. He threatened to strike Phineas with a heavy engine in his hand, and when Mrs. I. took this away, he said she was "horrid, and I'm not coming to this school any more." In this mood, for a part of the time, he pretended to be "an engine that ran over people."

1.12.26. Phineas was hammering nails into the door, and Conrad opened the door from outside, thereby pushing it against Phineas. The latter hit Conrad with his hammer. Conrad cried because this hurt, and when the other children came to see what had happened, he shouted angrily at them, *"Don't look."* They laughed at this, and he became very angry, and rushed at Dan as he was passing, and bumped him against the stairs.

17.3.25. During the morning, Mrs. I. told Harold and Frank that Priscilla was coming to lunch. They asked what her name was, and laughed at it very much. They at once spoke of "smacking her" and throwing things at her." When Priscilla came, Dan sitting opposite to her, said several times, "Shall we shout in her ear?" and "Shall we hit her?" After lunch, when they went into the garden, the boys stood round her at first in an affectionate way, but later in a rather hostile manner. They said they would "squeeze her." Dan stood with his arms open, saying, "Let's squeeze her." She replied, "if you squeeze me, I'll squeeze you," but later she found the boys rather overwhelming and began to cry for her mother.

10.2.27. Phineas and Lena were digging happily together in the sandpit. Lena began making her "pie" into a "castle." She made a little hole in the side with her finger and said, "There's a pussy in there." Phineas, looking in, "Where? Can you see it?" Lena: "It doesn't like you." Phineas, "Why?" *"Because it hasn't seen you before!"* Phineas, after a pause, "Does it like me now?"

20.10.24. Robert and Frank were digging in the garden, and found some worms. Mrs. I. was digging near them, and Frank said to Robert, "Shall we put a worm down her back, so that it will bite her?"

6.3.25. Frank and Harold had a squabble and Frank hit Harold on the head with a cardboard clock. Mrs. I. took the clock away according to her rule. Frank protested violently against this and Harold took his part against Mrs. I. Paul then joined in, too, with the others against Mrs. I., saying, *"Here* is the beast, I'll pull her down!"

Autumn term 1926. Miss D. joined the staff of the school half-way through this term. For two or three weeks a group of the children, including Jane, Dan, Conrad and Priscilla were extremely hostile to her, frequently calling her a "beast"—"Oh, here comes that beast"—saying they did not want to be with her, and creating difficulties at meal times and bed times. After two or three weeks this wore off and she was promoted to one of their "best friends" and a favorite member of the staff.

9.11.25. Frank and Priscilla were hostile to Penelope saying she was "dirty," "a faeces girl," and so on. Priscilla kept this up with more persistence and vindictiveness than Frank. All the children now just say they "don't like Penelope"; it seems to be a social fashion.

24.1.27. When the elder children heard that Lena had arrived, they said as if at some concerted signal, "Oh, that dragon has come," and ran into the schoolroom shouting in a hostile and intimidating way, "Oh, there is the dragon."

C. Friendliness and cooperation: The records showed fewer instances of this type of behavior than of the more hostile variety, for "the happiest days with children are those that have no history."[54] Conflict provided the drama in the school, although times of peaceful play occurred regularly, as did many instances of helpfulness and cooperation.

12.11.24. The children were all modelling, very quietly, and Dan made a boat and gave it to Benjie. Benjie told the others, "He has made a boat for me." Dan remarked, "Yes, I like you very much and I'm going to kiss you." He kissed Benjie's hand. Benjie told the others, "He likes me." Dan then said to Harold, "I like you and I'm going to kiss you," and kissed Harold's hand. Harold said, "He's a dear little thing," and all the others agreed.

6.3.25. Paul was in the garden, and wanting to come in when the door was shut, he called out to Mrs. I., "Open the door, my Princess dear, open the door, my Princess dear."

23.3.25. Dan cried at lunch-time because he had not been given a brown plate, and when Harold, who had a brown plate, had finished his pudding, he took his spoon off and passed it to Dan—"You can have my brown plate." He stroked his hand affectionately several times, and Dan said to him, "I love you, Harold, I love you."

1.12.25. Jessica was in the garden, and Priscilla and Dan wanted her to come in and join their play of "school." They kept inviting her, and after a time she did so. Priscilla took off Jessica's outdoor things and washed her hands for her. Dan said to Jessica, "You've come in because you love us, haven't you?"

16.3.26. When the children were drawing in the afternoon they arranged their tables very close to Mrs. I.'s saying, "Lovely Mrs. I."

5.5.26. Dan and the others were today very happy and friendly together. The children were digging in and near the sand-pit, with a game of "Making a new road." Dan voluntarily put his superior reading and writing at their service, and wrote a notice, "This road is up for repairs," and fastened it up where they were playing.

2.12.26. Priscilla had brought sheets of coloured paper to make streamers to decorate the school room. The other children wanted to join in this, and she generously gave them each some paper, and showed them how to make the rings. She gave particular help to Phineas, who was very anxious to do it, but rather inept. He struggled very hard to learn and spent all the rest of the morning on it, in the end making a long string of rings. The other children commented on his achievement in admiring tones, standing round—"Fancy Phineas being able to do that! Isn't it splendid!"

19.1.27. Jessica hurt her finger when moving one of the tables. Phineas at once went over to her and said, "Jessica, I'll rub it for you."

All the children at the school expressed their feelings of both love and hate toward others at one time or another. All the children were driven by the wish to possess, to assert themselves over others, to play one child or adult off against another, and so on. Overall, however, there was definite social progress during the first year of the school's existence. At first, when the children first came into this unusual and unfamiliar setting, there was a subdued, rather quiet period. Soon they realized that not only were they quite free to do and say almost anything they wished, but also that most of the prohibitions and punishments they were used to were missing here. Then followed "an outburst of disorder and boisterousness"[55] during which it seemed as if the majority of the children spent most of their time asserting themselves against others, destroying their play, or annoying the adults present. It was a testing time, primarily, although some constructive play did go on in the midst of the aggressive, acting out-behavior. Gradually, however, and not all at once, this disorder gave way and the group took on a definitely social shape, able to work and play together more freely and compatibly. There were constant free activity, the give and take of friendly relationships, and a newfound pleasure in inventiveness and creativity. At the same time that social progress of this kind was being made, individual children showed some remarkable changes too,

> a change from fear and peevishness and active hostility to calm and friendliness and freedom and play and cumulative activity.[56]

Even children who had seemed most anxious or hesitant were gradually able to enter with greater zest into the social and intellectual opportunities that the school offered. Here seemed to be the best vindication of the methods used with the children.

D. The next group of incidents recorded show the children behaving in ways that indicate the "deeper sources" of their feelings;

> It remains to consider the deeper sources of love and hate and anxiety in [the children's] individual minds, by examining the records of their sexual development, and attempting to use those occasional signs and hints of deeper unconscious mental processes which every now and then the children offer us in their words and deeds.[57]

The records, however, could not be full enough to form a systematic survey of sexual development in children, since although they enjoyed a great deal of freedom, they were not left "guideless"; some adult restraints were certainly enforced, and by the time the children came to the school, they were already well aware of other adults' prohibitions. Further, the work of the school was educational; it was not the special setting of therapy, but encouraged the children to express their fantasies and interests in the real world, thus objectifying them and diffusing the feelings of anxieties concerned with them. However, despite the fact that the records of children's sexual behavior as part of their social development were necessarily fragmentary,

> as these records demonstrate, far more such openly sexual behavior occurs among small children than is usually admitted, and quite enough to bear witness to the truth of the psycho-analytic view of the child's emotional development.[58]

In this section of the records, the children's behavior was grouped under two headings: "infantile sexuality," and "guilt and shame." The sexual behavior observed took a variety of forms; oral erotism and sadism; anal and urethral interests and aggression; exhibitionism, direct and verbal; sexual curiosity and masturbation; castration fears, threats, and symbolism; family play, ideas about babies and marriage; and "cosy places"—small, enclosed, private refuges.[59]

1. Oral erotism and sadism (i.e., biting and spitting)

> 22.10.24. George again put the rugs into his mouth when resting. He always puts plasticine into his mouth. At lunch, Robert said, "Shall we wee-wee on the table?" and then suddenly, "Here's the wee-wee," and spat on his plate.

> 28.1.25. George and Frank, having climbed up to the window overlooking the lane, to see a motor, began to spit on the window; Dan joined in: they all spat vigorously, and said, "Look at it running down." George also spoke of "belly," and Frank of "ah-ah-lu-lu," and "bim-bom," both laughing.

> 4.11.24. There was again much spitting and bubbling at lunch, and the children showed each other the food protruding from their mouths.

> Autumn 1927. Dan, throughout the term, was very fond of biting the finger of any grown-up he passed near, and unless prevented would bite quite hard. This was not done in apparent temper; and when one refused to let him bite, he would sometimes say, "Then I'll kiss you instead," and kiss instead.

> 8.5.25. George and Conrad were sitting opposite each other at one table doing plasticine and somehow excited each other very much. They began throwing plasticine at each other, putting it in their mouths and biting it and laughing in an excited, screaming way. This went on for some time until Mrs. I. took the plasticine away.

2. Anal and urethral interests and aggression

> 19.11.24. At lunch the children had a conversation as to what people were "made of," and spoke of people being made of pudding, pie, potatoes, coal, etc., and of "bee-wee," "try," "do-do" "ah-ah," "bottie."

> 24.11.24. Conrad took a bowl from Benjie, Harold said, "I'll hit you in the face if you take mine." Benjie, "I'll wee-wee in your face." Benjie and Harold said to Tommy, "We'll put bim-bom bee-wee water in your face." When he is angry with Mrs. I., he sometimes says to the others, "Shall we pee-wee on someone?" The children were getting water to drink in cups, and Harold told the others that he had given Frank some "wee-wee water" to drink. He often says, "there's wee-wee

water in the bowl" in which he washes his hands. Later he said he had drunk "wee-wee water" and that the water in the cups was that. Frank said, "Shall we make Benjie drink wee-wee water?" "Yes," said Harold, "and poison him." And another time, "and make spots come out all over him."

11.2.25. After lunch, Frank and Dan made a "house" with chairs. Frank said "and we'll have a little lavatory, a little lav-lav." Presently he went to the real lavatory, saying, "Shall we go to our little lavatory?"

27.11.25. Priscilla pushed Tommy when he was carrying something very carefully; when Mrs. I. held her arm so that she should not upset him, Priscilla was very angry, and the other children took her part against Mrs. I., all joining in saying, "Horrid Mrs. I.!—she's a faeces woman—ah, ah, bottie!" and so on.

3. Exhibitionism (either direct or verbal)

7.10.24. Robert and George were in the garden together. Robert pulled down his trousers and exposed his penis, saying, "Look at my wee-wee thing! Where's your wee-wee thing?" George did the same. On one occasion later, Mrs. I. went to join them in the sand-pit, after there had been a sing-song about wee-wee things, when George suddenly said to her, "Do you know where the wee-wee thing is? Here it is," exposing his penis.

22.4.25. In the lavatory in the afternoon, Dan passed faeces, and on wiping his anus, showed Mrs. I. the paper, saying, "Oh, much faeces! Would you like it?" And when she said, "No, thank you," he offered to wipe it on her frock.

16.3.26. Priscilla, Dan and Jessica wanted to take their clothes off. It was very cold, so Mrs. I. did not allow it. Jessica was very persistent, and Mrs. I. had to prevent her forcibly, although Priscilla had made the suggestion. After lunch, Priscilla shut herself in the lavatory and then ran out naked.

4. Sexual curiosity

2.2.25. In the afternoon, Mrs. I. was playing the piano, and Dan and Frank sat on the floor below her. At first, this was to watch the action of the pedals; then they suddenly turned up the edge of her skirts, saying, "Shall we see her suspenders?"—with laughter.

27.5.25. When Mrs. I. was stooping down to help Tommy with his shoes, he suddenly put his hands up, pulled the front of her frock forward, and tried to look at her breast, saying, "What is that?" very affectionately.

27.1.27. Jane and Conrad went with Mrs. I. to the ethnological museum today. When looking at a human figure made of bamboo, Conrad pointed out the prominent penis, giggling, and saying, "What is that funny thing, sticking out? We know, don't we?" They whispered and giggled about it.

5. Sexual play and aggression

17.11.25. When Mrs. I. was getting ready to leave, Priscilla and Dan made a fuss about her going, and insisted on kissing her "all over"—face and hair and dress and shoes. After this, Dan fidgeted about in a way that clearly indicated an erection, and asked her to "lie down and be a motor-bike," assuring her that he "wouldn't hurt her." (Of course she did not do so.) After Mrs. I. had said goodbye, she had occasion to return, and was standing on the bottom step of the stairs talking when Dan bent down and kissed her ankle, then suddenly thrust his hand up her leg. Priscilla then tried to do the same, which, of course, she prevented.

18.5.27. After lunch, the children bathed in the sand-pit. Three of them, when drying and dressing in the cloakroom, asked Miss D.: "Please go away and leave us alone." When she refused to do so, they were very angry and made violent protests; and ended by saying that *she* was "rude", as she insisted on staying with them, so that she could not see them—trying to dress under the towels—with an air of completely shocked and injured innocence!

6. Masturbation (only one incident recorded)

26.10.25. For a few days around this date, X. appeared to be masturbating at frequent intervals; he sat or stood about in a vacant, dreamy way, fidgeting with his genital, for half-an-hour at a time. On one occasion, P. saw him doing this, and said, with much contempt, "Silly little boy." X. was very angry, and replied, "If you say that again, I'll kill you."

7. Family play, and ideas about babies and marriage

29.6.25. In the afternoon the children made two houses, one in the old hen coop and one some distance away. They modelled telephones in plasticine, quite excellent models, and joined up the two houses with real wire, and telephoned from one to the other. They had the small rabbit as "the baby" in the family, and the two households visited each other with friendly conversation. The house on the lawn had two verandahs made of chairs. When Mrs. I. came out after a little time, they gave her the house in the hen-coop and from the other telephoned her and asked her to come to tea. This was repeated twice. She went to tea, and they ate apples which they had brought down from the trees. This was a long quiet play.

8.7.25. While Frank, Priscilla and Dan were dressing after being in the garden in bathing suits there was a long conversation about "being married." Priscilla said she could not marry Frank because she had already married Dan. Then Frank said, "Oh, but you promised to marry me," so Priscilla said to Dan, "I'm very sorry, but I promised Frank to marry him if he would do (something) for Duncan." Dan then said, "Well, I'll marry Duncan." The others laughed and Duncan said, "Oh, you can't, boys don't marry boys." Priscilla said, "I can marry any boy, can't I? But not a grown man." Duncan said, "Oh, yes, any boy, but you can't marry a girl."

24.9.25. When using the counting rods, Dan used them imaginatively, calling the smallest one "the baby," and the largest ones "daddy and mammy." At first he called the longest of all "the mammy," but said "No, that's daddy. My daddy is bigger than my mammy."

1.7.26. In the family game, Priscilla was the mother, Dan and Jessica her babies who had "fallen from the top of a taxi and been hurt." They were in the hospital, and Mrs. I. was asked to be the nurse. Presently they became "new babies, just born." Then Priscilla asked. "*Where* are babies born—how do they come out?" Dan at once replied, "They come out of the vulva—here," with the appropriate demonstrative gesture. Priscilla was clearly shy about it. Jessica and Christopher listened. Further conversation went on about this.

8.6.27. Penelope invited Mr. Y. to come and stay at her house. Mr. Y. said, "Oh, you haven't a room for me." Penelope replied,: "Oh, but you can sleep with me. I should like to have three, you and me and my dolly."

8. Castration fears and symbolism

30.4.25. In the afternoon, Dan and Frank played in the sand-pit. They took off their shoes and stockings and dug their feet in, so that these could not be seen. Dan then called out to Mrs. I., "Tell Priscilla to ask us to come and love her." Mrs. I. did so. His reply was, with much laughter, "We can't because our legs are cut off."

27.10.25. Dan bit another child, and Mrs. I. reminded him that he didn't like it when James bit him. He replied, "No. And a big giant bit me once, and bit my finger right off, and it was bleeding." He said this again soon, showing Mrs. I. his forefinger. "It was this finger, and he bit it right off, and it was bleeding."

14.12.25. Whenever anything is being cut—paper or sewing material or canvas—Priscilla is extremely anxious that no one should "have their finger or thumb cut off." The fear is expressly, "cut-off," not just "hurt" or "cut."

8.2.27. At bath-time, Conrad said to Dan, "Let's have some fur over our penises." He held his sponge in front of him and said, "Now I'm a lady."

9. "Cozy places."

8.12.24. George put two chairs together and sat alone in one on top of another for a long time, without joining in what the other children were doing. After a time Mrs. I. asked him what he had made. He said it was a "cubby-hole," and sat quietly there for a very long time.

112.2.25. Frank and Priscilla had a "house" with a rug. Dan and Tommy had another. Frank said to Dan, "Shall we be friends and visit each other?" and they did so.

24.3.25. The children piled up a tower of chairs in the schoolroom, piling them very high, and were very delighted with this, hanging a rug round the tower, and getting inside underneath.

8.12.25. When the children were reading, they arranged chairs all round their tables "to keep them warm," and called them "a house." When Mrs. I. wanted to sit near them, and turned a chair round to sit on, Priscilla protested, but Dan said, "It's all right—you can be the door to keep us warm."

24.3.26. When drawing and crayoning today, Dan and Priscilla arranged chairs round themselves, "to keep out the fox."

6.5.26. Several of the children went into the canoe house, and crawled through the small hole into the inner dark chamber, with some excitement and great pleasure—finding spiders' webs, saying, "Isn't it dark, isn't it lovely and dark!"

These sample incidents give glimpses into children's feelings about the various aspects of sexuality; the next ones center on their feelings of guilt and shame. Here they expressed remorse for doing "bad things" directly, by means of fantasies of punishment against themselves, or by projection of their guilty feelings and fears of punishment onto someone else.

> 8.10.24. The children were standing at the door, watching a heavy shower of rain. They heard the rustling noise of the rain on the leaves, and when something was said about this, George remarked, "Perhaps it's God saying He will punish us for doing things we shouldn't."
>
> 28.11.24. When the children were using scissors for cutting out, George applied them to his own finger and pressed sufficiently hard to make it bleed, Frank and Dan saying to him, "Harder, harder." Dan then took the scissors and also tried, George saying to him, "Hard, harder," but Dan could not make his finger bleed.
>
> 20.2.25. Frank made a "prison" out of plasticine. He pretended to put Mrs. I. in it, to "shut her up," and said he would "never let her come out," and that he would give her no food and then "she will starve." Then he asked Mrs. I. to "make my house" and a "policeman's house." When the houses were finished he asked her to put the "policeman's house" up on the "iron rod," i.e., one of the cross-beams of the schoolroom.
>
> 9.3.25. Paul wanted to urinate, when washing his hands, and his hands being wet, could not get his buttons undone in time, and he wet his trousers; bitter tears and sobs. "I'm *so* ashamed of myself, I'm *so* ashamed of myself," he said, and he could not be comforted for a long time.
>
> 29.6.26. After school yesterday Christopher and Dan had been hammering with large hammers which Dan had brought himself, and the prong end of Christopher's hammer had come down on Dan's finger, injuring it. Christopher was obviously suffering under a heavy feeling of guilt for this. He had run away when adults approached him after the accident, and then had said, "They won't blame me, will they?" All today, he tended to go off by himself, into the far part of the garden, staying alone there on his cycle. During the afternoon, Christopher became very bored and restless, saying, "What is there to do? What can I do?"
>
> 10.3.27. Lena and Phineas were poking a stick into a hole in the plaster of the wall. The stick came out covered with dust and cobwebs. They said in awed tones, "Isn't it a naughty wall?" Mrs. I. asked, "How is it a naughty wall?" "Look at the dirt on the stick." Mrs. I. said, "Yes, what is it?" (having in mind that they might see that it was cobwebs). Lena replied gravely, "Muck—isn't it a naughty wall!"

E. To the total, verbatim records from the Malting House, Susan Isaacs added, as mentioned earlier, accounts of children made by other observers. Again, her intention was to demonstrate that both love and hate are played out by all children in social situations, and that sexuality, guilt, and shame are also normal in their growing adaptation to the world around them. From letters written by mothers and nurses came accounts like these examples:

> Within the last month or two she has developed a habit of violently sucking any wool she can get hold of—chiefly in the bed or in the pram—but also at other times. She stuffs her coat or the blanket into her mouth voraciously, and sucks and sucks until she goes to sleep.

> She seems to love the feel of wool, and laughs and chuckles if one plays with the blanket over her face, or if one tucks it under her chin. She will suck the front of her nightgown until it is wringing wet on her chest, and this together with the fact that she swallows little pieces of wool, makes me feel that we must stop it in some way.

> Ages 8:0, 8:0, 10:0. Three boys bathing. All in bath together, getting out. X. sticking out his posterior at a boy and roaring with laughter. All three boys laughing. One of them sticking his front out slightly and then all three laughing again. Looking to catch my eye, then laughing again. So infectious was their laughter that I could not look solemn. Then as they jumped out to dry themselves, I said, "I really think boys are ruder than girls!" X., "Well, they've got more to be rude about, haven't they?" The air of superiority, lord-of-creation and tolerance for the other sex with which he said this set us all laughing again. By the time they were dry and had their pyjamas on they were deep in a discussion as to how to make stilts, and what wood they would need, straps, etc., and the next day they made them.

> Will you help me with my small charge? He is fifteen months, perfectly healthy and normally developed, usually very happy and contented, but he has occasions when he gets impatient, or when he just can't manage to do what he wants, such as open the door or climb on the chair, he will then start to bump his head against anything he is near. Soft or hard, it makes no difference, and just lately he has started to do it when either his mother or father leave the nursery. He will just throw himself on the floor and bump his poor head unmercifully. I am so afraid he will really injure himself. I try to attract his attention to something else and interest him in it. If let to go on, he just bumps and bumps until he hurts himself. Then he cries and all is over until the next time, but leaving him to hurt himself has not cured him.

From such authors as Helen T. Wooley ("Eating, Sleeping, and Elimination" in *Handbook of Child Psychology* of 1931) come comments like this:

> The function of urination is more likely to be indulged in too frequently than to be restrained for erotic reasons. The passage of urine affords a mild stimulus to the sex organs of the infant. The child may adopt the habit of urinating with unnecessary frequency just because of the sex pleasure derived from it. In my treatment of cases of enuresis among somewhat older children, I have encountered eight-year old girls who insisted that they kept on wetting the bed because they enjoyed the sensation. Ordinary urination on a toilet could not assume the same sex quality as the secret performance of the function in an assumed attitude.

Kathrine Bridges's important book, *Social and Emotional Development of the Pre-School Child,* which appeared in 1931, included many illuminating accounts of children such as the following:

> It is well known that young children claim or hold on to everything that appeals to their interest of the moment. When children first come to the nursery school they claim one toy after another whether a child is playing with it or not.
>
> Apparently, aggressive behaviour on the part of a new-comer to a group of pre-school children is really a definite stage in social development and is usually

followed by obviously social behaviour. The child who does not make such active and bodily contacts on coming into a group may be more socially advanced, but in all probability he is still unsocial, egoistic and indifferent to the group, and may be slow in social development. Children usually react to social situations . . . by hitting, pushing, stroking, pulling a child's hair, or knocking him over.

From J. B. Watson, author of *Psychological Care of Infant and Child* and a well-known behaviorist, comes a long account of masturbation in very young children and evidence of early sexual behavior. Here are two excerpts:

Masturbation is not, however, a problem that begins in puberty. For the parent it's a problem which begins at birth. Children as young as six months begin it.

Apparently a great many of the muscular responses later to be used in the sex act, such as pushing, climbing, stroking, are ready to function in the male at least at a very much earlier age that we are accustomed to think. In one observed case which came into the clinic, a boy of 3½ years of age would mount his mother or nurse, whichever one happened to be sleeping with him. Erection would take place and he would manipulate and bite her breast; then clasping and sex movements similar to those of adults would ensue.

Other accounts of similar behavior of little children were taken from Charlotte Bühler's "The Social Behavior of the Child," also in the 1931 *Handbook of Child Psychology,* and from V. Rasmussen's *The Primary School Child.*

A final source of illustrative material came from the mother of a child called Ursula. This mother had noted down much of her daughter's behavior and conversation between the ages of 3:2 and 5:6, during which period a new baby was born into the family. Here is one conversation between the two, when Ursula was 3:9 and her mother was already pregnant:

U. was with her mother while she was bathing. Her mother said, "U., do you know what's in here?" "No, what?" "Your little brother or sister." She went very red and said in a weepy voice, "Why, Mummy? I don't want one while I'm little. I don't want one till I'm big." This was repeated several times. Then followed various questions and comments: "Why do you have it there?" "To keep it warm till it's ready to come out." "When will it come out? To-morrow" "No, not for a long time, not till the summer." "Why not?" "It's not strong enough or big enough yet." "How big is it?" "So big, I should think." "Where will it come out?" "There." "How will it get out?" "When it's big enough and strong enough it'll push and I'll help it until it gets out." "How will you push?" "Like this." "How did you make it? Did Daddy plant a seed?" "Yes," "When did he? Last night?" "No, not then." "When we were on our holiday?" "Perhaps." "Was I there?" "No, I don't think so." "Was I asleep?" "Perhaps." "Why did you make it?" "Because I thought you would like a brother or sister to play with." "I like sisters best. How will you feed it? There?" "Yes." "You could make a brother and a sister." "Could I?" "One could feed that side and one could feed that side. Only they mustn't do a-a." "On me, do you mean?" "In your lap." "I expect they will sometimes. They don't know when they're tiny." "We'll have to teach them."

Some time later, she showed that she enjoys "cosy places" as much as other children:

> U. (5:1) U. had a new game from which she derived a mysterious pleasure. Nurse cleared the cupboard of her wardrobe. U. sat huddled inside with only a crack open, with a magazine on her knees and her electric torch in her hand. She came down to tea after about twenty minutes or half an hour, delighted, with flushed cheeks, and said she had been "reading" and telling herself a story. It was about a princess but was too long to tell her mother.

Clearly Ursula had been masturbating to her own satisfaction, and also imagining herself a princess, beautiful and powerful, rather than a little girl. Later she put her wish for power more clearly still:

> U. (5:1). Something U. wanted her mother to do that she didn't want to do. U.: "You *must*, Mommy, you *must!*" "Must I?" "Yes, that's what Mummies are for, to do what their children want them to." "Is it?" "Yes. And to look after them." "And what are children for?" "To play, of course."

In her play, she acted out inner fantasies, including the wish to exhibit herself, and thus prove that her body was acceptable, and also to see if her mother would reprove her.

> U. (5:3). U. had a friend to tea, and her mother overheard part of the following game. U. took S. upstairs when she arrived, to her room, where they undressed and redressed in some of U.'s clothes. Then they went into the garden and after a bit took off some of their garments. U. "Oh, ooky (a favorite exclamation), I want to go to the lav. Oh, I can't be bothered to go upstairs. I know, I'll bring the chamber down, and do it here." (She rushed upstairs, brought it down, put it on the garden path, sat on it and "did it" there.) U., "We'll keep it here." Mother (from the kitchen window, anxious for the susceptibility of her neighbours): "I don't think you'd better have it there. You put it behind the bushes." (a secluded place behind the dining room.) U.: "Good! We'll play schools and that'll be the lavatory." (She rushed up again and brought down toilet paper. They got umbrellas and hung them on a branch of a creeper, near the "lavatory," presumably for a cloakroom. They had out U.'s desk and the game went on peacefully for hours.)

Since her mother had not punished her but had only made a reasonable suggestion, Ursula and her friend could go happily on with their play, in response to whatever fantasy they shared.

Psychoanalytic Interpretation

Looking back over all these materials, one sees children behaving in characteristic ways, not always very pleasing to adults, but nonetheless natural. To understand what all this behavior means was Susan Isaacs's next task, since a major purpose of the school and the two books that described its findings was to contribute to genetic psychology in a way that no other investigation of children's behavior had done at that time.

> At this point . . . the need arises to pass from description to understanding. The facts observed must be linked genetically with each other, and with those coming before and after in the growth of children. . . . Taken as it stands, much of this descriptive material is unintelligible and carries no hint of its genetic significance. It raises many problems which call for further evidence from other sources for their solution. . . . Such further evidence, and an interpretative theory which suffices to bring order and meaning into our data, is offered us by psycho-analytic studies of the unconscious mental life of children and adults. That theory is the fruit of Freud's epoch-making researches into the technique of studying the human mind. . . . Freud himself first opened our eyes to the reality of unconscious mental processes and the whole inner world of the psychic life.[60]

For Susan Isaacs, and for other colleagues like Melanie Klein, Paula Heimann, Joan Rivière, and M. N. Searl, Freud's theory of the unconscious springs of behavior and his technique of psychoanalysis shed "a profound illumination . . . upon the outward behavior of young children."[61]

It is to the original family situation that Susan Isaacs turned to explain the unconscious and genetic significance of later behavior. She gives a straightforward psychoanalytic account of children's experiences from the earliest days of existence. For children's later relationships with adults are deeply influenced by their earlier feelings about their parents; their later attitudes towards their peers depend on the resolution of earlier sibling conflicts; their ability to work and play constructively in the real world is colored by the amount of anxiety and inhibition left over from earlier days; in fact, every aspect of their later interaction with the world has its roots in the experience of infancy and early childhood in the family setting. Therefore, the behavior reported in these records could not be considered as simply the result of the exigencies of the moment or the situation. It had its roots deep in the individual and family history of each child, and in his particular adaptation to the dynamics of the common situation into which he was born.

The human family is unique among higher animals, unique in ways that mean inevitable conflict and frustration for the infant and young child. In particular, the human couple has lost the sexual periodicity of lower animals, and can have intercourse at any time, rather than just during one season. This means that, when a baby is born, the mother is not devoted exclusively to it, with the father at a distance. Her attention is always divided between the baby and the father, and their physical relationship as well as the loss of attention that can result is intuited by even very little children. Also, because of the human child's long infancy, other children may well appear before the first one is independent and self-sufficient.

The infant is helpless at birth, unable to satisfy its own needs, wholly dependent on his mother for survival and nurturance, while at the same time she is not wholly his. And in civilized society, he is soon expected to give up and change the innate behavior that gave him pleasure, first through weaning and then through toilet training. Yet all through infancy and early childhood, his sense of reality is not strong enough to tolerate or understand much frustration or postponement of gratification. He is at the mercy of his desires, and can only feel that when he is satisfied, there is good. When he is not, there is bad. There is no neutral ground for him, and he feels that satisfaction withheld, even briefly, is a deliberate and malicious act. For survival, he must have satisfaction; the possibility of being permanently deprived and left wholly helpless seems a psychic disaster and death itself, and arouses great anxiety and wishes to destroy, bite, burn, or devour those at whose hands he suffers privation. At the same time, since he cannot yet understand anyone else except in terms of himself, he fantasizes that they wish to do the same to him for harboring such destructive wishes. So he is caught, at the mercy of his inner fears of deprivation, his hostile, defensive feelings against those who frustrate him, and his fears of retribution or punishment by the same people for his angry, aggressive feelings and fantasized actions.

His inner life develops, through all these difficulties, as a complex interplay of psychic forces: the id is the primitive wish-self, linked most directly to instinctual survival needs; the superego is the internalized parent-self, restraining his primitive impulses so as to avoid the retribution that their expression would bring about; and the ego is the representative within the psyche of the real external world, mediating and rationalizing between the powerful desire of the id for satisfaction, and the equally powerful and harsh superego or fantasy-parent.

This dramatic picture of children's early situation and the problems they must deal with within the universal setting of the human family is hard for adults to recall. For they have long ago repressed into unconsciousness many of the feelings that were characteristic of their early experiences. Yet, the method of psychoanalysis brings to light unconscious material, whether by free association and dream analysis with adults, or by symbolic play with little children. An understanding of the facts of early conflicts and their significance in later behavior provides the key to children's outward responses to and interactions with the real world. Teachers and other adults are seen as parent-figures; other children are sibling rivals; toys and games are either attractive or frightening; make-believe play provides a chance to express the fantasies of earlier times. A child's ability to make constructive use of these opportunities depends on the interplay of the early unconscious mental forces, and on the psychic mechanisms he has called upon to defend himself against his worst fears and anxieties. If his family experience has been harsh and punitive, he may have resorted to massive repression, shutting off unacceptable feelings from consciousness; he may have developed phobias, projecting his fears outward onto an object or person who then becomes terrifying to him. If his experience has been more positive, he may have achieved, by displacement, a way of dealing satisfactorily with his inevitable ambivalence toward his parents; he may have projected his feelings outward and found his worst fears unfounded; he may have found, in sublimation, constructive outlets for his libidinal energies that bring much satisfaction. All these modes of adaptation are played out again in school and later.

From this point of view, for example, it is no wonder that children seek to possess things and call them their own, for possession is power. As an infant, mere *having* what one wants was an end in itself: the infant must have his mother's breast for survival and therefore identity, at a time of total helplessness. If deprived, then possession itself becomes a crucial issue all through the child's life. Similarly, the wish to assert himself over other children is natural, for here the child is doing to others less strong what has been done to him (in reality or in fantasy) by more powerful figures. Self-assertion makes a child feel stronger, more potent, especially when he can achieve ascendancy over a rival. All actions of hostility that seem to have no immediate cause have similar, psychic origins in fears of powerlessness and inferiority, and the wish to defend against them.

One function of the nursery school setting is precisely to permit all this behavior to be expressed. Reality is, again, a "canvas" on which to project feelings, so the child can test out his modes of dealing with the world of people and things, and gain some realistic feedback from it. In fact, the hostile and aggressive actions of children toward one another must be seen as a positive step forward, for as long as a child is locked into his egocentric world, he is dominated by his own fantasies and can see others only as means to his ends. When he is thwarted, however, he brushes up against the reality of other people's wishes. He reacts defensively at first, but this is at least a recognition that others exist. Now all his ambivalence about other people and his feelings for them come into play, for as an infant he has loved parents and siblings when they satisfied him, and he has hated them when they did not. So now, again, he must deal with ambivalent feelings, "the psychological tension arising from the fact that he both loves and hates his fellows."[62]

A striking thing about the emotional life of little children is how quickly they move from love to hate, from "Oh, I do, do love you!" to "You beast! I hate you!" Each feeling is experienced fully at the time, and there is little stability of attitude, because a small child has not yet developed a reliable way of dealing with his ambivalence. Gradually, children do begin to develop a steadier attitude toward one another, but at first only by the device of hating someone else instead. By splitting his ambivalent feelings and projecting his hate onto someone else, he is able to love his playmate more fully.

> In other words, the child is able to love one of his fellows more wholeheartedly, more faithfully, more steadily, because he has turned his hostility on to another.[63]

Again, although children may join together for the express purpose of hurting or attacking someone else, this is actually a positive step, a forerunner of more stable and positive social relationships.

With little children, these joinings together do not last very long and are based on the same hostile feelings that individual children have. At first, they band together against other children, for the adults are still too powerful to defy; their authority is not only unquestioned, but also depended upon, since adults' frowns and smiles give little children their punishments or rewards. Therefore, at this stage, groups of children form around shared issues of possession or rivalry only against another child.

With latency, however, a newer attitude toward adults is achieved, since by that time the child has, in one way or another, faced the major Oedipal crisis in his life concerning his parents, and the primitive desires centering around them have been repressed. At this time, the group can come together against the adult, more watchful and realistic about the actual characteristics and limitations of adult power. Now the adult's authority is not simply assumed, but must be earned by fairness and real strength. Now, too, the group members' hostility toward others (adult, stranger, or child) gives the feeling of togetherness. Here again, ambivalence is dealt with by splitting it and projecting hate onto another person, thereby gaining a measure of solidarity with one's fellows.

> The hated enemy is not only a substitute for the friend; he is a scapegoat too, a representative of *my* bad self. *It is he hates my friend, not I.* I hate and condemn *him* for his hate to my friend, and feel justified in doing so by my own loyalty.[64]

This casting forth of hatred and aggressive feelings onto outsiders gives the members of the group a warm feeling of togetherness. Although it seems a hostile and disruptive act, it is an important developmental achievement, for egocentric isolation has been broken down and the children can begin to follow a common aim with some coherence. And the ability of a group of children to join in attacking an adult actually shows that they are moving beyond dependency toward self-assertion, drawing strength from one another in order to do so.

What of the times of peaceful play, of friendliness and cooperation? They, as well as the more conflict-ridden times, do occur with children.

How can they be accounted for, by this genetic analysis? Susan Isaacs believed that the role of the adult is also crucial here. With little children, still so oriented toward her and willing to accept her leadership, a group can come together in mutual tolerance and helpfulness from time to time.

> They find tranquillity in obeying her behests, and follow happily what suggestions she may make for composing their differences or furthering their practical aims. . . . Her prestige may indeed create and sustain a larger group than the purely spontaneous movement of the children would itself make possible.[65]

As long as the adults are friendly and understanding, most little children are able to be cooperative together for some periods of time. Any observer of groups of children, happily and quietly at play under the watchful eye of a sympathetic adult, knows that "such situations yield the happiest moments of their lives."[66]

As the children get a little older, they are even able to make gifts of services or objects to one another, and to make amends for harm they may have done, although littler ones are not yet capable of such reciprocity. Giving gifts means that one is a loving person, and receiving gifts shows love-worthiness, whether it be rubbing a sore finger or having a turn on the bicycle. The ability to give also shows that one is not needy, not made weaker by the loss of whistle or doll. So, too, the wish to repair damages done, to make good, is born of an increased and more realistic sense of self. Both giving and reparation are deeply social, positive acts, with roots in earlier group relationships, however hostile at the beginning.

The adult promotes this social development by acting as the good parent, as the positive side of the superego of the children.

> She is a true educator only when and in so far as she becomes the parent who offers the means and the encouragement to make good; that is to say, when her super-ego function works unobtrusively towards active and constructive ends in the group of children.[67]

When an adult is functioning toward the children as and in the place of the superego, they may project onto her all their aggressive impulses, but they also need her control:

> If they find her mild and loving as well as authoritative and reliable, then they feel themselves to be in far safer hands than when at the mercy of their own self-punishments, from the super-ego within them.[68]

They also identify with her, and begin to feel the possibility of acting mildly and lovingly too. This identification is the source of their being able to act reciprocally with their fellows, to give and to help, and thus move beyond the hostility earlier projected outward, which first bound them together.

She helps them to be good, and "to make good again those whom they wished to destroy in their moment of rage and hostility."[69] And when she is helping them to be their best selves in this way, acting as a strong and positive controlling force, "they love her most and follow her most contentedly."[70] She must, then, be good enough to them to satisfy their wishes sufficiently, and strict enough to protect them against their inner anxieties and outer aggressiveness. In this, she is a good parent figure, whose positive characteristics the children internalize more and more.

> The child's real growth, not only in friendliness and generosity, but also in personal responsibility and social skill, depends very largely upon his assured belief in the good parent, and in the possibility of himself becoming a good parent. The translation of the phantasy, the make-believe play, into real behavior and character traits, will largely depend upon the nature of his real experiences.[71]

The social progress of the Malting House children moved from quiet subduement to boisterous, aggressive behavior and finally to more settled, constructive cooperation. The methods used by the adults, providing a good deal of freedom of speech and activity but also sensible limits, clearly helped this progress along. They acted as good parent figures, unshaken by the children's hostility, firm yet fair, and always on the side of the ego, of reality, of constructive impulses.

Implications for Educators

The final part of *Social Development in Young Children* deals with the usefulness for educators of psychoanalytic theory about the unconscious significance of children's behavior. Few people questioned that it was important to understand children's overt interests and activities in order to plan wisely for them. Fewer were willing to look carefully at unconscious origins and meanings.

When Freud's discoveries became widely known,

> everyone will remember the shock and horror with which the public mind reacted to the idea that little children have sexual desires.[72]

Gradually, as the evidence accumulated and as people's horror was not enough to dismiss the idea of infantile sexuality, an opposite reaction set in: popular expositions of psychoanalysis were written, and teachers and parents were eager to grasp the truths of the "new psychology" and make use of it in their dealings with children. Schools were founded, dedicated to children's total freedom and the absence of "repression." Such overreactions proceeded to water down the theory, but since the proponents had not been analyzed themselves and had no serious understanding of psychoanalysis, they reinterpreted it to suit their own temperaments and values.

However, in more responsible hands, the work of analysis was going on and further discoveries were made, especially by Melanie Klein and her colleagues working with children as young as two years old. Her work made very clear the essential difference between the analyst and the teacher, between the setting of therapy and the school.

The analyst works with a child individually, for a definite period of time each day, in an environment specifically designed to make it possible for him to express his feelings, wishes, fantasies, and fears quite freely. Although he is not allowed to harm the analyst, even this restraint is not expressed as, "You may not," but rather, "Show me that in another way."[73]

> Once the analytic situation is set going, the child soon realises that here is a person and here is a setting whose sole purpose is to understand; he can then freely display his phantasies, whether wish or dreaded retribution, step by step, and show how these are evoked in him, moment by moment, by the real happenings of his outer life.[74]

Just as in adult analysis, the work proceeds by the gradual unfolding of the inner world of unconscious wish, fear, and fantasy, as the intricate interplay of id, superego, and ego becomes more clear. As this goes on, the anxiety of the child may mount and must be relieved by timely interpretation on the part of the analyst, who shows that she understands and does not punish. Thus she acts as a real person outside the child's fantasied world, and helps him to put his inner world into realistic perspective.

> The function of the analyst is, in essence, to act as the ego of the child in moments of stress, when it feels to him that he has no ego, when he is all feeling, all wish, all terror.[75]

The analyst also enters into the play fantasies of the child and accepts whatever role she is assigned, playing out the drama as directed by the child, and then interpreting the unconscious significance of what is being expressed.

All this is very different from the educational setting, where the emphasis cannot be on unraveling the unconscious fears, hostile impulses, or fantasies that may have inhibited a child's progress; in the school, the focus is on outward reality, and a child's ability to engage in constructive and rewarding activities there. The educator must play the part of the good but strict parent, by helping him control his hateful feelings and by encouraging his positive abilities. She must help him to be good and to make good, and thereby release energy that had been caught up in negative feelings. The therapist, on the other hand, must attract to herself by transference both love and hate, allowing each to be expressed, especially those feelings of hostility and aggression that have been most repressed. Only then can she unravel their meaning and interpret them for the child.

The analyst must also be on the watch for feelings that are being covered up by the child in opposite kinds of behavior: just when the child is at his most loving, the therapist must be concerned with feelings of hostility underneath and bring them out, to get a fully rounded picture. The educator, on the other hand, must ally herself with positive feelings, with a child's wishes to create and make good things and give good gifts. Such wishes are, in the long run, the most educative impulses, and the educator's task is to provide ways for their successful expression and development.* Unconscious wishes do not concern her directly, or the symbolism of daily behavior, even though she may be well aware of these things.

So the analyst, in the one-to-one therapeutic setting, plays out both the good and bad selves of the child at different times, as the child indicates, with the purpose of understanding his fantasies about these selves. Then she can interpret them for the child, without judgment or punishment, but in terms of the reality of whatever incident he is dramatizing. The educator must be the ideal superego, on the other hand, the good but strict figure, mild, tolerant, friendly, yet securely in control of destructive impulses and the fears about them that arise in the child. She is always on the side of the child's most positive capacities, and fosters them in every way. Clearly, no one person can perform in both roles, for while the therapist seeks only to understand and interpret what is expressed, the educator allies herself with that side of the child that is most conducive to his education. Analysis makes the child more educable, by relieving him of inner tensions that impede his entry into the real world and his successful dealing with it.

Thus one way in which an understanding of the unconscious significance of children's behavior can help teachers and parents is to sharpen the distinction between psychoanalytic treatment and education. There are other implications as well. In general, psychoanalytic theory had no new pedagogical truths or revelations to bring to education; rather, it supported the best educational practices then being used, the more child-centered, less restrictive or punitive methods of the progressive educators. It also suggested some correctives to the extreme and unwise tendencies current in some schools, especially those that advocated complete freedom for children.

In this regard, it was important, in Susan Isaacs's view, not to underestimate the reality and power of the superego.* This psychic force develops intrinsically and spontaneously, during the infant's oral period of growth, at the time when he begins to bite his mother's breast and suffers frustration for his biting. Again, he is at the mercy of his all-encompassing feel-

---

*See also Nathan Isaacs's "What Active Enquiry Means for the Child", in Part Two.
*See also "Original Sin" in Part Two.

ings, either of good (satisfaction) or bad (frustration), with no reality sense from his ego to help him understand what is actually going on. Therefore when he wishes to bite, he also wishes to devour and incorporate his mother; yet at the same time that he does so, he is pushed away from her and feels punished for such desires. He assumes that she feels as angry toward him as he does toward her, and must somehow keep down the aggressive feelings that he is sure will bring fierce punishment.

By the mechanism called *introjection*, he takes the parent into himself in fantasy (the mental connection between physical instinct and the conscious), and uses her internalized force to keep at bay the unacceptable impulses that he has come to fear. This is the superego, the parent inside the child in a fantasied form that may or may not have anything to do with the real parent. Its fierceness comes from the child's own strong wishes to attack a depriving parent at whose hands he is suffering bad things, and from his great need to keep safe from the attack of the parent figure whose retribution he greatly fears also.

Melanie Klein's psychoanalytic studies were able to show increasingly that this superego does develop in very young children, and does, from an early age, arouse fears and feelings of guilt for doing bad things. Those bad things were always specifically related to infantile, sexual wishes, as expressed in outward actions, and, in fantasy, deserving punishment.

All this sounds very exaggerated to adults, and even farfetched. Yet further confirmatory evidence came from the Malting House School records, for children of even the mildest parents played out fantasies of severe punishment far beyond anything they had ever suffered. There were two kinds of incidents that evoked feelings of guilt and shame:

> a.) the various forms of open aggression—screaming, biting, wetting, defaecating, breaking things, being greedy, being unable or unwilling to mend or tidy things; b.) certain forms of libidinal satisfaction, such as thumb-sucking and both anal and genital masturbation.... It can therefore be seen that the child's feelings of guilt are closely related to his aggressive tendencies."[76]

Punishment that the children felt was deserved took a variety of forms also, such as whipping, imprisonment, starvation, drowning, being scorned or laughed at, shut out from home and mother's love, and done to death in a variety of ways. Since actual experience of these harsh punishments of the children had little or no basis in reality, they must have come from the primitive superego, in all its severity, and therefore relate primarily to an earlier, fantasy-ridden period of emotional development as an infant.

Isaacs's point about the superego, then, was that it is real and not to be underestimated. Children do not attack one another or bite, hit, or destroy from a lack of conscience: they are projecting and playing out their inner fears of attack from the superego. If, in the real world, they do meet with harsh treatment, their fantasies of retribution are confirmed, and real psychic damage is done. What they need instead is parents and other adults who represent a stable and orderly world of social values, closely related to their actual ability at the time, and based on an understanding of their needs, but firm and secure in themselves. They need to feel that adults are stronger than they, and represent "not the forces of destruction but those of ordered creation,"[77] that is that

> those whom he loves are not at the mercy of his ungovernable instincts but are firmer and stronger and more reliable than he. . . . He finds relief from inner tension by being able to project his super-ego on the real adults who will excercise it for him. If that real external control is firm and secure, but mild and tempered, it enables the child to master his destructive impulses and to learn to order and adapt his wishes to the real world. If he neither finds fulfillment of his phantastic dreads in the outer world, nor is left at their mercy in his inner world by having no external support, but is slowly educated by a tempered, real control, mild and understanding, appropriate to each situation, as it arises, he is led forward on the path of reality and towards all those indirect satisfactions in the real world, the subliminatory activities.[78]

This is the corrective for the idea that children should be "smacked" to teach them a lesson, as well as for the opposite idea that they should be given total freedom. Neither position is realistic in terms of the child's psychic situation. "The child can bring out the good that is in him, provided he is given support against his fears of the bad."[79] Further still, if the adult in charge does not act with a group of children as their superego, though more mild and realistic than theirs, she is in fact seen as the ally of their own bad, aggressive selves. If she permits bullying and scapegoating, so that they are acting upon their worst and most feared impulses, she has supported them. Therefore, no educator can be passive and allow the children to do just as they please. Either she stands for or against the forces of aggressiveness and hostility, and there is no neutral ground.

A third bearing of Susan Isaacs's analysis of children's behavior on the work of the educator was the great importance of play. "It is supremely the activity which brings him psychic equilibrium in early years . . . it is the breath of life to him."[80] Educators have always known the value of play for children, as well as the value of creative activity, freely chosen, for adults. Here, the insights of psychoanalysis support this view, and illuminate the sources of a child's need for "quite free, unhindered, unorganised, imaginative play."[81] For if play is children's work, it should be remembered that when they are playing, they are indeed working, making sense of and gaining increased mastery of the world. As in the cognitive development of children, when they use imaginative play to try out ideas "as if" they might turn out one way or another, so in their emotional growth, the expression and testing of fantasy plays a vital part. By means of such play, little children move from a primarily egocentric situation more and more into the real world, as they express their fantasy world and receive feedback.

Whereas in acting as the superego of the children, the educator can and should be active, here she must be passive. She must provide a stable, safe setting and plenty of materials to stimulate play; then she must allow children to work out their own, individual fantasies, not cramped by adult suggestions about what or how they should play or behave.

A fourth implication of psychoanalytic understanding of children has to do with opportunities for sublimination. Again, the educator should be passive, except that opportunities and activities should be available to the children, so that they can find ways to redirect their instinctual energies in satisfying and acceptable ways. This is not repression, or shutting away unacceptable feelings or behavior: "Repression impoverishes life; sublimation fulfills and enriches it."[82] Still and always, the exact lines of his expression will be his alone, for no one can prejudge just how he will find his way happily out into the real world of work and play.

Opportunities for play are vital, then, and also for finding ways of creative expression of feelings. So is the company of other children. Cooperative play helps young children move from their early egocentrism, rivalries, and anxieties, eventually toward the real joys of social living and shared activities. While children do need the guidance of adults to help all this come about, such guidance must be of the kind that will reinforce their best tendencies and build on them.

Gradually, Isaacs felt, adults in society were beginning to accept children as they are, reevaluating their standards of dealing with children: "a modification of our cultural super-ego"[83] had brought about some acceptance of sexuality and aggression as normal aspects of children's development. "Little more is needed than deflection of interests to other pursuits and a chance for cooperative play in non-sexual directions."[84] The practical educator should only act for the child when he cannot act for himself. The child makes his own meaning of the world and his own way into it. Education (or child rearing) should not stand between the child and the world any more than is necessary for his security. The child must go through the phases of behavior that are natural for him and for all children, but within a protective setting.

The aim of the educator, then, is not to criticize, punish, disapprove, or mold the child's behavior into socialized, "acceptable" forms. Through his superego, the child already has a profound drive toward morality, not implanted from outside. The aim of the educator is to develop a technique that will help that drive to develop along constructive lines, more tempered and human than in infancy, more adjusted to the actual realities of the physical and social world. "She must be on the side of reality and of the child's own activity."[85]

4
Two Books for Lay Audiences

The two books dealing with Susan Isaacs's Malting House School work, *Intellectual Growth in Young Children* and *Social Development in Young Children*, were her most substantial contributions to genetic psychology, and formed the basis of her later educational works. Both were written for professional psychologists, educators, and other serious students of childhood. By presenting a mass of detailed observational data, together with her own analysis of them on developmental and psychoanalytic lines, Isaacs hoped to provide evidence to corroborate her findings and stimulation for further studies as well. She knew her sample of children was small and atypical, and that therefore much more broad work needed to be done; nonetheless, she believed that her insights into children's development had general validity. On the basis of this conviction, she also wrote the two books considered in this chapter, as well as others.

The Nursery Years (1929)

The Nursery Years was written simply, with a nonprofessional audience in mind—adults who had responsibility for children from birth to six years of age but not much background in child psychology. She hoped that by using her own work in the field as well as that of other professionals, her readers could obtain enough knowledge to care for young children. Otherwise

> we cannot be sure that we are dealing with him in the way most likely to help him. Without [such knowledge], we move in the dark, and may do much harm, with the best intentions in the world. Children need all our affection and sympathy; but they need also all our intelligence, and our patient and serious efforts to understand the ways of their mental growth. And we cannot leave this to their professional teachers, for they come upon the scene of the child's life too late in the day. By the time children go to school, some of the most important things that ever happen to them are already in the past. It is not too much to say, in the light of recent psychological studies, that the main lines of their behaviour are by then firmly fixed.[1]

Most of all, Susan Isaacs wanted parents and nurses to grasp the inner psychic significance to the infant and young child of outer events. She had noted in her experience as an analyst that the same developmental phases had occurred in the early life of every patient, together with the characteristic fantasies and defenses connected with each. Yet those for whom she was writing did not need a full, technical discussion of psychoanalytic theory and practice for their everyday handling of children. Instead, she provided a description of the child's inner world, from his earliest days, as well as general norms of development after the first year, phrased in simple language that would arouse her readers' sympathy and understanding:

> It would be the greatest mistake to think that the baby needed nothing but bodily care in his first year, and that his mind only began to grow, say, when he began to talk. Even the quite young infant has very powerful wishes and feelings and phantasies. And these have all the stronger hold over him, just because his power of making them effective is as yet so feeble. Far more goes on behind those wide-open infant eyes than most people imagine. Knowledge is lacking, understanding has not yet begun; but wants and wishes, fears and angers, love and hate are there from the beginning.[2]

Here is an example of her description of a child's earliest feelings, an account of the oral phase with which every mother could identify:

> At birth, the babe is adapted to his mother in his mental life, rather than to the outside world. Can we discern what his mother seems to him? She cannot well be what we should mean by a *person*. She must seem to him hardly more than a nourishing breast and sheltering arms, a vague large *Something* which comforts and caresses and feeds him.
> Mental life does not wait to begin until eyes and ears and active movement are bringing the outside world to the child, but is already active at the breast, and centred in his experiences there. . . . His mouth is his must sensitive part, and to it belong voracious nuzzling of the breast, and in the sharp turning away from things that taste or feel unpleasant to the mouth, *things that are not the breast,* we get a glimpse of how vivid and how much at the centre of his mental life the feelings and impulses of the mouth must be to the babe. If things that can be touched are the most real things in infancy, then things that can be touched *by the lips,* or, indeed, swallowed, are the most real things of all to the babe of the very earliest days.
> The mouth is thus not only the means of getting nourishment, but also of the babe's first knowledge of the world outside himself. For a long time, everything his hand can reach is brought into his mouth. He not only eats, but thinks with his mouth.
> Not only so: we can see too that the babe *loves* with his mouth, and feels his mother's love in her gift of the breast. His affectionate pleasure in the touch of the breast can be seen in his play with it after the first sharp pangs of hunger are satisfied. He will then suck a little, let the nipple slide out of his mouth, smile and gurgle and kick his legs with delight,

then turn back and caress the nipple again with his lips. But if the mother withdraws the nipple, how quickly the picture changes! His face puckers and reddens, he screams with distress and anger, his firsts clench and his body stiffens in protest. If then the nipple is returned to him, his body relaxes, the puckers fall away, he sighs or grunts with relief, and the busy mouth begins again to satisfy his hunger for nourishment and love. To give the breast is to the babe's mind in these early days to give love; to withdraw or withhold it is to withdraw or withhold love. When we understand this, we see also how important are the ways in which we manage all the business of feeding and weaning.[3]

In similar ways, Susan Isaacs presented the theory of infantile sexuality, moving from the first part of the oral stage to its second, biting phase and the beginnings of fear and rage, the rise of the anal stage and the use of feces both as tokens of love and of aggression, and the subsequent focus on the genital zone of the body as the source of satisfaction, and of fear and guilt. If adults could watch their infants closely as they pass through these stages, and understand that it is natural for children to be primarily physical at first and to find pleasure in bodily processes, they might be less eager to require them to give up such normal satisfactions faster than is appropriate. Also, the infant's mind does grow through these early bodily experiences, as it reaches out to engage with the world and make sense of it. Adults need to provide calm, gentle care and "avoid the harsh and hasty methods which may make him fear and hate us."[4] Unwise methods only bind the infant to his earliest ways of defending himself, for if he is kept by fear from moving ahead in his growth, then he is thrown back on his most primitive modes of protest and rage, and development is blocked. But steady and loving treatment will make him feel that the world is a safe place, and he will be able to make positive growth in mind and body.

There are certain general norms of development that characterize all children at each stage of growth, although individual children will differ from others somewhat along the way. There are the bodily signs of growth, increasing skills with hand and eye, awareness of other people and adaptive reactions to them, all becoming slowly more realistic and appropriate. Always it is the child's own activity that teaches him, within a settled framework of adult stability. And it is play that is the chief mode of his learning. Adults need to recognize

> how large a value children's play has for all sides of their growth. How great an ally the thoughtful parent can find it! And how fatal to go against this great stream of healthy and active impulse in our children! That "restlessness" and inability to sit still; that "mischievousness" and "looking inside" and eternal "Why?"; that indifference to soiled hands and torn clothes for the sake of running and climbing and digging and exploring—these are not unfortunate and accidental ways of childhood which are to be shed as soon as we can get rid of them. They are the glory

of the human child, his human heritage. They are at once the representatives in him of human adventurousness and hard-won wisdom, and the means by which he in his turn will lay hold of knowledge and skill, and add to them.[5]

Having described the feelings of the infant before he can speak for himself, and the general age norms of growth in little children, Isaacs turned to the inevitable conflicts and troubles that children have, even in the most mild and serene of homes. Her approach was to suggest that disturbances are normal, expected matters, that anger or harshness are to be avoided, and that calm, matter-of-fact handling will produce the desired results in the long run. For instance, thumb-sucking is often a problem with children, but an occasional or slight amount is not worrisome. The way to deal with it, as with any "bad habit," is by indirect means, not direct punishment or physical restriction. The adult in charge should be sure that the child is not deprived of oral satisfaction or of proper nourishment. Then he should perhaps be given more to do, more to see and talk about, perhaps more companionship. If his interests can be thus directed outward, his thumb will lose its value as a source of pleasure, since he will be moving ahead in development, beyond the oral stage when sucking was an absorbing satisfaction. Harsher methods can only convey to the child a sense of adults' anger at what he is doing, and although he can be physically prevented from getting his thumb into his mouth, it is "only at the price of continued nervous strain and helpless anger, which spreads most harmfully over the whole mental life."[6]

In a similar way, Susan Isaacs dealt with such questions as: What about punishment? What playthings should a child have? What and how much companionship? What should be said about where babies come from? What provision should be made for space and exercise? How should the older child be prepared for a new arrival? How best are weaning and toilet training managed? What about phobias, tantrums, and night fears? How much independence can children be given and when? To all of these questions, so central to child rearing, she gave specific, practical answers, aimed at increasing adult understanding of a child's frustration and conflict, as the world does not always bend to his desires. His anger when disappointed or thwarted is actually a good sign, however, for he is at least responding to the outer world, and if adults do not retaliate with equal hostility, his hate will soon dissipate:

> We can greatly increase the child's hate and give it a hold over him by despotism or lack of thought and understanding; or we can lessen it by patient friendliness and steady love. But we cannot rule it out altogether. The best-cared-for and happiest child will have his moments of anger, defiance, and destructiveness. Even if he hides them from us, they will be there underneath. And without some impulses to turn away from us,

how would he leave behind his infant's way of clinging to his parents? How come to feel himself as an independent person, free to turn to the adult social world and stand on his own feet as an adult?[7]

Similarly, in groups of little children, hostility to others has a positive side to it, since it is an early, though primitive, social response: the child realizes he cannot have everything his way and at first defends himself angrily. Later on, he will learn more socialized ways to achieve his ends and those of the group.

> Thus are little children in these critical early years torn and tossed between their loves and their hates, between the delights of possession and the fears and anxieties of loss.[8]

Nowhere are these conflicts more evident than at home, in relationships with parents and siblings. By the end of the first year, the child has been forced to recognize that mother and father have existences of their own, and perhaps that others share their parental care with him. And in those early months, too, his fantasy life is more real to him than the outer world, so his anger at frustration is the stronger because it is based on fancied loss or damage. Here Susan Isaacs described the origin of the superego, by the mechanism of introjecting the mother images, both the "good" mother who gives him nourishment and love, and the "bad" mother who is separate from him and not always satisfying, as well as the later psychic mechanisms by which he defends himself against conflict and danger, both from within and without, from real and from fantasied sources.

Again, her explanation of the problems with which every child is faced in the normal development of the first few years is couched in simple, nonprofessional language that carries a message of reassurance with it. For instance, when a child knows another baby is coming, an event he deeply dreads as if his mother had deliberately planned to have another child as a rival for her love, he begins to ask questions. He has also begun to have some dim sense of his own and others' history and growth, of life and change in persons. How could all this happen? Where do children come from? What is "having a baby"?

> How strange it would be if an intelligent observant child did not ask questions about the drama of human life in this way! He would have to be blind and deaf and stupid not to do so. Or (as alas! does happen only too often) to be locked up in solitary and fruitless musings by shyness and fear.[9]

These questions are to be welcomed, then, not evaded or laughed at. They are a good sign of growth, and should be answered as naturally and honestly as possible. In this way, the child senses his parents are truthful and dependable, people who will give him the accurate information he needs, not lies or fairy stories or shocked silence.

Intense and absolute in his earliest feelings, every little child feels the cravings for entire possession of a parent and jealousy for a sibling; so too when he has reached about the sixth or seventh year. Then the Oedipal conflict reaches its painful climax and must be treated with utmost gentleness, for upon its successful resolution depends the child's mental health during latency and beyond. At this time of his life

> children have to take the biggest and most difficult step away from the primitive simplicity and intensity of their loves and hates, their hopes and fears, to some sort of controlled and social ways of behavior; and have to learn the hardest lesson of their lives, in accepting the fact that they cannot have exclusive possession of either or both of their parents, as the ways of infancy would demand.[10]

He will not be able to verbalize, even to the most understanding adult he knows, his wishes and fears at this point in his life. They are too deep, beyond the reach of mere words or conscious formulation:

> They come to him in wordless organic longings for caresses, in desires to remove and destroy, in fears of rejection and retaliation. The guilt and dread bound up with these complex shifting feelings are indeed so strong that the child has to keep his own thoughts turned away from them. He comes to deny in himself, not only *behaving* angrily or possessively, but even *wanting* to behave so.[11]

Yet his longing for possession of the parent of the opposite sex springs from his deepest humanity, for on the satisfactory channeling of this desire depends the continuation of the human race. So vital is this conflict, and so much bound up with the child's earliest fantasies of loss of love and of guilt feelings that it is indeed "the hardest lesson," and even with the mildest and most forbearing parents, inward difficulties are inevitable. Again, play is his best outlet, a safety valve for his hidden wishes and fears, and also a way for the observant adult to glimpse something of his psychic tension. "The discharge in play of these inward tensions makes it easier for little children to temper their behavior in real life."[12]

And although children, in their deepest fantasies, see their parents not as they really are but fear and hate them as well as loving them, parents must nonetheless understand fully that what they are in reality makes all the difference.

> It is, indeed, of the utmost importance to them that we should be in reality gentle and just, kind, temperate and reasonable. This is the greatest help that as parents we can give them, towards learning to distinguish between their imaginings, desires and fears, and real things. If we are in

truth cruel and cold, capricious, unjust and tyrannical, our children are justified in their phantasies—and will become like us in their turn.[13]

Here, in fact, is the secret to character formation: identification with the important adult figures around the child. No amount of moralizing or preaching can change the fact that the parents' example is what counts. A grown-up cannot love well or wisely unless he has been well loved as a child.

This is the magnitude of an adult's responsibility in caring for children, especially in these early years. And this is the reason that Susan Isaacs was so anxious to make her message very clear. Here are her closing injunctions:

SOME DON'TS FOR PARENTS

Don't merely say, "You mustn't do that" if you can possibly add "but you may do this".

Don't call a thing "naughty" when you mean merely "it's a nuisance to me".

Don't discuss children in front of them; nor in general assume that they won't listen or notice or understand.

Don't interrupt anything the child is doing without giving him fair warning.

Don't show your love by constantly caressing the child, but by providing for his interests.

Don't "take" the child for a walk—go with him.

Don't hesitate to make holidays to rules sometimes.

Don't make a display of your concern when the child falls down, won't eat, etc. Do what is needed instead of fussing and worrying.

Don't tease or use sarcasm—laugh with the child, but not at him.

Don't show off with the child to others, nor make him a plaything.

Don't give moral lectures to the small child; if you find yourself doing this, don't be surprised or angry if he shows that he is bored.

Don't assume that the child understands what you are saying to him just because you do.

Don't, if you say or do something in anger, pretend that you did it "for the child's good"; humbug does more harm than honest ill-temper.

Don't break promises, or make any you may not be able to keep.

Don't lie or evade.[14]

The Children We Teach (1932)

The Nursery Years had been written to help a child's earliest educators—parents and nurses—to understand him better; *The Children We Teach* was written for his next educators, those in school. Here Susan Isaacs discussed the mind of the child from the age of seven to eleven, the years of the Primary School. Teachers need to know all about children—their general modes of cognitive, social, and physical growth, and their individual differences—when planning for their learning in school. And much work had been done to fill out the knowledge available, in developmental studies, in mental testing, and in psychoanalytic work.

> The really skilled teacher does in fact base his teaching upon an implicit understanding of these ways of the child's mind, whatever "subject" is being presented.... [This] is no longer an intuition of rare souls, but has become an everyday part of the everyday science of child psychology, based upon solid observations free to all. And soon it will be seen transforming every teacher's conception of the work of the school, and all the details of his practice.[15]

Then the barriers of an "anatomised" curriculum and schedule can be broken through, so these become servants of the child's growth and not the bad masters they have so long been. For "subject" and the "timetable" are mechanical contrivances that can foster a child's interests and organize them satisfactorily, or they can lose touch with him and hinder learning.

There should be no sharp break when a child leaves the Infants' School and enters the Primary School. It had been traditional to assume that the Infants' School's more relaxed, flexible atmosphere should give way to the "sterner, drier, more formal ways" of the school for older children, but doing so does not take the child into account. Although by about age six, he begins to want a "proper school" and to be held to more definite tasks and social control, still the newer school's ways should definitely link on to the old. While more can be expected from the children, both socially and intellectually, there can and should still be an easy, friendly relationship with the teacher, plenty of singing and dancing and miming, making things, free expression in paint or clay or dramatic movement, physical activity and games. For although children go through definite phases of development, yet these are not marked by hard-and-fast boundaries:

> There is nothing in human development corresponding to the metamorphoses in the life of the insect—the change from the larva to the pupa, from the chrysalis to the butterfly.[16]

Rather, development comes on many fronts and unevenly, so that a sudden change to emphasizing cognitive skills in school is a great loss to children.

Greater flexibility and more elasticity of method can also show the teacher her children as they really are, more than class teaching of a set lesson can do. Then individual differences become more clear, and can be more appropriately provided for. For while all children need activity and social opportunities, play and fantasy expression, and chances to find out about the world, all children are too different.

The actual differences between one child and another are a result of three factors: innate intelligence, social and economic background, and temperament or character. Every group of children will contain variations on these three themes, and the wise teacher must allow for them. It is a very hard task, however, to provide for the needs of all the children for whom she is responsible, so that ways have to be found to lessen the differences by grouping children of similar ability together. It is with this need in mind, Susan Isaacs said, that head teachers were turning to the new knowledge becoming available about children, in order to find a sound basis for classifying children. And "of all the differences between one child and another, inborn intelligence turns out to be the most stable and permanent."[17] It should never be the only basis for grouping, however, since home influences, differences in age, and temperament are important.

> But all those people who have been using mental age, rather than birthday age, as the *main* basis of grading, have found that the work both of individual children and of the school as a whole has greatly benefited. Such a classification makes it so much more possible to give to each according to his needs.[18]

Also, in the Primary School, the difference between children's mental ages is much wider than earlier, and it will go on increasing with the years of development. So it is just at this time that mental age needs to be ascertained, and grouping accomplished.

Here Susan Isaacs described Burt's tests in detail, explaining that they are chiefly aimed at finding out how a child makes use of the information and experiences he has had, by setting him some problems quite similar to those he might meet any day. She pointed out that, by and large, the results of widespread testing of children have proved quite compatible with teachers' judgments of their ability; and that therefore it is clear that

> ability as expressed in mental ratio is the soundest general basis for classifying the children in the Primary Schools. . . . no school could be run without some collective teaching and collective occupations, . . . they make the right background and general setting for individual work and personal progress. But as soon as children come together in groups, some mode of choosing the groups has to be found.[19]

Just how many groups there should be in schools, so as to provide appropriate education for each, and how the syllabus and teaching should be planned, she considered fruitful areas for experiment among schools, as there could be many possibilities that teachers and heads could work out together.

Yet while recognizing the value of mental testing and ability grouping, she continued to emphasize the need to treat children individually. Their specific interests will be powerful determinants both of learning style and of the direction intelligence will take. And difficulties at home or temperamental inhibitions of one kind or another may keep children from making the progress that they might. All these considerations reinforce the need for a teacher to observe her children carefully and develop ways of teaching them that will be individualized enough to meet their differing needs.

Especially important is providing opportunities for children to put to use what they learn in concrete activities. In arithmetic, for instance, a child may be having difficulty with its abstract symbols and need more play with building blocks, counting games, or measuring and comparing and weighing things. Or a child from a home with few books or little conversation may need extra time to talk with her playmates and with the teacher, to make up her own stories or shopping lists, to cook from a recipe, and the like. Many ways can be found to help children to see that arithmetic and reading connect with their real lives and practical pursuits.

> The interests of children in the Primary School years are still intensely practical. Formal and theoretical problems find little response in their minds, but the actual issues of practical life are real and compelling. If children have the chance to use what they learn, they learn far more rapidly and surely.[20]

All children, whatever their individual differences of intelligence or temperament, need to be active, to be doing. Not only in the Infants' School should there be plenty of opportunity for practicing bodily skills, developing more speed and accuracy of sense perception, and improving in manual skill. The Primary School child can do these things better and at a higher level, and can also manage the abstract learning of reading and writing, and it is important to blend the two. Activity is always the means of a child's education: "It is stillness we have to justify, not movement."[21] The appropriate attitude toward children's need for activity and experience is not to inhibit it but to use it.

> The problem is not just one of sandwiching periods of physical activity in between periods of immobile "headwork". The headwork itself is most fruitful when it is also handwork and bodywork. In these years, the child's intelligence is essentially practical. He thinks as much with his hands as with his tongue; and even with his tongue he can think better aloud than "in his head."[22]

Physical activity in concrete pursuits goes hand in hand with intellectual growth, and so too with social development, no matter what the differences may be between child and child. And a wise teacher will observe children's social behavior with care, not only in the schoolroom but also at play without adults present, where they reveal themselves freely and spontaneously, throwing new light upon their inner worlds.

Here again Isaacs differed with Piaget. Although she felt he was "one of the ablest observers of children,"[23] yet he believed that intellectual advance depended on social experience. At about age seven, according to Piaget's early work, children become less egocentric, more aware of and sensitive to the opinions of others, and hence are able to move from simple, unilateral seeing and handling of the world to more reciprocal "thinking in abstract terms, to reflecting upon thought itself, and so making it orderly."[24] For Susan Isaacs, there seemed to be no reason for saying that social development is the cause of intellectual growth, but rather that a child grows in all ways at once. Every sort of change is bound up with every other.

> It is always the whole child who plays and laughs, who quarrels and loves, who thinks and asks questions, through all the hours of his day and all the years of his childhood.[25]

Her experience with the children at the Malting House School had brought home to her so clearly the mutual influence of thought and social behavior in growing children.

Social development in the Primary School years grows directly out of experiences earlier. In the Infants' School years, groups of children form briefly and variously, and they are still individualistic and hierarchical. It is usually the stronger over the weaker, and the leader can be very hard on the followers. Rules are seen as absolute, not just conventions; punishments are harsh, and loves and hates strong. Children still feel much rivalry and ambivalence for each other, yet their very hostility and suspicion is, again, a sign of growth, of reaching out into the world of people with some recognition of their existence. When children reach Primary School age, these fleeting and naive social impulses become more organized. There are more stable modes of group formation, less antagonism, more realistic understanding of the feelings of others and of the joys of friendship. Earlier rivalries give way to more shared experience, and eventually to the even wider view of the adolescent, that begins to embrace all mankind. Thus, socially, the years from seven to eleven form a kind of "bridge," carrying the child over from the egoistic, self-centeredness of his earlier years toward a more truly universal social outlook.

> Our ultimate educational aim may be (and for myself I would say *must* be) to transcend all rivalries in national and international life. But to gain it, our children need the actual experience of smaller units of social life that lie within the compass of their sympathy and understanding.[26]

Children of Primary School age, then, begin to discover other children as allies, and to value their companionship and shared views. Here the adults' role changes: earlier, littler children were oriented very closely to adults, dependent upon them for praise and stability. Now children are more sensitive to comments from their peers, and they develop a kind of reserve toward adults. This is the age of secret clubs and special code languages that give children a sense of being apart from adults and even holding them at bay. Grown-ups are viewed with an appraising eye:

> Neither teacher nor parent can now maintain his prestige by mere virtue of being grown-up. Authority has to be won and kept by the real tested qualities of sense and firmness. . . . If we play the part of sensible, decent, friendly, perhaps remote but entirely human elders, free from humbug, from tyranny and from any fear of him, he will be content with us.[27]

This is a considerable change from the role adults played with the younger child, and it does not come all at once but unevenly and only gradually. Yet teachers should bear in mind that these attitudes are characteristic of the middle years of childhood, are a sign of real growth, and can be fostered by a gradual change in her behavior toward a somewhat less intimate, dependent relationship.

Another characteristic of the Primary School child, similar to his more detached view of adults, is his matter-of-factness. This is the age of wanting real skill, real achievements, real adventure stories, leaving fantasy behind in both play and work. He is, at the same time, more realistic and sensible in his judgments of others, and less intolerant of weakness or inability. Games are played with real team spirit, skills are practiced with more concentration, and attainments are realistically valued. Thus children of these years are capable of establishing more stable, cooperative, realistic relationships with their peers, and need opportunities to do so. Group activities like games and sports, drama, dancing, singing, should be part of the school day, as well as joint responsibility for certain aspects of the classroom materials or arrangements.

Children's matter-of-factness and interest in the workings of the real world influence their social behavior, and also point to the characteristics of intellectual growth in these years. For at this age (as indeed at any age), children want very much to understand the things and peole and events around them, and have an increased capacity and a natural impulse to do so. Less a prey to infantile fears, more stable in their sense of themselves, their spontaneous interests now come into their own, although not yet divided up into school subjects. By watching children outside the classroom, therefore, teachers can learn much about the spontaneous character of children's interests, when they are free from the heavy weight of the usual curriculum, with its abstract words and separate topics of study. Then perhaps "nature study" could be connected with walks in the country, drawing flowers in a vase, holding and caring for animals. For it seems that although children will vary in intelligence, yet "the movement of their minds remains essentially the same."[28] Children with more ability will range more widely in their understanding, express a more complex grasp of the world, and move toward abstract formulation more rapidly than those of less ability. But, in general, children of Primary School age share common interests that can be observed and provided for within the school, and that show themselves in those pursuits that are freely chosen outside school, or engaged in with enthusiasm inside it. As Dewey might have said,

> Whatever activity brings light to the eye and eagerness to the voice and gestures can be taken as a clue to some inner need of growth.[29]

Chief among these interests is the children's enjoyment of games and sports, both as means of increasing physical prowess and social reciprocity. Another group of activities that children of this age respond to with pleasure is singing, dancing, miming, acting out parts. Infants' Schools have always made room for these, but their interest does not lessen in the Primary School, although the subjects may change. Now there is much acting out of adventure, of hunting or piracy, of heroism or tragedy. Connected with this interest in dramatic representation of experience, there is a new desire to explore, often independently, to wander farther afield and look for wider experiences than the narrower confines of the neighborhood within which the child was content earlier. This is his wish for a greater and more systematic view of the world and should be treated as such—it is not vagrancy or truancy. Hardly less characteristic is the Primary School-age interest in making things. With increased manual skill and strength, boys and girls of this age will often be using materials that need a good deal of ingenuity and care. Instead of the plasticine, clay, or paper of earlier days, it will now be wood or metal or heavy cardboard. And they will be making real things, with attention to correctness of detail, to careful measurement, to exact fit. Perfection is not yet to be expected, but there is considerable satisfaction in doing a good job of work at this age. Boys are likely to prefer to make scooters or trains; girls may spend hours on their sewing and making paper dolls. All will enjoy free painting and drawing, if given the chance, for all are both craftsmen and artists.

Primary School children also enjoy having things that belong to them, especially collections of treasured tickets, pebbles, coins, moths and butterflies, which stuff pockets and satchels at this age. Pride in possession is strong then: a child enjoys owning a desk, a set of tools, an apron, a book, of his or her very own. And books begin to cast a spell over this age group as well. Littler children loved fairy tales and fantasy; these older ones reach out for books of adventure, of human experiences, of information about a great range of subjects.

Again, although levels of intelligence will vary among children, their general interests are similar, as can be seen clearly in the Primary School when they are free to choose and to act and to play according to their preferences. But how does their thought itself work? The old controversy comes up again—at what age can children be said to reason? On the one hand, those who believe that reasoning does not appear until later childhood stress routine activity, drill, memorization, habit training, so that when a child is able to reason he will have "the basics" to call upon, as well as habits of order, industry, and obedience. Understanding the whys and wherefores comes later. On the other hand, Susan Isaacs's experience at the Malting House School, borne out by Burt's problem-solving tests as well as Spearman's studies, seemed to indicate that this view of children's thinking is inaccurate. The main difference between older and younger children is chiefly the amount of experience that they have had and can draw on. Reasoning does not suddenly appear, either at age seven as a result of new social insight, as Piaget had felt, or in the early teens as others thought.

> It shows itself rather in a progressive increase in the child's power to handle issues that are relatively remote from immediate experience, less concrete and more general in character, more complex in type, needing a wider background of knowledge, and involving a greater element of "ifness", or hypothesis, than those he can deal with in the earlier years. . . . a child shows a growing ability to appreciate more and more complex relations, and to handle these relations more and more clearly and precisely.[30]

Put even more specifically, children grow in their ability to hold together in their minds a larger number of facts and relations among them, and to move from simpler relations to more subtle and complex ones. Memory and experience play their part in providing children with background information on which to draw. But, in this view, all the basic mental mechanisms needed for formal reasoning are evident long before children leave the Infants' School, and their development is chiefly a matter of an

> "increase in the extent and variety of the subject-matter to which those mechanisms can be applied, and in an increase in the precision and eleboration with which those mechanisms operate."[31]

Early reasoning can and does take place, if adults were to notice it better: indeed, whenever a new "capacity" seems to appear, its suddenness is due mostly to our not having observed its earlier stages closely. If this is true, then each kind of logical problem could be made simple and clear enough, even for very young children, while bearing in mind their small store of experiences and information.

> It is most significant for teaching method that even the younger children are not to be looked upon as creatures of mere habit and memory, but as

being able to reason and argue and draw conclusions, if we but make the appropriate opportunity for them.[32]

What differentiates children of different ages, then, aside from innate intelligence, is only the amount and range of experience that they have had. And reasoning powers can be seen very early in simple forms, so that hard and fast "stages" do not do justice to them. Higher levels of thought and reasoning develop organically out of lower, and it is always a question of more or less, not the presence or absence of rational thought.

For instance, one of the main stimuli to the expression of thought in words comes to children as a result of their practical interest in play, their arguments and discussions about it, and their questions. Little children cannot yet argue abstractly or make a sustained theoretical statement of cause and effect; but they will be able to do so as a result of earlier, concrete experiences. The beginnings of the ability to hypothesize, so characteristic of eleven or twelve year olds, can be seen in the imaginative play of much younger children, who act out their fantasies "as if" they were true, and thus see what might happen. Thus do high intellectual capacities grow from simpler ones.

In order to summarize and at the same time to focus her discussion of the mind of the child from age seven to eleven, Susan Isaacs closed her book with a brief statement on the practical implications that the study of children's social and intellectual growth have for the teacher. At every point, one is brought back again and again to the view that "it is the *children's activity* that is the key to their full development."[33] Whether it is the need for free physical movement and exercise, for wider experience of the world, for team play and social groupings, or for situations that provoke discussion, questions, or thought,

> it is the child's doing, the child's active social experience and his own thinking and talking that are the chief means of his education.[34]

The role of the teacher is to provide opportunities for children's activity, and for the means of solving problems or dilemmas that they are concerned about. In their natural interests in the world of things and events and people are all the necessary opportunities needed for their education. Segmented school subjects, formal, abstract teaching, habits of submissive behavior all have no place for this age group.

The children's activity will still begin by being practical and concrete. Real things need to be handled, measured, compared, and made, and real talk about these matters must be allowed for. Words cannot be substituted safely for things until direct experience has been ample enough. They should not be expected to talk instead of doing, but to put experiences of every kind into words, to ask, to describe, to question, to discuss. If the child is offered verbal teaching separate from experience, or if his free speech is forbidden, we take away from him one of the most valuable means of his social and intellectual growth. Conversation brings verbal fluency. One way to provide for it is to group children in small numbers of similar abilities, rather than attempt to teach large classes of various capacities, where silence has to be the order of the day. Smaller groups will allow for the varied free activity and talk that are a child's best means of development. And individual plans of work will allow for individual differences in progress, both in the early stages of reading and numbers, but also in practical, creative pursuits.

> In the making of real things, and in expressional drawing and modelling, far more interesting and effective work is done when each child follows out his own aims in his own time, than when all are forced into the same pattern.[35]

Other forms of activity are and should be communal, gaining much of their meaning from the sharing of the experience. Dancing, singing, and dramatic play are such; so are gardening, caring for animals, arranging the schoolroom, as well as joint projects in decorating the school or large construction plans. But even here, this does not mean all the children doing the same thing at the same time, as the old class methods insisted. Rather, this kind of cooperative experience means that each child is "making his own special contribution to the larger whole," especially when the goal is real and valuable to them all.

Thus Susan Isaacs came back to her basic point, namely, that study of children of Primary-School age (as well as younger ones) supported from a psychological point of view those teaching methods which built fundamentally on the children's need for activity and experience, as the best means for their growth in mind and body.

5
Further Practical Work

The work at the Malting House School had provided Susan Isaacs with data for her two extended studies of children's development, as well as for her more popularly written works. At the same time, she was also writing articles on psychoanalysis and education for a variety of professional journals, editing a series of handbooks called *Contributions to Modern Education*, and a set of pamphlets for the Home and School Council called "Concerning Children."[1] But her work was not confined to writing and editing. She also engaged directly in educational work: in 1933 at the Department of Child Development, in 1934 with the Wiltshire Education Committee, and in 1939 in Cambridge, studying the effects of the evacuation of children during the war.

The Department of Child Development, University of London (1933–1943)

In 1932, Sir Percy Nunn, then head of the Institute of Education at the University of London, discussed with Susan Isaacs the possibility of founding a department of child development within his Institute. There were important centers of research into children's development under Gesell in New Haven, Connecticut; Piaget in Geneva, Switzerland; and Bott in Toronto, Canada. England had a long-standing tradition of child-centered ideas and practices, but no university-based center for training and research. Nunn suggested that she should be the first head of such a facility.

At that point, Susan Isaacs was involved in her own second analysis, utilizing the fresh insight into early years that Melanie Klein and Joan Rivière had developed. She was also busy with patients and with the study of psychoanalytic technique, and was very interested in contributing to fundamental research in the area. So at first she demurred:

> I have had a taste not only of the satisfaction that comes from giving real help to minds in doubt and distress, but also gained a deep sense of the fundamental psychological research which the analytic technique with very young children makes possible.[2]

However, second thoughts prevailed. When she recalled that the post would be half-time only, and that she could rearrange her other lecturing and advising obligations, and still maintain her psychoanalytic work, she decided to undertake this new position. Her husband had always favored her doing so, and now she agreed.

Sir Percy was successful in persuading the university to establish such a department, and in 1933 Isaacs was appointed its first head. The purposes were twofold: to supply the demands of an increasing number of progressive training colleges for well-qualified lecturers equipped with the latest knowledge in the field of child development; and to establish a center for research into human development in general and sound teaching methods in particular. Initially, it had been hoped that a laboratory school could be attached, with opportunity for direct observation of little children in a nursery-school setting. Financial constraints made that impossible at first, but in 1938, the department moved into larger quarters and space was at last found for a small group of children to come each morning.

Finances were always a problem. Fees had to be kept low, since the experienced people who came were usually taking time away from their salaried posts. Despite many appeals to a variety of foundations for support, it was never forthcoming. Isaacs had to make do with one office for herself, her part-time secretary, many books, and for individual sessions with students. Many lecturers were willing to come for little or no remuneration, but she was never able to obtain a salary for a second instructor. Although in the years of her work at the department her advanced training program became known all over the world, it was never provided for very amply, as is tragically often the case with programs dealing with young children. (Not until 1944, when the program was reopened in London, was a full-time appointment made available to the new director, Dorothy E. M. Gardner.)

The students were few at first, some part-time and some full-time, but all came because they felt the need for the advanced work Susan Isaacs provided, even though at first there was no degree or diploma awarded. The number of applicants increased as soon as the program became well established and known, but she kept the numbers small so as to continue the high quality and personal attention that were important to her. Many of her students were already lecturers at training colleges, others were experienced teachers, some came from overseas, and all were people who had experience and concern for children. Although she was no longer in direct contact with children herself, as she had been at the Malting House School, Isaacs felt that this training program would mean that her ideas and practices would be disseminated to many others who would be working with children.

The work of the program consisted both of academic lectures and field experiences, and of discussions to link the two. Susan Isaacs herself gave lectures on the psychology of infancy and early childhood, as well as on methods of research into child development, including mental testing, and the educational implications of psychological research. There were also lectures by other authorities on the physiology of growth and medical care of children, on psychological factors in the physical welfare of young children, educational psychology, and basic philosophic principles of education. These lectures were given by such luminaries as Sir Percy Nunn, Dr. Flora Shepherd, Professor Samson Wright, Professor G. Hamley, Dr. Cyril Burt, Dr. D. W. Winnicott, and other leading experts in a variety of relevant fields.

Practical work included regular observations, systmatically carried out, at schools like the Chelsea Open Air Nursery School, as well as at schools for older children, with later discussion of what had been seen. There was also observation and participation at the nearby child-guidance clinic with disturbed children and their therapists and social workers; and individual research under Susan Isaacs's direction into a topic of special interest. Small seminar meetings were held weekly; students were expected to bring their questions or ideas, and to present their research findings. Individual tutorial sessions at which Susan Isaacs talked over the work of each student in detail and gave advice or direction were also held. And there were also social gatherings every week, especially when foreign students began to join the program, for Susan Isaacs felt "no little social responsibility" for them as visitors and strangers to London.

Beyond this bare outline, taken largely from the account given in Miss Gardner's book,[3] it is hard to get much idea of the program. The documents that would have given a fuller picture no longer exist. There are no lists of students and their backgrounds, no lecture notes or reading lists, no letters of application or recommendation, no inquiries about school visits, no schemes of evaluation, no program prospectus, or any of the usual documents that such a program would have generated. One account has been written by one of the first students, Dorothy May, who later won the prestigious Leon Fellowship for research into children's social development. Other former students have contributed their reminiscences,[4] but aside from these anecdotal and individual memories, only Gardner's book, a copy of Isaacs's official letter to Sir Percy Nunn accepting her position as head of the Department of Child Development,* and some miscellaneous correspondence are still available.

Her former students do remember her teaching well, however. In a letter to Susan Isaacs, who was ill at the time, one student wrote these comments:

> It is a bit difficult to write anything which is representative of the group, and is worth saying because we are so widely assorted in our

---

*See p. 16.

points of view and interests. As far as I am concerned, this term has been of tremendous value. In the first term one seemed to flounder.... This term things have come together in a wonderful way, and I am feeling that I have really captured and made my own a whole body of new knowledge, and with it seems to have come a new and more balanced outlook on life. I think perhaps the most remarkable thing about this course is that we one and all seem to be getting just the things we are wanting most from it. It does not seem to offer just one thing which we can take or leave, but it seems to reach each of our personal needs. I suppose this is what really creative teaching manages to do for people—but it is a rare achievement. I hope that you know how grateful we are to you for this.[5]

May's account of her experience with Susan Isaacs as a teacher reads, in part,

I well remember the heart-sinking with which I climbed those stairs for my tutorial knowing that I had reached a low ebb in my work, and having no idea what it was most important to discuss. Dr. Isaacs, I am sure would sense this, and with a quiet smile would look at one quizzically and utter quietly but challengingly, "Well?" Somehow one responded to the challenge, and at the end of the period one went away feeling not only that Dr. Isaacs had helped to clarify the issues but that she had made it possible for one to achieve this for oneself. It was in this that she excelled as a teacher—in her determination to foster one's self-reliance and at the same time in the skill with which, without seeming to give a lead, she made it possible for one to see the whole problem much more clearly.[6]

Gardner—Susan Isaacs's student, friend, and biographer—succeeded to the position of head of the Department of Child Development in 1944; her memory of working with Isaacs on an early research project into the meaning and effects of play for young children reads, in part, as follows:

As a tutor, Susan was superb. She identified herself completely with the students' need to find out and understand for themselves and encouraged their gropings for knowledge and insight with genuine respect for every discovery they made.... She encouraged me to choose a topic which appealed to me.... She was a perfect support to my own quest for finding out and would listen patiently when I gave her material from the play of children in the playrooms of child guidance clinics and tried, often in vain, to find a link between this play and the problems which I had learnt to be those of the children concerned. Only when I asked her specifically to do so would she interpret some of the behaviour.... I was left with the feeling that any discoveries I made were really my own, though she was by no means detached—in fact, I know she was deeply interested and involved.[7]

Susan Isaacs's teaching method was, in fact, similar to that developed at the Malting House School, now adapted to meet the needs of mature students: the framework of the program was carefully planned and made clear; extensive resources were made available, both at the department and in the field; independent exploration and discovery were expected; and opportunities were made for discussion of the results both with Susan Isaacs and with other students. One or two students found all this a bit too detached and wanted closer supervision and instruction, but most seem to have found it rewarding.

During the years of the program's existence, Isaacs was also called upon to provide expert help in other ways. For instance, once she was asked to testify in a murder trial: a father was accused of pushing his two-year-old daughter out of a train door. He claimed that, while he was in the corridor, she had opened the door herself and fallen out. Susan Isaacs was able to provide evidence that the child actually could have done so, and the man was acquitted.[8] She also worked with graduate students in psychology at the University of London under Professor Burt, examined for a variety of training programs and committees, consulted with child psychologists and educators from overseas, and still continued her daily work in psychoanalysis. And, in 1937, she went out to Australia and New Zealand, to lecture and consult with colleagues abroad.

The Educational Guidance of the School Child (1936)

In 1934, the Wiltshire Education Committee asked Susan Isaacs for help in developing record cards for teachers to use with the children in their classes. Over a period of two years, she worked with a group of Wiltshire educators on such a plan, refining it as they went along, until it seemed ready for wider use. In 1936, *The Educational Guidance of the School Child*, which embodied the fruits of their work, was published.[9]

Struckmeyer's introduction strikes a note familiar to all progressive educators, namely, a fundamental belief in democracy and the importance of education in building character for future citizens of a democratic society. In educational terms, this implies

> the belief that all true growth is organic, . . . springing from the life within; it must not be predetermined, nor designed according to a plan conceived for any extraneous purpose, but arise spontaneously within the consciousness of individual members of the social group.[10]

School practices must foster this growth by taking care to operate on democratic principles in every respect, not on autocratic ones that would defeat the central sim of education, which is character training. A democratic education attends to and fosters the real needs and attributes of children, by patient observation and thoughtful understanding:

> By supplying the right opportunities for development at the right moment, [it] fosters a growth of character in the child that is more vigorous

because it is more individual and natural, and more healthy because it is more free.[11]

Since a child's needs are both social and individual, the school has two roles to play: it must develop a school community that provides the optimum social climate for children's interaction; and it must be equally concerned with the development of individual mind and character.

These rather lofty aims were followed by the inevitable practical questions: How are they to be achieved? What are teachers to do to bring them about? Struckmeyer's answer was that, just as educators learn from physicians about the best care of children's bodies, so they must learn from psychologists about promoting their mental and emotional health. There was clearly a need for carefully planned ways to study school children in all their psychological variations and personality types. And concrete methods for dealing with both good and bad character tendencies must be worked out, but only on the basis of a thorough developmental knowledge. For, Struckmeyer contended, "education, after all, in its function of individual character-training, is mainly a process of diagnosis and treatment;"[12] This is reminiscent of Susan Isaacs's emphasis in her Malting House School methods discussion that teaching is, in an important sense, a matter of "deliberate technique," worked out on the basis of careful observation and understanding of children. In *The Nursery Years* and *The Children We Teach*, similarly, she had urged individual study of children by those who were responsible for them. Here was yet another opportunity to help teachers, in a very specific and practical way.

The cumulative record cards that Isaacs and her group developed were not like the complete anecdotal observations that were made at the Malting House School for primarily psychological research purposes. They were, instead, planned to be straightforward and useful tools for any teacher who wanted to learn more about her children. As Struckmeyer put it, the basic purpose of such records is

> to serve as an instrument of scientific observation for aiding the right selection of educational methods to meet the needs of individual children during various phases of their development, . . . and . . . [for] the removal of fixed notions about children's capacities and recognition by the teacher of new possibilities of development in children.[13]

Chapter 2 of *Educational Guidance* was written by Susan Isaacs herself, and discussed in detail how to use the sample record cards that appeared at the end of the book. For her, too, the value of pupils' records was to aid in the study of the individual child, so as to adapt the work of the school to meet his needs. Although this is important at all ages, it is of special importance with children under age seven, she felt, for at that age young children are more unstable in feeling and more sensitive emotionally than later on, especially toward their treatment by adults. As she so often reiterated in her writings, adults have an absolutely crucial role to play, with younger and with older children, though differently at each level.

> Their imaginings are very vivid, and they cannot always distinguish between the imagined and the real. Their experience is still so limited, their knowledge so meagre, that they misunderstand adult intentions or instructions. Confusions and fears are thus easily stirred up, in a way that may affect their learning and the whole of their development. When a child is afraid or suspicious, angry or impatient, defiant or obstinate, inattentive or muddled, we cannot find how to help him unless, as has been said, we can "think with" him, and feel with him. Only when we understand how things seem from this point of view can we straighten out his mistakes and calm his anxieties. And this needs individual study.[14]

Adequate records not only help a teacher understand individual children; they should also, when used cumulatively and comparatively, illuminate more clearly the general needs and characteristics of most children of any particular age, and indicate how some children vary from expected norms or trends in special ways. Records should be kept not only of academic attainments and of mental-test results, but they should also include observations of all possible situations that occur during the normal school day. Above all, children should be observed at play, for they will show themselves more freely and spontaneously during play than in any activity that is planned or controlled by others. "Play is for him a means of living and of understanding life."[15] In their play, uniquely, they show their fears, wishes, and interests, their ideas of the world and their imaginary dealings with it, their relationship with parents and family and with other children. It is also important to know what one can about children's home conditions, especially with the younger ones, since children bring their home troubles and feelings to school with them. Indeed, all areas of a child's life should be the subject of the teacher's observation and study.

The record cards that Isaacs and her colleagues developed included a number of simple headings, intended to direct teachers' attention to those aspects of children's behavior that should be noted. They were not intended, however, as norms for the purpose of judgment, but rather as broad, general descriptions of the type of behavior one might expect to see among children, although always with allowances for deviations. For all children will have difficulties in one or another area of growth, and these should be seen in the whole context of their developmental patterns. Nor should separate headings or topics be seen in isolation, for children's thinking is not separate from their feelings, or their learning from their imagination. Their emotions powerfully determine not only the direction of their interests, but also their ability (or lack of it) to concentrate and perform at their best.

Mental tests may be used with younger children, Susan Isaacs believed, as well as with older; but the younger the child, the less reliable are the test results. They should not be treated as more than items of information, which might be looked at again as he grows older and can be tested with more security. But with little children, it is far more important to make other sorts of observations. For instance, a child's special interest, noticed and followed up, may help him over a difficult time emotionally, by helping him find success and meaningful activity in the outer world. This positive step for him may one day lead to considerable attainment and high test scores, but it cannot be taken without a sound understanding of the child first.

Turning from these general remarks about the use of records by teachers, Isaacs moved on to make even more specific statements. When a child at five or under first enters school, he can be expected to show his personality in the way he reacts to the teacher, to other children, and to the surroundings. Most children at this age will be friendly toward an adult who seems pleasant and helpful, but some will be suspicious at first. Others will weep when left alone for what may be the first time; some will be nervous and a bit boastful to cover their anxiety; others may cling to the teacher and demand exclusive attention; while still others will chatter on excitedly but without much focus. All these are normal reactions to a new adult who will be the center of the child's experience at the school for some time to come. When meeting a group of young children, children under five will most often be shy and quiet with the others at first, and then will begin to open up and play and talk together with more ease. Often, too, their first advances toward each other will be boisterous or aggressive, and some children will tend to bully the younger or weaker, while others will show a more submissive or docile reaction. But these are only preliminary ways of reaching out from a still egocentric inner world to the social world that now contains strangers.

Many children entering this new environment will spend a good deal of time quietly taking it all in, watching or sitting still; others may simply wander distractedly for a while before settling down to play with one particular material or game; they may take hold of something possessively and want to call it "theirs"; they may try to get a toy away from another child or destroy the play of others. Within limits, again, these are all to be expected from little children from time to time, as typical first reactions to a wider, more varied setting. Although at times a child's behavior might seem antisocial by adult standards, then, those are not the standards to use in assessing children at this or any age.

Outstanding qualities of a child's personality should be noted, both positive and negative. Is he generous, frank, communicative, helpful, protective to younger children, adventurous? Or is he destructive, moody, apathetic, anxious, defiant, unable to play, overly excitable?[16] All these qualities appear in most children, at different stages, but what should be noted is when they occur in an intense, frequent, or unusual form. Similarly, such "bad habits" as thumb-sucking, nail-biting, masturbation, stammering, or enuresis should all be noticed when they appear more than might be expected under usual circumstances.

The bodily control of little children is always imperfect, and high standards of muscular coordination or of personal hygiene cannot be expected: "it is important to look at the aims and the effort he is making, rather than to judge the actual results by standards suitable for older children."[17] Can he balance himself well, relax easily on a mat, use scissors and paintbrushes freely, carry trays or cups of water without spilling, and so on? Or does he go rigid when trying to play with paint or clay, fiddle constantly while sitting still, hunch his shoulders, squint, duck his head, or trip over small obstacles constantly? Does he care for himself appropriately and keep reasonably clean and tidy? Are his table manners at least fairly good? Can he dress himself yet, and hang up his coat? Or is he excessively anxious about being clean and refuse to do any digging, modeling, or painting? Is he upset about a toy that is broken or lost? All children like to be messy from time to time, and an "excessive need to be clean and tidy is rather an unfavorable sign in a child under seven."[18]

Also, besides stammering, all speech should be noticed in children, whether it is clearly enunciated or not, pleasant and appropriately modulated for the situation, or, on the other hand, overly shrill, blocked in some way, fake in tonality or affect, or perhaps mature beyond the child's years in vocabulary or usage. For speech is, of course, the vital mode of interaction between the inner world and the outer, and must be carefully observed, although fully expressive and mature language cannot be expected as yet.

All these observations will show a good deal about a child's personality, and should be made upon his entry to the school, and again later on when he has settled in somewhat. The same is true for evidences of his intelligence, although it should never be thought of as operating in any way separate from his emotional and physical side. Most children, especially as they move toward the age of six or seven, take a lively interest in the things, events, and behavior of other people in the everyday world around them. Here special gifts or interests can be noticed, especially if a child is free to choose his occupation. Here, too, the teacher can decide whether to comment and help the interest along with fresh ideas or materials, or to leave the child alone when he is wholly absorbed. Again, a child's comments should be noted, since his speech about what he is doing shows his intelligence at work, and the teacher can listen with interest, and then clarify his words or suggest more accurate ones.

A child's intelligence is shown, moreover, not only in the concrete things that interest him and with which he engages; it is also shown in his ability to enter "freely and vividly" into an imaginary situation. Here is one of his best means to recreate his past and to hypothesize about the future. Children who cannot enter into imaginary play or show any quality of imagination in their creative work often turn out to be "either intellectually retarded or emotionally starved."[19] A child with little opportunity to play at home or with few playthings will have a hard time engaging freely, alone or with others, in make-believe; he may also be suffering from a deeper trouble that makes him unable to play, and the teacher needs to notice the quality of his hesitancy, if it appears, the duration of it, and what it is directed toward.

Originality and inventiveness in play are also clear marks of a child's intelligence at work, for the ability to add new details, to develop new games or make-believe situations, to adapt materials to different uses are all signs of creativity. The ability at this age to describe what is going on in words will be very much bound to the concrete and practical. Not until about age seven does any extensive verbal reasoning appear, or the ability to deal abstractly with logical issues like cause and effect. Even then, "verbal reasoning rises up from some manipulative situation in a crest of effort, and falls back to it again."[20] The ability to reason appears quite strongly then, but its simpler forms can be seen earlier, in brief, spontaneous comments, and these should be noticed and supported.

Personality and intelligence can and should be carefully observed, then, as they take on more and more stable forms over time, while the usual school "subjects" are of second importance

> The child is more important than the subject of instruction. The broad, all-round development of the child himself, his interests and efforts, are far more significant than the precise details of the level of achievement he has reached in this or that so-called subject.[21]

Yet a child's attainment in academic skills should nonetheless be noted, although by means of a relative scale, rather than by hard-and-fast levels, and only when he is working in an ordinary way, not under some special testing situation. Again, the records should be looked at as a whole, so that specific abilities in school subjects are seen in the entire context of the child's age and stage of development, not in isolation, since difficulties in intellectual attainments are so often linked to other factors in the child's life.

Only by looking at a child's whole record, then, both early in his school life and later on, can his special interests, his gifts of creativity and imagination, and areas of faulty development or disturbances be noted and dealt with appropriately. On the basis of this sort of knowledge, the teacher can get a dispassionate view of the child's needs and provide for them. She may wish to talk privately with an anxious or unhappy child and let him feel her interest. She may interfere with a child who has bullied a submissive younger one too long for the benefit of either. She may let a long stretch of time go by so that a child may play out whatever he is imagining. She may set down rules for the safety and cooperative harmony of all. She may decide to bring in fresh materials when questions are asked or interests shown. In extreme cases, she may wish to get the advice of a child-guidance professional, or confer with parents and suggest improved ways of dealing with a child at home.

> These are mere suggestions as to the sort of help which a fuller appreciation of the young child's difficulties by individual study makes possible. In the last resort, every teacher has to work out for herself her own technique of dealing with the individual children in her care, as well as with the group as a whole. And the wider and the deeper her general knowledge of the development of the young child's mind becomes, the more readily will she learn to adapt to the particular needs which face her in her daily work.[22]

Shown on pages 142–147 are three sample forms that Susan Isaacs and her group developed for use with children who have just entered the infant school (age five or under), children nearing the end of the infant-school time (age about seven), and those moving into the junior school (age seven or above). Bearing all the background suggestions and explanations in mind, the teacher can provide herself with a good deal of specific information, in a simple, single-page format. And although her comments will inevitably be interpretive rather than strictly objective, an experienced teacher's observations of her children, in Susan Isaacs's view, will be made without false judgments or moralizing about what the children "ought" or "ought not" to be doing, but with the more reasonable attitude that sound plans for children can be based only on looking systematically at them.

The Cambridge Evacuation Survey (1942)

In 1939 the war came, and Susan Isaacs's Department of Child Development, like many others, had to be evacuated. With her friend, Sybil Clement Brown, of the London School of Economics, she moved to Cambridge for the duration. There she was able to continue with some of her patients who also went out to Cambridge, to finish the work already started with some students in her program, and to continue as at least the nominal head of it throughout the war.

This move to Cambridge provided Isaacs with her next opportunity to be of service to children and to the adults who were responsible for them. In September of 1939, some 750,000 school children, 542,000 mothers with young children, 12,000 expectant mothers, and 77,000 other people were evacuated from urban areas threatened by heavy bombing.[23]

This great migration from town to country disrupted family life and relationships on a large scale, and was a cause of both interest and concern to professionals in the child-care field. Psychologists and social workers had a chance to observe what the loss of family life meant to both parents and children; teachers who went with their schools came to know their children far better, since they saw them on a twenty-four-hour basis for the first time; clinical workers had to deal with children who found evacuation especially difficult. Some investigators did surveys of the response of both children and adults to these strained and unusual conditions. For no sooner had the great migration been accomplished, often with much success but sometimes with difficulties, than its reversal began. Mothers and children began to trickle back even to endangered areas. Reports came in of distress and discomfort. "The town was ill at ease in the country. The country was shocked at the manners and morals of the town."[24] At the same time, there were reports that the country air and food were producing better health among city children, and that new relationships were being happily established among people even of quite different origins. Clearly, the evacuation had produced a "powerful social ferment."[25] Therefore professionals were eager to know more, and more exactly, just what the effects of this upheaval were.

In October of 1939, Susan Isaacs and other psychologists and social workers who had formed a child discussion group in Cambridge considered a plan to do a limited but focused study of the evacuation and its effects in their area, with a specific group of children.

> We felt that a detailed study of what was happening in one area might bring out causal sequences which would become blurred and lost in a larger and more comprehensive study.[26]

In Cambridge, then, an intensive survey of the successes and the failures of billeting into private homes the 3,000 children evacuated from two London surburbs (Tottenham and Islington) was planned and carried out between the fall of 1939 and spring of 1940; the study was published in book form in 1941; and in 1942, Susan Isaacs contributed a chapter to an American wartime study of the family, *The Family in a World at War*:[27] "Children of Great Britain in Wartime," providing a brief summary and discussion of the methods of the Cambridge study, the effects of the evacuation on the children, and the conclusions that could be drawn. Her book gave even more detail, and it also contained a practical and quite comprehensive set of recommendations for authorities planning similar migrations in the future.

The Cambridge Evacuation Study had two broad purposes. First, there was an immediate concern for the welfare of the children who had been evacuated and the families in whose homes they were placed. An attempt was made to understand just what had happened and was still happening

SCHOOL. Admission number B/G   Inf. Ad

Date of admission Class
Age on admission Attendance

Home Circumstances.

Occupation of parents   Pupil's position in family

Material condition of home | E | D | C | B | A |

Notes on special circumstances

Physical Condition.

Teacher's remarks

School Medical Officer's report and recommendations   Physique | E | D | C | B | A |

Intelligence.   Teacher's estimate | E | D | C | B | A |

Test	Date	Mental age	I Q	Average I Q. of class	Remarks

Personality.

Attitude towards

(i) Teacher

(ii) Other children

(iii) Surroundings

Personality—*(continued)*

Outstanding good qualities

Bad habits

Special difficulties in personality

Bodily control

Personal habits

Speech

Any Additional Comments.

Signature

94   THE EDUCATIONAL GUIDANCE OF THE SCHOOL CHILD

                                                                    Inf.
                                    SCHOOL.   Admission number B
                                                                 G
Age on 1st September, 19   Class
Average age of class   Attendance

Home Circumstances.
Occupation of parents   Pupil's position in family

Material condition of home | E | D | C | B | A |

Notes on special circumstances

Physical Condition.
Teacher's remarks

School Medical Officer's report and recommendations   Physique | E | D | C | B | A |

Intelligence.   Teacher's estimate | E | D | C | B | A |

Test	Date	Mental age	I.Q.	Average I.Q. of class	Remarks

Observation | E | D | C | B | A |

Imagination | E | D | C | B | A |

Inventiveness | E | D | C | B | A |

Verbal reasoning | E | D | C | B | A |

Personality.

Self-confidence | E | D | C | B | A |

Stability | E | D | C | B | A |

Sociability | E | D | C | B | A |

Reliability | E | D | C | B | A |

Outstanding good qualities

Special difficulties

Attainments.   Remarks

Reading | E | D | C | B | A |

Writing | E | D | C | B | A |

Number | E | D | C | B | A |

English | E | D | C | B | A |

Handwork | E | D | C | B | A |

Music | E | D | C | B | A |

Bodily skills | E | D | C | B | A |

Personal habits

Speech

Any Additional Comments.

Signature

SCHOOL.   Admission number ^B_G [   ]   J. & S.

Age on 1st September, 19
Average age of class

Class
Attendance

Home Circumstances.
Occupation of parents
Material condition of home | E | D | C | B | A |

Pupil's position in family

Notes on special circumstances

Physical Condition.
(1) Teacher's remarks

(2) School Medical Officer's report and recommendations   Physique | E | D | C | B | A |

Intelligence.   Teacher's estimate. | E | D | C | B | A |

Test	Date	Mental age	I. Q.	Average I. Q. of class	Remarks

Strong and weak points in special abilities

Temperament.   Vitality | E | D | C | B | A | Stability | E | D | C | B | A |

Disposition and characteristic moods

Outstanding features, including any special difficulties, of personality

Interests.

Social | E | D | C | B | A |

Practical and active | E | D | C | B | A |

Intellectual and artistic | E | D | C | B | A |

Attainments.   Number in class

Subject	Rating	Position in class	Remarks

Personal habits

Speech

GENERAL EDUCATIONAL OBJECTIVES.

Effective habits and methods of work | E | D | C | B | A |

Social adjustment | E | D | C | B | A |

Healthy attitude to self | E | D | C | B | A |

Development of moral qualities | E | D | C | B | A |

Any Additional Comments.

Signature

to these people, as they were seen in their home settings, in the schools, and in local child-guidance clinics. The hope was to discover what factors had contributed to success or failure in the billeting, and what sorts of help or support seemed most effective, so that future efforts could be better planned.

The second purpose of the study was more long-range: to understand more of the nature of family relationships and the family tie itself, which had been thrown into such sharp relief by this large-scale disruption. This understanding could well prove helpful during the war, but also later on: in peacetime Britain, some 40,000 children were boarded out into homes other than their own, and institutions provided for still more. Although wartime evacuation conditions were not similar to those of peacetime, still it seemed important to take advantage of this unusual and widespread social upheaval to increase available professional knowledge of families and child-rearing practices.

The methods by which this study was carried out had to be a compromise between the need to get the information published soon enough to be helpful, and the desire to gather truly valid and reliable data. Resources of time, money, and personnel were limited, and people kept moving about to a great extent, so exactness was difficult. As Susan Isaacs put it:

> Human relations cannot be arranged to suit the convenience of the person who is interested in finding out what they are like. Human beings will not stand still for the students' time exposure; they are always on the move, so that we must often be content with snapshots.[28]

It was, therefore, not the numerical or statistical significance of the study that was important, but rather the qualitative, personal assessments of the situation, as it was encountered and interpreted by trained observers.

The conclusions of the study were arrived at on the basis of different sets of inquiries, each carried out by a research committee that was set up for the purpose, under Susan Isaacs's leadership.

A general account of the local organization of Cambridge as a reception area for the children coming out of London was developed. This account included facts about the plans laid, the accommodations provided, the process of billeting itself, and so on. Also included were comments about how the scheme was working out in more personal terms, such as what difficulties were encountered and by whom, as town and country met and adjusted to one another. Among the children, for instance, the whole issue of cleanliness loomed largest; city children seemed dirty by country standards, table manners and personal habits seemed slovenly, and bed-wetting was a frequent occurrence. Yet, in the main, the survey showed that the people of Cambridge had responded enthusiastically and generously to the newcomers, and had made strong efforts to overcome difficulties and differences. There was much more success overall than failure, despite the serious lack of useful information about either the child who was coming or the family who was taking him or her in.

An assessment was made of the successes and failures of nearly seven hundred children, and of the general causes of their success or failure. Information was obtained from cards that were filled out by "friendly visitors" who made a number of visits to the foster homes; from similar cards filled out by the teachers who had come out to Cambridge with their schools; and from two essays written by the children themselves, "Things I like in Cambridge," and "Things I miss in Cambridge."

Using the children's essays, a detailed study of their comments about life in their new surroundings and their memories was done. The children ranged quite widely in age, so that younger children's responses were more fragmentary and impressionistic than older ones', but they remain vivid records. A little boy, aged 8 years, wrote:

What I like in Cambrdge

I like my dog I like my cat I like Granny dog to it is dead my Granny did not cry I made the grave the other dog run and run he nock the grave down.

What I miss in Cambridge

I miss my tortoise in LanDon he is Robert Taylor he bit me once he bit me. And I tod [told] him he wac [was] a note [naughty] boy and I fod [fed] him a lost [lots] of tam [times].

An older child of 14 wrote:

Things I like best in Cambridge

One of the most pleasant things that I find here is the kindness with which I was received. To receive town children who they have never seen was most difficult, yet within a week we were happy as if we were at home. When the first strangeness had worn off we seemed to be part and parcel of Cambridge. The historic buildings was another source of enjoyment to me, in my early days.

And a girl of 15 wrote:

Things I miss in Cambridge

One of the things I miss in Cambridge is when coming home from school in the evening if I'm not going to any school activities [e.g., Newnham College, etc.]. I know that the evening will be spent as usual knitting and sometimes reading. When I'm home in Tottenham I often go out to tea to a friend or relation of mine and spend an evening with them. Over the weekends when I feel as if I'd like to stay in by the fireside the lady I'm billeted with generally expects us to go for a walk, and as it is almost wintry it is not very nice. I miss my relations, parents and friends who are in Tottenham. And I often wish our foster mother wasn't so particular although she does that for our good, as she says.

In general, this portion of the study strove to present the children's own point of view when

> the fundamental relationships of life have suddenly been cut across—for an indefinite period, as the children realize; and moreover, under disturbing conditions.... In the experience of evacuation, ... many things help to support and confirm the child's dread that his parents may be lost forever, and that, before he can see them again or return to his home, all may have been ruined.[29]

Eighty-six children were then studied in more detail, forty who had made a significantly successful adjustment, and forty-six who had experienced severe difficulty in one form or another. In these latter, less successful situations, an attempt was made to assess the cause of the trouble, whether it was the child's temperament, the style of the care he or she received in the foster home, or some combination of the two. For instance, in some cases, the Cambridge people had rigid standards and found the city children's manners and speech intolerable. Or sometimes there was overcrowding and a lack of provision for privacy or for suitable activities.

Each child was interviewed by an educational psychologist personally. Mental and performance tests were given individually, to assess both intelligence and temperament. The children were encouraged to talk freely about their feelings about the evacuation, anxieties about the family at home, and positive experiences in Cambridge and the surrounding countryside, as well as their special interests and possible future career plans. A report was written up, and submitted to the teachers and heads of schools for their additional comments, which, as it turned out, were usually in broad agreement with the assessment of the psychologist. Meanwhile, a psychiatrist made a careful scrutiny and analysis of the school and foster-home records, in order to gain some idea of the temperament of each child, as well as any clear difficulties of personality. On the basis of this assessment, a few children were sent for special treatment to the Child Guidance Center or were seen in therapy by some psychiatrist.

In the study, a serious attempt was made to describe the different personality types of the children involved in evacuation, by means of objective tests, home and individual visits, records from the schools, and, where needed, clinical examination. A descriptive scheme[30] was then worked out delineating six types of children who had the most difficulty. The forty successfully adjusted children showed a normal balance of qualities and tendencies, which the others did not. The ways in which lack of balance appear varied a good deal, but certain definite types of behavior did appear and had led to unsuccessful adjustment in new situations.

Children who were anxious and at times depressed, sometimes to an excessive or unrealistic degree, fell into one category. They might show nervousness, diffidence, shyness, fear of failure, frequent crying, or constantly need reassurance. Also they might be unduly fearful of dirt or untidiness, set rigid standards for their own and others' behavior, or need an unvarying routine.

Another category included children who seemed closed off from the world, withdrawn, solitary, and often absorbed in their own daydreams, with little interest in or need for companionship. A third group included children who were excitable, jealous, sometimes quarrelsome, who liked to be the center of attention and threw temper tantrums at the slightest frustration or postponement of desire. They tended to be "hysterical, uncontrolled and suggestible,"[31] and difficult to manage in any reasonable way.

A fourth personality type was the aggressive, hyperactive child. Always ready to take on an adventure regardless of its danger, these children were anxious to gain power and attention at all costs. They seemed indifferent to others' needs or to relationships, but strove to win and readily took the lead in daring others, being openly aggressive, or engaging in wild forms of activity just for excitement.

The fifth type of child swung rapidly from elation to depression, from heights of excited joy to depths of gloom, often without much basis in reality. Some changes in mood are, of course, to be expected in all children, but these showed an exaggerated alternation, and seemed to have little insight into or control of their feelings.

Finally, there was a category judged "delinquent." This child was a special case, for although all children may steal or lie occasionally, in this kind of child there was a chronic wish to do so, and at the same time an affectionless, antisocial character. He seemed unable to make contact with other persons, to grasp the usual forms of social interaction, or to perform at the expected norms for his age or stage of development. He got into trouble with the authorities repeatedly and seemingly without caring about consequences either to himself, or to others who may have been his victims. This type of child, though few in number, was the most difficult to deal with, since the roots of his problem seemed to go very deep into his earliest experiences with others as an infant.

The other separate parts of the Cambridge Evacuation Study consisted of a description of the work of the Child Guidance Clinic in Cambridge throughout the emergency operation; an extensive survey of recreational facilities available to the transplanted children; a study of the homes and families of those children who did manage to go home to London and an assessment of the reasons for their return; and an account of the views and impressions of the London teachers who had come to Cambridge with their schools and who were therefore evacuees themselves.

On the basis of all this varied and detailed information, certain conclusions were drawn and recommendations made. The most general conclusion about the whole evacuation plan was

> that the first great scheme for evacuation might have been far less of a failure, far more of a success, if it had been planned with more under-

standing of human nature, of the way in which ordinary parents and children feel and are likely to behave.[32]

The authorities seemed more concerned with details of train schedules and housing than with the people involved; and every difficulty of adjustment turned out to be a problem of human relationships, not of arrangements. For instance, had better information been available about the children being evacuated and the homes they were going to, it would have been possible to put reticent, withdrawn, or somewhat anxious children into homes that were known to be quiet and relaxed. More aggressive, active children could have been placed in busy homes, with many activities and other children to engage their energies. Siblings could have been placed together more often, when their relationships were good. Foster mothers of over sixty years could have been avoided, or given only the most easygoing, friendly children to care for. Similarity in socioeconomic status could have been taken into account, so a child would not find himself in a home of very different material standards from his own. In these and other ways, difficulties could have been predicted and avoided, and happy relationships more often promoted.

One specific conclusion of the study was that the presence and assistance of trained human service professionals were very helpful in averting problems, especially if they were called on earlier rather than later. Teachers felt that their experience with children was at times ignored, and were happy to give help or information when asked. Social workers, similarly, were able to diagnose problems, provide insight and support, and thus enable a more successful adjustment. Had these people been involved from the beginning, their predictions and judgments might have made the whole enterprise go better than it did.

Another specific conclusion had to do with the necessity of providing plenty of activities for the children who were sent out from the city. They were used to the busy streets and shops of London, and often were bored or restless during long, quiet, winter evenings in the country, and tended to get into trouble as a result. Games and sports, swimming parties, boy and girl scout groups, cinema shows, handicraft classes—all were suggested to keep the children busy and happy, as well as to help them make new friends and develop new skills. For the real world is valuable to the child as a "way out" for him from inner anxieties and fears to the more stable world of facts and people and activity.

The most far-reaching conclusion of the study concerned the strength of the family tie and the great loss felt by evacuated children of all the intimate details of family life at home, even when that home was not ideal. The research committee had set out to study family relationships in general, and the findings went far to express their crucial importance, especially when parents and children are separated under conditions of stress. For many children, especially if they were not adjusting to country life as happily as might be, drifted back into the city in spite of warnings and real danger.

> Since the bombing of London's East End, we have seen how this need to keep the family together and to cling to familiar home surroundings may override even the worst dangers. Among the simple and poor, where there is no wealth, no pride of status or of possessions, love for the members of one's own family and joy in their bodily presence alone make life worth living. So deeply rooted is this need that it has defied even the law of self-preservation, as well as urgent public appeals and the wishes of authority.[33]

Strawberries and fresh milk in the country may be better for the child than fish and chips at home; but fish and chips are good because mother gave them and they are part of home life. His clothes may be poor and ragged, but they remind him of home when he is in a strange house. His speech may include city slang, but he learned it while helping his dad at the warehouse. These things point to

> the urgent need for skilled understanding of the individual child and of the child's point of view in general.[34]

The experience of evacuation in Great Britain, then, brought out very clearly the "depth and strength of family feeling in ordinary people"[35] on the one hand, and the equally clear need for some understanding of such feelings on the part of anyone planning a similar "social experiment," in war or in peace, that would separate children and parents.

Susan Isaacs closed her study with strong words for the authorities:

> This sharp lesson in the ineffectiveness and waste of a partial approach to a great human issue, one which from its very nature touches every side of human life, applies by no means only to the temporary crisis of dispersing urban populations during a war. It has an equally direct and urgent bearing upon the whole field of education and of social reconstruction during and after the war. We feel justified . . . in stressing our conclusion that a true understanding of the feelings and aims of ordinary human beings is an essential condition of success, whether we are concerned with the replanning and rebuilding of our great cities, the renewal of life in the countryside, the humanizing of our town schools, the training and teaching of youth, the education of adult citizens, the revision of economic structure.
>
> Every one of these purposes not only requires a co-operative effort from the departments and sectional authorities now so often working isolatedly; it demands also the full knowledge and understanding of human nature as a whole.[36]

6
Susan Isaacs and Others

Additional perspective on Susan Isaacs's work is gained by considering what her reviewers said about it, and by looking in more detail at some of her contemporaries—both those whose ideas had some affinity with hers, and those whom she specifically criticized.

Reviews of Susan Isaacs's Books

Susan Isaacs's books were reviewed by some of the leading figures in psychology and education of the day: C. W. Valentine, J. C. Flügel, Ernest Jones, Barbara Low, and others. Each had his or her own point of view: those with psychoanalytic experience were impressed by her account of children's social and personal development, in general, while those who were not of that mind found her descriptions harder to accept. All praised her lucid writing style, as well as the detailed presentation of the records about the Malting House children upon which her two major books were based. And other specific comments were made, as well, as reviewers' own interests dictated.

In 1931, the year following the publication of *Intellectual Growth in Young Children*, three quite different reviews appeared in three quite different journals. J. C. Flügel, who had been Susan Isaacs's first analyst, reviewed the book in *The International Journal of Psycho-Analysis;* C. W. Valentine wrote his review for the more experimental *British Journal of Educational Psychology;* and Raymond Willoughby of Clark University, Worcester, Massachusetts, reviewed it for *The Pedagogical Seminary and Journal of Genetic Psychology*.

Flügel's review was long, thoughtful, and favorable.[1] He felt that Susan Isaacs had collected much original material about children in her records of day-by-day events at the Malting House School: "No serious investigator of young children can afford to neglect it." From his particular perspective, he considered that the way in which the adults at the school worked with the children really paralleled the analytic process itself. That is, the role of the adult was inescapably important to children, who were always acting and reacting in terms of the adults present, and a mild but firm style of control by the adults was clearly therapeutic. So also was the degree of verbal freedom that the children were allowed, which gave them the opportunity to express their inner feelings, but not to do any physical damage.

Flügel went on to say that the children's natural "wish to find out," the dominant theme of this account of intellectual growth, was admirably fostered by the Malting House School but inexplicably neglected by most educators. For him, as for Susan Isaacs, reaching out to understand objective reality is an important step away from a child's egocentric, fantasy-laden stages of comprehension of his world. And he pushed further her explanation of children's greater interest in animal than in plant life: for him, there was at least the possibility that it stemmed from their sense that the adult world held prejudices and inhibitions about precisely the bodily processes that animals exemplified, notably excretion and reproduction, and that under this school's condition of free inquiry, their curiosity could be satisfied. Turning to Isaacs's criticism of Piaget, Flügel found himself convinced that "Mrs. Isaacs seems to have made out a good case against a too literal and uncritical acceptance of Piaget's interpretations." While bearing in mind the differences of situation, method, and level of IQ, he still saw Piaget's stages of development more as "general developmental tendencies" or "quantitative predominances," than as strict, chronological, self-contained stages of cognition.

As a psychoanalyst, Flügel was pleased with Susan Isaacs's discussion of thought and fantasy, and of the way in which fantasy helps the child try out responses that may then be confirmed in cognitive understanding. "There is thus," as he put it, "a constant fluctuation between the reality principle and the pleasure principle."

Flügel's final comments dealt with Nathan Isaacs's essay, "Children's 'Why?' Questions" and, characteristically, he criticized it from the psychoanalytic point of view. Sometimes, he felt, children use endless questions simply to exasperate the powerful adults around them, rather than out of an "epistemic" interest. More importantly, he wondered, "how far the actual questions asked by children are unconscious substitutes for repressed or tabooed subjects of interest—a process of unsuccessful attempted sublimation." For Flügel, therefore, Nathan Isaacs had ignored the possible role of the unconscious in influencing these children who had such verbal freedom, a role that Susan Isaacs had grasped with such clarity.

C. W. Valentine, a prominent experimentalist and professor of education at Birmingham University, reviewed Susan Isaacs's book favorably in 1931,[2] but in 1942[3] he expressed his opposition to her psychoanalytic views of social development. This later discussion of *Intellectual Growth* began, "Altogether, Mrs. Isaacs's work is a great stimulus to the study of the psychology of early childhood, . . . a most notable contribution." He picked up themes that Flügel had noted: one can never rule out the importance of the role of adults in the minds of children, as part of their environment—the question was not how to erase their influence but rather how to use it and how to understand children's reactions to it. Valentine agreed, too, that conditions of absolute freedom are neither possible nor wise, but that the very considerable "freedom of action and utterance" at the school provided a climate in which children could satisfy their curiosity about themselves and the everyday things around them. In such a setting, "children, when actively interested, can rise to a level of mental activity which they cannot reach under some formal tests when they are not so completely interested."

Valentine also agreed with Susan Isaacs that children's ability to reason and apprehend relations like causality begins much earlier than Piaget had stated; yet he disagreed with her belief that Piaget had made too much of the simple, innate force of maturation. While social factors do influence development of thought from an early age, in his view, the strength of maturation itself should not be underestimated. Finally, Valentine commented that Nathan Isaacs's essay about children's questions, while valuable, could even be broadened somewhat: children ask "epistemic" questions not only when they need information, but also when they ask about purpose or motivation. Still, although the section of school records seemed overly long to him, Susan Isaacs's book together with her husband's essay form "one of the most important contributions made to the psychology of childhood."

Valentine referred directly to the Malting House School records and interpretations of them, and attempted to refute the primarily psychoanalytic views put forward in *Social Development*. His own book was a thorough study of all aspects of mental development, based on his "almost daily observation of his own five children" over a long period of time, the kind of systematic observation that was customary by then. His genetic or developmental studies, he felt, provided "the best clue to innate propensities," and he detailed with precision the growth of reflexes, imitative behavior, early fears (which he considered largly innate), laughter, language acquisition, responses to parents, and the like. His extensive observational data, in his view, showed the inadequacy of theories like those of the behaviorists, the generalists, and the Freudians, especially the latter. Their emphasis on the symbolic character of speech and action went too far. He recounted a scene at the Malting House School:

> 30.4.25 In the afternoon Dan and Frank played in the sandpit. They took off their shoes and stockings and dug their feet in, so that these could not be seen. Dan then called out to Mrs. I., "Tell Priscilla to ask us to come and love her." Mrs. I. did so. His reply was, with much laughter, "We can't, because our legs are cut off."[4]

For Susan Isaacs, the boys were symbolically referring to their penises, and their apparent castration. But Valentine suggested:

Of course the idea of legless or footless little boys (as they would appear) hobbling towards Priscilla would appear funny to the children. Why should legs be regarded as *symbols* in such an otherwise comprehensible joke? . . . [as Burt asks] "Would any child at this age, however subtle, assume that either Priscilla or for that matter Dr. Isaacs realized the covert symbolism."[5]

Like many opponents of psychoanalysis, he preferred to take a common-sense view of the scene, rather than consider its symbolic, unconscious possibilities.[6]

The Pedagogical Seminary and Journal of Genetic Psychology had been founded in 1891 by G. Stanley Hall to publish studies of child behavior, animal behavior, and comparative psychology. Its international board of editors included Cyril Burt, Charlotte Bühler, and Arnold Gesell. In 1931[7] it published Willoughby's review of *Intellectual Growth*, whose basic summary of the work took a more educational tack. It was, he said, "one of the first collections of careful observational evidence tending to show the desirable effect in practice of the 'child-centered' theory of education." He also thought that Susan Isaacs has "the better of the argument" with Piaget about children's early ability to reason, and was impressed by her explanation of the reciprocal relationship between thought and fantasy.

Then Willoughby went on to wonder why it had to be that such a school, so clearly a positive environment for young children, closed down. As an educator, he was concerned about attitudes toward children generally, and noted that adults often show little interest in the all-around development of even their own offspring, let alone any children unknown to them. This indifference, he felt, shows up in negative reactions to progressive schools, even when obviously successful, and seemed to him to be based on the lack of "mental contact" between adults and children. Adults whose own education has conditioned them to traditional patterns cannot grasp the effect on children of a freer setting, nor see the point of letting their interests and developmental needs set the pace and direction of a school.

1931 also saw a brief note[8] by Ernest Jones, Britain's most prominent psychoanalyst, about the book that Susan Isaacs wrote jointly with Victoria Bennett, *Health and Education in the Nursery*.[9] Susan Isaacs had written the second half of the book, and Jones was especially interested in her simple account of little children's emotional growth. It shows, he said, "the care, knowledge, and comprehensiveness which we should expect from Mrs. Isaacs," from *The Nursery Years* columns and from her more technical journal articles. This book introduced "with great skill" the basic principles of the psychoanalytic account of little children's development, but not in such technical language as would either confuse or repel the reader. It was, in fact, the perfect book that he would recommend to anyone interested in "the care and understanding of young children."

When *Social Development in Young Children* appeared in 1933, it attracted a good deal of attention, although it was not as widely acclaimed as *Intellectual*

Growth had been. Again, its frankly psychoanalytic view was not universally shared. Yet one reviewer, M. Creak,[10] found Susan Isaacs's account "refreshingly free from the dogmas which are intelligible only to the initiated few." She liked the multiplicity of records, since she felt "their vigour and veracity taking us right into the vicissitudes of the child's social and emotional development." She applauded the author's emphasis at the school on using a deliberate educational technique, rather than scolding or moralizing, especially with regard to the children's aggressive behavior. It seemed to her that this was often a wish for reassurance that the adults really were stronger and would protect the children from themselves, and was not therefore the occasion for reproof, much less punishment.

With Susan Isaacs, Creak felt that the Freudian theory of the primacy of the early family situation was accurate, and that it was replayed in later life over and over again, as children move out from it into other relationships with adults and peers. But for Creak, the most valuable part of the book was the section on the relationship between psychoanalysis and education. Certainly a teacher or parent is not a therapist and can never take that role; there is need for a child's earliest educators to set realistic limits to his behavior, yet "a point often missed by advocates of 'free' education" was that repression is an *unconscious* mechanism. One cannot set up an environment that is free of all repressions, therefore, and the Malting House School's supportive but firm model of adult-child interaction provided a safer and more educative setting.

The book was, for Creak, "a serious and important contribution to the study of the development of both normal and difficult children," she concluded. And she closed with a moving account of the rewards that came "in due time" at the school: "free social cooperation, rich aesthetic achievement, and bold intellectual inquiry." "How often," she wondered, "is good behaviour and social conformity purchased at exactly the price of these qualities?"

Much less sympathetic was the review of Mary Sturt[11] of the same year. For her, *Social Development* primarily dealt with

> [the children's] social adaptation, their loves and hates, and their development, or rather lack of development, in what is generally called "decency." We feel that Mrs. Isaacs is chiefly interested in this latter point, and to this the greater part of the book is devoted.

Sturt was depressed that the school records reported gave so negative a picture of the children, "unrelieved by more than an occasional ray of friendliness." However, she very much admired the last section, on education, with its emphasis on the value to the child of developing skills, and on his wish to be good, to make good, and to be powerful.

Yet the central, theoretical section of the book "will not be so readily accepted as the other two," in her view. The problem with Susan Isaacs's psychoanalytic interpretations of the records, in Miss Sturt's eyes, was that they, like "so many of the psycho-analytic theories, fit the neurotic but seem very little applicable to the normal." She noted the centrality of Melanie Klein's recent studies in the book, but reminded her readers that Klein had always stressed that the children she dealt with were very abnormal. Those at the Malting House School did not have such extreme difficulties, and "the attempt to use theories based on one set of children for the interpretation of actions by the second seems rather pointless."

Although analysts would argue that "normal" and "abnormal" actually define two ends of a continuum, and that psychoanalytic theory is applicable to children of all degrees of normality, Miss Sturt felt that it was unnecessary to go into the "dark world of perversions" to explain what could be seen as normal and quite harmless "indelicacies," no more. Children's early interest in where babies come from is not sexual at all, but simple curiosity. And a child's attempts to separate or possess his parents is expressive of his wish to have power over those stronger than himself. Why, she asked, should unconscious symbolism be assumed in children's interests? Why do engines automatically symbolize a child's fantasy about parents and intercourse, and why not steamships, planes, and the like, which children also enjoy? Susan Isaacs's account of the early formation of the superego and sense of guilt, stemming from the oral-sadistic state, "strains the belief." A baby does not know he is hurting his mother any more than a puppy chewing a slipper. "One can attribute too much reasoning power to an infant under ten months!" Not being a psychoanalyst, Sturt missed the point that the formation of the superego is not a matter of "reasoning power," but entirely unconscious.

In 1934, another review of *Social Development*, by "E.V.J.," appeared.[12] Its style and tone suggest that it may have been by Ernest Jones. "This is an extraordinarily good book," it began. The author summarized the basic structure of the book, the material presented, and the analysis of the data, praising the extensive records as well as the lucidity of style. And for him, too, the last section of the book, "the educational problem," was "the most valuable and original part of the book, [showing] penetrating understanding and a superbly balanced judgment." Susan Isaacs's emphasis on technique, not morality, also caught his attention, for as an analyst he too believed that a child has a profound, unconscious drive toward morality from the earliest days, which cannot be implanted from outside by restrictions or preaching. Rather, a child needs to be shown how he can gain his ends appropriately, by developing his skills in the real world around him. He closed his brief review by saying, "I do not know of anything more precious in all pedagogical literature than this concluding section of a remarkable book. [We owe her] a deep debt of gratitude."

In 1934 also, however, Dorothea McCarthy returned to the attack.[13] To her, *Social Development of Young Children* was too narrowly the product of the Freudian and Kleinian "school":

Unless the reader who has been attracted by the title of this volume is an ardent disciple of Freud, he is sure to be disappointed by the author's narrow conception of the young child's social development which is made to hinge entirely around problems of infantile sexuality.

Further, McCarthy noted with some contempt, the records are "mere jottings," in no sense systematic or scientific. They had been taken down "incidentally, in diary fashion, admittedly without preliminary selection of the events to be observed." And in making such unsystematic records of this kind, Susan Isaacs had unfortunately ignored the new work going on in experimental psychology. The reviewer thus rejected both the basic theory of infantile sexuality on which the analysis of the data rests, and the method of systematic, long-term observation of children in a natural setting, preferring instead the more exact, quantifiable data that could be collected only in a more carefully controlled, experimental situation.

One other review of Susan Isaacs's work should be noted, for it raised some points not dealt with by others. Barbara Low reviewed *The Children We Teach* in 1933.[14] She was definitely involved in psychoanalysis and had already written *The Unconscious in Action: its Influence upon Education*, which contained an introduction by Percy Nunn. So she was especially interested in Susan Isaacs's account of the mind of the child from age seven to eleven, with its "characteristic directness of thought, lucidity of expression, balanced outlook, and a very human and sympathetic approach to her subject." Low, of course, grasped that Susan Isaacs's psychoanalytic understanding of children was the context and the underpinning of the whole book, although not expressed in technical terms, and that she also brought to bear her practical knowledge of children as a teacher. Low applauded the emphasis in the book on a gradualist approach to moving children from one grade to the next, rather than making too abrupt a change, assuming that a child is wholly ready to move on. She was enthusiastic about the discussion of the important influences of a child's inner life on his IQ, and of the need for "elasticity of method," since children's knowledge is so much affected by temperament, emotions, wishes, and fantasies.

However, Low took Susan Isaacs to task on two accounts: first, her insistence on the prior use of mental tests to classify children by innate intelligence seemed inconsistent with her desire for "elastic," holistic, spontaneous methods. Second, she queried the statement that teaching methods of the time were all right for the "general mass" of children, when she had also pleaded for recognition of individual differences. Clearly, standard class teaching of groups of children shut out the possibility of separate treatment to an important extent. Low was here pointing to an important difficulty, namely, how much should one rely on tests that claim to measure inborn intelligence and classify children on that basis? And she was also noting an equally serious pedagogical problem: how, in an ordinary public school, can one make use of the individual methods developed under such very different circumstances in the Malting House School?

Contemporaries

John Dewey

Prominent among the thinkers who influenced Susan Isaacs was John Dewey. As Isaacs herself said, he was "my active inspiration." Certainly by the time she began to lecture in psychology at the Darlington Training College (1913), Dewey's ideas had become well-known, as had the school that he and his wife founded in Chicago. A leading exponent of his ideas, M. E. Findlay, had been on the staff of the Froebel Educational Institute from 1898 to 1912, having spent three years in the United States chiefly working with the Deweys in Chicago, and also with the equally progressive Francis Wayland Parker School there.[15]

Dewey published his *Psychology* in 1887, three years earlier than William James's *Principles of Psychology*. In 1894, Dewey moved to the University of Chicago as the chairman of the Department of Philosophy, Psychology, and Pedagogy, and in 1896 he opened his famous Laboratory School. In 1897 he published his equally famous statement of the principles that underlay its operation, *My Pedagogic Creed*. Among his many other publications were *School and Society* in 1899, *The Child and the Curriculum* in 1902, *How We Think* and *The Influence of Darwin on Philosophy and Other Essays* in 1910, followed by *Schools of Tomorrow* in 1915 and his magnum opus, *Democracy and Education* in 1916. for the purposes of this study, however, it is Dewey's *Psychology* and *How We Think* that are important, for they seem to have had the most bearing on Susan Isaacs's work; she mentions both and no wonder, for they contain the very substance of her own beliefs about children's thinking and her method of promoting its development at the Malting House School.

Psychology was published when Dewey was a professor of philosophy at the University of Michigan, and it clearly laid the groundwork for all his subsequent psychological and educational writings. He wanted a psychology or theory of mind that was free from metaphysics, and that would also be useful for teachers in practice. Psychology, as he defines it, is "the science of the facts or phenomena of self,"[16] and self he defines as that which *"lies under* and holds together all feelings, purposes, and ideas."[17] In considering the self and its activities, which comprise the study of psychology, he finds that,

> all the other sciences deal only with the facts or events which are known; but the fact of *knowledge* thus involved in all of them no one of them has

said anything about. . . . Knowledge implies reference to the self or mind. . . . Knowledge . . . is an activity which the self experiences.[18]

Knowledge is not a bundle of received sensations, then, but an activity; it is concerned with relationships among the objects and events of the observable world, by means of which they are unified and connected into what we then experience as "an ordered, harmonious world, not a chaos,"[19] The processes by which the mind performs this relational function are two: apperception and retention. *Apperception* is "the reaction of the mind by means of its organized structure upon the sensuous material presented to it,"[20] while *retention* is "the reaction of the apperceived content upon the organized structure of the mind."[21] That is to say, by apperception, the mind organizes the world of knowledge by bringing the self to bear upon it, and by retention it organizes the self, in turn, by bringing the things known to bear upon it. Each process involves the other, and together they produce knowledge, which is active, assimilative, and experimental in nature.

Apperception operates according to the laws of association and disassociation. In *association,* "the activity of mind never leaves sensuous elements isolated, but connects them into larger wholes."[22] There is a tendency to shun isolated elements but rather to form relationships among them whenever possible, usually according to their contiguity in space or time, or their similarity to previous experiences, or both. Yet at the same time, "by associating sensuous elements, the mind never gives all the elements equal value, but emphasizes some, and neglects others."[23] This is *disassociation,* the process that distinguishes among elements and places more value on some and less on others, according to the "interest"[24] that the self takes in them.

> The interests of the self are the factor which is influential in breaking up the hard rigidity of a psychical life governed wholly by the principles of association, and introducing flexibility and perspective into it.[25]

Therefore one needs to look at what factors "render one datum more *interesting* than another."[26] The mind is attracted to one datum over another because of its natural or spontaneous interest, such as its large size or unusual loudness, but this soon gives way to an "acquired value . . . [which] necessarily leads the mind beyond what is actually present to other elements in our experience which gives what is present its attractive power."[27] An object or event is interesting because it is like earlier ones and fits into knowledge the mind already has obtained, or because it is at variance with it. When we encounter a novel experience, first we seek for what is nonetheless familiar in it and therefore connected to earlier experiences; yet at the same time, our minds grow and change as a result of new experiences and this leads us to differentiate and refine our knowledge.

Only the extent in which the old and permanent element is found in the new and varying can the mind deal with the latter. . . . On the other hand, without the new element there would be no change, no expansion, no growth.[28]

Familiarity thus gives meaning to novelty and makes an object or event interesting, while novelty in turn prevents stagnation. This dual process by means of which the mind identifies what is similar in experience and differentiates out what is new is a key mental activity and the mark of intelligence at work:

The activity of intelligence consists in identifying the apparently unlike, and in discriminating the apparently like; and it is through the relation of identity that the present experience is comprehended, and through the element of difference that past experience grows into richer forms.[29]

The connecting link between what the mind does and the objective world outside is *attention*, conscious awareness of or reference to the world. Yet it is more than simply conscious, but directive, seeking after knowledge and meaning, attracted by some things and passing over others.

[Attention] is precisely the relationship which exists in every act of knowledge, between that which knows and that which is known. . . . It is the active connection between the individual and the universal, [the source of] the activities by which the mind develops or realizes itself.[30]

Thus the world of known objects or events is an experience produced by the mind, acting according to the interests of the self in interpreting sense data as they enter it. Knowledge consists of interpreting such sensations, discriminating, selecting, relating, and adjusting.

Knowledge is not the process by which ready-made objects imprint themselves upon the mind, but is the process by which the self renders sensations significant by reading itself into them. . . . Growth in knowledge consists in discovering more and more fundamental unities, and thus reducing to ideal facts, events, and relations before separate.[31]

By means of the processes of apperception and retention, the structure of our knowledge is built up, using past experiences to make meaning of present ones, as the mind attends to each. Knowledge, thus conceived, is a useful, purposeful possession, for it serves to help the mind gain from experiences what there is of significance and interest in them, and thus grow progressively more adaptive.

The mind grows, not by keeping unchanged within itself faint or unconscious copies of its original experiences, but by assimilating something from each experience, so that the next time it acts it has a more definite mode of activity to bring to bear; one which supplies a greater content to whatever is acted upon.[32]

Elsewhere, Dewey admits that his central concept of experience is a "slippery word,"[33] since it denotes both what is undergone and the very process of doing so. But he is expressing his view of the essential unity between what is known and the mind that knows it, so as to avoid a dualistic view that opposes mind to reality.[34] In thus emphasizing the mind as engaging in continuous transactions with the world, receiving and adjusting as fresh experiences occur, Dewey was very much in tune with the emphasis on an evolutionary and experimental approach to human nature and to society that was characteristic of the scientific and psychological thought of his age. Nathan Isaacs believed that Dewey had been able to move philosophy ahead as well. As Dewey put it, in his essay "The Influence of Darwin on Philosophy,"

> The conquest of the sciences by the experimental method of inquiry; the injection of evolutionary ideas into the study of life and society; the application of the historic method to religions and morals as well as to institutions; the creation of the sciences of "origins" and of the cultural development of mankind . . .[35]

—all these have necessarily revolutionized the philosophy of the preceding generations, namely, British empiricism and neo-Kantian idealism. Philosophy now must use genetic and experimental ideas in its formulations, and even try them out in actual practice, in the arenas of social and political action, and of education. The Greek ideal of "natural excellence realized in social life"[36] can be achieved only in a democracy, which, for him, is "the crucial expression of modern life":

> [Democracy] is not so much an addition to the scientific and industrial tendencies as it is the perception of their social or spiritual meaning. . . . the conception of a social harmony of interests in which the achievement of each individual of his own freedom should contribute to a like perfecting of the powers of all, through a fraternally organized society, is the permanent contribution of the industrial movement to morals.[37]

With scientific methods of inquiry and the technology that results, our modern world now provides us with the means to develop a "fraternally organized society."

All this could hardly fail to have an impact on education, for if, as he put it, "intelligence is properly an organ of adjustment in difficult situations,"[38] a figuring-out, problem-solving tool, then its development is of the greatest importance if any hopes for democracy are to survive. Philosophy would also benefit from this pragmatic view of the mind:

(it) humbles its pretensions to the work of projecting hypotheses for the education and conduct of mind, individual and social, . . . [it] is thereby subjected to test by the way in which the ideas it propounds work out in practice. In having modesty forced upon it, philosophy also acquires responsibility.[39]

Just as Plato's philosopher-king, having climbed out of the shadowy cave toward the light, must then go down again and deal with the affairs of men and society, so must today's philosopher use the light he sees to do the same.

In *Psychology*, Dewey made philosophy of the mind into an experience-based study of man's transactions with the world, and his adjustments to it. In *How We Think*, he moves beyond cognitive psychology in general to school practices in particular, and to teachers' responsibility for training children in habits of what today we call critical thinking or scientific inquiry. In his preface he states the problems he sees in contemporary education, and the direction in which he feels it must move for solutions. Searching for a "steadying and centralizing factor"[40] that will focus the attention and direct the efforts of educators, he believes that it should be "that attitude of mind, that habit of thought, which we call scientific."[41] Further, that attitude is present, in simple form, in little children quite naturally:

The native and unspoiled attitude of childhood, marked by ardent curiosity, fertile imagination, and love of experimental inquiry, is near, very near, to the attitude of the scientific mind. . . . its recognition in educational practice would make for individual happiness and the reduction of social waste.[42]

Dewey's conviction about the natural capacity of children to wonder and experiment was born of his and his wife's experience at the Laboratory School between 1896 and 1903, during which time he had had a chance to see his psychological theories put into concrete practice, and to observe the results. *How We Think* not only provides educators with the fruit of this process, but is an example of critical thinking itself, integrating theory and practice into helpful interpretations for teachers.

Dewey begins by defining what he means by *thought*. He distinguishes it from beliefs, which are really prejudices or prejudgments acquired insensibly by imitation, or from tradition or authority, as opposed to reflective thought. Thought is a matter of conscious inquiry into the grounds and the consequences of beliefs, leading to a reasoned conclusion.

Active, persistent, and careful consideration of any belief or supposed form of knowledge in the light of the grounds that support it, and the further conclusions to which it tends, constitutes reflective thought.[43]

Usually life moves smoothly along "from true fit to true fit," as Nathan Isaacs put it later, with past experience being a sufficient guide to present events. But when we come to a novel "forked road situation,"[44] when suddenly what we are faced with does not jibe with our current knowledge, we are perplexed and doubtful. This is when attention is caught and thinking is aroused. We have a problem, we search this way and that for a solution, we apply prior ones to the present situation, we collect evidence and verify it—in short, we indulge in reflective thought. Good habits of thought, moreover, require that we do not take the first plausible idea that occurs to us as a way out of our difficulty. Rather,

> the most important factor in the training of good mental habits consists in acquiring the attitude of suspended conclusion, and in mastering the various methods of searching for new materials to corroborate or to refute the first suggestions that occur. To maintain a state of doubt and to carry on systematic and protracted inquiry—these are the essentials of thinking.[45]

Thought when trained to this level of discipline has great value for human beings: it allows man to escape from being governed by instinct or appetite, from action that is merely routine or impulsive. And it has characteristic modes of proceeding.

Present objects (or events) suggest or signify absent things, by means of which present things may be interpreted, found to have meaning, and acted upon. "Upon the function of *signification* depend all foresight, all intelligent planning, deliberation, and calculation."[46] As a dark cloud signifies the possibility of rain to an experienced traveler, so he quickens his steps toward shelter. We also develop artificial reminders of what things mean—as monuments signify past brave acts, as lighthouses signify dangerous rocks nearby. Language, too, is a set of symbols which signify objects and events of prior experience, and so aid us in developing ideas that may be successfully used in reflective inquiry.

Yet just because thought does free us from impulse or the dictates of instinct, it also opens us to the possibility of error, to false beliefs and superstitions, which rely on no sound evidence but which enter the mind unaware. "A long discipline in exact science . . . is required for their conquest."[47] This discipline must consist of the careful regulation of the conditions under which observation, inference, and verification take place. And this is the responsibility of education, to guard against faulty thinking and promote sound habits of mind:

> Education has accordingly not only to safeguard an individual against the besetting erroneous tendencies of his own mind—its rashness, presumption, and preference for what chimes with self-interest to objective evidence—but also to undermine and destroy the accumulated and self-perpetuating prejudices of long ages. When social life in general has

become more reasonable, more imbued with rational conviction, and less moved by stiff authority and blind passion, educational agencies may be more positive and constructive than at present, for they will work in harmony with the educative influence exercised willy-nilly by other social surroundings upon an individual's habits of thought and belief. At present, the work of teaching must not only transform natural tendencies into trained habits of thought, but must also fortify the mind against irrational tendencies current in the social environment, and help displace erroneous habits already produced.[48]

Education, Dewey believed, was the fundamental method of social reform, and it must proceed by the development of good habits of thought. It is not merely concerned with passing on accepted modes of thought or organized bodies of knowledge, to be memorized and repeated; it is fundamentally a training in good thinking, in methods of drawing inferences from evidence and solving problems. Otherwise, an individual's life and that of society at large will be governed by hearsay, prejudice, passions, self-interest, and authority.

> The very importance of thought for life makes necessary its control by education because of its natural tendency to go astray, and because social influences exist that tend to form habits of thought leading to inadequate and erroneous beliefs.[49]

But, Dewey says, such training must be based on "natural tendencies." It cannot create powers of sound reasoning; it can only recognize, enhance, and direct them. For teaching and learning form a transaction, in which the learner has the initiative. The teacher must have "an insight into existing habits and tendencies, the natural resources with which he has to ally himself."[50] He has to understand the fund or store of experiences that the learner brings to bear on a problem situation, his capacity for generating suggestions or ideas for solutions, and the appropriateness of what is suggested. Basic to all these is a child's natural curiosity, born of the desire to solve a problem, to choose in the "forked-road situation" which is the best path. This children have from the beginning. Little children are constantly active, "into everything," ceaselessly exploring and testing the things in their environment. They soon learn that people can supply answers to puzzles as they occur, and eventually they come to have an "intellectual curiosity" about problems as such. This open, inquiring attitude of mind is natural to the child, and the educator must seize and build upon it.

> To the open mind, nature and social experience are full of varied and subtle challenges to look further. If germinating powers are not used and cultivated at the right moment, they tend to be transitory, to die out, or to wane in intensity. . . . [The teacher's] task is rather to keep alive the sacred spark of wonder and to fan the flame that already glows. His problem is to protect the spirit of inquiry, to keep it from becoming blasé

from overexcitement, wooden from routine, fossilized through dogmatic instruction, or dissipated by random exercise upon trivial things.[51]

Given a problem, a child may come up with ideas for solutions quickly and variously, or not. Children are judged dull or bright on this ability, but Dewey reminds us that rapid generating of suggestions must be based on the degree to which an object or event connects with a child's experience and his interest, that is, what he thinks is worthwhile paying attention to. Therefore, anything that teachers plan to present to children must first of all connect with experience that they care about, and also lead that experience forward by encouraging attention, curiosity, and inquiry. In this sense, any subject may be used to develop critical thinking. There are also no subjects that are inherently more intellectual than others; rather, how a subject is dealt with to encourage reflective thought and inquiry renders it intellectual. If it is presented as a problem or puzzle, in the context of a child's interests, and if it is systematically used to train disciplined thinking, then it is intellectually valid. The problem for the teacher is to choose just those activities and experiences that will do so:

> The problem and the opportunity with the young is selection of orderly and continuous modes of occupation, which, while they lead up to and prepare for the indispensable activities of adult life, have their own *sufficient justification in their reflex influence upon the formation of habits of thought.*[52]

The teacher, then, knowing how the mind works and knowing how important it is to develop critical thinking, must deal with her special problem of the selection of truly educative experiences. Dewey contrasts such procedures with the current school practice that he had observed, and, not surprisingly, finds that formal discipline inhibits real thinking, in that it has no organic connection whatever to the way in which children's minds develop naturally.

Further, building on the way in which he believes reasonable habits of thought may be developed, he goes on to claim that such training will mean a better social situation in schools. The ways in which problems of behavior are treated in classrooms, as microcosmic societies, will lead (or not) to reasonable attitudes and sound character, based on an understanding of the similarities and differences among people, and an acceptance of them.

> Habits of active inquiry and careful deliberation in the significant and vital problems of conduct afford the best guarantee that the general structure of the mind will be reasonable.[53]

The teacher, in her choice of activities, must therefore bear in mind their present value as well as their social significance, for the cultivation of sound habits of critical thinking has moral as well as intellectual results, and both individuals and society may grow more reasonable.

> The final test is whether the stimulus given to wider aims succeeds in transforming itself into power, that is to say, into the attention to detail that ensures mastery over means of execution. . . . unless enlargement of mental vision, power of increased discrimination of final values, a sense for ideas—or principles—accompanies this training, forms of skill ready to be put indifferently to any end may be the result. . . . To nurture inspiring aim and executive means into harmony with each other is at once the difficulty and the reward of the teacher.[54]

Clearly, much of Dewey's work in his larger *Psychology* and his more focused *How We Think* is related to Susan Isaacs's ideas. One also sees some foreshadowing of Nathan Isaacs's study of knowledge and children's questions, and of Piaget's work as well.

Dewey, of course, did not make use of psychoanalytic theory, as Susan Isaacs did. For him, as for most psychologists of the day, the unconscious is simply that which has been forgotten or is not at that moment in the focus of attention. He was well aware that conscious awareness necessarily ignored such elements of knowledge, and that

> [there is] no reason for refusing to admit that what is not explicitly present makes up a vastly greater part of experience than does the conscious field to which thinkers have so devoted themselves.[55]

However, Dewey's view of the unconscious is hardly Freudian.

Nonetheless, the way in which Dewey described human cognition and what teachers can and should do was very close to Susan Isaacs's views as well. She saw, as he did, that the work of schools, to be effective in building good thinking, must be based on and proceed from children's natural tendencies—of which curiosity is preeminent. And they both fully grasped that helping children to be reasonable and effective in their immediate surroundings had long-term social and moral benefits.

Nathan Isaacs

Soon after the First World War, Susan (then) Brierly was in London, lecturing on psychology to evening students. One young man, after hearing her exposition, responded with a ninety-five-page essay "so far outside the usual students' calibre that she realized immediately she had caught a whale in her herring net."[56] He was, of course, Nathan Isaacs; among the contemporaries by whom Susan Isaacs was influenced, her husband ranks very high.

Nathan Isaacs[57] was born in 1895 in Frankfurt-am-Main, to a family of Russian-Jewish rabbinical traditions. His formal education went only as far as a Swiss gymnasium, but not university. His later extensive knowledge of a variety of fields (e.g., philosophy, psychology, languages, music, botany) was self-acquired. When he was twelve, the family moved from Switzerland to London, and he remained in England for the rest of his life. His vocation was metallurgy, and for his important role during the Second World War in the acquisition and distribution of the rare minerals needed for the war effort, he was awarded the Order of the British Empire.

Nathan Isaacs's avocation, however, was scholarship in epistemology, logic, and psychology, and the vital relationships that he believed existed among them. Although he was a member of the Aristotelean Society for years and contributed to their meetings and publications, he became dissatisfied with their, to him, outdated and incomplete psychology (still called "mental philosophy"), especially in the light of the revolutionary new findings being made in that field. He sought for a more concrete and reasonable account of human experience, of coming to know, to know about and to trust the objects and events we encounter in reality, while at the same time distinguishing experience from psychic reality, which is the source of memory, perception, and prediction, in short, of whatever equilibrium we are able to achieve in life. To him, scientific psychology was making strides in studying human behavior and intelligence. The experimental work of Piaget in genetic epistemology seemed to be moving toward an ever more adequate account of the cumulative growth world-model in each child's mind. The insights of Freud, too, provided an understanding of the inner world as illuminated by psychoanalysis, and of the important role played by significant adults in an infant's early experiences with the world.

For many years, Nathan Isaacs worked on an extended essay in which he tried to bring new psychological ideas and facts to bear on the old philosophical problems of epistemology, "setting out his theory of knowledge as a temporal distillation of experience, continually corrected by the confirmation or non-confirmation of expectation."[58] Although it was not published until the year after Susan Isaacs died,[59] the ideas that he expressed there were those he had lived with and worked over for years.

Why, Isaacs asks, in the face of all the philosophical criticism of man's view of reality, do we nonetheless stubbornly go on believing in what he called our "common sense" world? Philosophers themselves continue to act as if their books and papers were real and provide them with trustworthy information, while at the same time they discuss endlessly their doubts about the validity and reliability of man's assumptions about reality. Dualists claim that mind and world are absolutely separate entities, incapable of any contact that could be called real. Empiricists (or associationists) state that our knowledge of reality is merely a matter of joined-together, received sensations. All this is based on notions of "mind" and "ideas" that are faulty and outdated abstractions bearing little or no resemblance to our everyday psychological understanding of inner reality, outer reality, and their constant interaction, that is, experience. John Dewey escapes this criticism, although not wholly:

> A consistent and most penetrating psychological approach to the domain of knowledge has ... been carried through with invaluable results (not only in the realm of theory but also that of concrete application to the processes of education) by Professor Dewey. The writer believes that even ... Dewey is still caught up to some extent in the consequences of the defective empirical psychology which is so deeply entrenched in the entire history of the philosophical theory of knowledge.[60]

Nathan Isaacs wants an even more radical, "empirical-psychological approach"[61] to the whole problem of our knowledge of reality, a thoroughly phenomenological and genetic description of how we come to know, "an authentic, stable, and orderly subject-matter for our ultimate philosophical problems."[62] It is precisely the process of coming to know the world of reality that he set out to describe and analyse, and, in the end, to claim as the valid ground for our belief in the "common sense world."

> It is just the potency of the learning process, when followed right through from the start in all its breadth and through all its cumulative history, that our philosophy has in the past missed, since only an adequate empirical psychology can supply it.[63]

How, then, do we come to "know," to believe in our commonsense world? How build up the constituents of that belief? Only a complete account of experience, an account that is at once genetic, historical, and dynamic, can provide a description of observed states and events as they occur, and the pattern or structure that they impose on our subsequent assumptions, perceptions, and experiences. For "the mind" or "the knower" do not exist but as abstract summations of separate experiences within a focalized field of perception, each with a unique history and individuality; nor are "ideas" real things, but the final product (not always completed or realized) of a long, interactive, experiential process. Thus the content of any propositions that use such abstractions must begin with a phenomenological account of their origins and history. Such an account must do full justice to the crucial psychological characteristics of experience, to action as a mode of experience; to the temporal and historical nature of experience that precedes action, predicts its outcome, and corrects for error, and to communication, "the screen of language,"[64] which exists between ourselves and others, and is also the product of a long history, and, in fact, hardly to be distinguished from thought itself.

Cognition is based on previous direct contacts with reality. The mind takes hold of such primary experiences ("this requires attention"), remembers others like them ("this has happened before"), anticipates what may come next ("this may come again"), is either sustained or confused by what does in fact happen next, and makes what adjustments are needed. In the greatest number of cases, we go smoothly on "from true fit to true fit,"[65] but not always. This constant action and reaction is the psychological basis for our belief in the reality of the outer world, for our distinction between truth and falsity, and for the development and use of our logical concepts.

> Truth is correspondence of beliefs with objective facts. Knowledge consists of the beliefs of every kind for which we claim correspondence on generally dependable grounds.[66]

Our knowledge is always retestable and capable of being shown to be wrong, but it is based on a "solid structure of cumulatively verified belief,"[67] which is not shaken but is in fact confirmed by this very interactive, corrective process.

Certainly there are "margins and limits"[68] to this cognitive structure, fuzzy edges, dreams, fantasies, even delusions. But, in this scientific age, they are known to be such and can be explained, in a way that the taboos and spirits of more primitive societies cannot. The corrective processes of the mind can tell us that a new experience or perception is only fantasy, however pleasant, or else that our previous mental structure needs a little adjustment. The only limitation is the amount of experience one has had and can work from, not spirits and demons. And this limitation led Nathan Isaacs directly to a consideration of children's thinking.

Nathan Isaacs's earlier essay, "Children's Why Questions," anticipated in many respects this later one, and it was an important addendum to Susan Isaacs's *Intellectual Growth in Young Children*. In it, he focused particularly on the occasions when the children at the Malting House School asked, "Why . . . ?" Sometimes it was to ask for the motivation behind an action, or some purpose, function, or explanation not fully understood. Such questions arose from simple lack of information. But what he called the distinctively "epistemic" question was different: it did not arise from lack of knowledge, but from the sense that there was something wrong with the knowledge the child already had.

> This situation is that of a sudden clash, gap, or disparity between our past experience and any present event. Some fact is met which is contrary to expectation, . . . or creates confusion or difficulty as to what to expect next. Something has gone wrong with our habitual knowledge or assumptions. We need to find out what it is and to put it right. We are pulled up, thrown out of our course, caught unprepared, or left without any clear guidance, and we have to deal with the obstruction. . . . our knowledge suddenly fails us, or some fact actually contradicts or subverts it.[69]

When this happens, the structure or model of the world that the child has been building up in his mind is thrown into question. He needs to set matters straight, in order to go on relying on that structure: "The cumulative effect of the situations in question, of clash, jar, or disparity, is to stimulate the child to a genuine interest in the revision, extension, and reorganization of his knowledge."[70] Thus Isaacs found that children have a natural interest in the growth and accuracy of their inner world-model, since it provides them with meaning, a sense of an ordered and comprehensive world in which they hope to survive. And this early interest has all the basic characteristics of an organized adult knowledge.

The role of nearby adults is crucial for the child in this development, for they provide a bridge between his inner states and outer reality. They are objects "out there," but unlike any other they also possess an inner reality like his. Therefore they can understand an infant's feelings of disequilibrium and help him; and, with the advent of language, they can share common life experiences of noncorrespondence with him, and provide the corrective explanations he needs to adjust the mental structures on which he depends for interpreting the world. Not that language can communicate knowledge by itself: what matters is how children assign meaning to sound patterns, out of their own built-up store of experiences. Bearing this in mind, however, adults can be of vital assistance to a child, since "language and language-borne thought [are] the real keys to human intellectual development."[71] Without them, he would never get beyond copying the concrete immediate world around him.

Much of this description of children's ways of knowing is similar to Piaget's later work. Both Susan and Nathan Isaacs had criticized his early books (see below), but Piaget altered his method of obtaining data afterward, from "mere verbal questionings" to "concrete experimental situations."[72] That is, the child did things in front of him, and was only asked questions that arose quite naturally from what the child could not do, or could do rather imperfectly, or could do easily and well.

Once this alteration in method began to yield new data, Nathan Isaacs (with Evelyn Lawrence) led a strong movement of support for Piaget's work in England. In 1955, the National Froebel Foundation published a booklet, *Some Aspects of Piaget's Work*,[73] which contained four important essays. "Children's Ideas of Number," by Evelyn Lawrence, summarized and translated Piaget's work on children's understanding of the idea of number; T. R. Theakston's "The Teacher and Piaget's 'The Child's Conception of Number'" drew the attention of educators to this work, indeed, of anyone who "wishes to develop the child's arithmetical ability *through understanding*"[74] rather than through rote memorization. Two essays by Nathan Isaacs followed. In "The Wider Significance of Piaget's Work," he placed the new findings about number in the "wider framework of genetic psychology of learning and knowing as such."[75] So important was the work Piaget had undertaken, in Nathan Isaacs's view, "that we cannot in its light avoid thinking out our whole educational psychology and philosophy afresh."[76]

It was typical of Isaacs to take a specific enquiry like Piaget's into children's understanding of number and to see immediately what broader implications it had; this insight led him to believe that Piaget's work was so important.

> He has taken a great psychological region which had hitherto eluded sustained experimental study and by a vast series of systematically planned enquiries had now fully subjected it to this.... It is thus now an established finding of science that most of the fundamental structural ideas which we tend to treat as if we read them out of the nature of things ... have a long observable history of psychological growth behind them ... one which starts from their virtual absence or negation and goes through a succession of transformations before they reach the forms we imagine we just find in the nature of things.[77]

Piaget's bold combination of his own biological and evolutionary training, his philosophical interest in genetic epistemology, and his situational psychological experiments was "of *transforming* significance"[78] at this time.

The significance of these experiments went beyond psychological studies, however; they were crucially important for progressive educators as well, for they shared with Piaget, an "approach to the child in terms from the start of action, process, and growth,"[79] and an insistence that the child makes his own sense of the world by his interaction with it, not by outer coercion or explanation. As Nathan Isaacs made clear in the second of his essays in this booklet, "Piaget and Progressive Education," Piaget had provided progressives generally with some very powerful, scientific reinforcement and direction for their views.

After 1955, Nathan Isaacs continued to work toward increasing educators' understanding and use of Piaget's findings. He not only provided simply written explanations of them, but added his own comments and interpretations, especially with respect to his own observations of children's thinking.

Among examples of the many explanations that Nathan Isaacs published about Piaget's work is his "Growth of Understanding in the Young Child,"[80] and "New Light on Children's Ideas of Number."[81] Later they were combined, with a biographical preface by Evelyn Lawrence (Isaacs), and published by an American firm under the title *A Brief Introduction to Piaget*.[82] These two accounts of Piaget's basic contribution also included Nathan Isaacs's view of the misunderstandings and objections that had arisen about it, and his attempt to allay them.

In "Piaget: Some Answers to Teachers' Questions,"[83] Isaacs continued his effort to meet these problems with fuller explanation and interpretation, both of Piaget's work as he understood it, and of his own views about children's ways of knowing and thinking. In particular, teachers seem to have been concerned about two implications of Piaget's findings, which he set himself to answer. First, Piaget seemed to set the chronological age by which children are able to explain their grasp of basic concepts such as space, time, and causality much later than nursery or infant-school years. Teachers who were aiming to build those very concepts in young children naturally wondered if their work were futile, if the children were simply too young to profit from activity-based teaching methods.

To these teachers, Nathan Isaacs replied that they must remember the special circumstances under which Piaget's experiments were conducted, and with whom. For Piaget was describing only his findings with these particular Genevan children who had had their particular set of school and other experiences. Perhaps, in other educational settings, deliberately planned to enhance their thinking, their progress would have been more rapid. Also, in the experiments, children were asked to articulate just why they acted a certain way or did not; that is, they not only had to act but also to explain, demonstrating a conscious and verbal grasp of what they were doing. Further, however carefully arranged the experimental setting, it was necessarily an artificial one. All these factors meant that a child's explanation would very likely lag well behind his ability to act. This, in fact, Nathan and Susan Isaacs had observed among the Malting House children, in a more natural, day-to-day setting, planned to provide materials and activities that would enhance children's natural desires to find out, to make and build, and to test, but without the demand for verbalizing what they were doing spontaneously. At the Malting House, children somewhat younger than Piaget's Swiss children were clearly able to use logical concepts.

What was really important, then, was not at all the exact age at which cognitive levels were reached, but that they came along in a particular, unvarying succession of stages, each with its characteristic mode of thought.

The second problem that teachers were concerned about was the matter of maturation versus the effect of environment. Piaget seemed to be saying that children's stages of development came about by an innate force for growth, quite regardless of environmental conditions (within limits, of course). If true, this would mean that the careful work and planning for school settings that good nursery-infant teachers took so seriously were also futile. To this, again, Nathan Isaacs replied that one must look at Piaget's findings from a broader point of view. Although it is clear that Piaget concentrates on the inner growth in children's power of thought, it is equally clear that that growth can only come about by interaction with the environment. For thought is internalized action, leading on to further operations, and action necessarily implies an exchange with the environment. Children cannot make meaning and learn to think in a vacuum, so their active investigation of the world outside provides them with the experiences they need in order to develop. Assimilation and accommodation involve interaction with the world, or equilibration cannot be achieved.

Nathan Isaacs also had words of encouragement and support for teachers who wanted to provide children with settings that promoted their interests and activities. If they hold Piaget's description of the characteristics of children's thinking at different stages carefully in mind, they can see when a child has no understanding of, say, conservation, when he is just beginning to understand it, and when he has fully reached the stage at which he grasps it easily. The second stage, in particular, is ripe for teaching: at this time, a child can do simpler tasks involving a given concept, but not the more difficult or complex ones. A teacher who notices this transitional stage can provide the small steps and encouragement that will lead the child onward to a surer and surer grasp of the concept. Not that the next stage can be explicitly taught; rather, experiences that encourage its advent can be provided, in an atmosphere of support and expectation, both personal and linguistic. Being alongside the child, and using appropriate language, the adult can be of immeasurable help. For, in using such methods, the teacher is allying herself with the very stuff of the child's mind itself, with all its ability to grow and achieve the power that comes from understanding and control of the world and of oneself. With regard to such "activity methods," then,

> it can, I think, be fairly said that Piaget's fundamental psychology of mental growth not merely supports such methods, but decisively demands them. A radical "activity" approach over virtually the whole front of education is in fact now shown to be the only one that makes *psychological sense*—at least for all the primary period, and even well into the secondary.[84]

Finally, teachers possess, together with children, that special tool of language, which has a vital influence on the development of thought. But language can enhance thought if it is used in "living learning" activities; that is, both language and thought can only operate with success if

> a.) they habitually start from these activities; b.) they are continually kept linked with them; and c.) they remain in fact, up to a very advanced point, under their firm control. Where these conditions are fulfilled, language and thought do vastly enrich and multiply the child's living learning itself. Where they are disregarded, both are apt to trail off rapidly into mere verbalism and vacuity.[85]

This latter condition is all too often met with in schools that are governed by principles that do not understand or build upon the natural characteristics of children's thinking. When the time for "chalk and talk" does come, it should only be when the children have such a solid base of "living learning" that they can "meet verbal explanations three-quarters of the way."[86] Again, the mediation of experience by language is the adult's great contribution to children: "Effective thinking (and growing progress in this) needs the kinds of full-bodied meanings and ideas which can only emerge from the activities of living learning, worked over themselves with the help of language."[87] The teacher's job then, is to understand the stages of growth in all children, to provide the optimum setting for their development, physical, social, and verbal, and to allow for individuals to move ahead, in their own way and at their own speed.

Another essay by Nathan Isaacs, "What Active Enquiry Means for the Child," (1960) follows these ideas along; it is fully reprinted in Part Two since it shows both his clarity of exposition and the remarkable blending of his thought with that of Susan Isaacs, combining cognitive and psychoanalytic insights.

Among Nathan Isaacs's special contributions was his ability to set concrete facts about children into the broadest possible context, and encourage his audience to address ultimate questions about the ends of education and not merely the practical ones about the means. For instance, in 1957, he delivered an important lecture that was subsequently published as "What is Required of the Nursery-Infant Teacher in this Country Today?"[88] As a theorist rather than a practitioner, he talked of the broad problems facing human civilization, and their implications for training those who would teach the youngest children. The dominant factors of the present situation, for educators as well as for all citizens, are

> the principles of progressive education, as we have come to see them—our modern democratic conception of a free, equal and cooperative community—and our vast and ever-growing world of human knowledge and achievement.[89]

Around these, humanists, Christians, progressives, and liberals of all kinds can join. For whatever their differences of view, their "shared terrain" is

> that of the fundamental right of every person to arrive at his own ultimate beliefs, from his own inward necessity, without let, hindrance or imposition by anyone else, . . . the basic uniting bond from which everything else follows, . . . the postulate of the intrinsic value of individual human beings as such.[90]

This position has long been a cornerstone of progressive social and political thinking, as well as that of educators. Now the latter have learned just how to work it out in psychologically sound ways.

> It is they who are most aware how hollow its mere social proclamation must be, unless the reality of freedom of thought and belief has been built up from within. For the child is the father of the man, and the man is shaped by the child, and we have now begun to see what vital conditions must be fulfilled from early childhood onward, if the authentic capacity for freedom is to be achieved.[91]

Or put another way, "the integrity of a human person is one and indivisible, and if we mean to respect it, the time to begin is when he first begins.[92]

How shall this "authentic capacity for freedom" be achieved?

> Our problem is in fact how to achieve the *optimal reconciliation* of the social steering the child needs and the shaping he cannot escape, with the respect for his integrity as an end in himself which we accept as the very categorical imperative of education.[93]

Educators must open doors for the child, doors he would not otherwise find. By encouraging his own interests and activities, they must "enable him to enter into at least each major aspect of our civilisation."[94] Then he can choose and pursue his particular gifts and talents, while not ignorant of others whose are different. Thus he gains power or control of his own faculties while at the same time he learns "the lessons of reciprocity and co-operation in all his human relationships."[95]

From this common ground of progressive educational thought, certain implications for teacher training follow. The problem laid out is formidable. A teacher must have a thorough knowledge of educational psychology, especially that of Piaget and of Susan Isaacs, as applied in extensive observations of real children; the teacher's own education is also of the greatest importance, her own understanding of subject matter at a deep level of real, personal involvement.

> What the nursery-infant teacher, above all, needs is a big human-psychological globe; and then a big topographical model of her own continent, the child throughout his growth: and then another large map of her own country, the child from three to seven; but with the stress all the time on the major structural features, relations and proportions which no mere aggregate of separate detailed sections can bring out.[96]

Finally, she must also understand just how to bring the child from his present stage, step by step, toward "nothing less than the furthest span of present human knowledge, thought and feeling."[97] For it is vital that

> every teacher learns to link a clear awareness of methods and criteria with actual results, the knowledge and understanding and achievement, which we gain through them, . . . the bridges that lead from detailed inquiry to those general perspectives which, in so many fields, are alone open to her.[98]

A heavy responsibility indeed, but on it, in Nathan Isaacs's view, rests the future of all that is best in civilization.

There were still two other major topics, linking cognitive psychology, social philosophy, and education, that Nathan Isaacs addressed on several occasions: the child as a young scientist, and the nature of verbal communication and its relationship to the development of thought.

In his "Early Scientific Trends in Children"[99] Isaacs characteristically starts from a broadly conceived position, namely, that science is a fundamentally human endeavor, and its methods and goals should be known to everyone in this advanced civilization of ours. The case he makes is much like Dewey's:

> My case, . . . is that only by setting out from the young child's appropriate interests and drives, and working with these right through, can we reach the goal we really want. That is, neither a degree of scientific specialisation which for most of us is not even desirable, nor a mere worthless smattering, but some broad vision of what science means and—perhaps above all—how it is achieved.[100]

One must begin, then, with the natural interests of children that lead them to want to find out about things, and to ask questions about how things happen as they do. They should find each question answered in a way that takes them "further into a scheme of things in which new paths open, new questions arise, and new active curiosities and interests start up. . . ."[101] They should be learning all the time, by their own explorations and questions, how this "scheme of things" is built up and extended, how and when it needs to be tested and adjusted for, "towards science both as ordered knowledge and as method."[102] And modern scientists at work on the frontiers of knowledge demonstrate these same trends and activities in what is now called scientific inquiry, which dates from only about four hundred years ago. For about then, human thought was reoriented in two ways:

> First, there was the *turning* of thought and inquiry to the actual world of fact. . . . Secondly, there was the *testing* of anything believed or propounded for belief by what was actually found in the relevant field of fact.[103]

Alongside these two processes, there developed a "special alertness for everything contrary to expectation or in any way anomalous."[104]

These modes of thought—enquiring about the concrete world, testing belief by referring to that world, and adjusting for any error or noncorrespondence—these are exactly what, in simple and naive ways, children use every day. Advanced human thought and organized bodies of knowledge have their essential roots in the very nature of the human mind, much as Dewey had also believed.

All this Nathan Isaacs exemplified, again, by using some of the events and interchanges recorded at the Malting House School, especially the children's "Why?" questions.

> Why doesn't the ink run out when you hold up a fountain pen? Why does it get lighter outside when you put the light out? Why don't we see two things with our eyes?[105]

Thus the epistemic question shows "how close children come here to the very spirit and attitude of the scientist,"[106] in the pursuit of knowledge for its own sake. And so, to help the child attain some share of the achievements of scientific method and the heritage it has given to civilization, "surely few educational enterprises could be more worthwhile."[107]

But Nathan Isaacs did not rely on his own theorizing about children's natural trends or his observations at the Malting House School. In 1961, as a result of a lecture he delivered at the British Association for the Advancement of Science, he set up an enquiry into different approaches to science teaching in primary schools, especially the interests and topics that children expressed and developed with their teachers. The result was *Children Learning Through Scientific Interests*,[108] which provides teachers with many examples of materials and activities from which children learn successfully.[109]

Isaacs emphasized the importance of generating initial interests and extending or prolonging them by careful intervention on the part of teachers, as well as the value of real finding out, rather than looking things up in books or accepting explanations that do not connect with experience. Books should be used only as ancillary to "living learning"—true, first-hand, active investigations into the nature of things. "A view of our scientific knowledge as a living and growing whole is in turn among the main targets of any education in science,"[110] and a necessary possession of civilized man.

Closely linked to his interests in children's scientific development was Isaacs's careful discussion of language and its relationship to thought, for children's questions and adults' replies are vital modes of communication that either help or hinder the growth of understanding. In 1958 and 1959, he published the two parts of his essay, "Some Basic Reflections about Language"[111] and in 1961 he went back over much of the same ground, extending it as he went, in "Some Thoughts about Language and Thought."[112]

How, he asks, is verbal communication possible at all? How can we be sure that the meanings or ideas spoken to you do in fact correspond to one another? In particular, how can a teacher, by using language, help a child's mental world of meanings to expand and develop into what we call directed thought? How can she, while using words, nonetheless teach a kind of understanding that is more than "merely verbal"? Here Isaacs was dealing only with vocal language, but his analysis holds good for written language as well. And, characteristically, he goes back to "our learning-history," to the way in which we learn about the world long before language enters it in any understandable way. For the preverbal infant,

> what learning really consists in for the human child, from his first few weeks onward, is the gradual building up in his mind, mainly through his

own activities and their results, of an organized psychic schema of the world around him.[113]

The child explores and experiments, and gradually develops the earliest ordering concepts, on the basis of which he predicts, tests, and adjusts his actions and their outcomes. These first schemas organize his experience and make sense of it: objects turn out to be "persisting entities,"[114] space is a kind of framework in which both he and they exist, time is another kind of framework for various events as they come along, and cause and effect prove that if one thing happens, a result is likely to follow. From these early building blocks, all of a child's later adult, ordered knowledge ultimately flows.

> He must have his space relations right, his belief in the persistence of things right, and his time and causal relations right, otherwise his action will fail.[115]

When failures do occur, they are spurs to the child to make finer distinctions or allowances for new experiences. But the proportion of such failures, even in a tiny infant, as compared with his successes, must be very small, "or else his capacity for successful action would not so continually and spectacularly grow."[116] When language comes along, this "main groundwork of his learning" is in place, a "structured psychic model of a world of objects and happenings in space, time, and causal order which substantially *corresponds* to the real world around him."[117]

Then comes language, and the child's schemas get joined up with names provided for him by adults, the classifications of our society that it has developed in order to cope with the larger world, but built originally on these same early processes. "Both are drawn from the same real source and controlled by this."[118] This is how we communicate, and our only way; as human beings we go through the same learning history of making sense of the world, we assign sound patterns to our ideas thus developed, and they are shareable because they successfully correspond both to the child's experience of the world and our own. For a mother acts always, with her infant, on the assumption that he is experiencing the same world that she does and in much the same way; otherwise, her actions would not meet his needs and give him satisfaction. So too with language: it is "merely woven into a pattern of tested correspondences which is there already."[119] We act all the time on one another's communications, knowing that they correspond at the most basic level.

> The thought-patterns we form must agree with our informants', and theirs with the facts, so that ours in turn may prove in accord with these.... Our separate worlds of directed thought can thus be seen in essence as the directing organs of lives which are both continuously interwoven with one another and codependent on a common real

world. . . . [with the] important lifeline of language through which all these independencies have to pass.[120]

Once firmly based on correspondence with the child's early psychic schema, language can immensely expand his mental world. He can enlarge and enrich his own individual experience by learning about that of others, through people or books. He gains a new mode of organizing and manipulating his ideas so that they eventually become stable and sophisticated concepts. He can make use of language to compare and contrast, discuss and criticize his own formulations of experience with others. And, finally, he can participate in the human community, which does depend so much on the free flow of verbal communication.

Returning to the teacher's problem, then, we see how communication is possible, and how enriching it can be. And we also see that language which is not vitally connected with a child's psychic mode of understanding is exactly what is meant by "mere verbal learning."

> Ideas and knowledge which come to us at second hand, and above all through language, can truly become ours only to the extent to which we can turn them into our own living experience and thought. And this can only be done if we are able to integrate them fully into our own past learning history. . . . Knowledge remains merely verbal in the measure in which it fails to pass through these processes.[121]

Here again is Nathan Isaacs's repeated insistence on "living learning" and the importance of planning schools to provide concrete experience and activities, while at the same time giving children a community of others who are upon the same journey of growth.

Jean Piaget

Everyone in psychology and education now reveres the work of Jean Piaget, and it has given rise to a very large number of further studies that follow his lead. This was not always the case. When his first five books were published, they received not only praise but also some searching criticism from Susan and Nathan Isaacs, resulting in a long conversation between them, visits to one another's schools, and a group of publications that document their relationship. When considered in detail, their two points of view are not fundamentally opposed, however, but complementary; the Isaacses emphasized the importance of observing children's spontaneous activities; Piaget focused on the inner structure of the child's mind, by means of which he was able to understand the world around him.

Chronologically, Piaget's first five books were *The Language and Thought of the Child* (1924), *The Child's Conception of the World* (1926), *The Child's Conception of Causality* (1927), *Judgment and Reasoning in the Child* (1928), and *The Moral Judgment of the Child* (1932). In 1927, he visited the Malting House

School in Cambridge, and Susan Isaacs went to see his Maison des Petits in Geneva.

In 1929 Susan Isaacs wrote two reviews of Piaget's books, one dealing with the first three together, in *The Journal of Genetic Psychology* and one about *The Child's Conception of the World*, in *Mind*. In 1929, also, her small classic, *The Nursery Years*, was published, with Piaget's five books on its recommended bibliography. In 1930 her important work, *Intellectual Growth in Young Children*, appeared. It included an extensive explanation and critique of Piaget's theory of cognitive development to date, and Nathan Isaacs's famous "Children's Why Questions," which also dealt at length with Piaget's ideas of genetic epistemology.

In 1931, Piaget was invited to review Susan Isaacs's book in *Mind*, and he did so, both praising the work of the Malting House School on which it was based, and presenting his own responses to the Isaacses' criticisms of his own work. Another article appeared that year as well, in *The British Journal of Educational Psychology*. In this Piaget discussed at length Nathan Isaacs's essay on children's questions, in a piece called "Retrospective and Prospective Analysis of Child Psychology."

In 1932, *The Children We Teach* by Susan Isaacs appeared. This was her description of children's development from age seven to eleven, and it included a long section summarizing Piaget's views, followed by her own modifications of them. In that year, she also published in French an article* on children's social growth, which speaks of the fundamental importance of Piaget's studies in the area.

In 1933, the second volume dealing with observations at the Malting House School, *Social Development in Young Children*, came out, but here Susan Isaacs mentioned Piaget only in passing, since the theory behind this study was primarily psychoanalytic. In 1934, she reviewed his *The Moral Judgment of the Child*, in *Mind*, and she felt that this was his best book to date. In 1948, the year of her death, she brought out *Childhood and After*, in which Piaget's work is mentioned, but only his earliest five books.

In 1952, Piaget wrote an autobiographical essay, in which he spoke of his surprise at the serious way in which these early books were taken, since he meant them only as preliminary studies, and primarily for a French audience. He also gave an account of his own intellectual development, the change in his mode of studying children, and the different conclusions he drew as a result. Finally, it seems from his account that his work after *Moral Judgment* was largely unavailable to English readers, aside from academics and professionals. However, as already discussed, Piaget's work became more widely known and understood in England from 1955 on, especially through its interpretations by Nathan Isaacs and Evelyn Lawrence.

Such was the chronology of the published interchange of ideas between

---

*See Part Two for a translation of this article.

Piaget and the Isaacses. It was always marked with great respect, since each side knew that the other was breaking new and important ground in the study of children's thinking.

The criticisms that the Isaacses leveled at Piaget's first five books were basically variations on one theme:

> There is always more elasticity, more movement, more life, more variety, more foreshadowing of later modes within the earlier, than Piaget's preoccupation with types and stages allows us to see. [He] underestimates the richness and complexity of the emotional life and personal awareness of the child under two or three years of age, . . . and the relative importance of the social and physical factors in the child's movement toward objectivity.[122]

This lack of a fully rounded view of children was caused by the method by which he studied children. His "clinical method," as he called it, was to observe children at his Maison des Petits and later to engage some of them in long conversations, asking them questions that followed up on comments he had heard them make earlier, to clarify just what they had meant. His questions were all directed at understanding how children grasped the idea of causality in the objective world, the logical connection between events. Susan Isaacs stated in her review, "Upon the ultimate reliability of this technique rest the soundness and significance of his material and conclusions," and she then went on to raise serious questions about his method, and hence the conclusions he derived from them.

By that time, she and her husband had had some years of work with young children at the Malting House School, where, as she put it,

> the main character of our technique was to meet the spontaneous inquiries of the children, as they were shown day by day, and to give them the means of following these inquiries out in sustained and progressive action.[123]

At the Malting House, there was much spontaneous activity, discussion and expression of fantasy in play,[124] but relatively little adult interference or questioning, in contrast with Piaget's "sustained conversations" with individual children.

The Isaacses' descriptions of children's intellectual growth differed from Piaget's too. At the Malting House School, the children's activities and spontaneous expressions of their observations and ideas led Susan Isaacs to believe that they took a real interest in the physical world outside them and understood mechanical causality earlier than Piaget stated. Under what she termed his "negative" conditions of study, he found that children under the age of seven or eight were unable to formulate their understanding of causality, but she produced "proof positive" that they could act and comment spontaneously on just such an understanding much earlier. Piaget contended that, when children were able to think causally, they left their earlier, "magical" explanations of the world behind, but Susan Isaacs showed that these two ways of dealing with the world of facts exist side by side in the child's mind, depending on the circumstances of the moment, and the child's previous experience.

Piaget believed that children show a social instinct which emerges by virtue of increasing maturity in the middle years of childhood, and that until then they are locked into their subjective, "ego-centric" point of view which does not permit them to understand reciprocal relationships, that is, their action and the response it evokes. Susan Isaacs claimed that, as psychoanalysis had shown, children are involved with the outer world, especially that of people, at the earliest age. Their interest in objects in the physical world can be seen much earlier than Piaget had noticed, so that the emergence of a sense of reciprocity has a more complex evolution than his views would suggest, and is more dependent on the opportunities and events in children's lives than simple maturation.

In Susan Isaacs's view, Piaget's method of studying children was flawed, as were his conclusions, because they put the child at a disadvantage psychologically. The questions he asked, despite the fact that they might have been asked at another time by the child himself, had a directing force that he underestimated, and did not provide an opportunity for spontaneous explanation. The "prestige" of the adult is an inevitable and vital factor in any interchange between adult and child; therefore, when a child is pressed to answer beyond his sure knowledge, his small store of facts slips away and he moves into fantasy or "magical" explanations of cause and effect. Thus the affective aspect of this method can make the child bewildered and confused, so that he responds at a cognitive level lower than he might otherwise.[125]

> The conditions under which Piaget tried to measure them were very unfavorable. . . . Sustained conversations between one child and one adult in one place do not provide the circumstances which would provoke questions demanding causal explanation or inquiries about inanimate objects. . . . These occur rather in the course of free practical activity in a varied setting, and in play with other children and with adults who share in the practical pursuits. . . . His conclusions apply, legitimately only to the particular conditions of his particular experiments; and cannot, therefore, be taken as revealing stages of true *maturation*.[126]

Piaget's response to this criticism of his method of studying children's mental development was, in effect, to agree. At the time he was conducting his studies, he had no children of his own. When they came along in 1925 and 1927, he became much interested in observing their behavior and responses to the world at an age long before they could talk. In his 1952 autobiography, he wrote of the shortcomings he realized about his early work:

> One I was not aware of before studying infant behavior . . . [was] limiting my research into language and expressed thought. I well knew that thought proceeds from action, but I believed then that language directly reflects acts and that to understand the logic of a child one had only to look for it in the domain of conversations or verbal interactions. It was only later, by studying the patterns of intelligent behavior of the first two years, that I learned that for a complete understanding of the genesis of intellectual operations, manipulation and experience with objects had first to be considered. Therefore, prior to study based on verbal conversation, an examination of the pattern of conduct had to be carried on.[127]

Such an alteration in his method would have made him less surprised than he was when he visited the Malting House School in 1927. There he observed at first hand a child of 5:9 displaying two modes of thought, both causal and magical, on the same day but in different circumstances (see p. 78: Dan on his tricycle, and later spitting at the kettle). Here was clear evidence that this young child knew perfectly well what caused the forward motion of his tricycle, and that he also believed his spitting would have the power to stop the steam coming from the kettle. On the basis of such incidents, Susan Isaacs believed that children understand causality much earlier than Piaget had claimed, and also that several kinds of thinking can exist simultaneously in a child's mind. One type of thought does not preempt all others, even if it is at a more advanced level of cognitive development.

Piaget commented specifically on his observations at the school:

> . . . at the Malting House School the children proved their interest in the physical phenomena well before the ages indicated by our work. The formulation itself was found to be excellent: for example, Dan at 5:9 (IQ of 142) knew how to explain the mechanism of bicycles, etc., . . . Dan at 5 years, while quite able to explain bicycles, presented some examples of magical "precausality." It could not, therefore, be a question of successive (mental) structures, but the phenomena of syncretism or of egocentrism reappear wherever sentiment comes into play, or control is impossible, etc., and that is true among adults themselves.[128]

Later in this review of Susan Isaacs's book, Piaget defends his views as to the age at which causal explanations can be expected:

> Dan, at five years and nine months, explained the mechanism of a bicycle correctly, which fact, Mrs. Isaacs judges, contradicts the ages which we have assigned to mechanical causality. But we are told that Dan, at 5:9, had an IQ of 142, which gives him a mental age of 8. Now it is precisely at

8 years, according to our statistics bearing on a great number of children observed at random, that the correct explanation of a bicycle becomes possible! One sees that the example chosen by Mrs. Isaacs is unfortunate and tends rather to confirm the point established through our means.[129]

Later still, he also answers her criticism of his way of questioning children:

> We agree entirely with her three criticisms relative to the method of interrogation. . . . we have never considered the results of these interrogations as more than artificial enlargements of the beliefs existing solely in the form of tendencies in the child's mind. But these tendencies do exist! . . . How then is one to measure the intensity of these tendencies if, on principle, one never interrogates?[130]

While the facts that Mrs. Isaacs has observed and reported have great value and interest, he says, they are not enough to deny all value to others collected in a different milieu and with less-intelligent children.

Susan and Nathan Isaacs's criticisms of Piaget went further than this, however. They aimed to show that the development of a child's mental functioning was: (a) a total process beginning in the earliest years, not separable into discrete stages, each determined for its appearance by maturational timing; (b) not essentially different from adult thinking except in having less experience to draw on.

> Their thought is active and prehensile. It changes as their purposes change, and rests no longer in the static form of explicit judgment and inference than is momentarily needed for the momentary aim. It moves consciously on, developing and growing as their practical and social situations change and develop from moment to moment.[131]

Direct contact with the physical world is, of course, inevitable, and children learn about the limits that things set to their activities almost as soon as they learn about the existence of other human beings. Children and adults alike react to new or challenging situations at a more primitive level when prior experience is lacking or when anxiety or fear are provoked by what is happening. A more objective mode of response becomes possible when knowledge is more complete or when confidence is reestablished. This is particularly true in encounters with persons rather than with things, for our earliest feelings are bound up with people and remain to color all later relationships. Thus the movement from egocentricity toward objectivity is uneven, back and forth, and sporadic all our lives, and depends very much on prior, similar experiences and the feelings (old and new) generated by the situation in hand.

Only in the earliest years is a child's world entirely personal; very soon the inanimate world attracts his attention and reaction, and, in turn, serves as his educator.

> The disappointments and sense of impotence which *things* force upon him are as much a part of his education as the denials and thwartings suffered at the hands of adults. . . . Piaget, of course, altogether overlooks the denials and thwartings suffered at the hands of the parents, and allows himself to suggest that the infant lives in a world of satisfied desire until he is three years of age![132]

It is, then, the total environment that educates in the first days of life, and it is a child's entire mental activity that must be studied, as it interacts with environment. For Susan Isaacs, the process of cognitive and emotional/ social growth is a gradual, unified synthesis, involving all the faculties and dependent on experience with the real world for its development. A child is not so very different from an adult in his attempts to understand and to make sense of the world around him:

> The untrained, undisciplined and ignorant mind, is, *of course*, egocentric, precausal and magical, in proportion to its ignorance and lack of discipline. But after infancy it is not accurate to represent it as ignorant *because* of its ego-centricity—it is ego-centric in large part because of its ignorance and lack of organised experience. The difference between the younger child and the older child, between the child and the adult, is thus *not* that the former do not reason, or reason *only* in the form of perceptual judgment and practical manipulation. It is rather the extent to which, with the younger children, the higher forms of noetic synthesis rest directly upon and grow immediately out of the simpler.[133]

Piaget's reaction to all this was both to agree and to disagree. He paid tribute to Mrs. Isaacs's "fine book," and to Mr. Isaacs's essay which was of "primary importance," but he went on to raise questions: how is it that the mind in fact does experience the outside world? Is it not too simple to appeal to "raw experience," without inquiring what it is that, as the child makes sense of the world, does the sense making? For predictions are indeed made and expectations arise—where do they come from? By what agency? He insisted that mental structures, of developing complexity and character, do exist in the mind, through which experience is filtered and by means of which it is organized and made meaningful. This process is precisely aimed at reestablishing the equilibrium lost when a child is puzzled, so that in fact he feels the need to ask, "Why . . . ?"

Nathan Isaacs's essay, Piaget went on to say, is "one of the subtlest and profoundest," and his own views were "complementary and in no sense contradictory."[134] Whereas Nathan Isaacs had emphasized the "prospective" aspect of a child's approach to the world, in predicting and anticipating certain outcomes, Piaget stressed the "retrospective" aspect: a child brings with him to any event his earlier experience and understanding as well as his current level of mental functioning, that is, the mental structures that are characteristic of his age and stage of development. In this sense, these two views are indeed complementary, since it seems a matter simply of which part of the interaction one studies, in the complex process of describing mental growth.

Piaget's work on the development of moral judgment in children was more satisfying than his views on cognitive growth, especially to Susan Isaacs. Piaget brought genetic psychology to bear on ethical questions of right and wrong, inquiring just how moral judgments develop as children mature. For him, three clear stages appear as children gradually move from egocentric views of what is good and bad toward more abstract notions of justice. At the earliest level, what is just is what adults command; at the next, justice is what is fair within members of a cooperating group; finally, equity, a more subtle and abstract concept, appears as the basis for judgment. Certainly similar changes had been clearly demonstrated at the Malting House School, as the children grew from the earlier dependence on adults for direction, praise, and affection, toward their later reliance on group norms, holding adults somewhat at bay. But Susan Isaacs claimed that there are really only two levels: the period when adults exert (intentionally or not) a coercive power over children, and the time when their rules and conventions have been internalized and made rational by the child's own experiences. She again insisted that Piaget underestimated the power of adults in the world of the infant, and the strength and complexity of his feelings at that time; that the whole movement from egocentrism toward objectivity, in this area as in cognition, is gradual, unified, and uneven; and that all levels of moral judgment exist side by side all our lives, not in discrete stages, each one of which is outgrown when the next higher one is achieved. Nonetheless, she agreed with him that the final phase of mutuality and respect for human dignity is achieved by few individuals or societies: "Society as a whole is very far and will probably remain very far from such an achievement."[135]

The whole, long conversation between Piaget and the Isaacses can be seen in terms of the old controversy between heredity and environment. In this case, it is an argument couched in terms of the relative importance of maturation as opposed to experience in a child's gradual development in understanding and judgment.

For the Isaacses, again, maturation should be considered only as a limiting concept, which sets the ceiling to what a child can grasp but does not produce understanding unaided. By heredity, nature has endowed the child with a fixed level of intelligence or general mental ability, which mental tests can measure and which cannot be changed. But interaction with the environment, both animate and inanimate, is essential for whatever intelligence a child possesses to be called out. This view of maturation may be summarized thus:

> The process of intellectual maturation no longer wears the air of a mysterious or mystic happening. We are able to see that it shows, not a pseudo-

biological sequence, totally independent of experience, but a strictly *psychological* coherence of growth, into which experience is taken up more and more adequately. Maturation is in the first instance undoubtedly an affair of increase in the depth, breadth, and range of synthetic ability, or *noetic synthesis*, . . . I would suggest that all growth of noetic synthesis characterizes development at all ages, and can be seen in the progressive articulation even of perception in the very young child, as well as in the rise and elaboration of concepts.[136]

Piaget's view was that the mind grows in three distinct ways: it adapts itself to perceived experience, it reflects upon its own adaptation, and it "purifies" or clarifies its own conceptions of reality as it does so. Thus "reason changes structure bit by bit, not by chance, but following a line of evolution designed by its own function."[137] Development is not a matter of chance exposure to this or that situation, but rather a function of increasingly adaptive functioning marked by definite stages.

For us, stages do exist, but they are not at all due to a simple internal and inevitable maturation, analogous to embryogenic maturation. These stages are the expression of the three phenomena: adaptation to experience, reason becoming aware of itself, and the purification of reason.[138]

These stages, influenced by experience all along the way, appear in the child as "tendencies or attitudes" of intelligence, as "forms or organization or orientations of the mind."[139] Piaget's point here is that he is not assuming innate, a priori ideas or beliefs, which appear simply by virtue of maturational timing, but rather modes of thought and perception that may become more or less apparent depending on the surroundings that call them forth.

Thus Piaget is describing what the mind is and does, emphasizing the process aspect in a way not unlike the Isaacses. One may take the "prospective, functional" point of view as Nathan Isaacs did and say that a child learns something, just like an adult, by "making experiments and coordinating them."[140] Or one may take the "retrospective, structural" point of view, and ask oneself how a child's experiences, in their totality, are "crystallised" in his mind. There one finds structural differences, and he concludes:

"Structure", then, is no more than a crystallization of the moment, which the mind always goes beyond as part of its functioning. Presented in that way, the conflict between Mrs. and Mr. Isaacs and myself is much less acute than it appears at first glance.[141]

Melanie Klein and Anna Freud

Psychoanalysis took firm hold in England, thanks to the work of Ernest Jones and others, in the early years of this century. Jones's *Papers on Psycho-*

Analysis (1912) and his founding of the London (later British) Psycho-Analytic Society (1913) were critical events. As discussed in chapter 2, psychoanalysis became widely accepted, even beyond medical circles, especially after the First World War, until it became an important influence on intellectual circles and, to some extent, in the popular press.

In 1925, Ernest Jones invited Melanie Klein to come to London from Berlin, to settle in England and carry on the work she had already begun, developing Freud's theories further, especially with regard to the emotional development of young children. She did so, and became a dominant figure in the Psycho-Analytic Society for many years.

Anna Freud did not come to London until 1938, when, with her aging father, she escaped from the Nazis, who were moving toward Vienna. Before then, however, her differences with Melanie Klein had surfaced: in 1927 Klein had written "A Symposium on Child Analysis," summarizing her work to date; in 1926 and 1927, Anna Freud had published part one and part two of her *Psycho-Analytic Treatment of Children*, specifically referring to and refuting the Kleinian views; in 1932 Klein published her own *Psycho-Analysis of Children*, while Miss Freud continued along more orthodox lines, as is clear from her *Psycho-Analysis for Teachers and Parents* (1935), *Ego and Mechanisms of Defense* (1936), and subsequent works.

Susan Isaacs was in analysis with J. C. Flügel in 1921 when she wrote her *Introduction to Psychology;* she began taking patients in 1922 and became a member of the British Psycho-Analytic Society in 1923, so that, by the time Melanie Klein arrived, she was very much part of the psychoanalytic scene. Isaacs had also begun to see how psychoanalytic principles were corroborated in her experience with young children at the Malting House School, between 1924 and 1927. And, on the basis of Melanie Klein's new discoveries from analyzing very young children, she began a second analysis with a Kleinian, Joan Rivière.

Susan Isaacs was definitely in the Kleinian camp. Her chapter on "The Conscious and Unconscious" in her *Introduction to Psychology* begins by being orthodox Freudian until she comes to an account of the formation of the superego, which is Kleinian. In the 1928 edition, she added an appendix that detailed advances made in psychological studies by then, including the important work of Klein in the use of a "play technique" with very young children that uncovered the early processes of fantasy, introjection, and projection that are at the heart of the superego's formation in the first months of life. All Isaacs's writings on analytic topics, especially *Social Development in Young Children,* include Kleinian views. And during the years of the Second World War, Susan Isaacs and Melanie Klein shared a flat in Cambridge and worked together on the Cambridge Evacuation Study.

Melanie Klein's theory of the early formation of the superego was one of the major differences between her and Anna Freud. The other, closely related difference between them concerned the role played by the significant adults in a young child's life, and that played by the analyst in the therapeutic work with children whose normal emotional development was blocked in some way. Indeed, these differences were strong enough to divide the British psychoanalysts of the time. Flügel put it thus:

> In so far as [these] doctrines have been made the basis of a separate Kleinian school of analysis, they have had a somewhat disruptive effect on a psycho-analytic theory and practice.[142]

Anna Freud's clearest statements about these issues appear in the first four lectures in part one of *The Psycho-Analytic Treatment of Children*.[143] Here she claims that she cannot analyze children under the age of about two years in the usual way, because the effective tools of adult analysis are not available, namely, free association and the interpretation of transference reactions; for these, the young child has as yet neither enough "speech-faculty" nor a capacity for object relations. Small children also lack the capacity for reaction-formations and "cover memories," which are only constructed during latency, when the child's "ego-ideal" (superego) has detached itself from the parents by internalizing them. Prior to that time, the superego is still heavily dependent on the important adults in the child's life, whose demands press on him daily from outside, while strong opposing instinctual urges clamor for gratification inside. Yet until the resolution of the Oedipal conflict, the superego is not strong enough to stand against those instincts, and must rely on adult presence and direction. As she put it elsewhere:

> this detachment of the child from the earliest and most important of his love objects only succeeds on one very definite condition. It is as if the parents said: You can certainly go away, but you must take us with you. . . . Here, looking backward, we can say: The price which the child has to pay for detaching himself from his parents is their incorporation in his own personality.[144]

What can analysis do, before the superego has become an impersonal inner voice? Especially considering that those adults on whom it is still dependent are the very persons who are and have been responsible for a child's repression and possible neurosis, if analysis liberates blocked emotions and allows them fuller expression and gratification, there is "too great risk" to the adult-child relationship. Further, excessive gratification at any given stage leads to fixation at that stage so that:

> in the very interest of preventing neurosis, it is desirable to avoid too much direct gratification at any stage of a child's necessarily perverse sexuality.[145]

The analyst, therefore, should not permit regression to an earlier stage where blockage may have occurred, lest damage be done by overgratification of primitive emotions both within the therapeutic setting and in the outside world as well. On the contrary, the analyst must "succeed in putting himself in the place of the child's Ego-ideal for the duration of the analysis,"[146] thus becoming the child's superego and exercising appropriate adult control of the conflict between the child's ego and the instincts. This is done in the context of a positive relationship between the child and his therapist, so that the latter becomes a strong figure in the child's life and can actually mediate between ego and instincts better than the child's own parents did originally. If the therapist succeeds,

> he undoes a piece of wrong education and abnormal development, and so procures for the child, or whoever controls its destiny, an opportunity to improve matters.[147]

Again, if the analyst does not exercise this control, the child may mistakenly act upon his inner fantasies and feelings everywhere, so that not only will he encounter adult objections in the outer world, but also the material in the analytical hour will be "thinner," having been expressed elsewhere. Thus the analyst of young children must play a controlling, educative role, by encouraging the formation of "positive transference" only, an affectionate attachment to herself, but not negative transference also, as occurs with adult patients.

> Under his influence, the child must learn to conduct itself with regard to its instinctual life, and his views in the end determine what part of the infantile sexual impulses must be suppressed and rejected as unemployable in the cultural world; how much or how little can be allowed direct gratification; and what must be guided into the path of sublimation, for which process all the available resources of education can then be used.[148]

In short, the analyst must be a better parent than the child ever had, until the age when the superego is an internalized force and adult-style analysis is possible.

Anna Freud also criticized Melanie Klein's symbolic interpretation of children's play. Play, she says, is useful for observing children especially at the preverbal stages. Klein, however, also believed that she could interpret all play-actions just as she would adult patients' free associations, and translate for the child the "underlying symbolic function" of his play. But for Anna Freud, a child's play is not necessarily equivalent to an adult's free associations. A child who looks into a lady's purse may not be curious "to see whether its mother's womb conceals another little brother or sister."[149] The child may simply be reenacting an experience he has had. In adult analysis, symbolic significance of associations and dreams is ascribed only "to those which arise under the influence of the analytical situation which he has accepted."[150] A preverbal child in analysis lacks this purposeful attitude that adults have, since, after all, the decision to enter analysis is in the hands of adults, not children. Therefore, while play helps the analyst observe and understand the child better, it is not useful for analysis. Again, real analysis can only begin after the Oedipal conflict has been resolved, the superego is independent of the parental figures, and full transference is possible. Prior to that time, the analyst must be, in effect, a kindly, trustworthy, but firm parent.

The early development of the superego that Melanie Klein described, as it appears in Susan Isaacs's book, *Social Development in Young Children,* has been discussed in chapter 3. It is a dramatic picture of the infant, helpless between his instinctual urges and parental denial of them. In fantasy, he takes into himself external moral authorities around him, only in more extreme form than they could ever be, since for him feelings are all-or-none, without the gradations and shadings that the future will bring. Thus he has internalized the voice of the parent, which is directed in full force upon the instinctual self, and subjects it to hostile and aggressive punishment for transgressions that the parents (in fantasy) would punish. Since, by projection, the infant assumes that the adults around him feel as strongly as he does, he senses himself at the mercy of dangerous hostile forces within and without when he encounters frustration, which is, of course, inevitable. Thus the Kleinian view of the superego is of a force far more harsh than original external adult forces, and even the most gentle forms of education and the kindest adults cannot keep the child from its attacks; indeed, being kind and gentle may make dealing with frustrations actually more difficult for him, since such adults clearly deserve his aggressive behavior so little. Then massive repression occurs, and complexes arise.

Here is where the analyst comes in. Far from doing damage by unleashing and/or gratifying the strong emotions of infancy, Melanie Klein believed that such feelings must indeed be expressed in order for analysis to be successful.

> Analysis replaces the process of repression, which is an automatic and excessive one, by a temperate and purposeful control on the part of the highest mental faculties.[151]

Klein felt there was no reason to restrict child analysis by establishing only positive transferences; rather, the whole gamut of feelings must be expressed, in play or in words, and then interpreted by the analyst. Indeed, she even says that Anna Freud's technique with children is actually to use a child's anxiety and guilt about forbidden feelings to attach the child to herself, whereas her own technique is to use them in the service of the analysis to attract both positive and negative transferences. Since anxiety is a mode of resistance, it must be expressed and interpreted, in order for it to be allayed. When that happens, the child's ability to fantasize is liberated and can be followed out, until fresh anxiety resistances or symptoms arise. And play is particularly useful in this process, especially with the small child, since it affords him a chance to represent fantasy indirectly. Play, then, shortens the route to the unconscious for the therapist.

Whereas Anna Freud believed that the superego was weak and unstable prior to latency, so that the analyst must do its work for it, Melanie Klein believed that its formation had occurred much earlier and therefore the work of the analyst was to mitigate its early harshness. And, whereas Anna Freud believed that relationships between parents and children would be endangered if the analyst went fully into the conflicts and feelings of hostility that children feel for parents, especially during the Oedipal period, Melanie Klein held that it was necessary to go into every relationship, every early experience and feelings, in order to tone down the superego's demands and achieve a better balance between inner wishes and outer reality. For her, as Flügel put it,

> successful treatment of neurotic conflict always means the renunciation by the super-ego of the more extravagant of its claims, . . . and readjustment on the part of the libido in the form of sublimation.[152]

Such, in brief outline, were the fundamental differences between Melanie Klein and Anna Freud, in interpreting and developing the basic Freudian findings. Yet there can be no doubt that Mrs. Klein's views were dominant in England. Despite Flügel's concern about the "disruptive effect" of the Klein-Freud argument, his own account of the formation of the superego is essentially Kleinian.[153] John Rickman's influential work *On the Bringing Up of Children* (1936), to which Susan Isaacs contributed two chapters, "The Nursery as a Community" and "Habit," speaks of Klein's work in glowing terms:

> The new researches have done more for us than add to our intellectual knowledge, they have given us an insight into the mind of the young child which has deepened our emotional and living understanding of that all-important bond—the relation between parent and child.[154]

Ernest Jones himself wrote the preface to Melanie Klein's review of psychoanalysis over the previous thirty years, *Developments in PsychoAnalysis* (1952). Susan Isaacs also had an important chapter in this book, "The Nature and Function of Phantasy," and, with Paula Heimann, another on "Regression." Jones states:

> Mrs. Klein's work of the past thirty years . . . has been attacked and defended with almost equal vehemence, but in the long run its value can be satisfactorialy estimated only by those who themselves make comparable investigations. . . . As is well known, I have from the beginning viewed Mrs. Klein's work with the greatest sympathy, especially as many of the conclusions coincided with those I reached myself. . . .[155]

In 1957, Rickman published his *Selected Contributions to Psycho-Analysis,* in which he gives an account of the formation of the superego that is still vintage Klein, and reads in part:

> The experience of the small infant leads it to regard its own impulses as dangerous to its security, for in its phantasy-experience, which to it is a part of reality, love and hate both tend to the disappearance of the object of desire.[156]

Finally, in a talk presented in Los Angeles in 1962, the prominent pediatrician, D. W. Winnicott, gave an account of the teaching he had received at Melanie Klein's hands:

> [I was] astounded by the insight which psycho-analysis gave into the lives of children. . . . I had no idea that what was being taught me was highly original. The thing was that it made sense, and joined up my case history detail with psycho-analytic theory. . . . For her a specific play with the toys was a projection from the child's psychic reality which is localized by the child, localized inside the self and the body [and which] provides glimpses into the child's inner world.[157]

Melanie Klein's earlier arrival in England and her forceful expression of her therapeutic findings over the intervening years had made her work especially influential there. When Anna Freud did arrive, she set up a separate clinic in Hampstead, where she and her father settled, and developed her own training program for analysts. The clinic and program, in Maresfield Gardens, still exist today, although they are not connected with the British Psycho-Analytic Society.

During the Second World War, Anna Freud and Dorothy Burlingham ran the Hampstead Nurseries, for children without families to care for them. It was supported by the American Foster Parents Plan of New York City, and detailed reports were written to this organization regularly. From this important wartime nursery came *Young Children in Wartime* (1942) and *Infants without Families: The Case for and against Residential Nurseries* (1943). *The New Era,* which had a worldwide readership, published many articles that were based on the work at Hampstead, such as "What Children Say about War and Death" (December 1942). Freud and Burlingham were anxious to study and record their observations of the effect on little children of being separated from their families, and to share their findings from the unique laboratory setting. Anna Freud has undoubtedly the greater international reputation today: her popular *Psycho-Analysis for Teachers and Parents* is still in print, and her honorary degree from Harvard University in 1980 attests to her continued importance.

A final note: although Susan Isaacs was very much a Kleinian, both because of her professional agreement with Klein's views and her strong personal bond to her, it is interesting to note that she actually embodies both Anna Freud's and Melanie Klein's ideas about the role played by adults in children's lives, but with a difference. Specifically, in her *Social Development in Young Children,* as discussed in chapter 3, she carefully distinguishes between the different roles played by a child's analyst and his or her teacher. With regard to the analyst, her description is completely Kleinian. But the role played by the teacher, the mild-but-firm authority, who controls the child's most aggressive behavior since it is still too libinidized for him or her to handle, is very close to the "educative" role that the analyst plays, for Anna Freud.

Cyril Burt

> It is the duty of the community, first, to ascertain what is the mental level of each individual child; then, to give him the education most appropriate to his level; and lastly, before it leaves him, to guide him into the career for which his measure of intelligence has marked him out.[158]

Such a statement would not be made today. When Cyril Burt wrote it, in the aftermath of the First World War, it was more acceptable. There was a real concern for the structure of a democratic society, which seemed to be disintegrating or at least on the decline. It seemed, therefore, that the best interests of the nation and of each child would be served by careful assessment of children's ability, by classification into groups according to ability, and by providing the most appropriate education for each group. Then young people would be ready to move into their destined places, smoothly and efficiently. And mental testing was a key element in that process.

In our less hereditarian times, it is hard to grasp that this view was widely held by thoughtful and humane people. One needs to examine, without prejudice, just how the assessment of ability was to take place. It is also hard to imagine that Susan Isaacs, so concerned for the "optimal growth" of every child, could be a colleague and coauthor with Cyril Burt, who has come under such obloquy recently.[159] Here, one needs to examine their common ground, especially in the early years of Burt's career.

For neither Cyril Burt nor Susan Isaacs ever believed that mental tests should be the sole basis for classification and both warned repeatedly against such an idea. While they did believe that heredity governed a child's level of intelligence, they also believed that every influence on the child by his social and physical environment must be taken into account. As Burt later put it:

> In education, equal opportunity means opportunity to make the most of differences that are innate.[160]

Both started from the whole child, understanding that heredity and environment interact to make him what he is and may become. Susan Isaacs, in considering intellectual and social development. repeatedly warned against any separation of these two aspects of growth, knowing from long experience with children that they affected each other constantly, in complex and often fruitful ways. Nor did she believe that growth comes in discrete stages, but rather as a manifold but unified, gradual process, with later capacities foreshadowed at earlier ages. As she put it in *The Children We Teach:*

> It is always the whole child who plays and laughs, who quarrels and loves, who thinks and asks questions, through all the hours of his day and all the years of his childhood. . . . [We face] the most profound problem of mental life, that of the relation between understanding and purpose, between the activity of knowing and those of wishing and feeling.[161]

Burt put the problem thus:

> What influence is exercised upon the performance, from age and intelligence, by various extraneous factors—by sex, by social status, by educational opportunity, and by emotional and moral disposition?[162]

In 1913, Burt had been employed by the London County Council as an educational psychologist, to help with the "detection and training" of special children, particularly the subnormal and the supernormal. As already discussed, there was a concern that defective and retarded children were multiplying more rapidly than any other segment of community, and that they would one day pass on their genes, to the detriment of the whole society. And there was equal concern felt that the best and brightest should be detected and given every opportunity to move the top ranks where they belonged. Burt soon found, by his very thorough investigation, that children who are "backward" in school may or may not be mentally defective: it was much more likely that environmental factors were keeping these children from using their ability in school. This view is nowhere more clear than in his early and influential book, *The Young Delinquent* (1925), and many themes in that book were picked up and amplified later in his *The Backward Child,* (1937). Together with *Mental and Scholastic Tests* (1921), these works show Burt at his best.

The Young Delinquent was clearly written, exhaustively detailed, sympathetic and commonsensical in outlook. He disagreed with the classic view held by Havelock Ellis, that criminals are moral defectives, throwbacks to a primitive level of civilization, and should therefore be weeded out like any other defectives. Burt countered:

> Delinquency I regard as nothing but an outstanding sample—dangerous perhaps and extreme, but none the less typical—of common childish naughtiness.[163]

Further, crime to him was not a self-contained act, punishable as such, but a symptom, "a mental symptom with a mental origin."[164] Therefore, it was important to inquire into its causes, especially with a youthful offender who might be helped to return to lawful behavior. Such an investigation might turn up just what influences he had been under, what his criminal deed meant to him from a psychological point of view, and what plans could be laid for his rehabilitation. Along the way, a variety of tests could and should be given, so as to arrive at a just estimate of the boy or girl's abilities or deficiencies that needed either remediation or encouragement. The use of psychoanalysis was also urged, to fill out the picture:

> What the method of mental testing does for the study of intellectual capacity, that the method of so-called psychoanalysis performs for the study of the growing character. By this and other expedients, by a scrutiny of all available records and reports, by renewed interviews with the child and his parents and his teachers, the investigator should at last be able to trace in fullest detail, the whole biography of the offending individual, and so gradually to discover what forces in the past have brought the child to where he now stands.[165]

So struck was he by the need of these children for complete psychological services that in appendix 2 of *The Young Delinquent* he laid out a careful plan for a child guidance clinic. This became the model for the London Child Guidance Training Centre, established in 1928, the first fully staffed center providing training for future professionals as well as the full range of services for children and their families. "In this development," says Hearnshaw, "Burt had been the essential catalyst."[166] Later, Burt established a one-year graduate training course at University College, London, with both theoretical and practical work for mature students, very much like that of Susan Isaacs at the Department of Child Development.

Thus neither Burt nor Susan Isaacs used mental testing alone to assess and classify children. Further, both knew that giving tests and taking data required training, skill, a "knack." Susan Isaacs warned:

> Mental tests are far from "fool-proof," and must never be thought of as a simple foot-rule to be applied mechanically by anyone. They are of value only in the hands of a trained and experienced person, alive to all the possibilities of error, and knowing how to avoid them. . . . the whole art of the tester is directed to putting a child at his ease in the test situation.[167]

She had already criticized Piaget for judging a child's cognitive level after asking questions that could so easily put him at a psychological disadvantage. The observant eye of an experienced clinician was needed to gain the fullest picture. Burt agreed, as his biographer reports:

> He was himself an acute observer of facial expressions and of gestures, and when it came to emotional traits he believed that the psychologist still

had to rely largely on observation. He was sceptical as to the value of questionnaires, and he regarded the tests available to the psychologist in the area of personality (association tests, projective tests, and measures of psychosomatic function) as of somewhat limited usefulness. At bottom Burt was a clinician, who had imbibed clinical skills from his medical father at a very early age, and in the course of his experience developed them to a fine art. Observers of him at work are unanimous that he had a flair for establishing easy rapport with his "cases", and remarkable powers of observation and clinical assessment.[168]

When interviewing a child, he began not with a stern cross-examination but often a simple test of mechanical ability, focusing on something objective and noncontroversial, "before the child's fears or tears are reexcited by any allusion to the actual trouble."[169]

It was on the basis of such skillful and sympathetic study that he found that neither backward nor delinquent children, although they seemed deficient in school, necessarily lacked intelligence.

They may be scholastically backward; they may be emotionally unstable; they may be morally unsound; in general intelligence, they are not defective. In the causation of juvenile delinquency . . . the preponderant psychological factors are, as a rule, not intellectual but emotional, not mental deficiency as revealed by tests, but repressed complexes (on a basis of temperamental instability) revealed by observation and analysis.[170]

This being the case, he warned against the "misleading implications of quasi-scholastic tests,"[171] especially in the hands of untrained people. Indeed, he warned the Hadow Committee and others for years against overemphasis on the 11+ examination, for he felt that it was an oppressive force on the work of the teachers preparing youngsters for it, and that it discriminated against the late bloomer: one does not "root up a Christmas rose because it fails to blossom in the spring."[172] Nor could he give more than a "faint and faltering recommendation"[173] for the Binet-Simon scale, for much more research and development were needed. Indeed, although Burt's *Mental and Scholastic Tests* was long a classic in the field of test use and design, he felt that his own recommendations in it were no more than tentative.

Mental testing, however, did spread rapidly both in England and in the United States, and Burt's warnings went largely unheeded. It seemed, as has been discussed already, a scientific, accurate tool to use in organizing, classifying, and planning for increasing numbers and less homogeneous groups of school children, as well as for eugenic measures.[174]

Burt's position on the heritability of intelligence remained the same throughout his life: he believed that it was the most consistent aspect of a child's development, and he felt that, properly used, mental tests could measure it "with accuracy and ease."[175]

Yet despite later criticisms, Burt was not a supporter of the status quo; rather, he worked for a society in which social class and opportunities were determined by ability and not birth. Like Susan Isaacs, he had not been born into affluent circumstances, and like her, too, he had risen by hard work, self-denial, and sheer ability. Both believed that others could do what they had done. Although Burt's investigations did find a very strong connection between a child's intelligence and the occupational status of his parents, nonetheless he felt that was wrong: the very fact that the working class was numerous meant that, statistically, some children of high intelligence were necessarily born within it, and they should be discovered and encouraged to work for scholarships to grammar schools, and for entry to university. He was discouraged that some boys (especially) who managed to do so either failed to stay with the course or did not do as well as their intelligence would have predicted, yet he laid that fact to environmental influences that could and should be ameliorated, so that talent would flourish.

However, except for the unusual child at either end of the bell-shaped curve, scholastic attainment seemed a sound indicator of cognitive ability. The average child in school grew one year in achievement for each year of schooling. Hence, Susan Isaacs felt, "our methods of teaching and general school conditions are well adapted to the needs of the average mass."[176] For both psychologists, teachers' estimates of a child's performance and his overall school record provided, by and large, a sound picture of his mental ability, and coincided to a great extent with that revealed by mental tests.[177] Yet since temperamental differences matter just as much, teachers should always use flexible methods, careful observation, and individualized work with all the children. Burt said:

> In the classroom of 50 years ago, the teacher believed that he ruled by fear; he would have thought it crazy to leave a set of children entirely to themselves and expect them, not merely to behave, but to press on with their work. In modern schools, where the cane has been abolished and "free discipline" set up, that is an everyday experience. . . . internal control takes the place of external control. . . . [there is] a tendency to trust rather than coerce.[178]

Nonetheless, it was important to both that children be assessed and grouped by ability, especially between the Infants' and Primary schools. Testing them any earlier was unwise, since their emotions and dependency on adults made results too unstable; but by age six or seven, the long-term intellectual differences between children had begun to increase, so that that was the optimum time for testing and classifying. Here the experienced tester would have to be especially careful with the exceptional children: their performance might "scatter" more than the average child's, or they might show greater emotionality in their response. All this might point to the unusual influence either of specific abilities that the general curriculum had not called out, or specific defects or instabilities that had been unnoticed in the large group work. In such circumstances,

> the use of quantitative methods in psychology [should] not supplant but ... supplement qualitative, introspective assessment.[179]

Similarly, Susan Isaacs had described her method of observation at the Malting House School as "qualitative" rather than "quantitative," and had called for many more equally detailed, long-term records of children's behavior under relatively free circumstances. Again, both psychologists were convinced of the need for research into child development and wide dissemination of its results, so that decisions affecting children's lives could be made on the basis of the fullest information available.

Cyril Burt's work took him further into psychometry, especially factor analysis; Susan Isaacs' educational and psychoanalytic interests moved her in different directions. Yet there was much common ground. They served as members of the British Psychological Society's Committee for Research on Education, of which she was the secretary. While at University College, London, Burt lectured to Susan Isaacs's students on measurement and statistics; she, in turn, lectured on child growth and development to his graduate students and acted as a tutor for some. And in 1933, their joint memorandum to the Hadow Committee, for its Report on Infants' and Nursery schools, drew this response: "We attach particular importance to the evidence we have received from Professor Cyril Burt and Dr. Susan Isaacs."

Recent criticisms of some of Burt's work have inevitably cast a shadow on all of it. Yet the contributions of the early part of his career should not be overlooked. After the most careful investigation, his biographer states:

> Up to the late 30's, I see no reason to regard Burt's work as other than basically sound, and his conduct as other than acceptable. If there were weaknesses, such as a certain vanity, some overconfidence in his pronouncements, and the inadequate reporting of evidence in early articles, these are venial failings, and such as anyone might have been guilty of. Had Burt died at the age of 60, his reputation would have been unblemished, and his standing as a psychologist generally acclaimed, even by those who differed from him in viewpoint.[180]

From today's position of sophisticated research methods and statistical analysis, Burt's early work seems casual, primitive, unreliable. And it is certainly true that in later life, he changed his reported results, altered the wording of publications, and even invented some facts to support his strongly held convictions. By then, however, his illness (Ménière's disease) was taking its toll, both physical and psychological.

All the same, Burt's earlier vision was important, because it highlighted the essential task of the psychologist—to marry his humanistic insight with the logic and methodology of the sciences. . . . Burt insisted that both should play a part in psychology. . . . it was a worthy ideal to have put forward, and deserves wider recognition than it has received.[181]

Hindsight is never 20/20. Our current concerns about the effect of classification and selective education and the discriminatory nature of methods used to clarify and segregate—these have made it easy to look back and find a scapegoat. These concerns are not new, however, nor can they be laid at Cyril Burt's door, for all his failings. As early as 1922, Walter Lippmann was asking just what it is that intelligence tests really test, and the long Lippmann-Terman debate started.[182] There was mounting criticism of the use of mental testing to classify children and thus determine their future: in 1953, Brian Simon *(Intelligence Testing and the Comprehensive School)* summarized the social class implications of England's tripartite system of schooling. The impact of environmental influences on children's performance in school has been increasingly emphasized, as well as the social and political implications of differential schooling. Thus, whereas Cyril Burt had been in the forefront of progressive thinking in his younger days, by the time of his death, at the age of ninety-three, he seemed all that was reactionary and conservative.

Maria Montessori

Maria Montessori enjoyed a very considerable vogue among progressive English educators, although Susan Isaacs and others were critical of both her claims and her methods. Nonetheless, it seemed to some that "the future, even in the years of World War I, lay with Montessori."[183] Edmond Holmes *(What Is and What Might Be)* wrote an enthusiastic account for the Board of Education of her Casa dei Bambini in Rome, which he had visited in 1911. Her book, *The Montessori Method,* was translated in 1912 and widely read. When she came to visit England in 1919, a large reception was held at the Savoy Hotel, with H. A. L. Fisher, chairman of the Board of Education, presiding. A thousand inquiries came in for her training course that year, and enough interest continued for her to hold a similar course every other year until World War II. The very first issue of *The New Era* (1920) contained an account of her revolutionary teaching methods, "Montessori and the New Era," as well as an article by the editor, Beatrice Ensor, "The Schools of Tomorrow," with a description of the Montessori schools prominent among them. Percy Nunn's celebrated *Education: Its Data and First Principles* also contained a most laudatory section[184] on the wonders of the Montessori method. With such supporters, her importance and influence were established.[185]

The reasons for Montessori's impact are not hard to find. The groundwork for child-centered education had already been well laid. To this she brought:

> a carefully constructed system based on experiment (or if that is too pretentious a claim, on trial and error), equipment which she said embodied her principles, a powerful personality, . . . and the respectability of the scientist and doctor.[186]

She had worked successfully with very difficult children—those who were retarded, and those who were slum dwellers—just the children about whom authorities and educators, from Binet to Burt, were deeply concerned. She not only condemned class teaching, but had devised a way that made individual work possible in a classroom, by designing and creating a set of carefully graded, self-corrective materials for the children, as well as directions for the part the teacher ("directress") should play in their use. She planned the school as a child-sized environment that was appealing in its very complete domestic arrangements. And her aims for education were couched in the very terms that progressives also used: "To direct the development of intelligence, of character, and of those latent forces which lie hidden in the marvellous embryo of man's spirit."[187]

Specifically, Montessori held that her method helped children both to learn and to be "good" because, first, their work was organized with exact attention to their needs—motor, sensory, and linguistic—and, second, they were left free to absorb themselves with the materials, at their own pace and by their own choice. The Casa dei Bambini was, as she put it, "a real house . . . a set of rooms with a garden of which the children are the masters."[188] There was a central "working" room, a bathroom, dining room, kitchen, parlor, dressing room, even a shop and a gym. The furnishings were real but small.

In this pleasant setting, often so different from their own homes, the children not only worked but also shared in the routines of everyday living. The working room was, of course, the heart of the school, and there the didactic materials were laid out, easily available on low shelves. There were also pictures, plants, flowers, a drawer for each child's possessions, and a piece of carpet for each one, on which he knelt when working with his chosen material. Considerable care was taken in teaching the children motor skills, since at first their activity was "disorderly." The directress, with only "a hint, a touch," taught "very precise actions:" how to sit and rise, how to pour from a pitcher, how to set a table and wipe it clean, how to pick something up or offer a cup, all efficiently and without noise. A line was drawn on the floor for the children to walk along, sometimes with quiet music playing.

> Once a direction is given to them the child's movements are made towards a definite end, so that he himself grows quiet and contented, and becomes an active worker, a being calm and full of joy.[189]

This is "discipline" in its best sense.

Sensory education by means of the didactic materials comprised the bulk of the children's activities during the school day. And, again, the directress had a specific part to play. Kneeling beside the child, not in front where she might distract his gaze, she might take out one of the three sets of cylinders, which varied in height, in diameter, and in both. She took out the cylinders "without letting them fall and without making too much noise,"[190] mixed them together, and then began to replace each in its correct hole. The child, if this activity were just right for him, soon became interested and took over from the directress.

> At this point there begins the process of auto-education. The aim is not an external one, that is to say, it is *not* the object that the child should learn how to place the cylinders, and *that he should know how to perform an exercise.* The aim is an inner one, namely, that the child train himself to observe; that he be led to make comparisons between objects, to form judgments, to reason and to decide, and it is in the indefinite repetition of this exercise of attention and of intelligence that a real development ensues.[191]

Similarly with all the materials, the directress showed how they were to be handled, lightly, quietly, gently, and then allowed the child to go ahead with them, undisturbed: "[she] may be always ready to supply the desired help, but may never be the obstacle between the child and his experience; [her attitude] is respect, calm, waiting."[192] Each piece of apparatus was replaced when the child was finished with it, but, if he used it incorrectly, it was taken away on the grounds that he was not ready for it, and should direct his attention to another.

Sometimes the children were blindfolded, so that they could focus on one sense at a time and make very fine discriminations. From time to time, the directress led them in "the lesson of silence." She sat still and so did they, in a relaxed, balanced position; the room was half-darkened; and gradually noises dropped away until there was complete stillness.

> It is almost the discovery of a new world, where there is rest. It is, as it were, the twilight of the world of loud noise and of the uproar that oppresses the spirit. At such a time, the spirit is set free, and opens out like the corolla out of the convolvulus.[193]

The directress closed this meditative period by whispering each child's name; the children rose silently one by one, and walked towards her.

"These children, with the grace of pages to a noble lord, are serving their spirits,"[194] and many came to prefer quiet to noise all day long.

Training in language was similarly planned: the directress would take two objects, state clearly that, "this is the large (or small) one;" then put them down and say, "Give me the large (or small) one;" and then ask, "Which is this?" while holding one in front of the child. This progression, from naming to recognition to saying the word, always referred not only to the objects but also to some quality by means of which the children learned to observe and express differences of shape, dimension, and so on.

Such motor and sensory experiences preceded writing, reading, and number learning, but led up to them in careful sequence: "The didactic material, in fact, does not offer to the child the 'content' of the mind, but the *order* for that 'content'."[195] And when writing and the other skills did come in their due sequence, the earlier experiences had prepared the child and would transfer to them. Writing, for instance, came only after many exercises training the hands to feel and to touch, after tracing geometrical cutouts, coloring within lines, feeling sandpaper letters; then came the "explosion into writing."

Montessori felt her methods had proven themselves, because the children at the Casa dei Bambini did respond. They loved the work, the orderliness and "grace" of the environment, and developed "spontaneous discipline." Because they had a free chance to develop their motor, sensory, and linguistic skills through satisfying and progressive work within this prepared environment, they had no need for anger or rebellion. Here, she felt, was the answer to innate good versus innate evil.

This brief sketch gives a sense of the way a Montessori school operated: the experience provided, the use of the materials, and the function of the teacher. Not everyone agreed that her claims for the effectiveness of these three components were justified. For instance, in large part because of her indifference to children's play, the English Froebelians could not support her work. Their kindergartens were based on Froebel's fundamental teaching about the great importance of play for children's growth, whereas her attitude was very different: "If I were persuaded that children needed to play, I would provide the proper apparatus; but I am not so persuaded."[196]

Paradoxically, although Percy Nunn was enthusiastic in his praise of Montessori, he too was devoted to the idea that play for children was vitally important. His eloquence spoke for the Froebelians as well as for himself:

> The spirit of play is an intangible and elusive sprite.... Childhood is her peculiar sphere, and ... she manifests her presence there in activities whose special mark is their spontaneity—that is, their relative independence of external needs and stimuli. In play, the child gradually enters into possession of his own body, and raises his command over it to the highest possible power; ... he finds and exercises in play his intellectual gifts and powers, and often discovers interests that are to fill the central

place in his adult life; . . . he finds and established his moral and social self largely in corporate games; . . . in the understanding of play lies the key to most of the practical problems of education; for play . . . shows the creative impulses in their clearest, most vigorous and most typical form. [They] are, in fact, continuous in the development of individuality. . . . All truly effective reform, both in education and society, is motived [sic] by the desire to enlarge as much as possible the field in which that central function of life may find worthy and satisfying exercise.[197]

One can only assume that Nunn's agreement with Montessori came more from her respectful attitude toward children, her progressive rhetoric, and her demonstrated success at the Casa dei Bambini, and less from an exact study of the method at work.

As early as 1915, before Montessori had yet visited England, William H. Kilpatrick, a prominent American Deweyan, had criticized her work as well.[198] He praised her contributions to education, as demonstrated by her effective day-care center in the worst slums of Rome; he approved of her basic view of education as development from within rather than imposition from without; he agreed that there should be less intervention and direction of children, and more letting them do what they can for themselves; and he praised her attempt to apply scientific, medical knowledge of children to a complete school procedure. However, Kilpatrick felt that her didactic materials were too unvarying and precise, too formal and remote from the real world. By neglecting imaginative, constructive, aesthetic play, her school was actually repressive: "The proposed curriculum proves inadequate and unduly restrictive, . . . too limited and controlled [with] relatively mechanical manipulations of very formal apparatus."[199] Real-life situations or problems, games, or imaginative play had no place for her. Yet for him, education was more than just development from within: "intelligent, self-directing adaptation to a novel environment," and to the "race achievements,"[200] or what Dewey called "the funded capital of civilization." Montessori's methods were too simple in conception, too mechanical in implementation, and too far from "first-hand contact with real, vital situations."

Susan Isaacs also felt that Montessori was seriously at fault for dismissing the role of play and the imagination, that her materials were really more limiting than facilitative of children's growth, and that her broad claims were at variance with what actually went on in her classrooms. Yet she acknowledged those aspects of Montessori's work that were helpful and appropriate for the children at the Malting House School, and she regularly recommended *Dr. Montessori's Own Handbook* to readers of her *Nursery World* columns as a source of good activities for children, although never without recommending others as well. Indeed, she had started by calling the Malting House School a "Montessori" school, and, although she later abandoned the title, she kept a set of didactic materials at the school for the children to use if they wished. Her "summary of activities" at the end of *Intellectual Growth* includes mention of the children's use of these materials, but, characteristically, they played with them imaginatively, not as Montessori would have approved. For instance, the rods of graduated lengths were used as walking sticks or guns, and only after adult suggestion did the children appreciate the formal relationships that they were planned to exemplify.[201]

But the Montessori method as a whole could not claim Susan Isaacs's full approval. For her, a school has a far broader purpose than Montessori's idea of "the education of the senses."

> a.) to provide for the development of the child's bodily and social skills and means of expression; and b.) to open the facts of the external world (the real external world, that is, not the school subjects') to him in such a way that he can seize and understand them. With the first purpose, everyone will agree; the second is a little more novel.[202]

And while Montessori would also have agreed with the first, the second went beyond her. For Susan Isaacs, the school should never be a "closed-in place, a screen between the child and his living interests," as she felt most schools, including Montessori's, were apt to be. For rather than providing for the "direct interests of the child in the concrete processes in the world around him," Montessori had:

> unfortunately given her genius for devising technique to the narrow ends of the scholastic subjects. In the exercises for practical life her humanity broke through the conventions of the school; but even so, more for the purposes of practical necessity than for the purpose of knowledge. These practical exercises seem to be, with her, the field of morals rather than the field of intelligence.[203]

Rather than let the conventions of the school stand between the child and real situations in the world, the school should be a "point of vantage" for him, "a clarifying medium" through which he has "ample occasion for the actual movement of [his] mind towards 'finding out' about the world around (him.)"[204]

Montessori had a very unusual group of children to deal with—slum dwellers who benefited from learning habits of order, quiet, and cleanliness—and the Malting House School children were quite different. Yet Susan Isaacs's criticisms related to all children: Montessori lacked any deep, psychological understanding of child development, and this lack caused her, among other things, to underestimate the influence of the adult, no matter how passive, on the children. The Montessori directress could not be just a bystander or observer, but inevitably a participant, a controlling influence, who set the tone and the expectations for the child's behavior. Indeed, Montessori did speak of the teacher's responsibility to "suppress, destroy" any rough, ill-bred, or dangerous actions[205] and to inculcate the "invaluable habits of discipline and obedience." Here Montessori seemed to be making use of conventional aims of education, but instead of enforcing them by outside pressure, "turns them into the natural pattern of the child's own life" in her school, claiming that only by developing such habits can the spirit of the child be freed. That is, not until he is orderly, controlled, and quiet can he focus properly on the material which will be the means of his "auto-education."

Here both of the Isaacses and Montessori came to "the clear parting of the ways." The Isaacses began, like Montessori, with the individual child and insisted that he alone can ensure his own education, but their view of that child was radically different. Sense training, the centerpiece of Montessori's education, was for them an important but peripheral part of the whole process.

> Children from the very beginning are individual selves and agents, doers and sufferers, in constant interaction with the world—human and physical—around them. They have on the one hand their intensely dramatic and fateful affective history, yet on the other also their cumulative intellectual story of actively exploring and manipulating their world, experimenting and effect-producing within it, learning about it, and physically building up its pattern.[206]

Children are makers of meaning and, as the process of living shapes them, so they understand it and shape themselves as well. Educators can assist by supporting and strengthening all the self-educative forces within them, but not by Montessori's way of narrowing their experience, formalizing their modes of expression, or closing off the real world from them.

> The outstanding fact is the flat incompatibility of her proclaimed gospel of freedom and spontaneity with her intensely directive doctrine of actual training. [She says,] "Kindness consists of interpreting the wishes of others, in conforming one's self to them, and sacrificing, if need be, one's own desire. This is the kindness which we must show towards children." Only kindness is not enough, there must be true psychological understanding too, and by this criterion the main doctrine of her volume does seem to me just to fail.[207]

7
In Conclusion

During an unusually active and varied career, Susan Isaacs became an important figure in the expansion of child-centered ideas, in education and in child care, as well as in the growing fields of child psychology and especially psychoanalysis. Her ability to put complex theories into simple terms was in constant demand throughout her life. And she demonstrated in all the different arenas in which she chose to work the vital and interactive relationship between an understanding of the theory of human development and actual, helpful involvement with children and adults. The origin of her work lies in her early desire to do something to benefit humanity, a wish that gradually became focused on children. But Susan Isaacs was more than an interesting historical figure or even an exemplar: her work is still of value to those with responsibility for children. Two aspects stand out: her explication of the way in which children make use of the reality around them in the process of coming to understand the world and themselves; and the role of adults in that process, both in providing settings where the child's real needs and interests are met, and in interacting with the child.

Children, especially as infants, use reality primarily as a "canvas" on which to project inner feelings and fantasies; they are not yet aware of much difference between inner and outer reality. Susan Isaacs demonstrated how intensely children feel, how rich a fantasy life they have, and how they need the outer world for projection and a growing sense of self. Another use of reality is, of course, to provide children with ways to reach out, to test their abilities as they develop, to explore and figure out how things work. Reality is, then, the critical source of cognitive development. This reaching out and learning about the world has emotional benefits as well, and one remembers Susan Isaacs's long-held conviction that learning is an important way in which children achieve stability and happiness, especially if the reality that surrounds them appears in ways they can understand and master.

Here, also, her discussion of the relationship between maturity and experience is relevant: clearly maturity "sets the ceiling" to what a child can grasp, but it cannot produce understanding unaided by experience in the real world. A home that provides a little child with a variety of experiences and materials to engage with, in a well-protected setting, does much to help him grow in every way. Later on, the school can work in a similar way on a larger scale, especially if it is founded on the educational principles that Susan Isaacs worked out in such detail.

Further, an environment that is truly accessible to the child provides him with the chance to feel safe from his own at times frightening or hostile urges. In fact, he cannot destroy a real adult, no matter what his fantasies tell him, just as opening a real closet door shows there is no monster inside. Thus the opportunity to deal constructively with reality is critical in allaying fears and guilt. It proves to him that

> those whom he loves are not at the mercy of his own ungovernable instincts but are firmer and stronger and more reliable than he.... If the real external control is firm and secure, but mild and tempered, it enables the child to master his destructive impulses and to learn to order and adapt his wishes to the real world. If he neither finds fulfillment of his phantastic dreads in the outer world, or is left at their mercy in his inner world by having no external supports but is slowly educated by a tempered, real control, mild and understanding, appropriate to each situation as it arises, he is led forward on the path of reality and towards all those indirect satisfactions in the real world, the sublimatory activities.[1]

This analysis of the uses of reality for the growing child means, in practical terms, an emphasis on the importance of play, when that is understood to mean any activity chosen for its own sake. Play may mean building blocks for the little child, taking an engine apart for the older child, or paints and brushes for the adult. But the opportunity for free play, especially for children, provides practical situations for imaginative exploration, cognitive manipulation, and symbolic working through.

Susan Isaacs's discussion of the child's use of reality placed great importance, too, on the value of language. Since language is the unique tool that bridges the inner world and the outer in expressive experience, it follows that every chance should be afforded for the fullest use of language, spoken, read, or written, even at the expense of silence and order. Among early progressive teachers, in fact, conversation and informal discussions regularly preceded formal study of reading and writing, in the belief that oral use of language is a critical early step in both social and intellectual growth.

Further, it follows from this view of reality that every child has a unique way of learning, that subject matters cut up into apparently logical systems satisfy the adult mind more than the child's, and that any subject can be "intellectual," depending on the way in which it is handled—discovery and inquiry can be applied anywhere. Susan Isaacs speaks of "real reality, not school subjects," meaning a reality accessible to children. Since children use their own set of associations, fantasies, and intuitive processes to approach subjects, then room must be made for these ways of learning.

These ideas were not new. But Susan Isaacs was one of the first to provide a sound, thoroughgoing analysis of the deeper springs of the developmental processes, the sources of creativity and cognition, of love and hate, of hostility and aggression, of sexuality, guilt, and shame; she also pioneered in applying these understandings to specific situations in homes and schools, showing just what kind of reality can lead to a stable and serene approach to the world. In her work with children and in her advice to others, she always made very plain just how crucial adults are in a child's development. Again, this was not new, but her explication of the "prestige" of the adult in the child's eyes, and the need for wisdom and forbearance bears emphasis. The letters she wrote to troubled parents and nurses, her research methods and the data she worked with, her courses in child development, and the books that she wrote reflecting her experience—all delineate the vital contribution that a mature adult can make to the child.

In her two books about the work at the Malting House School, which one recalls was deliberately planned as both a school and a psychological laboratory, she describes the methods used there as they were gradually and carefully developed. There were positive conditions and also limitations for the children. The discipline was founded on a reasonable, concrete basis: children were protected from themselves and others; they had to put away materials they had finished with; they were not to interfere with the work of others; they must undertake communal responsibilities. But obedience was not demanded for its own sake, nor were moralizing or blaming used to gain compliance and control. Sometimes the adults simply withdrew their usual attention and support for a time. Whenever possible, the natural outcomes of a child's acts served as reinforcement.

Language was used carefully: requests or directives were kept simple, clear, and straightforward, and, when fully understood, adhered to with consistency; the children were given "almost complete verbal freedom;" aside from excretory talk and spitting, no comment was out of place, conflicts were talked over rather than fought out, and questions fully discussed. Adults used their own language judiciously to respond to and extend or deepen an initial expression of interest toward a more sustained inquiry, but not to give ready-made explanations, for they understood that the knowledge most worth having is how to deal with problems and grasp their meaning. They joined in with the children in their chosen activities, and they also engaged in adult-level activities, especially those that supported or might extend the children's own, such as systematic gardening; modeling in clay; playing the piano for singing, dancing, or marching; reading good stories aloud; arranging flowers and leaves attractively—in general, setting examples of civilized adult behavior that the children could identify with and gradually imitate.

In Conclusion

The adults also took seriously and recorded objectively every aspect of the children's behavior, pleasant or unpleasant, setting limits on language or actions only as needed. By providing a rich and varied environment, by encouraging children's activities within it, and by responding to them deliberately, they used what Basil Bernstein calls an "invisible pedagogy"[2] that allowed the children wide latitude in their choice of occupation, and gradually shaped them by indirection and example, rather than by direction or precept.

It may well be asked if there is evidence that Susan Isaacs's way of educating children at the Malting House School worked. Certainly it seems appealing and humane, if difficult to accomplish. Although the school was set up as a laboratory, no longitudinal study of any of the children has been done, so there is no evidence of that kind, aside from purely anecdotal remembrance. Yet daily records were kept, and *Social Development in Young Children* includes the results of the children's gradual development, over the three and a half years of the school's existence, toward "free social cooperation, rich aesthetic achievement, and bold intellectual inquiry." And although three years is not a lifetime, it is a considerable portion of the life of a young child. The road was not easy and there were definite phases in accomplishing this successful outcome,* but as one reviewer put it: "How often is good behavior and social conformity purchased at exactly the price of these qualities?" From Cambridge's "worst children" they became the most "amiable" and easy to manage.

Yet another source of confirmation exists: when Susan Isaacs began to teach advanced students of child psychology and practicing teachers, building on her Malting House experience (as well as her psychoanalytic work), her audiences felt that her theory and methods deriving from it provided them with a sound basis for what, in perhaps a less systematic way, they had long been doing effectively. The history of English informal or child-centered education[3] shows that such practices had been going on for a long time, with clear successes and high standards of achievement. So effective were such methods that when the Plowden Report was written in 1967, it reported that about a third of the maintained (tax-supported) schools in England were using them. While that is not 100 percent or even an actual statistic, it does show that a substantial number of teachers and heads in the mainstream of English education had found that they worked. And many have testified to the importance of Susan Isaacs's support of their work ("Then I knew where I was," said one) both in explicating the whole realm of child growth and development very fully and clearly, and in making practical suggestions for what steps to take in classrooms.

In the past few decades, there have been many books written about

---

*See also Part Two for an extended discussion of this development, "A Contribution to the Social Psychology of Young Children."

children and teachers who have worked together in schools that, while not always identical in method to the Malting House, nonetheless were essentially child-centered. Together, they show that such methods do produce results, that children learn better and are also happier, socially and individually. One much-neglected, quite long-range American study, the National Education Association's Eight-Year Study, considered students during the four years of high school and then in college: graduates from the schools that emphasized student choice and responsibility, creative arts of all kinds, interdisciplinary work, and informal relationships with adults showed significantly more self-reliance, flexibility, ability to solve problems, and creativity as well as academic achievement.

Further, Susan Isaacs's pedagogical method was not essentially different from the child-rearing practices she advocated, and there is modern research evidence that there are truly wise and effective ways to help children grow.[4] Adults who are able to establish good loving relationships and make use of their innate abilities are those who have been well and wisely loved as little children; and those who have difficulty coping with the world and abuse or neglect their children were usually badly treated themselves as children. In short, what DeMause described as the "helping mode" of child rearing does seem to bear fruit, both emotionally and cognitively, since it is allied most closely to children's natural mode of development.

Yet another question arises: why are not more schools and homes run on these lines? If Susan Isaacs's methods and those of like-minded teachers are so truly congruent with the developmental forces in children, and if they do in fact prove themselves in practice, why are they not more widespread, instead of being viewed with some hostility or at least suspicion?

For one cannot say that Susan Isaacs was a lone pioneer. She takes her place in an illustrious company: the history of Western educational thought includes a strong bias toward child-centered education. Philosophers from Plato to Dewey, whatever their other differences, knew that there is no vision of a good society that does not imply a philosophy of education, that is, a set of ideas about the nature of man, about knowledge and knowing, and about how the young should be reared to achieve the goal of a society that values maximum satisfaction and excellence for the individuals within it. Such an education must begin by observing and respecting the inborn nature of children, and then building on it as they grow in knowledge and character.

Among practitioners, too, one remembers Tolstoy at Yasnaya Polyana and Pestalozzi at Yverdun, both working with village children in natural, understandable ways that were based more on the children's experience than on the purely verbal, traditional education of the time. These are famous, if isolated examples, but toward the turn of this century and during the "progressive" era, there were scores of child-centered schools established, as *The New Era*'s lists prove, all over the world. Some were founded by single, charismatic figures whose schools could not outlive them; others by aristocrats and intellectuals who wanted a better school for their children than the locality provided; still others were taught by well-educated and devoted women in rural or small village settings, or in cities among the poorest children. There are, in fact, many examples of humane and effective teaching even in unlikely areas and with unpromising populations of students, as well as with the rich and well-born. For the dream persists that children, given appropriate adult help, really do know best how to grow themselves up; but the dream, however appealing, however well-adapted to the nature of children, has never been realized in the majority of the settings, home or school, where adults and children meet. It is not everyone's dream.

While one does not wish to indulge in socioeconomic stereotyping, there are sociological and psychological data concerning the social-class aspect both of child-rearing practices and school expectations that cannot be overlooked. Such data center around ideas of authority relationships, the tolerance (or lack of it) of play and playfulness, and the importance of the context in which language between adults and children is habitually used.

Nathan Isaacs himself saw the problem of the favorable sociological climate that child-centered techniques and values seemed to require. In his "Children's Why Questions," he discussed the inapplicability to working-class children of just those methods that encourage activity and the development of individual interests, and assumed that children bring to school a lively curiosity and a willingness to act upon it.

> [for] those under the economic and other pressures of our poorer classes, a very large proportion if not the majority of elementary school children . . . there seems to be an air of mockery about "epistemic" or "causal" interest in their case. Cognitive development remains overlaid in them by all of the environmental pressures, and usually gets no chance at all of emerging, beyond the minimum adaptation needed for survival, as an independent, voluntary interest.[5]

Susan Isaacs, too, was frank in recognizing that the children at the Malting House School were from professional families, with high intelligence and favored homes. Therefore, she knew that her methods could not be simply copied in any kind of school, but hoped that they might serve as useful starting points for other teachers' investigations of successful teaching methods in their own particular settings.

Yet it seems that poverty alone does not predict the failure of child-centered methods.

> Observers of "lower working class" culture have noted the arbitrary nature of child-rearing practices in this sub-culture. . . . A characteristic of arbitrary child nurture is the frequent use of categoric statements (for example, "Because I tell you," "Because I'm your father"), dependence

on which reinforces the personal at the expense of the impersonal or task-related. It limits the possibilities of future learning and of varied behaviour; it affects reactions to authority in general.[6]

If true, then educational ideas and practices that encourage learning through problem solving and inquiry, asking questions, following up on interests, and evaluating different explanations must necessarily be dissonant with what happens in the home, and children with different backgrounds will be likely to fail school. Independent behavior at school may be punished at home as disobedience; "messing about in science"* may be considered simply messy; asking searching questions of the teacher may be insolence to parents at home.

> Lower class parents are more concerned with good behaviour than with psychological states; they want obedience, cleanliness and neatness, compared with the relatively greater middle class emphasis on such psychic states as curiosity, happiness, and consideration.[7]

This is certainly not to say that working-class parents love their children less or are not anxious for their mental health and successful adaptation to the world; their child-rearing practices simply differ from those of the middle class, it seems. But when the classroom and its teacher are middle class, when this context is therefore filled with middle-class ways of behaving and expectations, the working-class child is at a disadvantage.

> In this climate of arbitrary [home] social relationships authority has either to be repudiated or obeyed: it functions as a moral imperative and not hypothetically as advice to be tested for its efficacy in promoting one's own objectives. And the child who accepts this sort of arbitrary authority will become disposed to see his mistakes not as things from which he can learn, but as shortcomings which indicate only a need for greater "training, instruction, and obedience," if he is ever to get things right.[8]

According to this view, the function of the school, for working-class parents, is to teach children the skills and behavior that they will need later at work, and teachers should be judged accordingly. This is what Bernstein calls a more "visible" pedagogy, where lines of authority are clear, skills and curriculum are laid out ahead of time for mastery, and grades assigned accordingly.

> The basic competencies which it is transmitting of reading, writing, and counting in an ordered explicit sequence, make sense. The failures of the children are the children's failures, not the school's, for the school is apparently carrying out impersonally its function.[9]

---

*I am indebted to David Hawkins for this phrase, which is in turn derived from Kenneth Grahame's *The Wind in the Willows*.

Yet while some aspects of this more structured pedagogy are "visible," others are less so: Philip Jackson's discussion of the "hidden curriculum"[10] lays bare the other "3 R's" that every child must master in order to be successful in school, namely rules, regulations, and routines.

Seen from a slightly different but closely allied point of view, in an industrialized, capitalistic society, school is clearly preparation for work; children may be considered raw material to be processed and turned out as nearly alike as possible, and schools are basically the institutional mechanisms for slotting children into future occupational levels on the basis of their demonstrated school achievement.

> Education was fashioned into an increasingly refined training and selection mechanism for the labor force. The schools' effectiveness then could be judged by how well success in school predicted success at work. While the character of work is changing, the schools' role as the primary labor training and selection mechanism continues.[11]

In the best interests of their children's future, then, working-class parents cannot afford to let them play around.

The distinction between work and play is critical here. For central to the concept of child-centered methods is the idea of play, which stresses individual self-expression, spontaneity, open-ended inquiry, activities engaged in for their intrinsic interest and reward. Schools that prepare children for work instill in them the behavior characteristic of the workplace: habits of obedience and conformity; deference to the authority structure; evaluation on the basis of external standards; the basic skills of literacy and numeracy without which no one can be employed. That is, school is work and not play.

> To the traditional notions of order, regimentation, and vocationalism, the child-centered school opposed spontaneity, freedom, and self-expression. . . . This more "natural" schooling process fits in nicely with the trend in middle-class ideas, away from repression and externally imposed discipline, toward greater freedom; and happiness in learning seemed to be linked with higher levels of achievement.[12]

For middle-class children, what goes on in school carries its own reward, just as the kind of work they will engage in later is expected to be intrinsically rewarding, combining "inner pleasure and outer prestige."[13] For working-class children, school is not a place to play but to work, just as later the job will be work, and playfulness must be confined to holiday times.

In successful child-centered schools, parental expectations were quite different. Looking at a number of famous experimental schools, one is struck by the fact that their founders were often of quite superior socioeconomic status; it was Count Tolstoy who taught children in his home; Lord and Lady Russell who founded Beacon Hill; and Harvard University's president Charles William Eliot who founded Shady Hill. And certainly Geoffrey Pyke was a millionaire who could afford to give his son the schooling he deemed best. The children in such schools could be allowed to play, and their future status was not the overriding issue.

At places like Summerhill, wealthy parents sent their children, especially those who had been troublesome elsewhere, to see what could be done for them. A. S. Neill insisted on absolute support for his methods and noninterference from the parents, or else he would not accept the child. The school's success clearly depended on a mutual understanding between master and parent. So too, although in a less extreme way, teachers in rural or village settings were careful to include parents in every way possible, so that there was communication and acceptance of the school throughout the community, whether it was Oxfordshire (Edith Moorhouse), Yorkshire (Dorothy Simpson), or rural New Jersey (Julia Weber Gordon). Parents came to the school to help or attend performances: the teacher visited the homes of her children and was a familiar and well-accepted friend. Again, the parents knew and approved of what the school was doing, for the children seemed to be getting on and to be happy about it. By contrast, perhaps one reason for the success of inner-city schools, where they have existed, has been in part the fact that the public schools had given up on the children, many parents were equally apathetic, and so teachers, like George Dennison in New York City, were not interfered with. But when "the system" did move in, however, such experimental "playful" schooling came to an end.[14]

It is hard to generalize about successful child-centered schools, since they do vary so much in location and in social class status. But critical to their success is the additional factor of the language they used. Bernstein's analysis[15] is instructive here, with regard to social class differences in linguistic performance. In schoolrooms, the medium of exchange is primarily language, in all its forms, but especially oral. If children come from an arbitrary, authoritarian home, in which the linguistic context is "restricted," they are not accustomed to using language flexibly, experimentally, spontaneously. Rather, the language that they know and can use tends to be narrow in focus, bound by a more limited linguistic context in which meanings are not to be questioned. Other children, with different home experiences, grow up in linguistic contexts that encourage an "elaborated" code of linguistic performance, more flexible and experimental, responsive, open-ended, and conceptual, so that the child can move beyond the given context to imagine others, and is thus released for wider linguistic experiences.

Since children perceive their relationship to the teacher as similar to those at home,[16] they generate language in school as they do at home. Often this means a conflict between working-class children, again, who face middle-class teachers and linguistic contexts with which they are unfamiliar.

And when the speech of the teacher and the school is valued as the correct or standard speech, the working-class child is in double jeopardy, and cannot gain the satisfactions from school that might otherwise be his. The problem, then, is not that a working-class child has a language deficiency or a different and unacceptable dialect, or that he cannot generate highly elaborated speech in other settings: the problem, is the conflict with the context in which the child has learned his language performance. "One of the effects of the class system is to limit access to elaborated codes."[17] Yet those codes are exactly what child-centered classrooms are built around, and to a very great extent are what conceptual thought requires for its development, as the Isaacses and Piaget made so clear; even moral character is based on conceptual progress, so fundamentally linguistic in nature:

> In fact, the moral achievement of man, the whole complex of factors that go into the organization of the conscience, is very largely based upon language.[18]

There is yet one other factor in the relationship between adults and children that makes child-centered practices less likely to be used: it is the sad fact that some adults do not or can not love the children for whom they are responsible, but actually resent them. They are authoritarian, anxious about control and obedience, intolerant of play, indifferent to children's needs even when openly expressed. This set of attitudes cuts across class lines and has little to do with language, and it is nothing new. Hostility between the generations is an old story both in individual family settings and in society at large.[19] It seems to stem from the deepest sources of our instinctual nature. Freud taught, and recent research by ethnologists and psychologists is corroborating,[20] that we are indeed the products of our biological and evolutionary past and that our most basic instincts are made of impulses to love and to be aggressive. Indeed, it seems that within species of animals where "stable and permanent partnerships for the propagation of the young"[21] exist, aggressive behavior also exists. Other behavior is developed among members of such species, however, to channel aggressive behavior away from the loved partner, in order to preserve that vital bond. So also with human beings, including the bond between the child and his earliest love partners, his parents.

> It is because the loved person is valued above all other things that the child gradually modifies his aggressive impulses and finds alternative modes of expression that are sanctioned by love. [This] has produced in man great love, great work, and the highest moral attainments.[22]

But where the basic bond has not been established early, there follow "diseases of non-attachment . . . the incapacity of the person to form human bonds."[23]

> Because tenderness or even obligatory parental postures were never a part of their experiences, they are indifferent to their young, sometimes "inhumanly cruel," as we say, except that cruelty to the young appears to be a rare occurrence outside of the human race. . . . in early childhood, the love bond normally serves the redirection of aggression from the love object.[24]

And where it has not successfully served this purpose

> the potential for violence and destructive acts is far greater among these bondless men and women; the absence of human bonds leaves a free "unbound" aggression to pursue its erratic course.[25]

Both Susan Isaacs's and Anna Freud's wartime studies of dislocated children show that, where the family bond is strong, it provides a stability and energy that stands the child in good stead; where it is weak, children do not thrive. They show poor attachment capacity, low intellectual and conceptual functioning, restricted or even retarded language, and poor control of their aggressive impulses.

Child abuse and neglect have deep roots, then. DeMause's description of what happens when an adult is confronted by a child who needs his help is again à propos: when a child is needy, frightened, dependent, or in conflict, adult anxiety can be aroused in response, bringing to the situation the leftover feelings of an unsatisfactory childhood, which have nothing to with the needs of the child himself. The promotion of a child's creative and intellectual faculties can help him overcome his inner fears and problems, as we know, but only if excessive and inappropriate demands are not made upon him by the adults around him, and if he can follow his own tendencies without dictation. This can only happen if those adults are relatively free from inner conflict or deprivation themselves, for where adults are not free, children cannot be.

Yet play also has very ancient roots, reaching far back in evolution. Animals play just as human beings do, and they also form love bonds and engage in aggression. In human culture, play is both a function and source of some of our most basic, assumed "forms of social construction."

> The great archetypal activities of human society are all permeated with play from the start. Take language, for instance—that first and supreme instrument. . . . In the making of speech and language the spirit is continually "sparking" between matter and mind, as it were, playing with the wondrous nominative faculty. Behind every abstract expression there lie the boldest of metaphors, and every metaphor is a play upon words. Thus in giving expression to life man creates a second, poetic world alongside the world of nature.[26]

So too with myth and ritual, developed and engaged in for their own sake, for the intrinsic efficacy which they possess:

Now in myth and ritual the great instinctive forces of civilized life have their origin: law and order, commerce and profit, craft and art, poetry, wisdom and science. All are rooted in the primaeval soil of play.[27]

Froebel had said that "play is a child's work." When Piaget was studying the moral development of children, he investigated the rules of games children play, and the stages they go through in understanding and abiding by them. Susan Isaacs, among many others, knew well how important play was for children: for working through fantasies and fears, for establishing social norms, for make-believe "as if" situations. Melanie Klein and Anna Freud, in their different ways, used play as an essential tool of therapy with young children. Children's play seems to be at one end of a long continuum, just as their early expressions of interest in the world are the beginnings of ordered adult knowledge. "Playful education," then, seems again, the method most in tune with children's nature, and most likely to promote adult culture.

However, there are the powerful forces noted above, both individual and social, that work against child-centered practices, and perhaps it is surprising that they have been successful at all. Some teachers, like some parents, are able to study their children realistically and objectively, grasp and work to meet their needs and overcome whatever limitations they possess, and help them move, step by step, "toward all those indirect satisfactions in the real world, the sublimatory activities," as Isaacs put it. For she knew, as Freud had written, that the redirection of hostile instincts toward positive, creative, and cooperative activities is the road to mental health, and ultimately the hope of civilization.[28]

Susan Isaacs's essay, "Modification of the Ego through the Work of Analysis," which describes the outcomes of satisfactory psychoanalysis, speaks of personal qualities that seem to be just those possessed by successful educators, whether parents or teachers. First, the patient comes to accept libidinal wishes more realistically and to find appropriate ways to satisfy them, either directly or through various modes of sublimation; second, all bodily pleasures become freer and more acceptable, and general health improves, as the patient is relieved of the need to resort to any physical symptoms to mask feelings, fantasies, or memories; third, the patient's sense of reality becomes firmer and more trustworthy, with an increase in the ability to judge things objectively; fourth, parents and other early adult figures of power are seen in their more just proportions, neither as monsters nor villains, but as real if fallible people; fifth, the distinction between inner psychic reality and outer objective reality is heightened and the denial of their difference is lessened; sixth, the patient experiences a "general lessening of rigidity of feeling and attitudes toward other people and towards himself, a lessening tendency to compulsive repetition of early patterns of his life," a freer ability to respond flexibly to changing situations in the real world; and seventh, there is a "great enrichment of feeling, in depth and variety and spontaneity." Anxiety is lessened; guilt, fear, hatred, and anger can be accepted and dealt with; and the capacity for feelings of love is much enhanced.[29]

Susan Isaacs must have experienced these healing changes in herself, in addition to having had the satisfaction of bringing them about in her patients. This is not to say that all parents and teachers should go into psychotherapy, but it is to urge them to take very seriously the emotional dimension of adult-child relationships in general, and the learning process in particular, for themselves and for the children. When this is done, homes and schools can be therapeutic for all their inhabitants. Adults and children can grow together toward a society, in Dewey's words, "more worthy, lovely, and harmonious."

Part Two

Selected Documents

Part Two presents some selected documents written by Susan Isaacs, and one by her husband. The first group includes sample columns from *The Nursery World,* a weekly magazine for parents and nursemaids, in which Susan Isaacs as "Ursula Wise" answered letters from subscribers who were having difficulty in bringing up children. The second group includes a number of brief pieces, on a variety of topics, that are relatively unavailable elsewhere. And the final selection is an essay by Nathan Isaacs, chosen because it shows so clearly his thinking in relation to his wife's.

1
"Ursula Wise" Columns

LEADER *or* FOLLOWER?
The Nursery World
November 13, 1929

I had a letter recently from a father, who wrote to ask whether I thought that anything could be done to ensure that his children "would not shirk responsibility" when they were grown up, and would be "leaders rather than followers."

Such a question, from one who has the wisdom to look far ahead into his children's future, reminds us that the nursery world is but a part of the larger world of social life. In our ways of helping the development of our children we have to remember what the larger world will demand of them. Even in the nursery years we need to think of what children are to grow into as well as what they are at the moment. We don't nowadays, for instance, live in the sort of society where everything is built upon authority. It would be much simpler for parents if we did. But, in fact, we have to prepare our children for a social life based very largely upon the responsibility of the individual and upon mutual services. And so this particular question lies very near to the heart of our problem as educators.

But it has to be said at once that there are no certain recipes for ensuring that any particular child will be a leader rather than a follower, any more than there are sure and certain ways of making him into an artist or a musician. Such things depend in the last resort upon one's native mental gifts and trends. But we certainly can do much to encourage the development of any social abilities our children may have, or to check and inhibit them.

To begin with, a little thought will remind us that the child can only learn to exercise responsibility by having it. He learns to walk by trying to walk; he learns to swim by swimming; to dance by dancing. He can't learn by mere teaching in words, nor by the power of our wishes, but only by his own efforts corrected by his own experience. Even the best teaching in, for example, writing or playing cricket or talking French can only come home to him through his own effort and actual experience. This is equally true of social behaviour. It is useless for us to say, "Be responsible, be a leader, not a follower," unless we translate this into real and concrete opportunity. We need to give him things to be responsible for. Even the young child can have the responsibility for the arrangement of his own toy cupboard, the spending of his own pocketmoney (no matter how little that is), the choice of what to do in his playtime, of the playmates he will invite to tea, of what he will do with his own piece of garden, of the places he will go to on his afternoon walk. If we want him to learn to choose for himself we need to give him the chance to choose on as many real occasions as possible. And when we do give him the choice in this way it should be a genuinely free choice, and not a pretence of one. If, for example, we tell him to choose whom he will invite to tea, and then try hard to persuade him to invite a child he doesn't want, because perhaps *we* think "he's such a nice little boy," or for any reason of our own, then it isn't really the child's choice, and it would be better not to pretend that it was. There are so many ways in which the child has to accept our views and our arrangements, that when we do give him choice and responsibility it should be a genuine gift. Such practical responsibility is a most valuable training.

Another thing is clear, also. If we want our children to be socially responsible, it is essential to give them plenty of the companionship of other children from their early years. The solitary child, or the child who only sees others at occasional tea-parties cannot learn either to lead or to follow well. He may try to get his own way by squabbling and fighting; but he can only become a real leader by understanding other people and by having learnt to co-operate with them. And this can only come about through the sharing of work and play with other children in everyday group life. For some part of every day young children between infancy and school age should enjoy a time of free play with other children, if possible not very much older or younger. And in that time of play they should be as free from adult interference as possible. Within the real limits of physical safety they should be left to play as they will. In this way, they learn vividly from each other that other people's wishes are real also, and that if there are leaders there must be followers. They learn this from the real, concrete experience of the give and take of social life in a way that no words of ours can possibly teach.

The child's need for companionship is as great as his need for shelter and comfort. Without such real social experience he cannot grow into a responsible social being at any age.

YOU *MUST* OBEY!
The Nursery World
November 20, 1929

Last week we were prompted by the question of a father to discuss the problem of training children in responsibility. This week I have had a number of letters from parents about a problem as old as parenthood itself—that of how to get children to obey us. This is really the reverse side of last week's question. We pointed out then that the ways of the nursery need to bear some relation to what will be asked of our children in later social life. And this applies here also. It would clearly be a mistake to train our children in ways of behaviour that would unfit them for the demands of the larger world, no matter how easy that makes life in the nursery itself. And yet, of course, they aren't *yet* responsible beings, and we can't treat them as if they were. What we ask of them has to be suited to their needs and powers at each stage as they grow. We should probably all agree about this in a general way; the problem is to see quite clearly what *is* the best thing at each stage.

Now, there can't really be any question as to whether or not the little child should be asked to obey us, in some things and for some purposes. The call for obedience, as and when it is needed, is part of the biological responsibility of the parent. It does not need to be justified. And it has its roots deep in the nature of the little child himself. Obedience comes quite naturally to him, if we ask for it in the right way. But it is not an end in itself. It is a *means* of education, not a final purpose. The problem really is one of *what* we shall ask children to do, or say they must not do; and of *how* we give our commands and prohibitions.

Many people's difficulties come from not being clear about these things beforehand. If we are muddled in our own minds about why we want obedience, and when and how we want it, we are very likely to ask for it when it isn't really valuable; or to demand it in such a way that we actually stir contrariness or obstinacy. Or else our own uncertainties get passed on to the children, and they never really know whether we mean what we say or not. And so we are liable to get into a vicious circle of scolding and nagging by nurse or parent, and of defiance and "answering back" (to use the words of one correspondent) by the children. When once this sort of mutual habit is set up, it is not easy to break. But sometimes it would help a little if we made a determined effort to get quite clear in our own minds what it is all about, and how and why and when we ask those things which the children have got into the way of disobeying.

In the first place, when we say that the child "should obey," we obviously don't mean that he should never do anything without being told, and never have any way of his own. Nor that we really want him to be docile to our mere whim and fancy. That would be sacrificing the whole of his future to our present convenience, and would make him a useless sort of person. What we surely imply when we say that he should obey us is that our particular demands are reasonable and just, and that obeying them will really be good for him. But are we sure that we are making no mistake about this?

Grown-ups very often *have* asked children to do what was bad for them, as, for instance, when we used to make tiny children "sew a fine seam" with fine thread. We believed then that we were educating them; but later on we came to see that in fact we were just damaging their eyes, health and tempers.

Are we sure that as parents or nurses we are not making any mistakes of that kind? Do we ask our children to do *only* what is really suitable for them at their age and stage of development? That is the first thing to think about. The second is the *way* in which we ask for obedience.

Do we remember, for instance, when making our requests, how much less sense of past and future the young child has, and how much more he lives in the immediate present than we do? If we remember this, we shall also remember how much more urgent his desires are than ours, and how much sharper a disappointment or a denial is to him than to us. And since he is necessarily given up more completely to anything in which he is interested, without thought of time and place, it means much more to him than to us when we have to interrupt what he is doing because we want him, for example, to come to dinner or to go out for a walk. If we remember this we shall not wantonly and suddenly cut across his interests, but shall give him a little notice, so that he has time to take in the request. If when he is in the middle of an absorbing game, and we have to call him to come to a meal, we can give him a few minutes' warning, "In ten minutes it will be dinner-time," he is much more likely to come cheerfully and readily than if we tell him only at the very moment we want him to come, and expect him to do it on the instant. We ourselves hate to be suddenly interrupted when we are reading or talking to a friend. The child hates it, too. And he appreciates our consideration very keenly. Such consideration can quite well go along with firmness about the request when it is actually made—and this, too, the child appreciates.

Again, having made sure that we are asking the right thing, do we take it for granted in a cheerful voice and friendly manner that he will do what we wish? Or do we show him by a doubtful or fretful tone that we are rather expecting him to grumble or defy us? If we ourselves are calm and friendly in our demands, he is more likely to agree, and to do what we want in the same friendly and cheerful way. But we *can* only be calm and confident when we are really sure that what we are asking is reasonable.

THE PUNISHMENT
The Nursery World
November 20, 1929

WORRIED AUNT writes: *"I would like to ask you what you think about this. My small nephew, four years old, got up early one morning, and found his way into the drawing-room. There was a small but valuable clock on the mantelpiece, which his mother prized very highly because it belonged to her (and my) mother. He must have wanted to look at it closely, and had climbed up on a chair to try and reach it. But he had slipped and fallen with it on the fireirons, and smashed it to pieces. He was very frightened, and when we went to find out what the noise was about we found him lying on the floor beside the broken clock, sobbing bitterly, although he was not hurt himself. My sister was so angry about the clock being broken that she scolded him severely and whipped him and put him to bed for the day. And when his father came home he, too, went up and reproved him. Do you think this was really necessary and wise? I wondered whether I was merely soft-hearted, but it worried me to hear the mite being scolded so gravely after he had shown how frightened and grieved he was."*

No, I don't think it is mere "soft-heartedness" to feel that the fall and the fright were probably enough punishment for the child in the circumstances. They would be quite a severe lesson to a sensitive child. After all, in judging the seriousness of what the child has done, we have to think of it in the child's terms rather than the adult's. A child as young as that could have no sense whatever of the *particular* preciousness of the thing he had broken. All the special value of the clock to his mother, with its long and tender associations, was something altogether outside his understanding. So, of course, was its monetary value. If we are really to educate the child we can only hold him responsible for things that come within his ken. Here we have to rule out the *value* of the thing broken. It would, of course, do no harm to tell him quietly that we *had* valued it: that would be different from treating him as if he could already have felt this in the full sense in which we feel it. Even our telling him won't make him understand fully, because to do so is beyond his mind at four years of age. We could, of course, try to make it clearer to him by refering to things of his own for which he has a special fondness. The best thing would have been to comfort him for the fright, and then when he was calmer to talk it over in a calm and undisturbed way, pointing out to him that we had treasured the clock, and that we would rather he did not touch things that were not his own when we were not with him. This, together with the child's own grief, should be quite enough to make it unlikely that this sort of thing would happen again.

But the other side to the matter has to be remembered. If we want children to respect our possessions we have to respect theirs. We, too, have to recognise the rights of property. In fact, the surest way of getting a child to be considerate about not touching other people's belongings is to treat his with courtesy. Children will always respond to politeness on our part. "May I look at your book? Do you mind if I move your bricks off this table? May I show your doll to Mrs. Jones?"

Our explicit order that the children are not to go into the drawing-room and touch things without permission is so much more likely to be effective if our general relation with them is satisfactory. And that depends upon our own true friendliness and our understanding of their ways.

CHILDHOOD PROBLEMS
The Nursery World
December 18, 1929

"TAFELBERG" writes: *"I always read with great interest your advice to other parents, and now I am writing to you for a few words of advice about my son, who will be seven next month. We have always done all we can to make his home life as happy as possible, and as we live on a farm he leads a very free-and-easy, healthy, open-air life. Lately I notice that he does a great deal of grumbling, and will insist on arguing with me whenever I tell him to do anything, and is almost rude to me at times. He has a small sister whom he really adores and of whom he is very proud; but whenever she goes near or touches anything of his, he gets very annoyed with her. I scold him about it and tell him he must learn to share his books and toys with her. It worries me to see him so irritable when he can and should be such a happy little boy. He seems very obstinate with my husband and me, too. I do not like to scold or nag at the child, as I feel it only makes matters worse. Do you think I should ignore his moods? One day I threatened to send him to a boarding school, and he cried and was very unhappy about it. He loves his home. He had his appendix removed in the spring and his tonsils and adenoids in July. His digestion is not too good, and, acting on my doctor's advice, I have been very careful not to give him fats; but I have given him plenty of sugar, which certainly seems to have improved his digestion. Otherwise he is a very healthy, sturdy child. His diet is plain and nourishing, and he goes to bed at 6:30 and sleeps well. I often make him rest during the day. He attends a Kindergarten class for two hours every morning, and seems to be doing quite well, although he is not too quick, figures appearing to be his worst subject. He is very interested in anything to do with machinery. Do you think this is a case for a psychologist? If so, can you tell me of one and give me an idea of his fee? I am told that as a child I had very much the same faults, and was very obstinate with members of my own family, although all right with outsiders. He is an affectionate little boy, always very sorry afterwards for any wrong-doing. Like myself, he is apt to worry very easily about things. I shall be very grateful for your advice."*

It does not seem to me that your little boy presents a very definite case for a psychologist, but I do think it would be a good thing to review all your own general methods of dealing with him. It was, for instance, a great pity to threaten to send him to a boarding school, for several reasons. First of all, when the boy does go to school, boarding or day, one surely wants him to go with eager anticipation of the new life. One does not want to start him off with a frightened or hostile attitude to the school, since that may easily affect the whole of his life there. And then to threaten to send the boy away at all does express a terrible condemnation, far more than one perhaps realises at the moment. Isn't it as good as saying, "I can't bear to see you or have you near me"? And what could be less encouraging to a child than that? How can one expect him to be agreeable and affectionate if one has told him that? One really cannot *command* a child's good behaviour; one has to create it by cultivating the attitude of mind in the child from which it springs.

And surely your little boy has had a great many physical causes for irritability—two operations within a few months, as well as the effect of the conditions which led to the operations, and a weak digestion, are a very big strain on any child. They do not justify "spoiling" and giving the child all his own way, because these are no help to him in the long run, but they do surely call for rather more patience and forbearance than a perfectly robust child needs. In general I can only suggest that cheerful firmness and patience without nagging will best help the boy to grow out of this difficult phase.

CHILDHOOD PROBLEMS, cont.
The Nursery World
December 25, 1929

MARY writes: *"I was greatly relieved to learn from another letter that there is somebody else with the same difficulty I experience with my little girl of 6½, who is very nervous. She has always been of a nervous disposition, and when about three years old, in the summer-time, she promised to go to bed without my remaining in the room. The first night she did so, but the following night she began to cry directly I left the bedroom. I decided not to give way, and waited for her to stop crying, but without results. I then punished her, but for all this I had to see her to sleep, which did not take place until after ten o'clock that night. This affair seemed to have completely upset her nerves, and to the present day I have to see her off to sleep every night. She began school last September, but only stayed three weeks, as owing to her extreme nervousness her health was affected through one or two bad colds. My doctor gave permission for her to remain at home until the spring, and I am trying to build her up ready for the time when she returns to school. I am unable to get her to go to children's parties unless I go with her. She seems afraid to go out of my sight, and certain kinds of noises disturb her. I don't doubt that after she has been to school for a time she will get out of most of these nervous ways. She is very quick to learn, and very thoughtful, taking things to heart quickly and reduced to tears over quite minor things. Do you think she should be kept quiet or let go into company whenever possible? I have a little boy, three years old, who is of an entirely different temperament, and I can't get her to go to bed with him."*

I wonder if you read my reply to "Puzzled," who wrote about the same sort of problem a week or two ago? As I suggested to her, one can only help a nervous child of this age to learn to go to sleep without mother, and to grow generally sensible and independent, by training her step by step, very gently and slowly, but quite firmly. And first of all we need to be quite clear in our own minds that it won't help to scold or reproach. A "promise" to go to sleep from a nervous child of three, or even of six and a half, means nothing at all. Going to sleep can't be done by a mere act of will, unless one is in a contented and peaceful frame of mind—as, surely, we all know from our own experience! But if one is contented and happy it comes of itself. So that we must begin by setting aside any idea of treating the child's wakefulness and dependence upon us as a *moral* matter. It is really a question of building up gradually a sense of confidence in the child herself, and this can be done if we go to work rightly.

It would surely be a mistake to try to send a girl of six and a half to bed at the same time as the boy of three. That would be treating her as if she *were* only three—and how then can we expect her to have the independence proper to six years of age? I should certainly give her at least another twenty minutes to play after he goes to bed.

And I see no reason why you should not begin now to train her to go to sleep without you. I should tell her beforehand, "Now you are getting a big girl, I am not going to stay in your room more than (say) half an hour, whether you are asleep or not. You will soon be able to fall asleep without me, even if you don't the first evening or two. Just don't worry—it won't matter a bit if you lie awake a little time. Sleep will soon come, and after a few days you probably won't mind being left alone. We'll have our chat together every evening after you are in bed, but I can't stay more than half an hour; and I shan't come back to see if you are asleep."

And then I should make the time I had with her as pleasant and companionable as I knew how to—letting her talk to me if she wanted to, or telling her a story or a poem if she liked that best. Then I should leave her, but *without* telling her that she *must* go to sleep, or pressing her; just simply taking it for granted that she would. And not go back once I had left, even if she cried. If she wanted a low light I should let her have it, of course. And the time I stayed with her would be gradually lessened down to, say, five minutes.

If along with this there was plenty of encouragement to independence in other ways, the child would not be very long before she accepted it happily.

The school will certainly be a great help, and I should myself be inclined to start her there again even before Easter, perhaps at first in the mornings only. And as regards her going out to tea without you, that will surely come about most easily through the growth of school friendships. There again I should not talk about it much, or say that she *ought* to go alone; but let it come quite naturally and as a matter of course as her friendships grow. That will be one of the great advantages of school life for her. And I should encourage her to see other children and play with them independently as much as possible. It will not help to keep her closely under your wing.

NERVOUS CHILDREN
The Nursery World
February 12, 1930

REASON asks: *"I wonder if you would deal with this problem. I have a son, aged seven, who has a dread and hatred of anything grotesque or unnatural, and until he KNOWS HOW IT WORKS he is terrified. After the first time and the explanation he can see it again unmoved. At his first pantomime, this winter, he minded nothing but the hurly-burly scene where chairs disappeared through walls, etc.; while other children screamed with laughter he was greatly distressed. At his one annual cinema he was enthralled by a motor race in which the car ran crowds of people down, etc., but he could not endure "Mickey the Mouse" and his unnatural antics. Yesterday at a party he saw his first Punch and Judy show; he grew graver and graver, burst into tears, and said 'I hate it; I hate it!' His kind hostess suggested that he should go away and play with trains; but I felt this was running away from, not conquering, his fear. I told him to remain in the room, but not look if he didn't wish to. He pulled himself together and did this, and later I told him to come and share my chair, and with my arm round him, watch the rest of the dolls being worked by a man in a box. He did this, and towards the end was laughing gaily. It is ALWAYS unnatural, grotesquely humorous things that terrify him. He is a child who goes off miles alone on his cycle, and will go out to tea at a strange house, alone, happily. He has never been afraid of the dark, and is the sensitive, trustworthy, conscientious type of child. He has a very keen perception of beauty—a beautiful sky, beautiful words, colour, fine scenery. Has this anything to do with his sheer dread of grotesque ugliness? And why is he not only disgusted, but AFRAID of unnatural ugliness, when 99 children out of 100 see it as humorous? I should be intensely grateful to know the cause and cure. Turning away from it does not help, surely, since it would have to be faced later."*

This is an extremely interesting problem, and to unravel it fully would take us very deep indeed into child psychology, much further than space will allow. But I want to touch on one or two points of psychology which may help in the practical handling of the boy's fear. In the first place, it is clear that with a boy who is in general so courageous and well-poised these grotesque things must touch off some extraordinarily sensitive place within him, or he would not fall so far below his usual standards of control and courage. These things that are supposed to be dead or inanimate, but that yet have a sort of magical life or power of an unnatural, mechanical kind, evidently stir up some very deep and hidden fantasies in the boy's mind belonging to the earliest period of mental development in infancy. In those earliest days of all, when the infant lies helplessly at the mercy of a strange and powerful world, and things happen without his being able to control or understand them, there is far more fear of imaginary things, even with a well cared for and tenderly treated baby, than most of us ever realise. But slowly the child comes to know what is real and what is not real, and to feel trust and comfort in the love of those big grown-ups who are so all-powerful and yet so kind, and his fears die away and he feels safe in the real world as he comes to know it with eye and ear and moving fingers. With some children, however, these infantile terrors of unimaginable things, belonging to the time when they did not know what was real and what was not, linger on behind the brave face they put on things. And if such a child is shown cleverly contrived imitations of life and reality that are yet only mechanical, these break down again, for the moment, the barrier between the real and the unreal, and so open all the floodgates of imagination and terror. Then *anything* might be true! For the ugliness means (in the young child's mind) *badness,* anger, cruelty. The child will not be able to put all this into words. It will not be clear even in his own mind. He will not so much *think it as feel* it, and that is why he cannot at first deal with it. Less sensitive children do not dread this mixture of reality and unreality so much. Indeed, the very fun for them and most of us lies in knowing that it is all pretence. Punch does not really hurt Judy and the baby; he is not *really* alive. Everything is really quite safe—and we feel all the safer for having pretended not to be!

But with your boy and some others these things get below the surface and stir those "old, unhappy, far-off things" of infancy. When a child *is* sensitive in this way it is best to avoid occasions of this kind, so far as this can be done without making him singular. But when occasions come along without your choice, as at the party, I think your method of dealing with the trouble is certainly the right one. He has shown that with your comradeship and the help of the explanation (which works, of course, by taking the magic and *unreality* out of the affair) he can get over the first shock. I think you did just the right thing in getting him to stay in the room and look at it while sharing your chair. But I should not press him too far. And the important thing is to avoid scolding or reproach. Do not hint that it is a social or moral misbehaviour. Just let him see that you can enjoy it yourself, and give him the support of the explanation and of your calm confidence that he also will not be afraid when he understands it. This is the only way to help him to grow out of the difficulty. As he gets older he is extremely likely (with the character you have described) to learn to control the show of fear; and as understanding grows the fear itself will lessen. But I think it is very likely that he will always keep a fundamental sensitivity to these things, and never be able to take the pleasure in them that some do. But what does that matter? The less sensitive ones may not have his delight in other forms of pleasure.

OLD-FASHIONED *or* MODERN METHODS?
The Nursery World
January 15, 1930

STUDENT writes: *"I have been very interested in some of the letters that have appeared once or twice lately in 'Over the Teacups' about 'old-fashioned' methods and 'old-fashioned' nurses. I should very much like to know what you think of this—are they really better than the modern ways? Some of the writers seemed to think that children are happier under nurses with old-fashioned ways. Do you think that this can be so? I've not had much experience myself, and never yet had full responsibility for any children, so I don't know what to think. But I'm very anxious to learn the best ways of dealing with them, and should awfully like to hear your views about this."*

I'm very glad you wrote about this, because I, too, was very interested in the discussion you refer to; and it is a far-reaching and important question.

What I wanted to say to the correspondents when I read their letters was, "But why lump everything together in this way, and talk about 'old-fashioned' and 'modern' as if either of these were *altogether* good or bad, and as if we were obliged to take *all* of one or all of the other?" If it be true that old-fashioned ways made children so happy and easy, it seems strange that anyone would have questioned them, doesn't it? Perhaps they were good in some respects and not in others. Is it possible to look at things in more detail, and find out *which* of the ways of the old-fashioned nurse were the ones that made little children content and easy to manage, and which of the newer methods really are an improvement?

One great quality of the old-fashioned nurse *at her best* was that she knew so well what she wanted in the way of good behaviour, and never doubted that she would get it; and so she did get it. Her views of what little children should be like were clear and simple, and she had clear and definite methods of getting them to be so. Now, if she happened to be mean and despotic (at her worst) the children were ruled with a rod of iron and their lives were closed-in and narrow. But if, in addition to being firm, she had a mild temper and broad, sensible ideas of good behaviour, then the children were indeed happy in having her; for they always knew what was expected of them, and what would happen if they didn't do it. They were not bewildered by being treated in one way to-day and another tomorrow. They were helped to be good by the calm belief of their nurse that *of course* they would be—because that was the way all ordinary little children behaved, apart from exceptional moments. And she never doubted her ability to deal with the exceptional moments. She was so sure of them and of herself and of the way to behave to them that her calm and content were passed on to them, and it was easy for them to do what she wanted.

Now, few mothers and nurses to-day are so clear-minded. They are not nearly so sure what they want for their children. This is partly because of changing ideas in the larger world outside the nursery, and partly because people have begun to realise that the idyllic picture of the old-fashioned nurse at her best did not always hold good, and that along with her good qualities there were often to be found big gaps in her knowledge, filled up with chunks of mere prejudice. And so people began to ask more questions, and to inquire more deeply into the real truths of child nature, what it is like, and what it needs for the most satisfactory growth. And since scientific methods of feeding and clothing the baby were turning out so infinitely better than the old ways based on tradition and rule of thumb, it began to seem likely that this might be true of social training too.

But, of course, the breakdown of belief in old-fashioned ways of punishment and such notions of good behaviour as that "children should be seen and not heard" has gone on much faster than the spread of the scientific knowledge that must take its place. Hence so many mothers and nurses really don't know what is best to do, what good behaviour in little children is, and how to bring it about. And, of course, children are less happy in these circumstances. They are as lost and confused as the grown-ups themselves.

The only remedy for this is the serious study of child psychology and methods based on child psychology. We have to try to bring back the old calm surety; and to find it our feet must be firmly placed in sound knowledge.

An expert in the treatment of emotional troubles and disturbances of behaviour in little children said to me recently, "What little children most need in their nurses and mothers is affection, stability and spontaneity." And of these qualities the stability and spontaneity spring very largely from a sure knowledge of what is good for our children and the best ways of handling them.

The MOTHER'S ATTITUDE to the CHILD
The Nursery World
March 5, 1930

FAIRHILL writes: *"I feel a real need of advice from you. Our little boy is two years and nine months old. He is very wilful. Whenever I cross his will he howls and screams and hits me, and even kicks me. We have read in your columns of a mother whom you told to ignore this in her child, and we have tried that, but he keeps on. We long to deal in the very best way with him, but he makes me feel quite incapable of training him when he displays such determination and obstinacy; and such scenes are such a strain on my nerves. He has a little boy two months younger than himself to play with, and he, on the other hand, is so docile and has such a placid nature. Our little chap shows selfishness in playing, and tries to get everything for himself. He also plays and works in the garden for hours on his own, and thinks out how to do things. On the whole he is a splendid little chap, if only we could get him cured of his wilfulness. When we tell him to do something he says 'No,' and if he gets smacked he howls for ever so long afterwards. And if it is I who smacks him, he does not want me for ever so long, but only his daddy. In fact, this has troubled us, too. When daddy is at home he very seldom will allow me to do anything for him and hits off my hand."*

I agree very warmly that such determination and obstinacy in a young child can be very trying, and the outbursts of temper very wearing to the nerves of mother or nurse. But we usually let ourselves be far more worried by them than we really need to be. Half our distress when the child is naughty comes from our fear that his behaviour is abnormal or unnatural, that he will go on like this when he is older, and in general, that things are going altogether wrong. And when *our* nerves get frayed with this worry the child either feels triumphant that he has power over us, or very frightened of what we may do to him, and so gets more frantic still. And then *we* worry more, and feel that we have mismanaged things; and the child senses our anxiety and gets crosser still, and he and we go on upsetting each other still further until we have lost the power of dealing calmly and pleasantly with his need.

So that the very first thing to do is to realise that a certain amount of such behaviour is perfectly healthy and normal in a vigorous child in these early years. The child has really a big task before him in the way of accepting other people's ways and wishes, and learning control of his own. And he can't possibly learn all this in a few days or a few months. It is not really a very terrible matter if a child of two or three does sometimes scream or protest when he can't get his own way. Rome was not built in a day, but we seem to think that the child should reach human perfection in two or three short years! After all, determination may turn out to be a very useful quality in later life if it is tempered by affection and reason. The docile child is certainly pleasanter and easier to deal with when a child, but it does not follow that he will be the most effective person when he grows up, does it?

We have thus to aim, not at an impossible present perfection, but at a steady growth towards control and reasonableness and friendly agreement. It does not matter if this is slow, so long as it *is* real and steady, does it? We should surely feel that we had accomplished our task as parents if we helped a naturally self-assertive and obstinate child to grow into a friendly, co-operative person as he got older, shouldn't we? Nothing we can do would make such a child merely *docile;* but if we are unafraid and steadily firm and friendly ourselves, we can hope to help him to reasonableness and active co-operation in social life.

I would therefore still suggest that you take no particular notice of the mere screaming, reminding yourself, however, that this way of dealing with it may not have its valuable effect in a minute or even in a month. I should certainly say quite firmly, "Please don't hit me," and if necessary hold his arm or leg to prevent it. You *can* prevent his doing that; you can't effectively prevent his screaming on the spot. But you can prevent his gaining any power or special attention by it, and so gradually lessen it. The smacking cannot be wise, for how is the child to see any difference between that and his own violence? He cannot understand *our* reasons for feeling it to be different. It must seem to him that we are no different from him, save that we are the stronger. And to try to rule an obstinate child by fear simply increases his obstinacy.

If you can show him your active sympathy with his interests and his play, avoid all *unnecessary* demands or thwarting, then you can also keep quite firmly and evenly to such demands and denials as you really have to make for health or practical convenience. But don't ask him to do anything that you are not prepared to insist on or really can't enforce. And, above all, don't let yourself appear to him as *just* the-one-who-interferes. Let him have the constant sense of your active friendliness and understanding, shown in letting him choose the games when you play with him, or the way you go when you are out for a walk, and in general giving him as much chance to choose for himself in the smaller matters as you possibly can. Then you can safely insist on the important points.

As regards his preference for his daddy, that often happens, and is to some extent understandable, since mother so often *has* to be the-one-who-interferes, hasn't she? Daddy has so much less time with the child that he seems new and exciting; and since he has not the responsibility of the daily routine of feeding and bathing and training, he is often a little more indulgent, or, at any rate, is less connected in the child's own mind with musts and must nots! The mother can prevent this from becoming too accentuated by being careful to be *also* one-who-plays, sharing the child's fun and laughter as well as training him.

THE VALUE OF COMPANIONSHIP
The Nursery World
March 26, 1930

AMERICAN writes: *"I have an unusually intelligent 'only child,' whose health and disposition have been, for the most part, good. He has little contact with other children, since we live on the edge of a very small town, inhabited by surprisingly few children. That is the trouble. When 'company' comes, my son (two years old) starts to 'show off,' running from person to person with self-conscious movements, talking louder than usual, trying to get special attention, smirking, watching faces for admiration. What can I do to stop this unpleasant performance? If I ignore it on the old plea of 'He's so young; he'll outgrow it,' I am afraid the habit will grow, become an integral part of his later character, and make life less fine and happy for himself, as well as for those around him. Thank you so much for any help you can give me."*

You have raised a very interesting psychological issue, and one that goes far beyond the particular problem you yourself have to face into general questions of educational method. First of all, it has, of course, to be said there is *some* truth in "He's so young; he'll outgrow it," although you are certainly right in distrusting that as the last word on the matter. It *is* true, in the sense that the behaviour in question is perfectly normal for an intelligent child of his age, one who is free from shyness and nervousness. And in the sense that the impulse will not necessarily go on expressing itself in just that form when he is a little older. It is not true *enough* in itself, because all the social value of such an impulse depends entirely upon *what* form of expression it does in the end grow into—and that in turn will partly depend upon how you treat the impulse now.

Many mothers of shy and nervous children would, of course, be ready to envy you for having a child who could be free and spontaneous in the presence of others, even if, for the moment, it is a form that is not altogether pleasing. If you checked the child's histrionic impulse too sharply, this might easily make him nervous and inhibited, which would be a great pity. It seems to me splendid that you have such a *positive* social behaviour to train, rather than shyness and unsociability.

The real difficulty does arise from the scarcity of child companions. Such a child would be an invaluable leader in the dramatic and imaginative play of a group of children of his own age, and a delightful companion. If you can't give him this (and I should certainly make a good deal of effort to do so), then I should try to use the child's love of display in the dramatic expression of stories and poems. Let him have a box of "dressing-up things," and help him to make swords and helmets, fairies' wings, policeman's or conductor's uniforms, or whatever is needed for the imaginative expression of his interests at the moment. Join with him in acting out his stories and fantasies, or sometimes just make an appreciative audience for him. In this way the child's love of attention will get some real satisfaction in a form that will help his general development in language and in artistic creation. It is surprising what even a quite young child can do in the way of expressive acting and in drawing and creating all the things that help in his dramatic play.

If you could sometimes have other little children to join in this, with your grown-up friends helping and sharing in the fun, both children and grown-ups would get great pleasure out of it. And then you could safely check the child's wish to be in the limelight on ordinary occasions that were not suitable for it, without the risk of shutting down a most desirable path of development. But even so, it would be best if you could find ways of *using* rather than inhibiting the child's social impulses. Within the next year or two it would be quite possible to train him gently to help you look after the comfort of your guests—for example, by carrying the plates or cups or sugar. If one has a young child present in the company of grown-ups, one has to find *some* way of making him feel as if he had a real place there. If he is there, and yet feels he is not really wanted, he is quite certain to be restless and difficult, and to find unpleasant ways of getting attention. We have to provide him with useful and pleasant ways of feeling that he has a real part in things. If he has to be with you when you are entertaining grown-up friends, then let him share by having definite things to do; however small these may be, let him feel that it is important that they should be done nicely.

TRAINING IN INDEPENDENCE
The Nursery World
April 2, 1930

C.H.R. asks: *"I wonder how you would advise us to deal with our little girl, now twenty months old. She is very active and always anxious to do things by herself,*

> which sometimes leads to trouble, though I do not want in any way to hinder her development. Ought a child of this age to feed herself? She is teething, and has always had a poor appetite, and now shows every sign of wanting the spoon in her own hand. She may eat a little at first, but soon begins to play. The same with her milk; she will drink a little, and then, without warning, turns the mug upside down, saying 'Spill!' 'Mess!' And waits to see what I will do. She also enjoys washing her own hands, standing on a high stool to reach the basin. Once or twice she has made a fuss when she had to stop and have her hands dried. Not long after, she went to the coal-scuttle, and then came to me saying 'Hands dirty! Wash hands!' This happened twice in one afternoon, although she has plenty of interesting occupations for the rare occasions when she is indoors. It seemed like giving in to her, but she could not touch anything until her hands were washed. She seems healthy and very happy, though several pounds underweight, which makes the food problem more difficult."

Such an impulse to independence and self-help in a child of twenty months is surely an excellent augury for her future development! If met with understanding and a little patience now, it will save all the endless difficulties that arise at a later age in the more helpless, babyish type of child who doesn't want to learn to do things for himself. It is a splendid sign of mental health and vigour. Even her making her hands dirty with the coal so as to be able to wash them again is surely the most welcome index of enterprise and intelligence! If such a child is handled with humour and good temper, and given plenty of real opportunities to be active and to do things for herself, she should develop excellently in every direction. If she were to be treated negatively and repressively, she would obviously spend her time trying to find ways round or through the "don'ts," and might well become obstinate and difficult.

Letting her do things for herself will, of course, take a little more of your time now than doing things for her would. But so much will be saved later on! Not only the actual time that had to be given to feeding and washing a more dependent older child, but all that would be wasted in useless friction and tears if the child's impulses were not taken seriously and used constructively from the start. I should most certainly let her wash her own hands, and learn to dry them. Let her start doing it in plenty of time, if they are to be washed before a meal or before going out, so as to avoid having to hurry her. The look and the feel of soapsuds are fascinating things to many little children. Why should they not have the fun of them? If there *is* a real reason for hurry, well and good. But if there isn't any reason, why shouldn't she play with the warm water and soap as long as she wants to? What possible harm could there be in it? If you are afraid she might fall off the high stool, could she not have a bowl of water on a low chair or table, and have a mackintosh apron or overall on, with a cork mat on the floor, so that a few splashes would not matter? When she is a little older she will probably love to wash her dolls' clothes.

And many children of her age are learning to feed themselves quite effectively. Eighteen months is the average age among healthy and well-trained children for being able to use a spoon with good control. If one fails to use this desire in her, one is holding up her normal development in skill and in social habits. If you give her the right kind of food, and leave her to eat it herself, without urging her at all, or making any comment on whether she does or not, she will soon learn to feed herself efficiently, and will eat *at least as much* as she would if you stood over her and pressed her to eat, and showed your anxiety when she ate less than you thought she ought. She will, indeed, almost certainly eat *more* than if a fuss is made. Give her plenty of time, of course—she will at first naturally take longer to feed herself than if you gave her the spoonfuls. Unless she is a very greedy, urgent feeder (which would not be good for her digestion), she will not go at it steadily and uninterruptedly, but is certain to play a little after the first few mouthfuls have taken the worst edge off her hunger. But there is no harm in a little diversion between the bites. Let her have enough time to finish, but not an unlimited time. Give her, say, twenty minutes or twenty-five minutes, or even half-an-hour, to begin with, whilst feeding herself is novel. Then a few minutes before you are going to take the plate away, give her a warning: "Soon I'm going to take your plate away. Will you finish your food?" And after a little interval take it away, whether she has finished or not, and *make no comment* on the amount she has eaten or has left untouched. The appetite of any healthy child who has plenty of exercise in the open air and plenty of sleep and rest can *always* be trusted—if only mother or nurse does not spoil the situation by worrying and calling out contrariness.

As regards the turning of the cup upside down, I should put only a very little milk in the cup at a time. And once the habit of feeding herself is happily established, I should definitely tell the child that she could hold her own cup to drink from *only* if she did not turn it upside down and spill the milk deliberately.

A CHILD'S WONDER *of* LIFE
The Nursery World
April 23, 1930

A week or two ago I promised A.E.G. and E.M.M. to take up again the points of their letters on the subject of children's questions as to "where babies come from," and I should like to go into the problem more fully now.

It cannot be denied that the problem of how best to deal with little children's questions on these matters is one that demands a good deal of honest thought. It cannot be settled off-hand by anyone. The difficulties that my correspondents and the letters in "Over the Tea-cups" have raised are perfectly genuine ones, and have to be frankly faced from the outset. No one can offer simple ready-made advice which clears away all future difficulties and makes everything quite easy and straightforward. After all, we are in contact here with some of the most intimate aspects of human relationships, ones that have always been fraught with the most significant emotions, and the deepest moral and personal issues. It is very hard for us to be as calm and objective when the child touches upon these things as when he asks about engines or birds or butterflies. It is a great help if we *can* be equally calm and dispassionate; but it is not easy for the ordinary parent to be so. The trained biologist can look upon birth and marriage, life and death in human beings as objectively as upon any other facts of the science of life—when he is dealing with them *as* scientific questions. But I have known even trained biologists, with a great store of knowledge at their command, feel embarrassed and hardly know what to reply on the spot when their own children asked for information about their own origin. So that we must not pretend there aren't any difficulties, or that one or two easy instructions to parents will sweep them away altogether.

The one thing that has to be remembered, however, is that the child's difficulties are even greater than the parents'. His questions are not a mere matter of idle curiosity, nor of pure desire for knowledge as such. They spring from deep ponderings about his relationship to his parents and his brothers and sisters, and the relationship of his parents to each other; and from a groping and searching after some meaning in what he dimly senses of his own history and growth, his own past and future. He sees around him men and women, old and young, big children and little. He sees new babies arrive, or hears of them in other families. Where did they come from? How did they begin? Will they grow up too? What *is* growing up? what is "having" a baby? What does it feel like? Here is mother, loving and caring tenderly for someone who was not there before—does she love the newcomer better than him? There were brothers and sisters before him—will there be some after him to displace him from mother's lap and arms? And will he himself ever have this wonderful possession, a little baby of his own? How does one get such marvellous things? And so the child ponders on youth and age, on his own birth and growth. (I have a large number of recorded observations of such questions from both boys and girls).

How strange it would indeed be if an intelligent observant child did *not* think about the drama of human life in this way! He would have to be blind and deaf and stupid not to do so. Or (as, alas! does happen only too often) to be locked up in solitary and fruitless musings by shyness and fear.

What happens in the child's mind if he asks his questions trustingly and gets no answer, an evasive answer, or an answer that he will sooner or later (and it is usually sooner rather than later) find out to be untrue?

If he gets no answer, or an evasive one, he is lost and bewildered by the sense that his grown-up friends either don't know the most important things that he wants to understand, or (and this is the more probable) that they won't tell him. And if they won't tell him, *why* won't they? It can only be that there is something wrong and shameful about the knowledge they withhold. And, indeed, the voice and tone and expression of mother when she told him to "hush" and "not to ask such things," or turned away and talked of something else, did suggest that there was something dark and terrible about it. Then that means that behind this great mysterious pageant of youth and age, behind the love of mother and father, behind even mother's love for the child himself, is something shameful and hidden, too shameful and hidden to be spoken of. What can it be? And in this way the springs of life and love may be poisoned for the child. What could be more destructive of goodness and happiness than to be led to believe that one's own very existence was rooted in shameful mystery? How infinitely preferable to be helped to understand that babies take their life from the mutual affection of father and mother, and are at first shielded and nourished within mother's own body!

Of the evil effect of actual untruths, I spoke in my earlier reply. But how dreadful for the child to discover, not merely that mother would not help him to understand, but that she would rather let herself tell a lie to him than answer his groping questions! How terrible the truth must be if mother feels she must lie about it! How much truth or love is there left in which one can really believe and trust?

These difficulties of the little child—all of them only too real, as my own observations and those of many other people show—are surely much more serious and far-reaching than any temporary embarrassment that can come to us. It is the foundation of the child's confidence in us as true helpers and honest friends that is at stake. It is worth a little trouble on our part to find the best way of answering, and worth a little courage of facing any momentary possibility of social embarrassment among our grown-up friends.

Let me sum up briefly some of the chief reasons for dealing with the child's questions as clearly and straightforwardly as we possibly can. The first is that only by doing so can we keep the child's confidence and belief in our love and genuine desire to help him. There is no good our *telling* the child we love him, and then failing to meet his needs. He knows whether we love him or not, by our behaviour to him. He will sense our true wish to meet his difficulties and help him understand, or our fear and evasion and unwillingness.

The second reason is the great value of the actual knowledge of the biological unity of human life, and the facts of biology in general. What serious grounds can there be for failing to open up to the child's interest and understanding such a delightful field of knowledge? He naturally has an intuitive sense of his oneness with the animals he loves. Who could doubt the child's spontaneous delight in other living creatures who had ever seen children with their own pets, or watched their eager interest at the Zoo, or told them stories of animals? And it is the family relationship of animals that chiefly wins their attention in the early years, "the little baby pigs," "The daddy and mummy bear," the cow and her calf, the mother swallow feeding her young. These things make it relatively easy to help the child understand the story of human birth. As I suggested previously, the keeping of pet mice and rabbits, the cat and her kittens, the hen and her chickens, help the child to answer most of his own questions, and are much better than long explanations by the parents. If the child has this experience, one does not have to say much more to him than that the human baby is sheltered in mother until he is old enough to grow and feed in the outside world, just like the chicken in the egg, or the kitten in the mother cat. Some of my correspondents have found this the best way of getting the child to understand, and I have myself no doubt that such a contact with animals and their young is an essential part of the little child's education. I would have families of animals in every kindergarten and school and home if it were in my power to arrange it! Even in his early years the child can be gathering knowledge about animal life which is a joy in itself, and an intellectual stimulus to further effort and inquiry, and which will later lead on to the more serious study of all those facts of biology which underlie health and disease, both in man (e.g., in modern infant welfare itself) and in the plants and animals upon which his life depends.

In this I am looking many years ahead for the little child of course. The four- and five-year old is interested only to feed and watch and play with animals, and to sow his seeds and gather the blossom and fruit of the garden. But these are the beginnings of what may in later years become a serious pursuit and permanent intellectual delight, to add to the pleasures of literature and art and music. What a pity not to open the door to such a range of knowledge and pleasure! But we may shut that door if we do not let the little child enjoy contact with living creatures, if we bar his interest to some of the central facts of their lives, the facts of mating and parenthood, or if we deny him the knowledge of human birth and make him turn away in shame from his own origin instead of letting him feel the vast interest and beauty of the great pageant of life as a whole.

There are two practical points raised by my correspondents. One is the age at which to give the child the true answer. Some have suggested that six or seven is better than three or four. But surely the only age is the one when the child asks! There is no particular virtue in six as against three. If the child does not ask until six or seven, well and good: but if he does (and the age in fact varies a good deal according to the child and the circumstances), then it can only do harm to postpone the answer on grounds which the child cannot possibly understand. To do so is to give a false weight to the curiosity, and will usually only make him hide it. If the child does ask at three, it means that he is unusually intelligent and observant, or that some special circumstance has drawn his attention to the problem. And (as far as I have been able to observe) he will nearly always have thought a good deal about the question *before* he asks. That means he is ready for the answer, no matter how young he be. I have no doubt that all of us greatly underestimate the intelligence and power of observation of young children—largely, perhaps, because it suits us to do so!

The other point is that of what to do or say when the child embarrasses us by speaking about these things in front of visitors. Now here is a point on which I believe that a little courage should be astonishingly rewarded! Why should we imagine that we are the only ones in our social circle who are trying to face these questions? Are there not perhaps other mothers with young children among our friends? Isn't it possible that they, too, are concerned with these issues, and are trying to find out what is the best way to go about things? Might we not be doing them and ourselves a great service if we used the occasion of any remark by a little child to talk over all the problems arising from it, and so pool our difficulties and our wisdom? One would not need to rush into things—it would soon be possible to tell what the attitude of our friends was by their first response to a tentative remark. Their children will after all be very much like ours, and together we may be able to find a better answer to their questions than each of us would by ourselves.

In any case, it is quite certain that no "sniggering," or even scolding, on the part of other children or grown-ups could be as important for the child as a lie or evasion or refusal to help on the part of his own mother. Nothing matters as much as that.

A CHILD'S POINT OF VIEW
The Nursery World
June 4, 1930

PUZZLED writes: *"I have read with great interest your answers to others in difficulty, and would be so grateful to have your opinion of mine. My little charge, aged four and a quarter, is a highly strung, nervous child. I find fault as little as possible, but when she has to be corrected she has a most puzzling way of behaving. For instance, if I tell her in a very serious voice I am very displeased, she will come to me a few minutes afterwards and say 'It is not nice of you to speak to me like that. Now I am very displeased and shall not smile or talk to you. You see you have made me displeased and I am looking very cross!' On one occasion she called me to look at something. I replied I would soon come but was very busy just then, consequently afterwards I found a very offended little mortal. I tried to make her understand that to get cross when I was unable to come was not right or reasonable.*

A few days afterwards when I called her she kept me waiting; when I said that she ought to come when Nannie called, she replied with great firmness that she had been very busy showing something to her dog, and if she did not come I ought not to be displeased over it. She evidently feels that if I express displeasure she is entitled to do likewise, and also that if I can offer a reason for not going when called, she can do the same. If she happens to fall, she will generally hit the floor hard with obvious bad temper which seems mingled with hurt feelings. She is generally responsive to reason and persuasion where she loves. Will you please tell me how best to manage her with regard to these little difficulties?"

This is a very interesting problem, and one not easy for a busy grown-up, who has to get on with practical necessities, to deal with. But it is by no means an uncommon reaction in children of high intelligence and a certain sensitive temperament. In finding out how best to deal with it, I think one has first of all to recognise that there is a certain amount of reason and justice in the child's point of view. It isn't just perversity, it is in part a real attempt to understand the moral values and intentions of adults. The child is reflecting upon what you have said to her, and trying to get the inside point of view about what you think unreasonable, or what you disapprove of. But, also, she is defending her dignity. It is painful to her to be subject to the judgment of other people, and by saying the same things to you she is trying to get her balance again and to get away from the painfulness of being small and dependent. To be so very sensitive does not make for social ease, and one cannot but feel sorry for children who find it so painful to be corrected. She may grow out of it to some extent, of course, particularly when she mixes with other children at school.

I think there are three ways of helping her. One cannot, of course, altogether avoid having to show that one doesn't like or approve of certain kinds of behaviour. Nor would it in the end help her if you avoided correction when it was really needed. But one should admit to the full whatever justice there is in her point of view. As far as is really practicable, one should be as polite and considerate to the child as one expects the child to be to others. One should not cut across her play, for instance, unless this really cannot be avoided. It is no good expecting such a child to be a model of *automatic* and unreasoning obedience, because she is simply not capable of being that, and to try to make her so would only cause deep resentment. It would help her very much, for instance, to explain how much depends upon *your* being able to get on with your work, and to talk this out with her without reproach.

Another help you can give her is the utmost good humour! Such a child often suffers from a lack of the sense of humour. She takes herself and everything else too seriously, and if one can get her to laugh a little at her own tremendous wish to be as important and as morally powerful as the grown-ups, it does help her development. I don't mean you must laugh *at* her. One would need to go very gently indeed. But I have found that when children feel the need to . . . assume this great self-importance, one can ease things a little by a friendly good humored smile or laughter, in one's voice, of the sort that is *with* the child, not *at* her.

And the third form of help is undoubtedly plenty of the society of other children of her age. Active play with other children would probably help to lessen her special sensitivity a little, and to give her more confidence in herself, and therefore greater ease & a better sense of proportion.

FIRST OCCUPATIONS
The Nursery World
July 19, 1930

M.E.L. writes: *"May I seek your kind help with regard to my little daughter of just one-and-a-half years? The last week or so she has commenced biting her finger nails: not a very great deal, but persistently enough to make me feel I must try and stop this at the outset.*

"She always has been and is a very good, contented baby, and never indulged in thumb-sucking. Now she is walking well, and although she does not talk properly, yet is most intelligent and alert, and wanting to see and do everything she can.

"I feel her new habit is very likely that she gets bored, and needs more outlet mentally than she gets; at this stage I find it rather difficult. She is no longer satisfied to play longer together with a toy complete in itself, but is always wanting something that will come to bits, etc., and she is still too young for much of this.

"I would be ever so grateful if you would suggest what one might allow at this age. Is it too early for a little sand heap in her pen in the garden?

"I do like her to be out as much as possible. She loves roaming round the garden, but cannot be left alone, and I am almost single-handed with a lot to do in the house, and sometimes have to bring her in with me: she will not play contentedly with her toys in the pen in the garden, but is continually asking to come out.

"I always feel you are so helpful in dealing with mothers' problems, and shall be so grateful for any suggestions for mine."

If your little girl can be gently weaned from her nail-biting, it will be an excellent thing. It is, of course, very important not to scold or punish her for this sort of nervous habit, but, as you rightly suggest, to try indirect methods of keeping her active and content.

She is certainly old enough to have a heap of sand, and two or three pails of different sizes to fill and empty, with a few sticks to poke with or stand up in the sand, some pebbles and shells, and a small wooden spade. She would enjoy a funnel, too, for pouring the sand through, and any old pans or tins or boxes that you had to spare (provided they have no splinters or sharp edges). And these warm days she could wear peddlers or a bathing suit, and have a large zinc bath full of water, with her pails and cans. This would make her happy for a long time. When she is indoors she would enjoy two or three old boxes and a supply of dried beans to pour into them, and wooden bricks of different sizes and shapes. She won't yet build anything in particular, but will like to pick the bricks up and move them about, to pile one on top of another, and to knock down a tower which someone builds to give her this pleasure. Another interesting plaything for this age is the nest of boxes—a series of five to ten open cubes fitting loosely one inside the other. These are to be got in most toy shops quite cheaply. She might also enjoy the Montessori cylinders—hers is the age when they have the greatest appeal; and they will satisfy her particular wish to take things to pieces. Soon she would be ready for the "pink tower," too. A wooden cup and ball, and a strongly made wooden cart that she could fill with her other toys and pull about would be very attractive. And a box of old buttons (large ones, of course, so that there is no risk of her swallowing them) of different sorts and colours, or a collection of clothes-pegs. Little children love all sorts of odds and ends that have no value for us—all they want is a variety of things to own and handle. But when she is with you in the house, couldn't you let her "help" you in the dusting and cooking, or play with patty-pans and spoons? I have suggested this to other mothers with young children and they always find it successful.

If the nail-biting did seem to be setting in as a regular habit, it would be as well to have proper advice about the difficulty; but for the present it may be a great help if you can give your little girl plenty of happy occupation in these different ways.

NERVOUS HABITS
The Nursery World
August 27, 1930

... problem number two is that he has to be played with all the time, otherwise he cries and cries. Bricks do not interest him, neither do bottles with corks, or tins with lids. Only balls he loves. I know this description is of a thoroughly spoilt child. I have tried so hard not to make him one. He is only corrected when necessary, but then firmly and kindly, such as in his habit of throwing things at people, but he does it out of perversity, looking first of all to see what effect his threatened hitting is going to have. I'm afraid his crying lately has got rather on my nerves, and on his, too, I suppose, and so things go on in a vicious circle, and no nearer a solution. I am so sorry to trouble you with all this, but would be so grateful for a few hints. I have found your articles in "The Nursery World" most encouraging and illuminating. Thanking you very much for whatever help you give me."

With regard to the feeding difficulty, the only way is to leave the child to eat by himself, and not to try to force or coax. Whenever we do try to coax or force the child because we think we know the amount he should eat, what we are really doing is to come between the child and his food, and to turn the whole thing into a *social* question, instead of letting it be a direct relation between the child and the food. If the child is not ill nor sickening for any illness, and if the food is of the right kind and attractively cooked, and the child is left to eat it or not as he wishes, he always will (apart from very rare cases of severe psychological disturbance) eat what his appetite demands. He will nearly always eat more when left to himself and the food than when nurse or mother try to insist on his eating, and he will digest and assimilate what he has eaten far better.

Whenever I get a letter about this problem I wish I could do with mother or nurse what is quite often done in some of the splendid American nursery schools, where they have made a careful scientific study of all these problems of feeding children and training them and educating them. There are certain of these schools staffed by experienced teachers and psychologists and doctors, where they have also the closest co-operation with the mothers of the children, and have made arrangements by which the mother can go and watch her child amongst the others in the school, playing and learning and eating at the routine times. They have a special sort of screen across one end of the room, behind which observers may sit. The screen is transparent in one direction and opaque in the other, so that mothers and visitors can see the children without the children being disturbed by their presence. In this way mothers have the rare chance of seeing their children as they are in themselves, so to speak, or rather as they behave in the hands of highly trained and experienced educators. And this question of feeding is the one that has been most often helped and improved by this method.

When the mother who comes to the school saying, "My Tommy won't eat. You'll never get him to touch his dinner. He doesn't like this, and he won't eat that. He never eats anything unless I stand over him and make him"—such a mother is given the opportunity of seeing just how her boy does behave when, amongst the other children, he is given a dish of the right sort of food, and left alone to eat it or not. Only the other day the head of one of these schools was describing to me how the particular mother had behaved under these circumstances. She sat behind the screen watching the children, and when she saw her Tommy opposite a plate of food like the other children, she said "He will never eat that; he never touches carrots at home." But presently she saw him take up his spoon and begin to eat like the other children around him were doing. When she saw a glass of milk of the prescribed size put beside the boy she said, "Well, anyhow he won't drink that," and was surprised when Tommy actually did drink the milk. Thee were no adults at Tommy's table; he was just alone with three or four children, and as there was nobody to mind whether he ate or not, or to scold and fuss if he did not, his appetite acted naturally, and he ate his food with enjoyment. And the mother went home really believing for the first time that it was far better not to make a fuss, nor twist the whole situation by making eating a question of obedience and disobedience.

In the case of your little boy, I do not think there can be any doubt that the tantrums and general perversity are, at any rate, in part, due to his having lost his nanny. After all, young children get very attached to a competent nurse, and the sudden loss is often felt very severely, far more than mothers often realise. The child may not understand why he is upset and cross. He may not remember her in the way in which a grown-up vividly remembers a lost friend, but it acts on him, nevertheless. Everything may seem wrong to the child under these circumstances, and it is specially difficult if the new nanny is not quite so good as the one who has left him; not so motherly or firm. The child has to be given time to get over the change. Probably the reason why he will not play alone is because he is seeking for the comfort he has lost. I think that the way to deal with this difficulty is to give him your companionship as much of the day as you can conveniently arrange, remembering that his need is great. And then when you really cannot be with him and play with him, just keep firmly to it, see that he is supplied with playthings likely to amuse him, and leave him to cry, if he must.

But for a time I really should try to give him plenty of companionship and play. There is no doubt that we often go too far in our idea that the good child is the one who is content to play quite alone and does not show any active need for other people. That is, of course, convenient to us if we prefer to do other things rather than play with him, but I do not think there is any ground for thinking that it is an essential virtue of early childhood, or that all should be alike in that respect.

CONCENTRATION: IS IT A HABIT THAT CAN BE ACQUIRED?
The Nursery World
December 17, 1930

"CONCENTRATE" writes: *"I have no particular trouble, I'm pleased to say, but I would like advice on the following points:—(1) Concentration. A small girl friend of ours has just commenced school at our local High School. The teacher says she is a very bright child, but will not concentrate. Now, I'm wondering if this state of affairs is 'quite the usual' and with careful school training the child will learn to concentrate when she is older. To me it seems such an important point in a child's training. I have a small girl of three, who, like all healthy kiddies, is very busy and active. What I would like to know is 'can I' or 'how can I' train her to concentrate? Daddy says, leave her 'quite free,' but is it best to leave matters to take their own course? (2) Toys. Can a child have too many of the simple variety? We seem to have collected such a lot—a doll's pram, dolls, tea set, iron, rolling-pin, etc., a really nice counting frame, balls, bricks, a lovely piece of old blanket, which is a work of art with its bright wool stitches, and so I seem to be able to go on and on. If I turn out the toy box I hardly know which to dispose of, as they are all loved. Usually the toys are brought out a few at a time, then the 'stale' ones go back and a few fresh ones come out. I'm quite certain in this particular case the apparently large number of toys is not destroying the creative impulse; rather the reverse. Several of my friends allow their children 'half a dozen toys and no more,' but I think one can err in this direction. I think my question of concentration will be of general interest, and if you could answer through 'The Nursery World' columns I should be grateful."*

As you suggest, a great many people worry themselves about this question of teaching children to concentrate, but as a rule the whole problem tends to be wrongly conceived. We can't teach concentration in the way we can teach reading and writing. Concentration means one of two things: either being so interested in what one is doing that one has no thought for anything else, or being able to go on doing something that is not in itself enthrallingly interesting, but is done for some further end which has real value of its own. Now, the first form of concentration is undoubtedly the most valuable. All the great creative achievements of men and women in art and music and literature and science and sport are achieved because they are of absorbing and spontaneous delight. They have not sprung from a will or act of concentration, but from their inherent attraction. Now, the child, at any rate over five or six years, shows plenty of concentration of this kind. He can be completely absorbed in his building or modelling or games or make-believe, or in listening to story or to music. The other kind of situation in which one has to do dull or irksome or routine work that has no appeal of its own, but is part of a larger whole which has an intrinsic value, plays a very large part in the world, too, of course. Every mother, every nurse, every business man, and even the artist and scientist, have plenty of drudgery as well as creative delight. But the drudgery and the ability to go on with the dull routine are really only possible for us when we have some further attractive purpose to serve. The mother slaves for her children's welfare. The business man, the engineer, the scientist, know well that they cannot gain their greater ends without the dull routine. And yet none even of us grown-ups, unless we were stupid, or machine-like in our own natures, or except when driven by economic considerations, could carry out continuous drudgery that did not serve some greater end that we valued.

Now, of course, the child has to learn to be able to carry on routine activities that have no intrinsic appeal if he is to be able to achieve the greater ends and if he is to hold his place in the world. But it is useless to expect him to "concentrate" in a vacuum. According to his age he will be able to go on with, for example, the drudgery of learning to spell, to write clearly and legibly, etc., if he has some vivid sense of the value of such things, if they have some meaning and purpose for him. The ordinary boy of ten or twelve years of age has a great capacity for sustained routine work, provided only that he sees the motives for carrying it out and has a lively sense of an intelligible end to be achieved. The younger child has less ability for concentration of this kind, even when he wants to gain something by it. The periods of effort must therefore be shorter, and the results more immediate. With the younger child still, say under five or six, concentration is hardly a normal possibility. With all his abundant interests in the world around him, and his great delight in the exercises of his senses and his muscles, the little child's attention normally moves on from one thing to another. He may have short periods of complete absorption in some kind of play, but to expect him to stick to one thing for any length of time, or to demand that he should stick to something which has no appeal in itself, is simply to violate the normal laws of his growth. Only the dullest child will go on doing the same thing over and over again.

Concentration in the second sense, of sticking to a task, even when it does not hold one's spontaneous interest, thus only comes to be possible as the child grows older, and is really only to be expected in the later years of childhood. The first task of a teacher who has a bright child who will not concentrate is to inquire into her own methods of teaching. She should first make sure that she has found the right sort of appeal to the child's interest before blaming the difficulty on the child. On the other hand, it is perfectly true that there are occasional children who don't seem able to develop any steady interest in any occupation. This is not, however, a normal characteristic of children, and there is usually some conflict or inhibition behind it which should be inquired into.

(2) Toys. No, I don't think that there is any harm in a child having plenty of toys of the simple variety that she can use either in make-believe play or in construction of some sort. Children can certainly have too many of the merely mechanical kind with which there is nothing much to be done, but I don't see that there is any reason to be niggardly with the kind of toys that you mention. I don't see any virtue in the "half a dozen toys and no more" theory.

"CRITIC" writes: *I should be very grateful if you would tell me what you consider a suitable time-table for morning lessons (9:30 to 12) for children of five and six. I am particularly anxious to know how much actual brain work (such as reading and sums) is advisable, and what length each lesson should be. My little girl, aged six, is very quick and intelligent, but is bored with her lessons, and I think the fault may lie in the arrangement of the time-table.*

The problem you raise is linked up with the question asked by "Concentrate." Everything really depends upon the way in which the lessons are handled. If they are formal lessons with no elements of play in them, then they should certainly be quite short, a quarter of an hour or twenty minutes. The child will learn far more from short periods of such work than from long ones. If she gets tired and bored, then her time is more than wasted, because there is the risk that she will get a real distaste for lessons. But with children of five or six there should in any case be very little formal work. The sums, for instance, should be as far as possible of a practical kind, worked out with number material of the Montessori type, or in actual practical problems connected with the child's constructive interests. For example, in making dolls' clothes, in making and furnishing the dolls' house, there could be a great deal of practical adding and measuring and subtracting. So in learning to cook simple things, which children of this age love to do, there could be lots of arithmetic in the weighing out of the ingredients, in buying them in the shop, and counting up what they cost and reckoning the change. This sort of practical arithmetic is of infinitely more value than formal sums. I should strongly suspect, if a quick, intelligent child of six was bored with her lessons, that the lessons themselves were of the wrong type. Intelligent children love games of counting, learning the time, working out dates and the number of days to Christmas or a birthday party, and reckoning the cost of things. There is really no need for sums to be boring to a bright child. So with reading and writing: if use is made of the words the child can read in games and stories, she will not be bored. I am, however, going to discuss the whole question of reading and writing in my talk next week. Meanwhile, I should, if I were you, be inclined to go into the question of the method by which your little girl is being taught, and would certainly keep any formal lesson very short indeed.

LEARNING TO READ AND WRITE: SOME MODERN METHODS
The Nursery World
December 24, 1930

I have had a letter from a correspondent who is an advocate of the Montessori method of teaching reading and writing, and who appears to feel that I have not done justice to the merits of this method in my recent remarks about it. As the subject is undboutedly one of general interest, I am quoting extracts from her letter (too long to print as a whole). I am naturally anxious that my readers should feel that in these columns they do get a representative view of such modern methods as have any serious claim to respect.

But in the end, of course, one judges between rival methods on the evidence as one sees it, and when correspondents ask me to advise them about methods of teaching reading and writing, I can but offer them the fruit of my own experience with children and my knowledge of the general consensus of opinion among practical teachers and psychologists.

(My correspondent) gives a clear account of the initial steps in the Montessori method of teaching and writing.

At various times in these columns I have suggested quite other ways of beginning reading and writing—those that are known as "word-whole" or "look-and-say" methods. In these methods one does not begin with sounds and letters, but with actual names of things and people and actions in which the child is interested. The most natural unit of speech in the young child is the word. There are some psychologists who suggest that the real unit of speech is in fact the sentence, and some very interesting experiemental work is now being carried on by one psychologist with a "sentence-whole" method in which the child is taught from the beginning the written forms of short, simple sentences that are of vital interest to him. Most of us, however, think that the word is a more practicable unit for the young child, although we are awaiting the result of this experiment with great interest. For the young child, of course, a word very often does the duty of a sentence. "Down" may mean "I want to get down"; "Out," "I want to go out." Even "Daddy," when said with an expressive gesture, may mean "Lift me up" or "Come along and play with me." In any case, all through his early years the child has a great passion for naming all the things around him, and clearly gets a delightful sense of power from knowing the names of things.

Here, then, in starting with words as the unit of reading we are on very firm psychological ground. It is perfectly true, as "X." suggests, that many little children are spontaneously interested in sounds and parts of words, and when they are so interested there is, of course, no reason in the world why this should not be followed up. And, even when we start with the "word-whole" method, we very often go on to the analysis of the sound-whole into its parts, and the linking of these phonic sounds with movable letters which represent them. But I have always found—and here the great majority of psychologists in England, Germany, Belgium and America agree—that this interest in separate sounds is less sustained, less vital, than the interest in names and word-wholes. A name is a real tool. With it the child can express his emotions, his wishes, and his thoughts. It is the unit of communication. That is why it makes the best jumping-off point for learning to read.

I have described on several occasions in replies to correspondents the various stages of this method: how we label all the common objects around the child in clear, printed letters, each name on a separate card, and play games with him, using these labels, such as by saying aloud, "Give me the (pin)," here supplying the printed name, or "Where is the (cup)?" "It is on the table." Then we go quickly on to simple commands (which are, of course, also used in the Montessori method at a later stage), printed as a whole sentence on different cards. For example: "Shut the door," "Pick up the pin," "Lie down," and so on. We can then pass to a series of pictures of different sorts, with names printed below them and boxes of movable letters with which the child can make the names himself. Then, too, we print for the child, on a blackboard or large piece of brown paper, simple sentences dictated by him about things he has seen or done: "I saw a bunny," "We went to the shops," "Johnny is coming to tea," and so on. Very soon little stories can be composed by the child, which either he or we print on the paper made up into a little book, or on to a large sheet of thick paper hung on the wall. These are used over and over again for reading practice.

These methods are being used to-day in many of the more progressive schools and are found to be most fruitful and stimulating. In some cases, though not all, the children are also encouraged at a later stage to analyse the words they have learnt into separate sounds, and I think it is always useful, in fact, to do this. In every direction the living interests of the child should be appealed to and made use of, and our sense of the value of one sort of method need not blind us to the merits of another. They can always be combined.

This word-whole method of teaching reading and writing is also in wide use among the more progressive schools in Belgium, particularly those that have been influenced by the leading psychologist there, Professor Decroly. And in further confirmation of the special value of the word-whole approach to reading, there is the interesting fact that in child guidance clinics, where they have to deal with special backwardness and disability in reading amongst older children (often up to fifteen or sixteen years of age), their corrective methods are mainly of the word-whole type.

As to my own practical experience, I have in fact worked with all these different methods, giving the Montessori method itself a thorough trial with different groups of children, and this experience led me to the conclusion that the word-whole method had a far more general appeal, and links up far more fruitfully with the child's practical motives for learning to read and write.

In the schools run on strict Montessori lines it is perfectly true that, as my correspondent says, children do acquire a great facility in recognising the different sounds and representing them with written or printed letters. But in these schools a very definite morale is built up by suggestion, which leads the children in this direction rather than in any other. Children in a freer environment, where a greater spontaneity of behaviour and a greater variety of occupations are allowed, do not so light-heartedly take to sound analysis and word building. As Stern, the leading child psychologist in Germany, has pointed out (quoting with approbation another psychologist): "It is the paucity of other games in the Montessori schools which makes the children take to this new occupation. In the Froebel kindergartens, with their incomparably greater variety of occupations to exercise the child's powers of intuition and imagination, his interest and independence, as a general rule, scarcely any instances of liking for reading and writing exercises are to be observed."

THE NEED FOR CONSISTENCY
The Nursery World
April 15, 1931

My general point is one I wish I could make so clear that everybody would understand and remember it in connection with practically every aspect of nursery training. It is this: the great need for consistency in our ways of handling a child, and steady pursuit of a method of training based upon the awareness of all these problems of *learning* and of *growth*. What so often happens, in the desperate anxiety of mother and nurse to make their children clean and docile as quickly as possible, is a sort of blind search for a panacea, an almost magical method of scolding or punishment or appeal that will bring about the result *at once*. First one method is tried for two or three days, or perhaps a few weeks; then it is abandoned and another taken up. If this doesn't work immediately, it too is dropped and a third tried. This haste for a quick and easy method springs, of course, from an intense wish to help the child and to make him good and happy. But as so often happens, an apparently short cut turns out to be the longest way round. In the training of a little child it is very rare indeed that panaceas can be found which will cure things in a hurry.

Learning control of the sphincters of bladder or bowel is essentially a matter of slow growth. It is not even a straightforward problem of habit building, but essentially a social problem, bound up with the complex processes of the child's love and trust in us and his of fear and defiance. Some children are certainly by nature easier to train than others, but we have no means of ensuring that this nature will be of that easy kind from the start. We can, however, steadily and consistently follow methods of regular and cheerful suggestion, knowing with reasonable certainty that they will effect the desired end with time and patience. Changing horses in the middle of the stream bewilders the child, sets him on his guard against us, and compels him to defend himself by being independent of our wishes and defiant to our commands. But cheerful, friendly, consistent routine sets his mind at ease, puts him in a situation he can understand, sooner or later wins his trust, and gives him the chance of finding what he needs so much, the firm support of an orderly world based upon love and understanding.

Sometimes I feel that mothers who hastily change their methods in the way described are themselves rather like little children digging up a bulb they have just planted in order to see whether it is growing! Patience and confidence in the future are just as essential to successful training of children as to successful gardening.

"M.S.H." does seem to have tried patient training, but, I would suggest not long enough. She doesn't seem to have allowed for the fact that some children are more difficult to train than others, and need longer time before settled habits are built up. One has, moreover, with many children, to expect occasional lapses due to anxiety. It is not in the least surprising, for example, that the child has become worse after the circumcision. After such a psychological shock as circumcision always is, he is bound to be more disturbed and difficult. He needs extra patience and extra love. I hope very much that "M.S.H." will now feel more confident in not punishing the child. I would not suggest altogether ignoring the problem, but rather using calm positive suggestion without any reproach or undue urging.

NERVOUS HABITS AND MASTURBATION
The Nursery World
June 10, 1931

"WORRIED" writes: *"I have always read your articles in 'The Nursery World' with great interest, and many times have had benefit from them. I am now going to ask your help in a problem of my little charge, aged five, a girl. Ever since I have been with her (about eighteen months) she has had nervous habits, which, try how I might, she does not give up, namely, nail-biting, nose picking and eating, and, lastly and most worrying, she is continually playing with herself—in bed especially, although I give her toys to cuddle. I have never scolded her for it, but have told her that nice little girls don't do those things; but I don't keep at her about it in case she is attracted too much to her faults. Can you tell me if this particular habit be masturbation, and could you explain to me what it may lead to if allowed to continue? 'N.'s' mummie says every little girl does it, but I had two little girls before I had 'N.', and they did not. She is a happy child, has a wonderful appetitie, and is a generally healthy, intelligent child. If you could help and explain, as I must plead ignorance where this is concerned, I would be most grateful."*

I am very glad to hear that you have never scolded your little charge for these habits, nor even pressed too heavily on the idea that "nice little girls don't do these things." None of these habits—nail-biting, nose-picking and masturbation—can be cured by scolding or punishment. They invariably get worse if one adopts that method. With regard to the masturbation, this is far more common than many people realise, and I am constantly being asked about it.

Now, the very first thing to be said is, don't worry too much about it. Most people are far more distressed than there is real cause for being, largely because they think that their own child is the only one that does it, and must therefore be abnormal. And when the mother or nurse gets worried the child gets frightened, and that makes her do it far more frequently. The more ashamed and worried the child is about it, the more likely it is to happen! It is very important *not* to focus her attention upon it by talking about it or scolding her. She has to be weaned from it, and cannot be forced. The children in whom the habit becomes firmly fixed and uncontrollable are nearly always those who *have* been scolded or frightened about it in the beginning. The more undisturbed and calm you yourself can be the more you will be able to help the girl grow our of it.

That is why I first of all assure that the habit is much less harmful than many people fear, or even than doctors used to think some years ago. It is far more common in both boys and girls than we used to realise; and *in itself* it does not do anything like the harm we used to imagine. The harm it does comes chiefly from the child's guilt and terror about; that is why it helps to avoid scolding her. This has been proved over and over again, among children of all ages, including boys and girls in their teens.

The best methods are indirect ones. Don't let yourself be persuaded by anyone, whatever happens, to try any ways of *forcibly* preventing it. I heard from a mother recently of a little girl who had had her legs put into splints to try to cure the habit. After months of misery this had been given up, and had not helped in the very least. On the other hand, I know several splendid children who had the habit in very early years, but who are free of it now. Their mothers and nurses followed the indirect way of helping all their interests in the outer world during the day—building and modelling and running and playing; and as their skill and knowledge grew, they tired themselves out with happy play, and got to falling asleep as soon as they went to bed.

I don't think it would do any harm to suggest to the little girl, quite calmly and cheerfully, without scolding or reproach, that it is better not to do this. A quiet word without fuss is often a help; but you have to allow time for her to grow out of it, even with the best methods and conditions. It will probably disappear quite normally later on, if not too much fuss is made.

If, however, this or the nail-biting and nose-picking went on indefinitely, or became more marked, than it would be as well if you could persuade the little girl's mother to have definite advice from a medical psychologist. No one but an expert is qualified to deal with any of these problems, and if the child doesn't grow out the habits, then such advice is really called for. If, presently, you would like to know the name of a suitable medical psychologist, and will write to me again, I shall be very pleased to give the necessary information.

CAN SELF-CONTROL BE TAUGHT?
The Nursery World
August 19, 1931

"M.E.P." writes: *"Can you help me bring up my wee daughter, as I find great difficulty in doing this as well as I should like? I must explain fully. She is one year old, her brother is two years eight months (he is of a sweet-tempered disposition). Just lately she has become very bad tempered. Throws her food away when she has licked the butter off, and so on. Screams when put on the chamber very often, and always* wants to be picked up. She has only two bottom teeth, and is cutting four at the top, I think. She is remarkably strong, plump and fit, and as brown as a berry. She has always had a temper from her earliest days, and she does not care for strangers. She is full of determination, and is obviously 'able to take care of herself' even at this age. She always wants to come to me as soon as I enter the room. She is, on the other hand, a very happy child, quite fearless in her bath, and splashes and kicks, not caring if she falls over or gets her eyes wet. How am I to treat her so that she grows out of this temper? I will add an important point. It is inherited. I have, and did have as a child, a terribly hot temper (soon over). My father also has it. It has been my one great sin in life, my one and only trouble. It has caused many regrets in my life, and I do not want my little baby to have such a curse in her life. I was spoilt, for peace' sake, as a child (and even, now, I think) because my mother's heart was not strong. When the children scream and are very naughty I get very irritable and very often lose my temper. I know how wrong this is, but I am anything but a perfect mother. I always read your articles and the letters of Sister Morrison; try to live up to this high standard, but it is not easy. I have only a smallish home and one maid, who is far more patient than I am. They are good kiddies really, but as I can see this trait in my baby. I do most earnestly want to guide it rightly. I shall be so glad to hear your answer. Baby sometimes stays awake and wants to play for two or three hours in the night if she wakes, and will not lie down. She doesn't cry, only coos and talks. Now I strap her down and she goes to sleep. You will, I hope, excuse this long letter, but I am very anxious about it."*

I sympathise very much with your difficulty, as it is never easy to handle a child who has such a ready temper, especially if one feels guilty oneself over the same sort of thing. I agree too with the importance of trying to train your little girl so as to curb her temper. There is, however, only one general piece of advice to be given—that is, to be perfectly firm in not allowing the child to tyrannise over you or other people because you are afraid of her hot temper. If she finds that she gains advantage by her outbursts she will naturally go on indulging in them. If, however, she finds that they bring her no gain, and she does not get any privilege or consolation through her temper, she is much more likely to control it. In your own case this policy of firm control could not easily be followed because of your mother's delicacy, but I gather there is not the same reason in your case for indulging your little girl for the sake of peace. I know that the problem is more difficult for you because you find it hard to be both firm and patient, and children screaming can be extraordinarily trying when they are vigorous and strong. But there really is only the one way to train a child of this kind, and that is a calm, steady firmness. If one can possibly attain this it does gradually make the child more sensible and controlled. I am sure you know this quite as well as I do. What I wonder is whether you are not worrying too much about your own temper and striving after an impossible perfection. I sometimes feel that my remarks in these columns do suggest a standard of perfection that cannot possibly be attained by anybody. But, after all, all I can do here is to point out the direction in which wiser handling of children lies. I don't imagine that children need perfect parents, or that they have a right to reproach us if we are imperfect and sometimes lose our tempers and get impatient. I think you probably get a feeling of hopelessness when you see the child screaming in temper because of your own difficulties, and that makes you less able to cope with her than you would be otherwise. But there is no need to give way to your little girl for peace' sake, and so you should be able to train her gradually to greater sense and self-control.

"I SMACKED HER"
The Nursery World
January 22, 1936

"NANNY" writes: "*After reading two letters on the question of smacking children, I would like to tell you my experience. My charge was nearly a year old when I took her. She was eighteen months old before I had a good night's rest. She would wake up every night and cry, sometimes for hours. As she was a healthy, normal child, I put it down at first to teething time, and tried to soothe her to sleep again. But it was of no avail. Sometimes mummie would come in and take her into her room in order to give me a few hours' rest. She would cry for an hour on end without a tear in her eye. Then one night, instead of petting her, I gave her a smacking instead. For the rest of the night it was effective. She was very quiet. So every night after that, when she woke up and cried without reason, I smacked her. At the end of three weeks, I found I had nights of undisturbed rest. She is getting on for two and a-half years now, but I have no more trouble. I found when I took her on that she would not go to sleep without being rocked, even when she was put down after her bath at night. Why? Because until I came, mummie brought her up. It is my opinion that where the upbringing of children is concerned, the present-day mothers are hopeless. If my little one sits and dreams over her meals instead of eating her food up, I give her hand a sharp smack, but this is very rare. If I say to her, 'Nannie wants you,' she comes straight away. I never have to tell her twice to do anything. If ever she is really naughty, I put her to stand in the corner. 'Alison's Mother' should try this. If she is going to feel 'awful' every time she punishes her child now, it is nothing to what she will feel when her child defies her and makes a scene in public. This is exactly what my charge does when mummie takes her out alone. But mothers think if they smack their children they will lose their love, little realising that the hand that loves them must sometimes hurt them for their good. In spite of the 'brutality' I have shown to my little one, she always says when she sees me going out without her, 'Nannie no go away. Nannie stay.'*"

I am glad to have an opportunity to take this subject up further, and I am going to say quite frankly what I think about the methods described by the writer of this letter. I will begin by saying that I would allow no one with such a point of view and such a way of handling a tiny child to come anywhere near a child for whom I was responsible. The method works for the practical convenience of the nurse. It is convenient to have a child who will do everything one wants at a moment's notice, and who will hide all troubles and difficulties instantly by going to sleep for fear of smacking. But the duty of a nurse or the responsibility of a mother does not lie in finding the shortest way to her own practical convenience. It surely consists in finding the way that will not only help the health and happiness of the child at the present, but will ensure satisfactory development, health, happiness, independent social responsibility, and full development of skills and interests in later childhood and in grown-up life. Now, the experience of all the Child Guidance Clinics and of all the people who have to do with difficult children in later years, say from four or five onwards, and above all, with delinquent children in the middle years of childhood and early adolescence would confirm me in saying that just this type of method with tiny children is responsible times out of number for these later difficulties. I do not say, and no one can say, that in every single case such stern and stupid methods will result in anti-social behaviour or severe neuroses. There are children who can come through the worst treatment successfully, just as there are children who become ill and difficult even with the most understanding nurses and parents. Human development is so complex that one can never predict with absolute certainty, but all the experience, as I say, of the Child Guidance Clinics, and of those who have to advise and treat ill and difficult and unhappy children in the later years, would confirm the view that it is extremely probable that a little child treated as this one is treated would grow up with some serious neuroses or anti-social character. The risk is so great that, as I began by saying, I myself would not allow anyone with such methods to have anything to do with the child for whom I was responsible. Such complete inability to understand the child's point of view, to have any glimmer of imagination with regard to the child's problems, to see the child as a person or to think of the child's future, as distinct from the nurse's present convenience, would in my mind entirely disqualify a person for dealing with children of any age. I know that I am speaking very strongly, but I do so with a full sense of responsibility, and with the knowledge of all the experience of other people, as well as my own, behind these statements. Recently, a psychiatrist who is experienced in the remedial care of delinquent girls and adolescents, and who has a home where a certain number of such girls are kept, and treated with every helpful method known to psychological science and medicine, has told me that after six years' experience she has gone over the results of her treatments and the histories of the girls concerned. She finds that she has had fifty per cent. successes, that is to say, half of the delinquent girls in her care have been returned to life responsible and sensible and happy people. The other half have to be counted failures, and she has found that in every single case of these failures the outstanding fact in the girl's history was lack of love in the first two years. This took various forms. Some of the children were illegitimate, some of them had really cruel parents, some of them had stern and un-understanding treatment. But in every case the children failed to experience a really affectionate relation with some human being during the first two years. Now I am not suggesting that the writer of this letter fails altogether to give affection to the little child in her charge. The child has had some affection from her mother, so that this case does not illustrate the situation of not having been loved at all during the first two years; but to have a nurse who treats one with such severity and such complete lack of understanding is getting very near the case of children who suffer from lack of love. And I would not venture to hope that a really happy and successful child in later life is the outcome of such treatment in the early years.

2
Articles and Talks, 1929–46

THE TRIALS OF THE CHILD
BBC talk
1929

Let us take any ordinary situation. Suppose, for example, that we travel with a little child of three or four in a crowded railway carriage, and try to feel things as they seem to him. First of all, you see all round you the faces of big grown-ups who are quite strange, and because they are strange they are terrifying. As one little girl said to a boy friend—"These people don't like you because they've never seen you before." You look shyly at them, and turn away again quickly if they glance at you. If one of them smiles at you in a friendly way, your heart grows shyly warm. But it may be a long time before you feel quite sure that they are really smiling, and you dare to smile back. Most of them don't smile, but really do frown when they find that you, and perhaps your baby brother, are in the carriage. And as soon as you begin to jump about—and your legs *will* jump whether you want them to or not—these big strange people frown more and more. And so you get a bit more frightened, and a bit cross, and find it still harder to sit still. Then the seats are so high that if you do try to sit still, your feet dangle over the edge and you can't find a comfortable way of tucking them up. And if you stand on the floor, you soon grow tired and fidgetty. There's something about your legs when you're small and young which simply refuses not to move about and change their position all the time. You *must* move them—that's what young legs are like.

If you are allowed to kneel up on the seat and look out, you can see all sorts of exciting things going past. Some of the fields are full of cows and horses and poppies, and you would like the train to go slowly so that you could watch these a long time, and count how many there are. But it goes ever so quickly past these lovely things, and then there are a lot of dull things that you don't a bit want to see, and the train goes much more slowly past these. You think they'll *never* pass, and there'll never be any more cows or horses. And if you get impatient and call out "Want to see more cows", the grow-ups say, "Be quiet—don't be a naughty boy", although you can't a bit understand what's naughty in that. All you know is that you want them to come, *very badly,* as one small child said.

Then you begin to feel very tired, and the noise and jerking of the train won't let you fall asleep even on mother's lap. And you begin to cry just because you feel so miserable and they all look so cross.

Or perhaps you are being taken for a walk by mother, when she's going to the shops. She's in a hurry, and you put your feet as fast as you can one in front of the other. She holds on tightly to your hot little hand, although it makes your arm ache to stretch up so far all the time. She doesn't stop when you see a lovely brown dog that you would like to stroke and talk to, nor let you climb up on that nice high wall and walk along the top. What are walls for if not to climb on? When you did climb on it once, you could see all sorts of exciting things—big trees, the pond in the field and some ducks on it, motorcars on the road beyond. Mother's tall enough to see this without climbing on the wall, but all *you* can see when you're down in the lane is the wall itself, it's so high and long and dull. Then you come to the shops, and mother hurries *past* the toy-shops, and takes you into the butcher's. And then into the grocers, where there are biscuits in tins with glass lids, and brushes and candles. You put out your hand to feel these, and she says "Don't touch, John". Coming back, you have to go near the station, and you want to stop and watch that engine shunting. They're such lovely wonderful things to you, you could watch them for hours. But mother doesn't see anything exciting in engines and signals. She hurries you on impatiently, because it's time for dinner.

One day, when you are six you and big Jack next door go fishing in the brook over the fields. The water gurgles and runs so quickly over the stones, and the sun shines and you're so hot and happy. Your foot slips once and you get your shoe all wet and muddy, and on the way home you tear your trousers when you're crawling through a fence so as to get back quicker. But you feel so important carrying tiddlers you've caught that you *forget* all about that, until mother, who is watching for you because you're late for tea, says "What have you done to your trousers, you naughty boy—and *look* at your dirty shoes! Come right *in* and take them off—you won't go *fishing* again if you can't keep cleaner than that. And she takes no notice of your wonderful tiddlers—they don't seem *anything* to her.

Before this, when you are three, just when you've been learning about letters for the first time, and are very proud because you can make the letter A, you see a piece of chalk on the table, and you feel at once that you *must* write A. You see the nice big space on the wall near you, looking just as if it was *made* for writing on, and you forget that you're in the parlour, and your fingers go on to make the marks—"up-down-atross, up-down—atross", you say, while the wallpaper gets covered over with chalky A's, and a piece of the chalk breaks off and gets squashed on the carpet. Mother hears you saying it, and comes in to see what you're *doing*. She's very cross and takes the chalk away, and doesn't seem to understand how *pleased* you were to have remembered how to make A. If *only* you had something of your *very* own to chalk on!

Suppose you're Mrs. Jones' little boy of three—the one who has been so naughty since the baby brother came. You were very happy before. You could climb on mother's knee whenever you wanted to, and it was *all* for you. When she had tucked you into bed at night, she stayed with you a little while and told you stories. If you had a pain she nursed you and coaxed you happy again. And when father came home he picked you up and laughed at you and said "Isn't he a fine boy?" Then mother was shut *away* in her room and left you all alone with Mary, who is cross when mother's not looking. And one day, after *ages* and ages, you were taken into mother's room to see her, and she had that other baby in her arms. Now she hasn't *time* to hold you on her lap or to stay with you and tell stories when you go to bed. She has to feed the *baby* or wash it. And she smiles at *it* and nurses and coaxes *it* more than you. And when dad comes home, he goes and looks at *it* and says "Isn't he fine?". And you mayn't shout now because you'll wake the baby; and you have to go walks with *Mary*, who won't let you do anything you want. It's *hard* to stop crying when you feel lonely and wretched. It's *hard* to stop wanting to do things to that baby who pushed you off mother's lap. And when mother puts you down to go to the baby, you feel such an awful blind rage and misery, you just bite. If *only* mother and daddy would make you feel sure that they love you as much as ever, you might feel happier and be able to like the baby more.

When we try to see things from the level of the small child in this way, we very soon discover two most important truths. First, that most of the things which as unsympathetic grown-ups we find rather trying are nevertheless real *needs* of the child in the way of growth. It would, for instance, be very bad for the young child with soft bones and weak muscles if we *could* make him sit still or stand up in one position for more than a short time. His limbs would either grow crooked or not grow at all. And the eager interest he feels in engines and horses and things in the shops and what he can see when he climbs on the wall—these are what his *mind* grows on. He can become skilful and wise only by trying to do things and satisfying his interests. To say to him "Don't touch, don't ask questions" is really to say "Don't grow, don't *try* to be intelligent".

And the second thing we learn is that his questions and his desire to move and see and do things becomes annoying to us most often when we fail to give him the right surroundings. Let him have a piece of board to chalk on. Let him wear old clothes that don't *matter* when he goes climbing or fishing. As often as possible, go at *his* pace when out for a walk with him, and stop to look at what he's interested in. Make it easy for him to do all the things his mind moves out to, and let him see that we are really interested in his pursuits. Then we shall begin to find as much pleasure in the growth of his skill and knowledge as he does himself.

No doubt many of us do these things from time to time; but we tend to look upon them as special privileges for special occasions, instead of the everyday needs of the young mind. They are just as important to the growing body and mind of the child as sunshine and rain to growing plants. There are some things we can't help, of course. Occasional railway journeys, for instance, can't be avoided. But if we *do* feel things from the child's point of view, if we share his fun in what he can see from the windows, if we answer his questions in a friendly way instead of saying "*don't*" all the time—then he will fidget and cry far less. And the journey will have been time used instead of wasted for him.

But all this points to the fact that we ourselves need the help of some knowledge of the ways in which children in general grow well and happily. Nowadays we add to the natural affection of nursing mothers as much knowledge as possible of the baby's digestion and good and bad ways of feeding him. And in the same way if we plan our ways of training his behaviour on a sound knowledge of the needs of his mind, we shall be more able to help him grow into all we want him to be.

Many people are trying to find out these things by applying the methods of scientific research to the study of all the different aspects of children's growth from infancy onwards. We can learn both from children who have developed satisfactorily, and from those who for one reason or another have got into difficulties. The Child Guidance Clinic will be studying chiefly the children whose development has not been quite normal and happy, the children who are doing badly at home, in school or in social life. The trained workers there will try to find out what has led to the difficulty in each case, by inquiring into all the circumstances of outer history, and into the inner development. The knowledge they thus bring together will help to lessen the trials of the child, as well as those of his parents. Children as well as parents have everything to gain from the spread of real understanding of their ways of looking at us and at the world.

CORPORAL PUNISHMENT
THE NEW ERA
July 1929

At this time of day, it may safely be taken for granted that the only motive for corporal punishment which claims the serious attention of liberal educators is the motive of 'cure' or 'reformation'. Two questions may then be asked: Does corporal punishment in fact, 'cure' or 'reform'? If so, and in so far as it does so, how can we understand this, psychologically? (With the important correlative—if, and in so far as it does *not*, how does *this* come about?) In this very brief paper, it is not possible to do more than glance at these questions; but it may be fruitful to bring them into relation with some recent developments in psychology.

The verdict of the history of crime and penology, and indeed of social history in general, is conclusive that corporal punishment and bodily degradation are not effective means of moral reformation. So convincing, clear and now generally accepted is the evidence for this that nothing more need be said about it here. There are, it is true, some Head Masters and magistrates who still *believe* flogging to be effective; but their belief does not in itself constitute evidence since it is rarely supported either by the concrete history of cases or their psychological analysis. Investigators[1] who take the trouble to follow up the later history of flogged offenders, or to find out what happens in the mind of the delinquent in response to the punishment, very rarely recommend the method. The wisest are not, of course, too completely dogmatic as to its invariable failure and harmfulness. Professor Burt, for example, allows that there *may* be occasional instances where the sharp and immediate experience of physical pain may be the needed stimulus to fresh habits and self-control. But he safeguards this admission with every sort of proviso and warning, and looks upon the method as exceptional and the last to be tried.

The detailed study of individual delinquents in recent years has made it quite clear that delinquency springs from definite conditions, of mind or body or circumstance. It can in each case be remedied by finding out what specific conditions led to it, and changing these positively and constructively. Corporal punishment is thus, in the vast majority of cases, either (or both) (a) beside the point; or (b) injurious (since it tends to confirm the psychological causes).

(a) It is, for instance, irrelevant in all those cases where the specific offence (or difficult behaviour) is mainly neurotic in character, although even here it may have evil reverberations on the general social attitude of the child. Such are cases of kleptomania, compulsive arson, truancy and vagrancy, many types of lying, enuresis, masturbation and other sex offences, violence, aggression and general intractability. The cleavage between neurosis and delinquency does not, of course, lie along the line of the type of crime, but along that of its psychological setting. Any one of these offences may be neurotic in origin, and, in such cases, corporal punishment is certainly powerless directly, and probably harmful indirectly.

(b) In other cases, it confirms and aggravates the psychological springs of the delinquency. For example, it justifies and develops the Ishmael attitude wherever the offence arises from misplaced personal aims and undesirable group ideals—friendship with older delinquents, loyalty to a gang, heroic defiance of the policeman and the law, and so on; or wherever it springs from 'stepmother' fantasies or real social isolation. Again, in the not infre-

---

1. V. Professor Burt: *The Young Delinquent,* p. 120 et seq. Also W. Clarke Hall: *The State and the Child,* pp. 23–31.

quent cases among delinquents and difficult children, where bodily pain has itself an erotic value, corporal punishment at the hands of the father or his representatives enhances the wish to provoke it, and thus confirms the evil it seeks to uproot.

Such are some of the psychological grounds for rejecting corporal punishment as a general means of the cure or reform of delinquents and difficult children.

Yet there still are to be found some psychologists who would give the infliction of physical pain a place in the earliest years of childhood, as an integral educative method for specific behaviour and under particular conditions. Among these, Dr. Watson's view represents, a new and very interesting phase of the belief in corporal punishment—and one likely to have a popular vogue under his influence. Let us hear his own words about it.[1]

"I think some fears and other negative responses should be built in . . . I do not hesitate when children begin reaching for objects not their own to rap their fingers smartly with a pencil. To get the right psychological condition, the parent should always apply this painful stimulus just at the moment when the undesirable act is taking place. If you wait for father to spank when he gets home it is practically impossible to establish a conditioned negative response. Unless negatively conditioned in this way, how else will children learn not to reach for glasses and vases? How can they learn not to touch strange dogs, fondle strange cats, to walk out into the water? But the building in of these necessary negative responses and gentler fear responses, both by the word 'don't' and by rapping the fingers smartly, must not be looked upon as punishing the child in the old sense. The word punishment should not appear in our dictionaries except as an obsolete word, and I believe that this should be just as true in the field of criminology as in that of childrearing. The parents' object in rapping the child with a pencil is to get it to react in conformity with certain social usages—to behave itself. Why, then should the parents ever be angry? Why should they ever punish in the old Biblical sense? Such things as beating and expiation of offences, so common now in our schools and homes, in the Church, in our criminal law, in our judicial procedure, are relics of the Dark Ages. The parents' attitude should be positive, should be that of the instructor. We can sum it all up by saying that the behaviourist advocates the early building in of appropriate common-sense negative reactions by the method of gently rapping the fingers or hand or other bodily part when the undesirable act is taking place, *but as an objective experimental procedure*—never as punishment". (Watson's italics.)

There are thus two points emphasised—the exactly right penalty at exactly the right time; and the mental attitude of the person who inflicts the penalty. (Dare we say, the name he gives to it?)

1. J. B. Watson: *The Psychological Care of Infant and Child*, pp. 58–9.

Now does this mental attitude and exact science of inflicting pain really make any difference to the child who suffers it? Is it thus made less unpleasant emotionally or less seemingly cruel? Is this modern form of the old intolerable humbug, "it hurts me more than it hurts you", really less bad? Does the supposed absence of anger and revenge in the parent leave the child himself equally undisturbed and matter-of-fact? Surely not. The likelihood is that it does far more psychological harm than straightforward anger. The child understands and easily forgives direct annoyance, since he feels like that himself. But this cold, calculating, deliberate hurt puzzles and frightens him, far beyond the extent of the actual pain. He does not, and cannot, understand our reasons and justifications for it, and that his loved parents should behave so is to him merely strange and terrifying.

Watson's moral blunder springs, of course, from his naïve and inadequate psychology, which does not take any account of *the child,* but only of a set of isolated reflexes, each one of which can be dealt with without reference to the others. Even on his own behaviouristic ground, Watson is clearly making a crude technical mistake in assuming that the pain inflicted by other people, and particularly by parents, produces exactly the same type of effect on the child as pain suffered directly from the physical environment—burning one's finger, or bumping one's knee. He leaves out of account the whole of the child's actual perception that *his mother* is the active source of the pain, the whole of his generalised affective response to her, and the whole of his previous experience. In other words, Watson here treats the child rather like a decerebrate preparation.

The child himself, however, makes no such mistake! *He* knows the difference between the experience of bumping or burning himself and having his mother rap his knuckles—as one has only to watch him in the two situations to see. And such behaviour on her part will certainly be "built into" his view of her, and his future responses to her.

No! It is clear that whatever value Dr. Watson's methods have (and we believe they have a great deal) as true "objective experimental procedure" for the discovery of some sorts of behaviouristic fact, they are as yet worlds distant from being an adequate psychological basis for education. And this new sort of apology for this new sort of corporal punishment is even less psychologically convincing than the old.

It is in fact far less soundly based. For the recent detailed study of the deeper psychology of young children, whether delinquent, difficult, or ordinary, by the psycholoanalytic technique, has shown that the old view of punishment as expiation has its deep psychological roots in the child himself, which have to be recognised and dealt with by the educator, if not in one way, than in another. It might, indeed, be possible to state the whole question of aims and technique of social education in terms of the child's internal problem of guilt and responsibility. For this problem arises for him in the earliest years—from the earliest time when he begins to be aware of his parents as persons, and to enter into love and hate relations with them, i.e. from at least the second year of life.[1]

It is only now beginning to be possible to understand how the earliest anxiety and guilt arise, and we have here no space to do more than refer to what is the most central problem of genetic psychology. Such guilt is, however, the forerunner of the developed 'conscience' of later life, but far more tyrannical, automatic and inarticulate; and it relates to guilty *fantasies*, not to real social responsibility. It is found in every child, and the difference between one child and another—between the normal, the neurotic and the delinquent—is not as to the presence or absence of this primitive conscience or 'super-ego', but as to (a) its rigour and sadistic quality, which depend upon the phase of libidinal history reached by the child when the super-ego was most strongly fixed; and (b) its manifold and variable inter-relations with the instinctual life.[2]

The delinquent and defiant child is not seldom suffering from an *excess* of conscience, i.e. of this primitive guilt and unconscious 'need for punishment', set up as a barrier against libidinal and aggressive impulses. Such unconscious need for punishment—and this is the real difficulty from the point of view of our present discussion—enters into a circular movement with the forbidden fantasies themselves, from which many children can hardly escape without analytic aid.

The educational problem in early childhood is thus not to *create* or foster the sense of guilt, for this is a given psychological factor; but to tame it and reduce its severity and automaticity, to alter its incidence and bring it into relation with a developing perspective and sense of social realities. The child has to be freed from the tyranny of his neurotic conscience, and the unconscious need for punishment. Only deep analysis can do this fully, and for the more neurotic child, little else is of permanent value. But in proportion as the child is free from severe neurosis, and therefore adaptable, the constructive methods of liberal education will help to this end.

Such considerations, based on the deeper studies of developmental processes, reinforce the view that corporal punishment is either idle or harmful. They strike more deeply, perhaps, at the Watsonian refinements than at an occasional hasty action on the part of any unpretending parent. But, what is more important, they enable us to understand far better than before *why* coporal punishment is uneducational, and to grasp the psychological realities underlying this judgment.

---

1. See:—(a) M. Klein: "The Early Stages of the Œdipus Conflict": *International Journal of Psychoanalysis*, Vol. IX, Pt. 2., pp. 167–180.
  (b) M. Klein, J. Rivière and others: "Symposium on Child Analysis": *I.J.P.*, Vol. VIII, Pt. 3.
  (c) E. Jones: "The Early Development of Female Sexuality": *I.J.P.*, Vol. VIII, Pt. 4, pp. 466–7
2. M. Klein: "Criminal Tendencies in Normal Children": *British Journal of Medical Psychology*, Vol. VII, Pt. 2, pp. 177–192.

THE CHILD AS SCIENTIST
The Spectator
1931

(Mrs. Isaacs is the Chairman of the Education Section of the British Psychological Society, and the author of *Intellectual Growth in Young Children*.)

Discussions recur from time to time among scientific men and educationists as to the best way of teaching science in the schools. The problem is usually envisaged as arising in the later years of childhood, at say, anything over ten years of age. And it is thought of commonly either as the problem of how to acquaint children with certain important selections from the body of scientific *fact,* or how to introduce them to full-fledged scientific *method*. Sometimes, and rightly, as both. But whether the stress be put upon fact or method, science is thought of chiefly as something which has to be brought *to* the child from outside.

But the behaviour of intelligent young children in fact suggests that, at a very much earlier age than is usually supposed, they are actually reaching out themselves to a view of the world which, when it is fully developed and articulated, can only be called a scientific one. Take, for example, their questions. Here is one of the many recently put to his mother by a boy of four years. "How can the hippo get down the steps into his tank, when his little front legs are such a long-way off his little back legs?"

Should we feel surprised and impatient that the boy cannot see how obvious it is that even such a creature as the hippopotamus can manage his own legs, since they *are* his? Should we let ourselves be amused at the child's "quaintness"? Or should we take the question as showing a serious and active interest, limited in its intellectual scope, but none the less genuine, in the mechanics of the hippo's movement?

A few months earlier the same child has asked "When a building has a corrugated iron roof, why is the corrugated iron always crinkly, and not flat like the other sorts?"

Here are questions from other children, all under four and a half years: "Why does the soap look smaller in the water?" "Why can't we see the stars in the daytime?" "Why do you see the lightning before you hear the thunder?" "Why does the glass look different in the water, but it doesn't if you just put water in the glass? The water can't really bend the glass, can it?"

And here is a spontaneous inductive movement in the mind of a child of three years and eight months: "I'd like to see dogs' teef and cats' teef and cows' teef and horses' teef and fwogs' teef and camels' teef and mice's teef." Mother: "Why?" "To see if they're like ours."

All intelligent children of about this age spend a great part of their time in such wondering comments and queries, especially if they have the good fortune to live with adults who show some sympathy with their interests.

Nor is it only special experiences like a visit to the Zoo that awaken their active attention. Every ordinary happening of daily life draws their inquiries as to How and Why.

Nothing seen is stale or obvious to young children. Buildings and bridges and road repairs, railway stations and trains, motor-cars and aeroplanes, the water in the bathroom taps and drains, soap-bubbles and smoke, the gas-fire and the electric light, the rain and the sun, the life and movements of animals, even our own behaviour to the child, come under his scrutiny and his effort to understand.

The extent of even the small child's devotion to this wondering interest in the world is always surprising to the sophisticated adult. The child will stand and watch some happening that interests him in the street or the fields until our patience is long exhausted, and on coming home he will play out what he has seen in dramatic repetition that bores the grown-ups but enchants the child himself. He will be in turn "The fastest express in the world," "The R 100," "the crane moving the big stones," "The man with the Hoover," "Mr. Jones to mend your typewriter," "a tiger coming to bite you," "the doctor coming to see your little boy who is very ill," and a host of other moving things or people.

Nor is the little child's interest in real happenings confined to passive contemplation, verbal questioning, and dramatic expression. If he has the chance, he will try to "find out" by practical handling and experiment. Take, as one instance, the following record of a group of young children in a favorable environment: "Some modelling wax having been dropped on a hot-water pipe, the children discovered that it melted, and tried some more. When they found that all the wax would melt, whatever colour it was, they went on to try other materials—plasticine, wood, chalk and so on, talking about it together and telling Mrs. I. 'Plasticine melts. Wood won't melt,' and so on. The whole of this was entirely spontaneous. (Ages four to five).

To many it may seem monstrous to try to bring science and the little child together. The world of science is cold and hard and abstract and indifferent: that of the child is warm and tender and dramatic and full of lovely imaginings. How can they be brought together without doing violence to him? Leave at least the young child alone with his charming beliefs in fairies and Santa Claus! Cold, hard reality will snatch his dreams from him soon enough, without our forcing his attention to it prematurely.

Yet the child's active questioning about the How and Why of things, did we but listen to it, would show us that, woven in with his love of creating and expressing, is this delight in inquiring and knowing about the real world. He bears within himself the seed of the patient discoverer no less than that of the creative artist and practical doer. And we do violence indeed if we fail to welcome this movement of his spirit, as well as those others. How can we meet and welcome it? Obviously not by *lessons* either on science in general or on parts of it in particular: we should but stultify and disgust the little child if we took his impulse of inquiry solemnly and didactically. His capacity for absorption of presented facts is very limited. If we began to teach him systematically, he would soon protect himself by boredom and inattention. The vital impulse of curiosity itself, although so eager and persistent, is shy and wayward in the young child. It is a wild animal rather than a tame and disciplined beast of burden.

The time for the teaching of science is indeed much later, but the time for meeting the child's active interests is here and now, when they arise. If we meet his questions with frank sympathy and respect, answering them as well as we can, and understanding their meaning to the child, his knowledge of real things will develop and grow as happily and easily as his skill in games and the arts and crafts of childhood. It is not so much information we need to give as the comradeship of interest in the world. Our sharing of his enjoyment of the adventure of discovering the world is what the child seeks in us.

Such a response on our part, frank and good-humoured, free from all pedantry and system, helps to foster in the child's mind, that attitude to the world which will later be one with the methods of thought we call Science.

Let the child play and sing and dance to his heart's content. Let him make-believe and act and draw and dig. Let him read of fairies and ogres and princes and sleeping beauties. But let *us* not deny his active interest in the real when he shows it, not fail to give to his first impulse to subject himself and us to the authority of facts the understanding and sustenance with which we meet his other needs. Let us not bar the door to the world of scientific thought when he himself essays to open it.

THE HUMANE EDUCATION OF YOUNG CHILDREN
XIXth Annual Conference of
Educational Associations
University College, London
January 1931

I want to plead that the term "humane education" should be interpreted in a very wide sense. It should not be thought of simply as a matter of building up the sentiment of "kindness to animals," but rather as the education of children to biological understanding. The mere sentiment of kindness to animals, no matter how thoroughly it may be inculcated and how strongly felt, is liable to a form of excess leading to real unkindness, and liable, too, to break down at times, either through lack of imagination or lack of knowledge.

The humane sentiment needs to be built upon an active constructive interest in the life-histories and life-cycles of animals, as an interest for its own sake. This attitude of mind, which might be described as the "birdwatching" attitude, is becoming increasingly widespread among intelligent people. Even those who at one time went out with a gun may now take a camera instead. We should try to build up, too, an active interest in the whole fascinating nexus of biological relations between animals and men. In biology we open up to children a vast field of intellectual delight, and one of the utmost practical importance.

If this be accepted as the aim of humane education, there comes then the question of method, and next the question of the age at which to begin such studies. The answer to this lies in the psychology of little children themselves, their native interests and impulses. All intelligent children have an eager and spontaneous interest in animals from an early age. There can be little doubt that children are interested in animals earlier than in plants. They have a far more vivid sympathy with animals, sensing the unity of nature between their own impulses and those of animals, and they spontaneously want to know the why and the wherefore of the animal world. One boy of four years, for instance, coming home recently from the Zoo, wanted to know, "How can the hippopotamus get down into his tank when his little front legs are such a long way from his little back legs?" Another intelligent child of three years and eight months said to her mother, "I would like to see dogs' teef, and cats' teef, and cows' teef, and horses' teef, and fwogs' teef, and camels' teef, and mice's teef." When her mother asked "Why?" The child said, "To see if they're like ours." Here one obviously has a very vital interest in the structure and the life of animals—something very real and solid to build upon educationally.

Along with this native interest, however, there are in the child's mind contradictory impulses of actual behaviour also. In all little children there are to be found impulses both of cruelty and of tenderness, although one may show a readier tenderness and another a more frequent cruelty. It is safe to say that if one observes from the beginning the whole behaviour of any little child to all kinds of living things, including lowly creatures like worms, both these tendencies will be found at work. The great majority of little children, for instance, are interested in the worms turned up in the garden, but sooner or later they will cut them in two with the spade. One might say, of course, that this should not be called cruelty, but rather a failure to realise that the worm is a living thing. That might indeed always be true of the very little child; but later on the intelligent child does undoubtedly have some sense of what the animal is feeling. And he gets definite pleasure from the feeling of power, of being able to cause pain. Mixed up with this there are always sudden waves of tenderness, too. I have seen a boy of four hug a puppy affectionately, and then suddenly throw it into a pool of water and laugh to watch it struggle out. As in older people, so in little children, both these trends of behaviour occur, and the question is how best to deal with them. What is the most fruitful way to direct them, so that the outcome shall be satisfactory both for the development of the child and for the welfare of animals?

Now, if we merely say, "Don't be cruel. You must be kind," that does not necessarily achieve the desired result. Sometimes the cruel impulse is temporarily checked; but without a constructive education, the child may be cruel when we are not there to prevent him. Merely negative methods may result in the attitude of mind which some women show, when, for instance, they have to get rid of a family of unwanted kittens. They may throw them into a pail of water without putting a lid on top, and then go away because they are not able to bear seeing pain and suffering, and are so sensitive that they can't even take steps to see that the kittens are drowned quickly. This sort of result is clearly not a desirable one. If we ourselves, moreover, use aggressive methods in trying to teach children to be "kind," intelligent children can be trusted to see through that sort of inconsistency. One little girl, for instance, had been in a violent temper and had bitten her brother, and her father had smacked her. She said to her mother, "He smacked me all over." The mother said, "It's an awful pity to bite," and the child replied, "It's an awful pity to smack."

The problem of dealing with the contradictory impulses of the child is made more difficult because of the great inconsistencies of grown-up standards. I have elsewhere tried to make a list of the different sorts of behaviour in which we adults indulge towards animals under different situations.[1] They are surprisingly confused and contradictory, and it is worth while trying to realise what effect they may have on the minds of children who are struggling to order and control their own conflicting impulses.

Sully recorded some years ago a vehement protest of one little boy on this matter. He was looking at a picture of some seals:—C.: "What are seals killed for, Mamma?" M.: "For the sake of their skins and oil." C. (turning to a picture of a stag): "Why do they kill the stags? They don't want their skins do they?" M.: "No, they kill them because they like to chase them." C.: "Why don't policemen stop them?" M.: "They can't do that, because people are allowed to kill them." C. (loudly and passionately): "Allowed, allowed? People are not allowed to take other people and kill them." M.: "People think there is a difference between killing men and killing animals." C. was not to be pacified this way. He looked woebegone, and said to his mother piteously, "You don't understand me."[2]

The little boy who had made the remark about the hippo at the Zoo asked his mother recently whether she wouldn't like a moleskin coat. When she replied, "No, I wouldn't like the little moles killed for it," the boy, after

---

1. Susan Isaacs, *Intellectual Growth in Young Children*, pp. 161–162. (Routledge & Sons, 1930.)

2. J. Sully, *Extracts from a Father's Diary.* (Longmans, 1903.)

a pause, said reflectively, "Mummy, wasn't there a mole in the garden, and didn't granddad trap and kill it?" "Yes, Colin." "Well, wouldn't you kill a mole if one came in your garden?" The mother said, "Yes, I suppose I should have to." "Then why not make the little skins into a coat?"

Behind these queries, there lies not only a feeling of real distress on behalf of the animals, but also a deep bewilderment about adults' views and behaviour. Such questions and wonderings in the child are clearly very relevant to the problem of how to build up a humane attitude. We obviously need to aim at a much greater consistency in our own standards and our own thought as educators. It is indeed one of the aims of this Society to bring such a change about. If the public mind were more consistent and humane, it would be easier to educate children in these respects.

As regards direct teaching, it is important to take a wide biological point of view with children from the beginning, not turning their minds away from death when it appears to them, but helping their interest in the whole life-cycle and in the causes of death when they meet it. I have found in my work with little children that if we do not shut out the children's interest in any of the biological phenomena they meet—life, birth, death, all the processes of their own bodies, and the biological unity of human and animal life—we are more likely to achieve the end we have in view, that of making children consistently humane to animals. By building up a sustained interest in biology we can ensure the welfare of animals far more securely than if we content ourselves with the simple teaching of kindness. Mere sentiment needs to give place to knowledge and intellectual understanding, and in this way we may open to children the whole significant world of biological fact and discovery.

A CONTRIBUTION TO THE SOCIAL PSYCHOLOGY OF YOUNG CHILDREN
Le Journal de Psychologie, 1932
(translated by Denis Brearley, 1980)

The observations hereafter described were made, during the course of three and a quarter years' work, upon a group of very intelligent middle class children aged between two and seven years, in an experimental school[1] where it was attempted to create and develop a special technique of education. The aim of this article is not to describe this technique nor yet the work of the school as a whole[2] (for example, there will be no consideration of its important intellectual aspects), but simply to report certain facts regarding the conduct of a group of small children placed in these

1. The Malting House School for Young Children, at Cambridge

2. I have described the aims and methods of this school in my book *Intellectual Growth in Young Children* (London, Routledge, 1931), to which I would direct the reader desiring a detailed description of the actual conditions of group life in which these observations were gathered.

conditions. I will say simply, that, so far as social education is concerned the methods employed were such as to stimulate to the utmost the intelligent observation and judgement of the children, so as to found the social requirements upon objective factors and thereby to diminish the tendency to the sentiment of guilt.

As will be seen, this technique has offered to psychological enquiry a very rich and varied social life, expressed with a rare clarity and distinctness. What the children said and did was noted down in a complete and detailed manner. Inasmuch as this was probably the first time that such a group of children had been systematically observed in conditions leaving full liberty to the expression of social (and anti-social) sentiments, these notes have great theoretical interest. What follows represents only a very limited selection, intended to illustrate certain general points.

The experiment began with a round dozen children, all boys, aged 2½ and 5½; their numbers afterwards rose to eighteen. The first girl came in the third term of the first year, and others followed; the average proportion of boys to girls during the three years was two to one. Among the children of the original group, there were half a dozen boys of definitely "difficult" type; the rest were what are customarily called "good" children.

During the first and most critical year, the behaviour of the children at the school passed through a succession of well-marked phases. The first, which was very short, was a period of appeasement and submission, due in part to the effect of the unknown, the novelty of the people and places; and in part, at least so far as the difficult children were concerned, to the fact that they expected the same kind of prohibitions and punishments as they were used to in their own homes. Then they began to notice that they could give way with impunity to most of their desires and impulses. They discovered that not only were they free to run about and shout, and occupy themselves as they thought fit, either with real objects or by using their imagination, but also that they were not separated against their will at the first sign of a dispute, to reprimand or punish them. Then came an overflowing of disorderly and noisy agitation, in which the fighting instincts of eleven or twelve healthy boys were given free play. During all this period, there was a great deal of constructive play and many moments of happy collaboration and contentment, of friendship and affection towards the adults. But there were times when most of the children thought only of fighting to affirm the superiority of one over another, either by direct attacks, provoked or not, sometimes by the destruction of others' work, and by open hostility towards the adults present. Then little by little, with some returns to the disorderly agitation, the group began to take a definite social form, and the conduct of every child altered in the most remarkable way; by the end of the year, the days were entirely occupied by constant free activity in an attitude of friendship and complete understanding. The children showed a marked keenness and pleasure in all their activities, and an uncommon inventive power, in conjunction with a concrete appreciation of social realities. The change in some of the most difficult children was most remarkable; fear, sulkiness and active hostility were replaced by calmness, affection and freedom in play and in collective activities. In some cases, the change was quite dramatic, and led to a remarkable contrast between periods at school and the holidays. For instance, two children from different families who from a very early age had suffered from insomnia and night terrors, began to sleep all night shortly after returning to school, and continued thus during the whole term, but lost this power during the first two or three days of the holidays.

In affirming these remarkable changes in the social behaviour of the children I do not rely on any vague and subjective impression, or even on the comments of the various visitors who came at different times to see the work of the school; but on the detailed notes reporting the acts and attitudes of the children.

During this time the ordinary children grew and developed normally, but showed more freedom and spontaneity of expression, imagination and inventiveness, and more freedom in all mental processes and the appreciation of social realities than are obtained by most of the usual methods.

We may now consider certain general aspects of the behaviour of young children in such conditions, always bearing in mind that all the following affirmations are subject to individual exceptions, and to differences due to age and to the effect of conditions at the school as a whole.

A. *"Egocentrism"*

The content of this study illustrates certain aspects of the particular character of early infancy that J. Piaget has called "egocentrism". Piaget's works are today well enough known for it to be enough simply to refer to them. I have formulated in my book *Intellectual Growth in Young Children* certain reservations which I feel about this work, notably the part that concerns the intellectual aspects of "egocentrism". In my following book (*Social Development in Young Children*) I shall examine more deeply the various social aspects of this question, and in particular the relationship between the intellectual factors and the social factors in mental development. For the purposes of the present study, I accept in their general lines the phenomena of Egocentrism. The behaviours here described show how egocentrism manifests itself in the activities of play and in the earliest social relations. In particular, they indicate ways by which the child passes from this primitive phase to more developed group relationships.

As one might expect, a number of small children brought together and free to move about and play as they wish do not immediately form a group in the full sense of the word. The important question is to know by what factors and through what stages group relationships develop. Each child is, in the first place, concerned chiefly with his own interests. These interests may be opposed to the present interests of the other children, or may temporarily bring together several of them for some particular object, if the affective phase of one child is in agreement with those of one or several of the others. As the children get to know each other better and a common history between them is constructed, these emotional communions occur more frequently, but on the whole and except for certain rare moments of fusion through common interests, each child is preoccupied by the carrying out of his own imperious fantasies and uses the other children as a means to attain this end.

It is these individual inventions which, in so far as they can be adapted to each other, provide a background propitious to the initial development of group relationships.

For example, one of the older children wants to play at being mother and tries to recruit younger ones to be her children. If this agrees with their feeling at the moment they joyfully accept, and it happens that the most active ones, those who usually will not let themselves be dominated, play at being docile children for hours and days, often with a very tyrannical "daddy" or "mummy". On the other, hand, if the proposal does not agree with the younger child's passing fancy, even the most agreeable child will revolt. A little girl of four, J . . . , who had spent months in being the child, suddenly revolted and began to cry, in a piercing voice; "No, I want to be the daddy!" And a gentle, peaceful little boy of the same age, taking part in a game in which he had been appointed the daddy, wanted at all costs to be the mummy! When this sort of thing happens, the older children may use the active means of persuasion or corruption, either by making or promising a present, or by threatening the child not to love him any more, or by showing him active hostility: "I wont sit next to you at dinner!", and so on. J . . . , for instance, got tired of her subordinate position in the game, or of the game itself, and went off on her own devises. Her former playcompanions tried at first to make her and threaten her, from which I protected her. Then they told her: If you come, J . . . , we'll bring you something tomorrow": she replied: "All right, I'll come", and rejoined the group. Another day she was to be the "little dog", but she declared: "I don't want to be your little dog, P . . . , I want to be your little girl". "Then I shan't bring you anything". Another little girl had promised to marry a boy, D . . . , when they were grown-up. For some time she used this promise to make him do what she wanted. For example, during a period of authority she decided how he should pass his time at school; and when he did not want to finish his needlework, she said: "Then I won't marry you!" One morning he wanted to be a carpenter and repair the floor, and asked her "Can I mend the floor?" She replied "If you like", in the tone of a grown-up who accepts no responsibility. He said "Oh, then you won't marry me, will you?" and went on with his needlework.

These examples show clearly, on the one hand, how at this stage of evolution the playing-together of little children is a sum of individual caprices, sometimes adapted more or less well to each other and sometimes not so adapted; and on the other hand that this fortuitously collective play is the means by which real social relationships develop. The latter grow thanks to the real experience not only of the communion of interests bound to a shared fantasy or emotion, but also and perhaps especially to the very sharp clash between aims and desires; the discovery of this clash brings the child to adapt himself to the wills of others than himself so as to obtain what he wants. Here as everywhere else, a refusal, suffering and lack of satisfaction are the effective factors in the development of the sense of objective reality. Such clashes between objects are an active stimulant in the evolution from egocentricity to social adaptation.

B. Ambivalence

The alliances that little children form in the course of carrying out their common notions, or imaginative games, or in helping each other in the handling of real objects (for eample, in modelling) are very changeable and ephemeral, and capable of being dissolved at any moment under the effect of some fighting urge,—unless at the right moment there appears a child who does not belong to the little group upon whom can be concentrated the warlike humour of the others, so that it is turned away from fellow-members of the group. One of the most striking things is this need that the children forming a temporary group have for an exterior object upon which they can direct their hostility. They unite unreservedly in the most dramatic way in their aversion and hatred for a child or another group of children, as the case may be, so as to love and appreciate all the more the members of their own narrow circle. Thus, you may hear some children saying to others: "Shall we imprison X. . . in the castle?", or "Shall we kill X. . .", "Don't let him come in!"; or else "We hate X. . .!". "He's a beast!", "He's horrible!". Some child may start running through the room singing about the children who don't like his group: "Dirty old X. . .!" Again two rival gangs will quarrel and say they will "put each other in prison". The older boys will sometimes try to shut some of the younger ones in a shed regarded as "the prison". It was for a time fashionable to draw enormous crocodiles on the floor with chalk, their mouths open and teeth well in evidence, and the artists threatened their temporary foes by saying that the crocodiles would "bite off their legs" and so on. Another time, when a group of children had united against an older and stronger boy, they tore up his drawings and tried to pull him from the stair-case where he was sitting, and teasing him in many ways all morning. On this occasion the boy, knowing himself to be older and superior in strength to the whole group, found great satisfaction in enduring them with good humor. Another boy of four and a half said of his enemy of the moment: "Shall we make X. . .

drink some wee-wee?" and his allies replied, "Yes, and we'll poison him", "yes, and it will give him pimples all over". One of them aged four was accustomed to say, when he was ill-disposed towards someone: "Shall we wee-wee on him?". Another time, a girl served as a contrast to members of the group, and had to endure all the time hostile remarks such as: "Oh look, here comes the dragon", "The dragon's here".

If a child excluded in this way wanted to join some particular group, as was sometimes but not always the case, he had to try to concentrate their hostility upon another child, playing to the gallery in the most amusing way. For instance, a little girl X and little boy Y were, one afternoon, very hostile to another boy Z, who at other times was their principal playmate. X was helping to dry the feet of children who had paddled in some water, when she declared that she "wouldn't dry Z now". Z cried: "But you must, because I've got to go home to tea", and he embarked on a series of explanations and claims. X and Y began to laugh and said contemptuously that Z "doesn't know what he's talking about". Z stamped his foot and said: "Oh yes I do, but I'll tell you who doesn't know what he's talking about, and that's C". "Oh yes he does". Then Z made a heap of mud on the path, explaining to the others that it was "so that C would slip on it when he was running." It was clear that this was done to turn the hostility of X and Y against C and away from himself, though until then C had been Z's best friend.

Another child, a boy of five who was fat and ill-made, nervous but very intelligent, was excluded from the various groups for some time after entering the school. None of the children liked or accepted him, for several reasons. It is interesting to note how he tried to win their favour, by offering to put his ability to read and write at their service. He stood and carefully watched their games, and seized the least opportunity of helping them, for instance writing out a ticket or a notice which could be used in the particular game they were playing. In this way he succeeded in overcoming their hostility and penetrating their society.

This fixation of negative impulses upon someone exterior to the group appeared as one of the procedures by the aid of which little children overcome the ambivalence which dominates their very first social relations (I mean here the manner in which they are pushed by affection and aversion, by positive and negative impulses, towards the same persons;) and by the aid of which friendship within the group is cemented. Naturally, the more difficult and nervous the children are, the more this is true; one or two of them, indeed, could not like A except by detesting B. But the difference between such children and normal children was merely a matter of degree. To watch them reminded one constantly of the intensification of patriotism during wartime; the increase of brotherly love by hatred of the enemy; and that makes it easier to understand more clearly, the part played by love and hate in party politics.

The same aspect was presented by the relationship of the most difficult children with adults. The fact that, in the early days, there were two adults constantly at the school evoked love and hatred strongly and precisely and thereby intensified the opposite tendencies—or more exactly showed them in clearer and more precise forms. Some of the children in the early days always hated me, while they loved my assistant or reciprocally. This was true even of the older children, and among the most normal ones, though to a much less degree, the hostility being expressed almost entirely in the form of mischievousness, consisting for examples in the form of nicknames or the imitation of personal peculiarities. For some children it was a proof of a marked improvement if they could show affection to both of us at once.

C. "The horde of brothers"

The reciprocal action of the sentiments the children felt for each other and those they felt towards us as representatives of their parents were both equally striking and evoked very sharply Freud's theory regarding the relationship between the brother-group and the primeval father. Every time one of the adults acted as the accepted head of the activities of a group, for example in a game with machines or motor cars, we had the typical picture of the "representative of the parents", the "ideal ego", causing the group to unite in a common devotion and a fraternal love. An interesting example is the way the children reacted when we joined with them in working with natural clay or modelling-clay. Every time that quarrels or angry behaviour broke out, it was enough for one of us to pick up the modelling clay and start to use it, for the children to come to us after a few moments, and for peace and constructive play to be re-established very quickly. The opposite picture, the union of the group in a common hatred of a "tyrannical" parent, appeared in other circumstances with the same clarity. If we intervened in the activity of certain children, or refused some request, they would immediately turn towards the others and a group would be formed, united in common opposition to the "tyrant". An amusing illustration of this theme was given by one of the children aged three. Another child of the same age had threatened to hit him with his spade, and in conformity with one of my principles—which were few but strict—I took the spade away from him. He stormed, cried, and held on to the spade. Whilst I gently insisted on taking the object, I suddenly received a blow from his friend, a child ordinarily very affectionate with me. When I turned round to say to him: "Don't hit me, please X. . .", he replied: "I shall hit you if you are naughty to Y. . .!"

Another child, one of the most nervous ones, often said slyly to his friends: "Shall we put a worm down her back so that it will bite her?"

Yet another child, when I had opposed his wishes in the least, immediately reacted by inciting the others to say to me: "I'm going to wee-wee in your face!" or else: "Shall we spit on her pudding?". This was particularly striking every time they had been talking to each other about their excretions. On these occasions there always appeared a tendency to bursts of hostile feeling against the adults present, as the following incident shows: A boy of five, X. . . , went to the W.C.; another aged four ran after him. I was sitting with the class, painting. X. . . and Y. . . had a little conversation which I could not hear very clearly. Y. . . came back and came and spat on my picture. I said: "Don't do that please, Y. . ." Y. . . ran back to X in the W.C., and I heard X say to him: "Give her a kick!" Y. . . ran up again and made for me as if to do it. I said to him: "If you kick me, I might perhaps kick you back!" He ran out again to X. . . , who asked him: "Did you kick her?". He replied "Yes", though of course he had not. X. . . cried: "Do it again!" and Y said "Yes" and ran towards me again. The whole incident was repeated in detail three times, the hostility gradually softening down into fun—to which my method of action had been orientated.

Sometimes the sense of solidarity among children united against the intervention of an adult to allow a child who had suffered a little from occasional attacks by the others to join with the others in their opposition. Here is an example: the children had been very rough with J. . . I intervened to say to them: "I won't let you do that to J. . ." They got very cross, and J. . . joined with them to declare that I was "a beast", and she added: "And then we won't go and have dinner with you". Another time, two children had quarrelled, and P. . . had hit H. . . on the head with a cardboard clock. Following my rule, I took away the clock, whilst P. . . protested violently. H. . . took P. . .'s side, and H. . .'s little brother immediately joined with them, saying: "She's a beast, I'll make her fall down!"

It is very interesting to compare this with the behaviour of the children when they are separately with the adult in question. They were, naturally, relationships full of friendliness. The weakness of the little child needs the support of his equals to be able to express his opposition, even against an adult who is always friendly, tolerant and gentle. In fact, it was clear that these defiances and attacks simply covered the deep anguishes that every child necessarily experiences, in his weakness and feeling of inferiority compared with the superior power of the coolness and the effective activities of the grown-ups.

When the first critical days of schooling have passed, then among the most normal and least ambivalent children these tendencies naturally become much less apparent; but their essential features always remain perceptible to attentive observation.

D. *The Feelings of Fault and Inferiority*

We can now pass on to the study of the psychological factors that determine the choice of some object as the target to the aversion and the attacks of the group, and which provokes them on every occasion.

As must be expected in view of what we learn from the studies we know of relating to gregarious behaviour in general, the latest comer to a school often finds himself in this position, unless he possesses something, some object or quality specially agreeable either to one of the leaders or to the whole group, which does not hold it against him that he is new.

It is very often on a younger or weaker child that the temporary hostility is directed. "We don't like X. . . , he's too silly": "I hate him, he cries too much"; two or three children will start pulling faces behind their hands, or openly scoff at the drawings of a younger child.: "He can't draw machines!": "Isn't he silly?"; "That's not a nice machine!" "He says 'likkle' instead of little!". The little boy we have already referred to who all the others detested, was singled out as the object of this hatred because of his heaviness and clumsiness at games and modelling and dancing. The other children were very scornful, for instance, of his difficulty in holding the cards; "He's so silly!"; "I really don't like him!"—and they hated a kind of loud groan that he allowed to escape him sometimes. The first time he tried to do modelling, as he was making great efforts to model a railway, which was in fact more shapeless than any of the others, they called attention to his inferiority to the rest without mincing their words, so that he demolished all he had done and started again.

If a child began to cry, the rest would shout: "Baby, baby, baby!", or surround him crying: "What a funny face!" Or if one of the very little ones, unable to control himself, wet his knickers, the rest laughed and jeered at him. In this field, the absolute nature of the childrens' judgments is severe, and more than one small and backward child has had to be protected against the severity and cruelty of these value-judgements. Such a picture, of course, does not always appear; there are many occasions when older and more advanced children show themselves as tender and protective towards the weaker ones, and may experience pride and pleasure in seeing the efforts of the latter. For example, on the day when on of the smallest and least developed children made a great and long-sustained effort to make a paper-chain out of paper rings, and succeeded well beyond his usual level of achievement, the other children were delighted for him: "Just think, P. . . did that! Isn't it good?"

The positive or negative character of group reaction in given circumstances seems to be determined by a certain number of influences, some of which can be specified. These are: (a) The usual relations of the group with the child in question, for example, whether he is or is not a member of the group at a given moment; and whether his relations with them are good or strained; (b) The child's general reaction to the group's behaviour; if hostility does not trouble him and he goes his way without being upset (in which case they tend to be friendly and admire him), but if he shows fear and distress at hostile words they exploit it; while if he courts their friendliness they end by according it generously; (c) The general orientation of their imaginative life at the moment, determined to a large extent by one or two of the most influential members. For instance, one of the leaders in the early days was an altogether charming and very gifted boy, the oldest in the school at that period, who had a very great influence by way of suggestion over the rest, by reason not only of his age but also his rare gifts of imagination, invention and expression. Unfortunately he was subject to fits of ill-humour and morose hostility, his character varying from day to day and even from hour to hour. Naturally the group of his younger friends tended to share his humour.

However, a deeper study of the content of these group hostilities and an examination of the following examples suggest that these facts should not be interpreted in the superficial sense of a simple gregarious exclusivity, but rather in the direction of the transfer of feelings of culpability upon a chosen victim. For example, a little girl who noticed that a boy was playing with his genitals turned to the others, saying: "What a fool!". The boy, a charming and docile child, replied angrily: "If you say that again I'll kill you!" (Naturally, in his turn he displayed the same superiority over other children when favourable conditions arose). The group hostility is often directed against some child who was recently the leader or a partner in games that were forbidden or that the children suspect would be forbidden.

An example relating to other social values is that of a rather older little girl, who had induced her group to hate and exclude another little girl, and who took an opportunity to say to a member of the school staff when she found herself alone with her: "Do you like X. . . ?" "Yes, very much."—"I don't, I hate her, she's so selfish and tries to get something for herself every time!". It was explained to her that this was not a rare fault (it need hardly be said that it was one of the traits of the little girl who was speaking); but the child replied: "Well I think she is worse than the others, and she's very naughty and sneaky".

In addition, the terms in which hostility is usually expressed, especially by the smallest children, show very clearly that its principal content is a transferred fault, most often concerned with matters of excretion and with masturbation. "She's a dirty little girl!" "He's horrid, he wet his knickers!"—and so on. It is clear that the smaller child, who has less control over himself and less resources makes a favourable target; the others can protect and punish their own selves, whom they already despise but have not yet triumphed over securely.

This recalls the absolute character of the moral ideals and judgements of adolescence, compared with the more tolerant, calm and secure way of looking at things of those who have come to maturity.

In my article "The Function of the School for the Young Child" (*Forum of Education,* Vol. 2) I have given several proofs of the precocious development of the consciousness of being at fault in young children. I would wish here to stress that fact and to complete my remarks. One of the most remarkable things for an observer who has had no experience of neuroses would be the extreme tyranny and severity of the children who take the part of mother or father in games, even in the case of children who have themselves enjoyed the most gentle of bringings-up. For example, a boy who had never heard such words as "naughty" before the other school children had used them to him, who had never been reprimanded, nevertheless used these words himself very frequently to his pretended children; and a little girl, who had a mother with the kindest of temperaments, took a younger child to play with and shook her roughly on her chair, saying: "Naughty child! Nasty little baby!" The relationship of this to the sensation of fault is clear from the following extract from the notes: P. . . , a little girl of seven, had been playing with dolls, and said that her own had been "a dirty little horror!", that she would not keep quiet in her pram for a minute and was going to have "a good hiding". She washed the doll, then told it: "Say good-night to Madame!"; she held the doll up to kiss me, and then said to it: "Go straight to bed and keep quiet, and don't do such dirty things!". Just before this incident, P. . . herself had shown crossness and indiscipline and had declared that she would tell her father not to pay me any more money, and that she "would come to school just the same." She threatened me at the same time to tear up some pages of figures. Then followed the episode with the doll, after which she calmed down and became more friendly and active.

Another time, two boys and a girl were playing at families with dolls. They left their "children" at home while they went to play hockey. When they returned they said that their children had been "dirty" and had done all sorts of horrible things. Another boy, actually the one who had been caught masturbating, asked about a year later if he could learn to read and write, and wanted to learn, at his first lesson, to write "Johnny is a naughty boy". He wrote it in large letters on a sheet of paper, which he proudly affixed to the classroom wall, laughing with pleasure when the others asked: "Who has written this about Johnny?", and he could reply: "It was me!" More seriously, another boy, aged five, whispered a promise to another to "bring him a present" if he did not "do in the garden what he ought to do in the W.C."

Severity towards other children finds its counterpart in a very striking way in the ardour with which all the children, even those who had never been scolded at home, welcomed the idea of the tyrannical parent or master, when it was presented to them, for instance, in the form of Father Whiphard, and the way in which they asked me to "do Daddy Whiphard" and chase them around the room with a stick, amidst boundless laughter and joy. They invented a whole series of games of the same kind, pretending to be compelled to work—though they never worked unless they wanted to—and sometimes saying: "Oh, she will hit our fingers if we don't do all this!". When I said to them, laughing: "Shall I really do it?" they replied, "Oh yes, do!", and I had to join in the game and pretend to rap their knuckles. Again, in the middle of a piece of work they had imposed on themselves: "Oh, I *hate* Mrs. Isaacs; she *makes* us do this!" Other times they would pretend to be "naughty children" who would not put away their bricks, and would ask me to go and fetch a policeman to make them do it. Playing at policemen was an altogether favourite game, and I had to put them in and out of "prison" to their great delight.

One particular example—the exterior form of which had been fixed by family conditions, but which by its spontaneity on this occasion and the way in which it was expressed, showed the strength and the action of the sensation of being at fault—was that of a charming boy of four, one of the most docile and agreeable in the school. He was standing with the others watching a heavy shower of rain and listening to the sound it made in the trees; as as to this agreeable sound he remarked: "Perhaps it is God saying he will punish us for doing what we ought not to do!"

Space is lacking here for a longer discussion of the theoretical consequences of these facts of behaviour. It is clear, however, that they are essential for the development of social relationships in young children.

In conclusion, it is worth while stressing the fact that, if I have chosen, for the objects of this work, particularly those aspects of social conduct which were negative, hostile or aggressive (partly because these are the facts one passes over or omits to cite in books of child psychology, and partly because of their theoretical importance) these examples in fact stand out against a daily background of friendship, mutual help and constructive play, which made life with these children most agreeable. The freedom and spontaneity with which they could express their negative impulses, may, indeed, be considered as an indication of a vitality and animation which were equally apparent in the keen pleasure which they took in collaborating and in loving each other.

ORIGINAL SIN
Lecture published in
Twentieth Century
1933

The problem of original sin is one of the very greatest psychological interest.

When I was young, I used to hear a great deal about original sin, and the sense of guilt was looked upon as an essential preliminary to happiness. One of my most vivid childhood memories is of an old Methodist woman who used to pray aloud at Sunday evening prayer meetings with great vehemence: "Oh God, make the young men *miserable*".

This, however, is not fashionable now today. The sense of guilt is regarded rather as something to be got rid of as quickly as possible, something that need never be felt by a properly educated child. We have issued an edict, "Let there be no more sin and guilt." Indeed, we look upon the notion of original sin not merely as an evil and undesirable doctrine, but as an old wives' tale, a mere invention of the theologians.

But how did the theologians come to make such an invention? This is the psychological problem, and it is that to which I want to provoke your attention this evening.

A close psychological study of young children, even those in the twentieth century houses, suggests that this notion of original sin and feelings of guilt have a deeper origin and more permanent character than many of us like to believe. They appear to spring not so much from the accidents of human history or the confused attempts of early man to understand the world, as from an inevitable and recurrent conflict within the individual psyche of each human being. They have to be regarded as endo-psychic in origin, a largely inevitable outcome of the interplay between the earliest and most primitive psychological tendencies in every child and his external environment. We cannot by a mere edict or by waving a magic wand of words, banish all feelings of guilt from the human mind.

In my own intensive studies of individual children in ordinary life, and a special group of little children in a nursery school, I have gathered evidence suggesting that even with children brought up in the most liberal homes a feeling of guilt will arise spontaneously. It is possible for children brought up with practically no moral teaching, and certainly no punishments or open reproaches, to feel a quite acute sense of guilt in certain circumstances. I must content myself with one or two examples of this general conclusion. One boy of four and a half years in my own school, for example, who had the mildest of parents, came with the request to be taught to read and write, and as soon as he was able to write insisted upon making a large poster saying about himself, "Tommy is a naughty boy", and fixing this up on the wall of the schoolroom. When other children came in and asked "who put that up?" and why, Tommy proudly replied "*I* did". There we obviously have a complicated state of mind. Making this statement himself and found drawing people's attention to it can only be understood as an attempt to control and lessen an inner feeling of guilt by forestalling a similar statement by other people. Another small boy, brought up in a fanatically free home, lost control of his bowels one day when he was on the river with his father. He showed the utmost distress and with bitter tears cried "Daddy, Daddy, *what* shall I do?" just as if he was accustomed to being scolded and reproached for such a happening.

A survey of the kinds of behaviour that are considered reprehensible by little children is worth making. All forms of dirtiness, for example, are felt to be bad. One amusing case was that of two little children who poked into a hole in a plaster wall and brought out a stick covered with dust and spider's webs. Their comment was "Isn't it a *naughty* wall?" And when they were asked why it was naughty they replied, "Look, *muck! isn't* it naughty?"

All kinds of breaking are considered to be bad. So is looking at anything one is not supposed to look at. For example, one small boy made a model railway train, and when another boy wished to look at it, the first one said, "You are not to look at it. It is *rude* to look." Biting is felt to be bad. So are screaming and scratching. Amongst older children such social faults as crossness, slyness, selfishness, are part of the content of feelings of guilt. One can in fact summarise the main content of feelings of guilt as including all forms of aggressive behaviour, screaming, biting, wetting, being dirty, breaking things, and so on and so forth. But along with the sinfulness of this open aggression go certain forms of early sexual satisfaction, such as thumb sucking and masturbation. I have no time to give you the evidence for the following conclusion, but must content myself with offering you the apparently dogmatic statement that the guiltiness of these sexual satisfactions belongs not so much to the purely libidinal element in the experience as to the aggression that is also bound up with it. In masturbation, for example, the child feels that he is secretly stealing pleasure that his parents will not give him. It is this aggressive element in the total activity which gives rise to the guilt and anxiety about it. On is therefore led to the general conclusion that *there is a very intimate relation between aggression and guilt in the human psyche.*

Another interesting study is of the kinds of punishments that are feared by little children for such guilt behaviour. The phantasied punishments will of course bear some relation to actual experience and teaching, but they are also very largely determined by the nature of the guilty wishes themselves. When a little girl says that if she is naughty in school "God will drown the world", we can be quite sure that this notion arises not only from hearing stories of the Flood, but from her own primitive wishes to attack the world with urine, in the days when wetting and dirtying is an effective instrument of aggression towards other people.

The ways in which feelings of guilt are expressed in children's behaviour are of three main types. The first is that of simple *direct* expression of shame. "I was *so* ashamed", sobs one little boy when he has dirtied the floor. Another child quite spontaneously inflicts a punishment upon himself when he accidentally breaks a cup. He says, "Now I can't have any cocoa," keeping this up for a week, in spite of repeated invitations from the grown-ups and other children. Another is the expression of guilt in various forms of *play*, for example, the play of putting each other in prison, or playful threats that "the policeman will come" and put someone else in prison.

The third form, the most frequently occurring, and perhaps the most important for an understanding of social life amongst adults as well as children, is that of projected guilt. One sees one's own faults in other people, not in oneself. One says, "Hang the Kaiser!", "Boycott the Jews!" This projected guilt is very often seen in a group of small children, and is quite the most important factor in their quarrels, whether between individual children or between rival groups. With children under seven or eight years of age such rival groups of two or three children occur spontaneously wherever you have a larger number playing under fairly free conditions. The children within each group love and admire each other all the more, because of the scorn and dislike which they turn on to those of another group. Such group hostility is clearly to be understood in terms of projected guilt. A group which is feeling the need to dislike or disapprove of other children will go to almost any lengths in teasing or tormenting. They will for example exclude a particular child from their group on the grounds that he is "horrid" or "naughty" or "stupid". Tiny children can be extraordinarily cruel to each other when this psychic mechanism is at work. There are indeed hardly any limits to which human beings will not go in savage attacks upon those enemies who at the moment bear the burden of projected evil as we know only too well from current political events.

The group behaviour of little children shows another phenomenon, too, very clearly, viz. the way in which one individual, or a smaller and weaker group, will attempt to gain the approval and patronage of a bigger child or a more powerful group by turning the hostility of the latter on to a third party. As one example: Two children had banded together against a particular boy and told him he was "stupid" and "quarrelsome" and they were "not going to play with him." This boy was very distressed and attempted to win their good feelings by saying "I am *not* horrid—but I will tell you who *is*. X is." He hoped in this way to enlist their regard for him by getting them to join with him against the absent X, who in the ordinary way was his own good friend. At the moment his friend had to be sacrificed to his more pressing need of winning these two powerful individuals over to his side.

If now we should ask how such situations come about, and what is the ultimate origin of these phenomena of guilt, we should be led into the deepest regions of the human mind and the most primitive aspects of individual experience. We do know a good deal about the psychic sources of the feeling of original sin, but that is unfortunately far too long a story for me to tell this evening. The sense of guilt takes origin within the first year of life. It is bound up with the child's identification of himself with his parents, the parents who are unable to satisfy all his surging instinctual desires.

In the first few months of life, these primitive desires and feelings are enormously strong. Since the child's satisfactions come to him from persons, so it seems to him that dis-satisfactions also come from persons; even the most liberal parents are at times inevitable agents of frustration. But the feeling of frustration is too painful to be borne and the child builds up within his own mind parental images in order to lessen the psychological tension of unsatisfied desire. What we have come to call the super-ego, the most primitive archetype of the later adult conscience, is formed within the mind at a time when the child has very little experience of ordinary reality and knows only his own intense primitive wishes and the equally primitive rage and hate which the frustration of his wishes stirs up. Already within his first year the child experiences what St. Augustine called the 'divided self'. Already there is a complicated inter-play between the wish-self of primitive desire and the parent-self, built up in order to control desire and make adaptation to the real world possible. It is this parent-self from which the dictates of conscience and the sense of guilt issue. This is why even an education that is in reality most liberal is not altogether able to prevent the feeling of guilt from arising within the child's mind.

These conclusions will not, I know, be entirely acceptable to progressive educationalists, since they suggest so strongly there are definite psychological limits to the reforming zeal of the liberal educator. Some of our most cherished educational hopes have to be modified and moderated. Love and kindness are not such easy universal solvents of psychological difficulty as in our most optimistic moments we have hoped. We cannot recreate human nature quite so simply and readily as we could wish. I do not of course suggest that liberal education is fruitless, or that we cannot do a very great deal to lessen the tyranny of conscience in the little child. I do suggest that we are not as omnipotent as we have sometimes thought. But above all, I suggest that the essential pre-condition of our being able to achieve this end of liberal education, is to understand in far greater detail than we have hitherto troubled to do, the actual processes in the little child's mind from which the sense of guilt and sin take origin.

My purpose tonight has been mainly to provoke your interest in this issue as a psychological problem and to suggest the need for deeper and fuller understanding of early mental development.

PERSONAL FREEDOM AND FAMILY LIFE
The New Era
September—October 1936

The belief or disbelief of the adult in personal freedom, his success or failure in achieving it, is very largely the fruit of his early feelings and experiences with his father and mother, his brothers and sisters in the family circle. The primary issues of desire and frustration, love and hate, and all the child's ways of dealing with these varied feelings, are the starting

---

NOTE by D.E.M. Gardner
In lectures given later, Susan Isaacs often stressed the connection between feelings of guilt and those of love.
In 1948 she wrote of the psycho-analytic research:—
"In the last six or seven years the chief advances in this field, mainly the work of Melanie Klein and Joan Rivière, have been in the direction of deepening our understanding of (1) the child's early love tendencies, early sympathy and identification with his parents; (2) the complex interplay of love and hate tendencies in the earliest days, and the immensely varied modes of controlling, deflecting and diffusing the love and hate tendencies; and (3) the study of the "reparation" tendencies, the wishes and efforts of the child to make good any harm that his aggression and hate have done (in reality or in phantasy) towards those whom he loves."

point both of individual development and of social adaptation. In the unconscious mental life of every one, persons and powers, governments and servants, the poor and the rich, the state and the individual, the larger issues of personal and public life still carry these intensely concrete and direct meanings of his own relations with his father and mother and the other children in his own family. The result of development (whether in those who become free in their emotional life and secure in their social purposes, or in those who fail to serve others happily or to find fulfillment for themselves) may seem very far and very different from its beginnings; but the continuity of social life with individual experience can be traced; and can always be seen arising in the family situation.

The essential problem is thus the same for all peoples and all times. Every child, whatever his race or culture or circumstances, has to find a solution to the primary conflict of feeling towards his own two parents. But, of course, the precise terms of that conflict will always depend upon his actual circumstances, upon the conditions of his parents' life, upon their behaviour and attitudes.

The young child's life hangs upon his parents' response to his needs. Without them he is completely helpless to satisfy any of his wishes and longings. He shows us in his earliest behaviour how greatly he dreads his own helplessness, how intense and urgent his appeal to his parents becomes in moments of hunger or loneliness or lack of power. At first his mother fills the world for him; and it is because he has found how much he needs her for nourishment and comfort and tender love that he resents her concern with his father. Yet his father means also to him strength and wisdom and support, both for himself and for his mother. In the child's mind, his father's love for his mother ensures her safety and satisfaction, and hers for his father keeps him strong and wise, and thus again ensures the life and happiness of the child himself. Even from the beginning, the love of the parents for each other thus has its beneficent aspects for the child. But, on the other hand, since he needs each of them so deeply and inexorably, their concern with each other also distresses and terrifies him. All he can then do to express his distress and terror is to rage against them. And since he has as yet not knowledge of cause and effect, to attack in feeling means to his feelings to damage and destroy in reality. His rages and attacks thus arouse in him the greatest anxiety, anxiety of having altogether destroyed the parents who are at the same time the only source of life and of love. He comes to fear the destructive forces inside himself and thus to need all the more intensely to find good outside, to counteract the bad within.

The infant's picture of the world is an absolute one; parents seem *either* good or bad. He himself is either altogether good or bad. Only slowly is that picture modified to admit of degree and measure and differences in quality. During at any rate the first two years, and to a large extent throughout early childhood, the child is intolerant of failures and shortcomings in himself and others, seeking always to find and hold the absolute good and to drive out and destroy the absolute bad. He feels overwhelming anxiety at any hint of destructive forces, greed or anger or hate or rivalry, or criticism or self-assertion in himself of his parents.

Even those impulses which *we* know bring growth and achievement—the wish not merely to get good but to do things for himself, to move and talk and learn to be worthy of admiration and love, to become independent of help from his parents, or as skilful and knowledgeable as they, all the indispensable means of his personal development and social achievement, the instruments of freedom, may, to his deepest and most primitive feelings, mean simply getting things for himself, turning other people out, being greedy and jealous and destructive; and be therefore forbidden in his feelings.

The child sometimes becomes so terrified of his own angers and greeds and destructive wishes that he cannot bear to own them his in the slightest degree and must project them on to his parents. His father and mother are bad, he then feels, not he. They wish to starve and hurt him, to deny him pleasure and opportunity, to tyrannize over him and interfere with his wish to do good and be good.

Every child feels this at times; but with some it becomes to a greater or lesser degree a settled way of life. Sometimes the child retains this picture of all parents and all those who stand for parents in later life—teachers, employers, governments, kings and presidents, the state or the economic system. All parents are to be met by private defiance or public denunciation, or their place and existence is to be altogether denied. All men are brothers, but none of us has, and none of us shall be, fathers and mothers. Those who assume the place of parents are to be defied and denied. In such cases the complusion to destroy the bad is always felt far more strongly than the need to preserve the good.

The preoccupation in feeling and behaviour is always with the necessity *first* to get rid of the bad, by force and destruction, before there is any possibility of preserving or using the good.

In some persons, indeed, the good *within* has to be so carefully guarded from greed and desire, from being used up or spoilt by the bad, that it never can be acknowledged or brought into the realities of everyday life. It remains a phantasy, and is not seen in actual behaviour. These are the difficult, the delinquent children; these are the adults who fly to arms and unloose the powers of death as a means of creating a new heaven and a new earth. But freedom cannot live in such a world.

Sometimes the child rejects his own real parents but retains the hope of finding others, the perfectly good parents, elsewhere in real life. He turns with passionate attachment to new friends, new teachers, new leaders, new movements. But alas, as soon as he sees a flaw, as soon as the frailty of ordinary human nature reveals itself, these gods and heroes become again devils and betrayers. He flies once more to newer friends and newer loyalties. And his life is spent in this compulsive search for the ever-new and wholly good, and the repeated rejection of real men and women, of actual embodiments of his ideals in living flesh and blood. The dust of daily life is for him a fatal blemish upon the absolute good. He is a slave to his own anxieties: and freedom passes him by.

The insistent demand for the perfect parents, unharmed by the child's own hate and greed and jealousy, is often expressed in the indirect form of an absolute standard of perfection for himself. He too must be altogether pure and wise and loving; and again, he forges chains for himself which make freedom, a free choice of ends or free interchange with other people, unattainable in any form in the world of reality.

The second major mode of dealing with primary conflict regarding the parents is that of loving and clinging to the one and hating, defying and turning out the other. Here the child is in better case, since he has loving contact with one real person and can do something actual for this one, whether it be father or mother. Yet since he then projects the whole of his own evil on to the rejected parent, his anxieties are centered there and a loving identification with that one can never be accomplished. Not only will his development be incomplete and one-sided, but he will be scarcely less chained in the vicious circle of hate and fear, of attack and defence, of turning out the evil and endlessly protecting the good, than the child of our first description. He will have too little trust in himself or in any other who may seem to represent the parent who has been turned out and denied.

He has separated the one parent from the other; the need to make up this loss, to serve and defend, thus becomes insistent and enslaving. He is often unable to find a mate, or to trust real friends freely, to value any person or group or social function which may become identified in unconscious meaning with the parent who has been made the representative of evil, condemned and turned out. There are many people in this psychological situation. They accomplish much of noble service and achievement by identification with the one good parent. They are often a power in the world. But they do not attain freedom; nor are they able to confer it upon others.

Personal freedom in adult life is only possible when a new solution different from these two has been found in early days, when the vicious circle of greed and hate and anxiety and the desperate need for love, which leads to further greed and hate and fear, has somehow been opened out, when the child has learnt to bear some degree of frustration without this meaning to him the fear of death, when he can not only tolerate but can love and cherish his parents in their love for each other, when he can believe that the good is not wholly destroyed, either within himself, in his parents, or in the world as a whole, because bad is also present.

This central problem of the co-existence of love and hate in the child's feelings towards his parents arises as early as the second half of his first year; but its solution occupies all the early years of his development. If he can in some degree learn to leave his parents free to seek each other, if he can feel them joined in good, not only for his good, but for theirs and that of their other children, he can then identify himself with the two parents, with all their diverse attributes and their particular contribution to the family life and to his happiness. If he can admire his father's strength and wisdom and bear to know himself weaker and more ignorant, less able to help and love his mother, if he can delight in his mother's fertility and tenderness and know himself less skilful and loving, and if he can see the failings and faults of others without regretting them; if, above all, he can learn to know his own faults, his greedy wishes and pleasure in destruction, his rivalry and hate, without complete self-disgust and despair, then he can come to trust himself and others.

He has then less need to project evil upon others and therefore less ground for fearing and wishing to control them. He is then less bound by the need to control himself, the dread of being spontaneous, for fear of what may come out of him if he is free. If he attains a greater balance of loyalty to his two parents, he then also gains a greater harmony within of those feelings and aims in himself which are identified with his parents. He can become free because he can first allow his parents to be free. He can believe in good in himself, because he can allow them to be good to each other as well as to him. And so feeling is slowly tempered by real experience. He finds that moving and talking and doing things for himself may actually help and not destroy others. He becomes free to challenge and to assert his own choice because this may cherish and serve the good in himself and in others.

Psychologically speaking, personal freedom does not mean being bound by no attachments, no loyalties, no obligations, having no parents. It means, in its deepest aspects, having learnt to acknowledge *both* parents, to admit their claims and to believe in their goodness in spite of fault and failure, to allow them to love and give to each other, to believe in one's own powers of serving and cherishing them, to exercise a just authority over oneself or others, in their likeness, to serve the needs of our own children and the future, as they have served ours. And above all, to allow these varied needs and loyalties to reach some degree of harmonious balance in our own minds and hence in our real behaviour in a real world, limited and faulty as it may be.

We are, indeed, not born free, but we may learn to become so. It is only on this basis of belief in both parents and the resulting inner balance of loyalties, that a psychological stability can be achieved in which change can occur without cataclysm and freedom be exercised without a later reaction arising from anxiety.

Now the child cannot reach such a happy solution for himself. Nor, if he is not helped by his parents in his earliest years, can the wisest schools and teachers ever bring him fully to it. And so we come to the educational problem and especially to its earliest phases in the life of the young child at home.

Experience has shown that the regimented life of institution yields no adequate education for the young child towards personal freedom. Whether it be resorted to because no family life is available or because someone believes that family ties bind and hamper the growth of a free personality, it remains true that that deep sincerity and generosity and balance of feeling and aim in the inner psychic life, upon which personal freedom in its manifold aspects of external purpose and achievement ultimately depends, rarely grows except through the actual experience of normal family life.

What then can we say briefly as to the conditions in the early life of the child which will foster personal freedom most fully and securely? I must confine myself to a few of the broadest considerations.

First of all, I would say that the humanity of the child, the reality of his feelings and wishes and anxieties, even though they be childish and inarticulate, need to be recognized by his parents and nurses. No theory which regards the child as a reflex machine to be conditioned, a plastic clay to be moulded by habit, can train him to freedom. Such theories are themselves the outcome of anxiety in their progenitors. They hint at a profound fear of real people, real emotions, real contact between living personalities. It is only when we are willing to recognize that the child is, from very early days, a real person, a whole person, with real feelings and purposes that we shall, on the one hand, be willing to try to understand the mode of his development and so gain the skill necessary to aid his growth; and on the other, to be able, without extreme anxiety on our own part, to exercise our natural authority as parents, and ask him to recognize our rights and privileges as real persons.

This suggests the second main service we can render the young child to aid his freedom, viz., the exercise of control where control is appropriate. A blind indulgence and the absence of just control do not help the child—whether they spring from a doctrinaire worship of the name of freedom or a masochistic suffering of the infringement of the liberty of the parents. We have to remember that the parent is a psychic reality to the child, whether he has none, or whatever sort of parent he has, in external fact.

We may for some reason of our own inner life wish to abrogate our authority; but we cannot alter the fact that the little child seeks to find a good and helpful parent who will help him by control where control is just and appropriate. If we feel the need to deny our own parenthood, to deny the function of parenthood itself, the child knows what we are doing. He feels us to be aiders and abettors of his own defiant moments, to be bad children like himself. If we cannot defend ourselves against his encroachments, the whole burden of control falls upon him; and will be too much for him. If we show him that we cannot or do not want to take care of ourselves against him, he does not trust us to take care of him. The resulting anarchy and anxiety in his psychic life cannot give birth to freedom.

The child needs our help in creating a rhythm and order, in his external relationships and his inner psychic life. By identification with the just and protective parents, who can keep themselves and him safe against his aggression, he becomes able to trust himself to act justly and helpfully; and lessened anxiety brings the possibility of freer relationships.

But, one hastens to add, this control and authority needs to be both appropriate and loving. Mere harsh control for its own sake will imprison, not free, the child. It needs to be exercised with understanding of what the child can really do for himself at each age and in each situation as it arises. And this requires knowledge of the normal phases of his growth in physical and social skill, in the normal spontaneous expression of his impulses in play and effort. It requires not only knowledge of these things, but also sympathy with them, joy in the child's natural interests, pleasure in the ways in which he seeks to help and learn, to make and do. Above all, it needs an appreciation of the social value of the child's wish to grow and become skilful and independent, a willingness to allow him to become free of our help, to be in due time an adult and a parent in his own right; without wanting to hasten this process or refusing to let him be dependent upon us while he does need us. We have to be willing, as the child grows from infancy to adolescence, to give up control as and when he shows himself able to take it over and we have to be willing to allow him to make mistakes, to do things prematurely here and there, with the knowledge that we are standing by so that errors need not be irretrievable.

It is surely true that from the very beginning the child needs to be given some genuine responsibility, some freedom to make mistakes and to learn by failure and the effort to retrieve failure. Only his actual experience of effort and activity in a setting of security and love can lessen his anxiety about his own aggressions and insufficiencies and give him the trust in himself which will make him free. Even the little child needs opportunities of free choice and the following out of the consequences of his own wishes. Our wisdom lies in knowing when to leave him free and when to guide and control him in his play and work.

It is important moreover, that this increasing self-determination in the child's life, as he grows through childhood to youth, and indeed the freedom of choice and activity we allow him at any age, should not be wrested from us by his protest and defiance, but should be given freely to him by us, as his natural right. It should be the fruit of love, not of fear, should be based on his identification with the good parents, not his defiance of the bad. Then the child himself will wield it without anxiety and without guilt and will not need to renounce it in later years or to deny it to his own children.

Finally, I would say that the actual relation between the two parents themselves is of the greatest possible importance. If each can allow a freedom of feeling and opinion and action to the other, if each value the other, not merely for his own psychological needs and satisfactions, but as a real person, then the child can grow into freedom naturally and securely. His daily experiences build up a balance of loyalties within himself, a belief in the good father and mother whose goodness does not demand an impossible effort of devotion to preserve it, but can be used and acted upon in everyday life. I have seen the most tragic enslavement of real gifts, the most pathetic binding to obsessional ritual, in those whose life had confirmed the need to defend one parent against the contempt or encroachment of the other. What the parents are to each other is surely as significant as what they are, together or separately, to the child himself.

I will end by repeating that the child best learns to be free when his parents or earliest educators are themselves real persons with sincere emotional responses and can allow each other and the child to be real persons too; when they are not only self-controlled, adaptable, loving and understanding of his needs, but also unafraid of their parental standing.

In summary:

  i The infant's picture of the world is an absolute one. Parents seem either good or bad; he himself is either altogether good or bad.
  ii Personal freedom in adult life is only possible . . . when the child can believe that the good is not destroyed, either within himself, in his parents or in the world as a whole, because bad is also present.
  iii If he can learn to know his own faults, his greedy wishes and pleasure in destruction, his rivalry and hate, without complete self-disgust and despair, then he can come to trust himself and others, to seek freedom and pursue it.
  iv What conditions in early life will foster personal freedom? First, the recognition of the humanity of the child; second, the exercise of control where control is appropriate; third, a willingness to allow him to become free of our help.

"SAFETY FIRST" EXAMINED
Home and School
October 1938

In response to Mr. Lyward's invitation, I began to write this article on the evening of the Nuremberg speech. I found myself unable to settle down to it. The Nuremberg voice crying WAR seemed to make an article on Safety

First for little children a mere mockery. But the mood passed, and I reflected that the very reverse point of view might be nearer the truth. Is not peace itself a mockery if there is no safety, even for the brightest and best of our children, when on their journey to school or about their innocent pleasures? The toll of the roads in the ordinary course of daily life is in some ways even more shocking and disturbing than the horrors of warfare. It seems to hint at a persistent hidden strain of carelessness and callousness in civilized man about human life, and above all, the lives of little children, which might give one more ground for despair in looking on the future of the human race than even the unbridled passions of our war lords.

No question can seem so urgent to anyone who cares about children than their bodily safety on the roads. The need to safeguard life and limb must take precedence even of mental health. There is little use in helping our children to grow well and happily if at any moment they may be killed or dismembered by the swift and crowded vehicles in the street. We are bound to put this first in our care of children.

Our purpose and the urgency of the need are clear; but how to achieve our aim is not so clear. It is natural for those who look at the appalling statistics to say "Teach the children to look before they run. Give them lessons on how to cross the road. Find ways of impressing on them the principle of "Safety First". But will this do what we want? Will this make them controlled and sensible and skilful?

Some critics of "Safety First" teaching in the schools have raised objections to emphasizing the dangers, lest this should over-stimulate the child's imagination and fill his mind with fear and horrors. The answer to these objections is that everything depends upon the way in which the teaching is given. If we over-stimulate the child's fears, neither are we helping him to keep himself safe on the roads. A frightened child does the wrong thing, not the right. To keep him safe, we must not fill his mind with the feeling of danger. If, therefore, we avoid injury to the child's feelings and imagination, our Safety First training will be far more effective.

To begin with, in our approach to the problem of children's safety, we must not put undue emphasis on the part which the child himself plays in the situation. Of the three partners in the situation—the driver, the community and the child—the child must come last and least in responsibility. The first charge must fall upon the community, responsible for all the physical conditions of the roads, the rules and regulations, the public opinion, which sets the stage and ultimately controls standards of behaviour among motorists. The second part of the burden must rest upon the driver, who can never be exonerated, no matter what children do, since children are children, and no one—motorist or other—has the right to assume that they can and will behave as grown-ups.

"Safety First" propaganda amongst children very often seems to assume that they could be controlled and reasonable if they would, or that little songs and tabloid lessons will alter their fundamental characteristics, and make them wise like men.

I do not believe this. We shall never reduce road accidents amongst the very young unless we are willing to come to terms with children as they are, with their natural ways of feeling and thinking and acting.

I am thinking particularly about that peak in road accidents amongst children between four and seven years of age. The problems of cyclists' accidents in the teens and motor cyclists' in early manhood have to be considered on their own merits. These have something in common with the problem of the young child, but are more amenable to teaching and public opinion. It is in the case of the little child, above all, that we have ourselves to learn and to accept, if we are to save the child from the results of his own natural ways of behaviour.

What does the little child himself contribute to the awful dangers he runs on the roads? What is it in his very nature which lays him open to inescapable accident? Some of the characteristics which hamper him in the face of modern traffic are intellectual, ways of perceiving and knowing or not perceiving and not knowing. Some are matters of feeling and imagining.

First of all, the child of four to six is an impulsive creature, whose wishes are urgent and compelling, who runs far more easily and naturally than he walks, and who has very little foresight or self-control. He not only runs before he walks, but he leaps before he looks. Foresight, steadiness, sober pace, self-control, come later. At nine to ten years he will be cool, sensible and clever, but at five or six years he does not walk with wariness and circumspection.

He is often bold and challenging. He loves to climb a high wall, a ladder, a tree. He will often attempt feats which make his mother quake to watch him. But left to himself he very rarely comes to harm. He comes of climbing ancestors, and his body is naturally adjusted to the tasks he sets himself in this adventure. But there is no natural adjustment between the pace and direction and changes of direction of a swift-moving motor car, and the pace and control of the little child. He has nothing within himself to enable him to solve that problem successfully. Moreover, without years' more experience, his eyes and ears do not bring him the necessary knowledge. He cannot judge as the older boy does, the pace and distance of the approaching lorry by its sound or visual appearance. His perception of space and movement, his sense of time, are still very imperfectly developed. He has not the means of judging correctly what he ought to do, even if he were controlled enough to do it. Nor can he attend to several things and the complex relations between them at once, as the older child and the grown up do. His span of attention is narrow. He sees his ball rolling in the middle of the road and this occupies his mind and controls his movements to the exclusion of other moving objects not yet within the field of his vision. Time and growth and experience will make it possible for him to remember that swift-moving cars may come upon him and that the speck now so far away may be on top of him before he has had time to retrieve his ball and get back to the pavement. But he has, at four and six years of age, no means of feeling or remembering all this. And we cannot put it into him by any magic of our own teaching. Only time and growth can make such knowledge, such memory, such skill, really secure.

The swift moving traffic of a crowded street presents unnatural and incalculable problems to the small child. Teaching and demonstrations can reduce the discrepancy, but cannot remove it, except through time and growth. But the fast-moving car takes no account of the child's immaturity. It behaves in exactly the same way to the child of four as to the child of eight or nine years. This is what the driver must learn not to do, and the community must see that the driver learns his lesson.

This is not yet the whole story. Not only has the child's immaturity of perception and knowledge and skill and self-control to be considered, but also his imagination and his feelings. The young child is not yet ready to regard physical objects in an impersonal and detached way, to understand them as problems in mechanics. Neutral physical objects, determined by neutral mechanical laws, have no place in the young child's feelings and imaginings. It is true that even the very little child gains a certain amount of intellectual understanding of physical events for their own sake. He adapts to space and time in his action, and to some extent in his thought; but his *feelings* and phanatasies about chairs and tables, fire and water, the railway train and the motor car, are as of persons. The chair is hard and unkind when it bumps him. The fire wants to attack when it burns, the moving vehicle represents a father, a mother. It has purposes towards him like a person, and he has personal aims in return. He wants to dash across the road and defy the moving car, just as he wishes to assert himself against his parents. The imaginative play of little children with physical objects, bricks, cars and engines, shows us how the child naturally vents his feelings and phantasies about people in manipulating these objects. When the boy of seven or eight climbs on the backs of moving lorries, he is doing this not only to solve a problem in physical co-ordination, but to prove himself against the authority of his parents and teachers—all those powerful beings upon whom as an infant he depended for life and love, who were powerful and dangerous to him just because of his dependence.

So profoundly true is all this that the psycho-analyst has learnt to read the meaning of the child's play with physical objects, and through it to understand his feelings and purposes and phantasies regarding his father and mother, his brothers and sisters, and so to change and modify the child's relation with his family and the balance of his emotional life. But the playing out of a personal drama by means of physical objects goes on all the time, not only in the presence of the analyst. As the child grows older, his interest in physical objects for their own sake, in the problems of skill and understanding which they set, becomes emancipated from its first moorings to his personal life. But at these ages, when from his very nature the child is subject to such dangers from moving objects, his actual behaviour towards them is determined much more by his feelings and phantasies, by their symbolic value, than by his knowledge of them as physical objects in their own right.

And this, too, cannot be changed by Act of Parliament. These ways of thinking and feeling have to be reckoned with. Time and growth, but *only* time and growth, can bring a change favourable to the child's survival.

All this holds true of every child. Lack of skill and perception, the compelling imagination, are the normal characteristics of children between four and seven. And every child loves to defy and challenge, to adventure, to prove that he is not afraid and helpless.

But some children are more firmly held in the grip of phantasy than others; and with some children there is not only a strong urge to defy and to challenge principalities and powers, represented by the fast-moving omnibus and lorry—there is also a strong impulse to self-injury. Even amongst little children there are to be found those who are prone to accident because they seek it. There are children who will always tumble and hurt themselves, cut themselves with a knife, bump against the furniture, or fall out a window. And there are those who will seek the utmost danger in the street through an unconscious impulse to hurt and even kill themselves.

Not every child, fortunately, has this need to hurt himself. But those who have it are by no means uncommon. No amount of safety teaching will lessen the risk which such a child runs in crossing the street, or for that matter in playing with fire or water. Such children have to be reckoned with, and must always be allowed for in any customs or regulations about road usage. They are completely at the mercy of their phantasies and unconscious impulses, and we alone, the community and the drivers, can safeguard them.

Before we come to the teaching of young children, therefore, we MUST attend, first, to the roads—regulated crossings and speed, road bridges and the like; and secondly, to the motorist—to *his* teaching in the principles and techniques of Safety First. The onus must rest upon him and upon public opinion.

Then, when our own burden of guilt towards young children is lessened, we may hope to come to their teaching and training with a clearer vision and a surer aim.

To young children, mere words are of little avail. They need concrete help in actual seeing and understanding and responding. Any method which shows the traffic situation to the child as a concrete and positive problem of actual skill, rather than as a matter of authority and obedience, or personal risk and challenge, will increase his safety on the roads. Models of moving traffic and traffic controls, which the child can manipulate and respond to impress the eyes and nerves and memory far more effectively than verbal instructions. Some authorities in this country and elsewhere are now using such devices with good results. Once realise that the child needs, not so much warning and command, as technical help in seeing and learning and remembering and co-ordinating, and right ways of teaching will be found.

Again, the child will be safer if we make our emotional appeal, not to authority or fear, but to the interest and fun of co-operating to reach a common aim with all those others, the policeman on traffic duty, the lorry driver, the people who plan and make the roads and traffic regulations, the parents who watch the crossing so sensibly when out with their children, and teachers who show them the how and why.

Yet children *need* the chance to defy and challenge, to pit themselves against exciting difficulties. There is in any healthy happy growing child an irresistible urge to find risks and measure himself against them. And if we do not want him to attempt those in which the odds are too heavily weighted—dodging in and out of buses, retrieving a ball "just in time", tantalising the lorry driver by climbing on the back board—we must give the child space to run and jump, trees or ladders to climb, adventures and fun on school journeys and country holidays, play equipment in his gymnasium and school playground.

If, by giving up mere authority mongering, we take the personal excitement out of traffic dodging and defying the policeman, if we show the technical problem to the child as one which he and we must needs solve together by discussing and learning and practising, if we give him other good places for play, other ways of proving himself against physical risks, other means of expressing his feelings about people, if he *knows* by the way cars and buses behave and the way we teach him that we do not put upon him the responsibility of being "good", but co-operate with him to solve a common problem—than he will be much more likely to act with such measure of sense and self-control as is within his grasp—at less than seven years.

But remember! sense and self-control are and always will be meagre and unreliable in any child of less than seven years; and in quite a number of children, the self-hurting impulses are not lessened by any safety teaching—they may, indeed, even be provoked by it.

We may and we should ask the children to help us in avoiding accidents; BUT THE RESPONSIBILITY IS INALIENABLY OURS.

THE ESSENTIAL NEEDS OF CHILDREN
The New Era
November 1946

The essential needs of children can be considered under the two headings, human relationships and activities. Under the former may be grouped: affection, security, mild control, and companionship with other children; under the latter, the natural activities of a family home, stimulating materials and their free use, contact with the outside world, and emotional and intellectual development.

Affection

Throughout early childhood the world is a *personal* world, for the child's mind. The whole structure of the young child's being is orientated to personal relationships—first of all to his mother, and later to his father and other adults as well. Everything is for him, centered in persons. Neutral things and impersonal happenings come into the child's awareness only slowly and relatively late. As the work of Piaget as well as that of the psychoanalysts has shown, things happen in order 'to keep people good' or 'to punish them because they are bad'.

Feelings in the infant and young child are very intense and overwhelming, and imagination is very vivid. The child's behaviour and his picture of the external world are more determined, in the early years, by his inner world of feeling and imagination than by what is real from the adult point of view. What people do to him and around him is necessarily interpreted in terms of his own feelings. This makes the behaviour of the grown-ups not less, but *more* important. The child is even more dependent upon the goodness or badness of the adults around him than he would be if he had an adult sense of reality. What from the adult point of view is a mild deprivation or small discomfort or punishment may be felt by the child to be overwhelmingly severe. The morality of the very small child is an intensely severe and strict one. It has often been observed in the spontaneous dramatic play of little children that the young child feels his parents to be *either* ideally good *or* terribly severe, inflicting lethal punishments. All that happens is thus (in the child's mind) the outcome of the goodness or badness, the lovingness or cruelty, of his parents (or other grown-ups) and of his own feelings and behaviour towards them.

In the young child's mind, moreover, people are *always* either good or bad. Mere indifference on their part is felt by him to be a positive badness. If they satisfy his needs by loving and caring for him, they are felt to be 'good' parents. And not only if they tantalize or hurt him, but if they neglect him or leave him without guidance and control, they are felt to be 'bad'. In the very young child, these patterns of 'good' and 'bad' are extreme in character. Mother is (at first) felt to be either *wholly* loving and helpful or wholly hostile and cruel. If she is cold and neglectful, then he feels starved and helpless, and everything becomes bad to him. In other words, the world as it appears to the young child's mind is very like that of the old fairy tales. When he feels loved and satisfied, the world seems full of fairy godmothers and helpful genii, bringing good things by beneficent magic; when he feels neglected and unloved, the world seems full of witches and ogres, terrifying giants, bad fairies, who deprive and destroy by an evil magic.

What the child will become as an adult citizen is determined quite as much by his feelings and his imaginative apprehension of the people around him as it is by his being fed and medically cared for, or given good schooling in later childhood. It has been established, for example, that delinquent children at any age are still living (in their inner beliefs) in the world of giants and ogres. Their anti-social conduct is partly the result of their hidden (largely unconscious) terror of cruel tyrants and extremely severe punishments, which yet paradoxically they feel compelled to defy. Or they may be led to provoke punishment in order to exchange their awful phantasies for a less unbearable reality.

Only as his (the normal child's) sense of reality slowly develops through the early years, fostered by the real experience of affection, security and mild control from his parents or those who stand for parents, does his inner world of feeling come closer to the actual human world of ordinary people who are neither fairy godmothers nor evil giants; a world of social realities in which the child can take his own place.

Children become adapted to this real world, become social beings themselves, able to exercise self-control, and to co-operate with others in an active and friendly but responsible way, *not* by virtue of what they are taught in words, but by living experience of people, by absorbing the pattern of behaviour shown in the actual personalities of those around them. The child cannot judge father and mother and teacher except by their behaviour and their emotional attitudes towards him. Words, verbal commandments, abstract principles, have no significance except in so far as they are embodied in the actions and the personalities of the people upon whom he is dependent. What parents and teachers are, and his real experience of them, is infinitely more important than what they profess or claim to be, or tell him he ought to be. This fact is no new discovery—'Example is better than precept' is a well-known truth. But the experience of the psychologist has confirmed and amplified this truth in a new way by his understanding of the deeper, more hidden processes in the child's mind. Put concretely, it is useless to tell the child to be kind and loving and self-controlled, considerate with others, and so on, if he does not experience these virtues in the day-to-day conduct and attitudes of the adults about him, towards him and towards other children. If he is in fact treated coldly and distantly or harshly, starved of affection and natural human contacts, he cannot himself become a social being, trustful of other people and confident in his own ability to be decent and generous.

His first essential need is thus *affection*, the experience of loving care, either from his own actual parents or from those who take over the function of parents, whether in a foster home or an institution. The experience of love is just as necessary for the child's mental and moral growth as good food and medical care are necessary for his bodily health and development. Even his bodily health is greatly influenced (especially in infancy and early childhood) by the happiness or unhappiness which comes from experiencing love, or the lack of it.[1]

Security

Another essential need of the infant and young child is *security*. He needs to feel safe in his environment, safe not only from physical dangers and discomforts, but also from shocks in his personal life, such as frequent and unexpected changes in the people upon whom he is dependent, and to whom he has become attached. He needs not only a regular routine in his daily life, a rhythm of bodily care suited to his age, but also a stable relationship with people. If his nurse is frequently changed, as may happen in an institution, (or in comfortable families which employ nursemaids), this shocks his feelings in a way which is very hard to bear, and makes it difficult for him to build up stable attitudes of affection, of trust in others and confidence in his own feelings. Many children who have this experience tend to withdraw from affectionate relationships altogether, becoming suspicious, distrustful and aloof, since they never know what to expect. What is the good of loving if one so often loses the object of one's love and has constantly to make a fresh start? In the ordinary home this sort of thing does not often happen; but there is sometimes an insecurity arising from changeable moods in mother or father. The mother who indulges one day and scolds the next is a great trial to the child and arouses similar feelings of insecurity and uncertainty. The 'spoilt' child is an anxious child. He is 'spoilt' not by too much loving but by fickle indulgence and a mixture of

1. 'The hospitalized infant sleeps less, passes more stools, is more liable to respiratory infection, than the infant at home. Also there is a dulling of response to emotional stimuli, e.g. these infants do not smile in response to mother at 3 months of age. There is a lowering of resistance and delay or distortion in development.

'When a child's mother is excluded from hospital, even though there be a high level of bodily hygiene, mortality is high. When children were mothered by nurses and doctors, and parents' visits were allowed, mortality fell sharply.

'This applied also to toddlers. E.g. there was a hospital case in which a young child went steadily downhill until "so weak that it seemed he might stop breathing at any minute". The child then returned to the mother—rapid and complete recovery followed.'
(*Loneliness in Infancy*, Bakwin, *American Journal of Diseases of Children*, 1942)

'The book stresses the importance of mothering in the emotional life of the infant as being "as vital to the child's development as food". By expressing consistent tender, caressing love, the mother teaches the small baby to love, and this has far-reaching effects on later life, for "the capacity for mature emotional relationships in adult life is a direct outgrowth of the mothering which an infant receives". There is need to stress this phase of child care. There are advocates of institutional or group care of young children; many professional workers with children and many mothers who do not appreciate the importance of the emotional attachment of mother and baby.'
(*The Rights of Infants: Early Psychological Needs and their Satisfaction*, Margaret A. Ribble. Columbia University Press, New York, 1943.)

uneasy and changeable feelings in his mother. A steady emotional attitude and consistent ways of teaching and training are very necessary support to the child.

Mild Control

The great help which consistent methods of handling and training the child bring to his development links with another essential need, the need for a steady but *mild* control. This is another aspect of good parenthood. The good parent not only gives love to the child but helps him to control his aggression and his destructive impulses. The small child *is* aggressive; he is greedy to get all he wants, he is full of rivalry and jealousy towards other children and grown-ups, he gets angry and often feels great rages if he cannot get what he wishes for, and even in cooler moments he may hate other children or may damage physical objects or destroy things he values. He is at the same time very frightened about these aggressive impulses. He becomes very anxious if he believes that the grown-ups cannot control him, since he feels he cannot control himself. Self-control does develop later, although even the adolescent boy or girl suffers acute anxiety about his wishes and impulses and the feeling that he cannot yet control the uprush of his instinctual life which new bodily development is now bringing. The young child feels even more the need of some controlling influence. That here should be such an influence is a familiar fact, which is in no danger of being overlooked in institutions or in most foster-homes. We all know that it is chiefly fond mothers who are over-indulgent with their own children. What is not always realized, however, is that if the control which the child seeks, as a help in keeping himself in order and saving the persons and objects he loves from his destructive impulses, is to be really educative and help him to become an independent, self-controlled citizen, it must be a mild and loving control. Severe punishments are quite as unwise and unfruitful as indulgence and the lack of control. Mild control by a firm and just authority is always felt by the child to be a help. This educates him in self-control. Harsh punishments, rigid prohibitions of natural pleasures and healthy activities serve to increase the child's hate, aggression and anxiety, and are far more likely to turn him into a delinquent than into a useful member of society.

Moreover, control should be primarily a *positive* control (as it usually is in the hands of a skilful school teacher), relying upon the provision of positive means of activity rather than upon negative prohibitions. Not so much: 'You must *not* do that', as 'You *may* do this, and here is the means to do it.' To provide for constructive and co-operative occupations and responsibilities is the best form of control. (This point links with what we shall have to say in the next section about children's activities.)

If, then, the child's parents are so enormously important to him and his need for affection, security, and a wise control is so great, how does this bear upon the needs of children whose parents are either dead or absent or so unsatisfactory that society decides to remove the children from their care? It means that whatever substitute we make for the child's own home and own parents, these must, if they are going to help his development, come as near as possible to being good *parents,* and must be felt by the child to represent *good* parents. In the case of bad homes, it is not enough to take the child's own parents away and then supply simply the physical basis of life. To have no parents at all (as in a formal institution) is a positive evil and scarcely less undesirable for the child than having actively bad parents of his own. If the representatives of society decide to take the grave step of separating a child from his own parents, they must realize that this *is* a very grave step and that they then have the further responsibility of recreating a family life for the child. Otherwise they themselves become *bad* parents both in fact and in the child's mind. Again, if the child has no parents of his own and society takes the responsibility of putting him in a home where his bodily needs are met, this still meets only one partial aspect of his needs as a human being. To shirk or evade the responsibility for satisfying his emotional and social requirements is for society's representatives to act as bad parents themselves.

Companionship with other Children

There is, however, still another essential need of the child in the world of human relationships, viz., the need for active *companionship* with other children. It is largely by means of an active sharing of work and play in a genuine social life with other children that the young child learns to overcome his distrust of himself and of others and his rivalry with them, to build up a true social feeling of comradely affection and group loyalty. Here again, it must be emphasized that the transformation of the child into a social being does not come about by his being talked to and preached to, but only by active *experiences* in making and doing and sharing and playing and working with other children in day-to-day social participation.

Natural Activities of a Family Home

Having the chance to develop bodily skills and to co-operate in play and in learning is of tremendous help not only to the child's physical health but also to his emotional life and mental balance. It gives him hope and confidence in his own future as a grown-up, and trust in the parents (or parent-substitutes) as people who will allow and encourage him to become grown-ups like themselves.

This applies not only to the development of manipulative skills in creative handwork but also to participation in the daily activities of the home, helping to keep it clean and orderly. Every young child wishes to help his mother in the work of the home, especially at the nursery ages. Later on he may rebel against too much of this, especially if it is treated as an obligation and takes the place of free, natural play out of doors; but within the limits of his ability, he does wish to share in the daily routine of the home, and to become independent in caring for himself.

Moreover, active social participation, playing with other children and talking to grown-ups, such as happens naturally in the everyday life of an ordinary family, makes a great contribution to the child's intellectual life as well. It stimulates his wish to speak and his understanding of language, and by the asking and answering of questions it stirs his interest in the multifarious activities of the real world and continually adds to his knowledge and enlarges his perceptions and understanding in a pleasurable way.[1]

Stimulating Materials and Free Use of Them

The ordinary comfortable home, moreover, provides many playthings and materials for inventive play and creative activities—not only by way of the toys, tools and stuffs specially bought for the child, but also in the ordinary objects and utensils and odds and ends of the material of the day-to-day household life—such as pots and pans, pebbles, matches, dough, cotton reels, paper, rags and boxes. The very poor home has much less to offer, but may still be rich in this respect as compared with the war nursery or the regulated institution. These often provide extremely little in the way of materials for the child's imaginative use and pleasurable enjoyment. It is essential in any environment to provide for the children's manipulative and imaginative play and their creative activities, by generous material, which need never be costly, but should be suitable for each successive age.

It is of comparatively little value for young children in the earlier school years to follow a prescribed programme of formal work. The value of

---

1. A comparison was made some years ago in Chicago by Mrs. Alschuler of two groups of young children of nursery school ages: (a) those from their own homes where the children were allowed to help their mothers up to the limit of their ability—feeding, washing and dressing themselves, dusting, sweeping, washing crockery, etc. (Positive ideal of children's goodness.) (b) Children from (own) homes where they were expected to be very obedient, very quiet and mostly passive. (Negative ideal of children's goodness.) It was found that children from the first sort of homes had fewer tantrums, were less liable to be obstinate or disobedient, or to refuse a request from their parents, and had better bodily health than those from the second type of home.

In a valuable study made some years ago by two parents of the various questions asked by their boy between 3 and 7 years of age, it was found that by far the most active questioning, the greatest number of questions which could be called 'scientific', questions as to how things were made, what they did, what they were for, how they worked, were asked in the moment-to-moment interchange of questions and answers with an interested mother and father in the two fundamental situations of ordinary life in a home: viz. (a) being bathed and cleansed, and so on; (b) eating, cooking, shopping and everything to do with food and feeding, at the meal table, and in the kitchen.

active methods of learning has been fully demonstrated by a number of recent experiments and investigations, such as Miss E. R. Boyce's account of her very valuable work in an Infant School in a slum district,[2] and Miss D. E. M. Gardner's comparison of different educational methods in Infant and Junior Schools.[3] Miss Boyce's book is a clear proof of the value of those methods which make use of the children's activities; and Miss Gardner found that schools using 'activity methods' were superior to a greater or lesser degree in every significant test with the exception of writing (at six years of age).

Contact with the Outside World

Another important aspect of the intellectual stimulus afforded by life in a family—one which the institution mostly lacks—is contact with the larger world outside the home, with opportunities for learning about the real life of adults.

In most institutions, there is little natural stimulus to active interests and questionings arising from such contact with the ordinary world. Many institution children have never seen any of the basic processes of maintaining life under ordinary conditions. They have never watched mother washing, cleaning, cooking, nor gone shopping with her, watched the bus conductor clip the tickets, admired the driver, nor gone to the pictures with father or older brother, and enjoyed all the varied and exciting life of the streets. They have no idea how an ordinary mother contrives her spending of the household money,—nor learnt to manage their own pocket money. They have not had questions stirred in their minds by these interesting events and processes connected with the satisfaction of fundamental human needs, nor been stimulated to speech and to knowledge by their wish to understand these things. A colleague of mine, talking recently to an institution child, found that the child had no idea that washing ever *could* be done except in a fully equipped laundry!

Emotional and Intellectual Development

It is difficult to separate social and intellectual growth, the development (or lack of development) of character and of learning and thinking. These aspects of children's growth and of their education interact at every point. Deprivation of the chance to develop bodily and manipulative skill, and of the active means of learning and co-operating, handicaps alike the child's bodily health, emotional balance and the growth of intelligence.

2. *Play in the Infants' School*, by E. R. Boyce, Methuen, 1938. 'Contributions to Modern Education Series.'[3]

3. *Testing Results in the Infant School*, D. E. M. Gardner, Methuen, 1942.

Active methods of making and doing and learning are of great value in the child's character development. They help him to learn to control those natural impulses of greed and aggression and rage to which we have already referred, and to overcome the anxieties which these destructive impulses of his own arouse in him.

For example, in considering delinquency, it is important to realize that it is not the mere lack of private possessions (although this may itself be a serious deprivation) which causes a child to steal, but often the longing for love and lack of the means of loving and creating.

A clear example is that of a girl (an orphan) who had been an inmate of a Poor Law Home from early infancy until she was fifteen, when she became a servant maid in a comfortable household. She was an extremely inhibited and unresponsive personality. She did what she was asked to do, but showed no open sign of feeling, no wishes or ambitions. It was, however, discovered after some months that she appropriated various family possessions—*not* money or clothes, but family photographs and devotional books from the library of her employer: her drawer was full of photographs of the family she lived with. Nothing could show more clearly her longing to be a member of a family and to have kind and loving parents and brothers and sisters of her own.

The young child often shows us that he not only feels anxious about being helpless and about his own greed and aggression, but also feels doubtful about his ever becoming controlled and skilful, able to do and to create in the world as he desires. He has so little hope and confidence in his own future that he sometimes feels that the only way to get the good things which the grown-ups have (not merely possessions but abilities, being able to learn and understand, to create useful things, to have children of their own) is to *steal* them. Much of the actual thieving of children is an expression of these feelings. They may steal money, food, etc., but in the child's imagination these things stand not only for things to eat and money to spend, but also for the means of being powerful in well doing, in creating and giving. For example, one boy in the top class of an infant school was discovered to have stolen money quite often; on one occasion it was a ten shilling note from his teacher's pocket. He readily confessed that he had taken it and had given it to a poor man in the street who, he said, 'needed it more than the teacher'. This is an unusually clear instance of a fact familiar to psychologists, that the hidden motives of the child who steals may include constructive wishes as well as greed.

The child needs to feel that he belongs, that he is wanted and valued as a person, for what he is and what he can give. If he has the chance to develop manipulative and creative skills, to share in the social and practical life of his home, to be active in learning in school, he gradually becomes to believe that he can contribute to others as well as take from them, can make a real return for what had been done for him when he was weak and helpless.

Only *active* learning, however, and active social participation and interchange with those who love him and give him responsibility can build up in him a confidence in his own future.

(These notes were part of the evidence submitted by me to the Home Office Care of Children Committee in 1945. The rest of the evidence consisted in comments which related more specifically to children in institutions, with quotations from technical researches. The tenor of my main arguement was that the essential needs of all children include the experience of family relationships, with the emotional and intellectual experiences and the practical activities which normal family life affords; and that any institutional substitute for the home must be organized to meet these needs, if it is to foster healthy development.—AUTHOR)

3
What Active Enquiry Means for the Child*
by Nathan Isaacs
(1960)

I

We have seen in earlier chapters [of Isaacs's book] the questions which children of the Primary School ages ask, the interests they express and the capacity they can display for following these through. We have watched them pursue far-reaching explorations with great zest and enjoyment and end up with the most worthwhile achievements.

The keynote of this volume has been that all the main activities required for both the pursuit and the appreciation of science are spontaneous natural interests in most normal children. The present chapter aims at showing how we can go a vital step further. We can say that not only are these interests commonly present, but where at all marked, they represent important *needs* of the child's inward poise and happy growth. Thus in helping these interests to thrive to the utmost of each individual's capacity, teachers are not merely achieving invaluable educational ends, but also strengthening some of the main stabilising forces within the child.

From such an angle, however, we must look afresh at the five year olds who enter our Primary Schools, and what these schools can do for them. Naturally if all we want is to drill somehow into large numbers of them certain elementary skills and information, we hardly need to concern ourselves with them as persons. We know that they all differ in character and temperament, but our very aim is to get them as similar as possible, at least to the extent of this basic equipment. Anything more is not really our affair.

But once we do think of each child as a person and aim at getting him really interested and carrying him with us, we have to give a new attention to what everything we are trying to do for him means to him. And if we are to start from his own interests and to help him to advance educationally

---

*A chapter from *Approaches to Science in the Primary Schools* (1960) edited by E. Lawrence and N. Isaacs.

through the most constructive use of these, the need to understand how things look and feel from inside his mind becomes paramount.

We are of course still faced with individual differences of capacity and temperament which we have to accept. But we must now attempt to grasp at any rate the background needs and problems which most of our children are likely to share; that is, which as a normal result of their history during infancy and early childhood, they are likely to bring with them as they enter the Primary School.

In the course of the last decades, we have in effect greatly deepened our understanding of their first eventful years. We have therefore a far fuller and truer picture of what things signify for him, what he needs and why, and what can best serve his further growth. Above all, we have learned to appreciate, as never before, how the story of every child is one and indivisible from birth; how closely feeling and acting and learning, real inward learning, are intertwined in this story and depend on one another; and how impossible therefore it is to understand any one of these aspects of children's mental life without taking into account the interacting history of them all.

II

This story cannot be considered in any detail here; all we can do is to pick out a few main points that seem most important for real sympathetic grasp of the typical mental phrase and outlook reached by the ordinary Primary School child.

(a) In the first few months an infant's life must mainly consist of alternating feeling states, with only the barest rudiments of the outer world entering in. These feeling states would seem to be already capable of great intensity: eagerness-joy-bliss-contentment-craving-distress-pain-disappointment-rage-fear are all strongly manifested in turn. But one thread that tends to run right through is the infant's state of almost complete helplessness and dependence which can get linked even with his bliss, that may be *withdrawn*, or his satisfactions, that may be *withdrawn*, to say nothing of the distresses, fears or pains that may be suddenly *thrust* on him. Yet over against this there are also the first faint beginnings of the future answer to helplessness: the first active turnings towards stimuli in the outer world, the first absorbed and following attention to what goes on there and even the first exercises of the infant's powers of *action*. Within a few months indeed these achieve their first great triumph: the hand learning to grasp what the eye perceives ushers in a new world of achievement. There is now really something to set off against the earliest all but complete helplessness; and the infant, as we know, makes the very most of this new *sense* of power.

(b) As the first year progresses and the second unfolds, the same sort of alternation of feeling-states continues, but in addition there are also thrown up particular protracted crises; for many infants that of weaning, for all the drawn-out process of teething. Again, these come on him helplessly and painfully. At the same time, however, he is making the most exciting and prodigious progress in what *he* can now do and achieve in the outer world. He learns to stand, to walk, to accomplish a variety of successful and satisfactory actions, to recognise more and more persons, things and situations and to foresee what is going to happen next. All this supports him and buoys him up against those other states of helpless dependence. Yet these become in a way more acute too; for as his scope and powers in the outside world grow, so does his awareness of it and with this his sense of all the things he cannot do, and above all of everything which he is restrained or prevented from doing. Indeed, as we know but he does not, the more his powers grow, the more does he need, in those early days, to be kept in check in his own interest. Moreover, his resentful but impotent chafings against such restraints become just one element more in a deep conflict of feelings inside himself, in which he is peculiarly helpless. From perhaps the latter part of the first year onward, as his sense of the main persons round him grows more and more distinct, they become for him the focus of directly opposite emotions and impulses; his mother means everything to him, yet also very often denies and thwarts and constrains him; his father, besides playing a similar alternating role, provokes his special hostility by frequently drawing the mother away from him. With these warring feelings, whenever they lay hold on him, the infant has no means at all of coping; but comes nearest to getting away from them as he exercises and further expands his rapidly growing powers in the outward role.

(c) In the course of the second year, these powers gain the further accession of the vast new one of language and communication. This quickly multiplies a hundredfold all his capacities for real achievement and all but creates for him a new capacity for phantasying and imagining, thus opening up for him a kingdom of make-believe might and accomplishment stretching immensely beyond everything—however much—he is now really able to do.

However, here once more there is an equivocal side to his advance. With his new powers come new lessons in dependence and impotence. He suffers a daily training in submission to an order of things constantly growing more unlike that of his "feather-bedded" first year. He must accept his mother's going about her own business, adapt to rules and routines, and learn to subordinate his will to other and superior ones. In particular he has to learn one great adaptation which often comes anything but naturally to him. From a very early state he has taken the most absorbed interest in all parts of his own body and all that happens to them, not least among them his own eliminatory functions, which readily get charged with specially strong feelings for him. These are of course for him experiences like any others, since he knows nothing yet of our taboos. However there comes a time when he becomes aware of ever heavier pressures on him to change his ways altogether about these functions. He is expected to learn to behave quite differently and even to feel differently, and though presently he learns to do so, this happens rarely without some struggles and often only after a long and severe battle of wills.

This struggle is an important part of his inward history and indeed may well bring home to him in the most pointed way how powerless he still is. How reluctant his submission is apt to be and how superficial, may too frequently be evidenced by subsequent relapses. But he may be tried even more severely, especially should he be a first child, if during his first few years, a baby brother or sister comes on the scene, and he finds himself, virtually overnight, turned out of the place which has so long seemed all his own. It is not difficult, if one really tries to relive the whole experience with him, to grasp the catastrophic difference—all the losses and all the fears—which the sudden dramatic dislodgement *must* mean to him.

This succession of dramatic experiences, in all of which his mother is so centrally involved, add their own further complexities and tensions to the tangle of contradictory feelings in which the child is already caught up. They discharge themselves to some extent through his phantasies and make-believe play, but can also all too easily manifest themselves through every sort of arrest or disturbance in the tenor of the child's life: temper tantrums or night terrors, feeding difficulties or stubbornnesses or hostilities and aggressions, shyness or phobias, or obsessional habits. In a large proportion of cases these, if not too severe, are happily left behind in the ordinary course of growth. But an essential part of this growth consists precisely in the child's sustained orientation to the world outside him and steady ever-increasing advance within it. From two to five he progresses by giant strides. Through his physical play he continually develops his powers of co-ordination and control and acquires new manual skills; at the same time with boundless curiosity and interest he explores, experiments, takes to pieces, puts questions, tries to build up and construct and mold and fashion, compares and sorts and arranges, seeks new experiences and new worlds to know and conquer.

These are the very processes by which psychologically he grows and they constitute a natural hygiene to which he constantly turns. In this fashion he can break away from conflicts and oppressions and fears within himself and expand freely in a limitless larger world. But to understand all that this world means for him we must also be able to put ourselves back in his place, go through all the vicissitudes and drama of his early years with him, relive ourselves imaginatively his first utter helplessness and dependence, his slow struggles out of this, the plunges back into it which he suffers and the incessant outwardly directed activity by which he alone can make good his eventual emancipation. This sort of attempted view from within is what the present thumbnail sketch has tried to indicate.

By the age of five to six, if he has come through reasonably easily and successfully so far, his worst crises may well be over. He has normally established a tolerably settled relation to the world around him, both human and physical, and this would go with a fairly stable balance in his feeling life and a large measure of security and confidence both in people and the scheme of things. To the extent of his habitual surroundings, he would have a reasonable notion of that scheme and would know generally what to expect of it and also what was demanded from him. We should see him as a typical five year old, running and playing, talking and asking questions, dramatising and pretending, eager to be taken around and shown things, but also to find them out himself, to do things, to construct and so on. But the familiarity of this picture should not lead us to take it for granted and should not mask from us the fact that our apparently carefree five year old has behind him a long history, on the one hand of inner storms and stresses and on the other of intellectual growth and advance, in which he has accomplished a vast miracle of learning. This miracle we need to understand if we are to contribute anything towards continuing it. The attitudes of mind, the interests and activities which have enabled the child to achieve the miracle, largely for himself, drawing whatever help he could from those around him but not class-educated or even tutored by them into it: These are assets still available to us. Ought we not therefore, by full understanding and co-operation, to make the utmost possible use of them.

III

If now, in the above broad sketch of the child's background history, we go back to the question of what the outer world means to him, we can sum up its value to him somewhat as follows:

(a) This world as the child advances in it, proves to be one which is mainly stable and solid and bright and open, and to which he can turn with security and confidence. Things for the most part remain constant in it and he can rely on them and look ahead and act accordingly. In addition he can always go on exploring further and further; there is more to find out in every direction. Moreover his new gains very generally join up with what he has already discovered in such a way that his sense of understanding and of security is both consolidated and further extended. And all the time his activities secure him a double reward. First there is the excitement and satisfaction of each success achieved; secondly, there is the opening out of the field for more activity of the same kind, with the renewed sense of stimulus and forward-looking interest which this can bring.

(b) To these two rewards there is added the great further one of the child's expanding power of actual *doing* things. The "finding out" process itself leads him to acquire all sorts of new skills and abilities each of which carries with it new pleasure and a fresh zest. Any one such conquest moreover often serves as a bridge to others, so that the child's range and level of reward-bringing activities are constantly stimulated to advance in an ever-widening field.

(c) Moreover as part of the same cycle of processes he is always coming up against difficulties, obstacles and problems which act as a challenge but which—often with no more than a hint or a simple question from the cooperating adult—he can himself learn to resolve. This again can be a great exhilaration and triumph and at the same time a renewed spur and encouragement to go on.

(d) These trains of activity, in which one thing leads to another and the child can so readily become completely absorbed, have in exceptional degree the power of "taking one out of oneself." They are thus among the most effective means of breaking away from inner tensions and stresses and a means which the child's teachers can help him to put to the fullest use.

(e) There is also a less apparent way in which many of his "finding out" activities can render large aid to the constructive progress of his mental life. We know only too well that in most of us, children and adults, there is pent up a mass of disruptive and destructive impulses (strongly nourished, if not produced, by our emotional vicissitudes) which present us with a most difficult problem of control. We recognise the importance of finding directions where they can be given their head so that they may as far as possible be diverted from disastrous channels. Now the one direction which most clearly stands out for its positive value is that of scientific knowledge. To advance this we must break things up to see what they are made of; we must take them to pieces to find out how they work; we must in fact practise the most varied forms of destruction and even keep learning new ways of destroying, precisely in order to learn. To serve its scientific purpose, it has of course to be a strictly controlled and carefully limited destruction (which, in the case of children, we should not allow at all to be applied to living things), but this fact itself can enhance its psychological value. For in most of us the very impulses to destroy are themselves deeply linked with strong impulses of remorse and contrition—impulses to repair and rebuild and make whole again. And the peculiar worth of destruction for the sake of learning and understanding is that we can so justly feel that it is being done for a positive and constructive cause. Scientific knowledge enables us to put right what has gone wrong, to relieve and cure ills, to synthesise and build and create in a thousand different ways.

All this of course need not be present to the minds of those who find special satisfaction in the more forceful ways of inquiring into things; but it is not difficult to see evidences of the processes at work, particularly in children. In them we can readily follow through all the transitions from just destroying to doing so *in order* to find out and then often *only* for this purpose, together with an increasing desire to use the "finding out" in order to restore, set right, to construct and build. This kind of transition can then be encouraged and fostered, to the enduring benefit of the child's mental well-being as well as his educational progress.

(f) Finally—and here we may well have a particularly valuable bridge between the child and the community around him—the activities by which he enlarges his knowledge and understanding are usually "combined operations." At home there are most often co-operating adults; at school we have group or team enterprises led by a teacher. These operations give the child all the satisfactions of "doing things together," a continual sense of harmony and unison and an enhancement of power. And this is strongly nourished by the actual productiveness of such "finding out" missions and the manifold rewards which, as already described, they bring. Moreover as the team form develops, there is the feeling not only of working in cooperation, but of being carried along in a great enterprise. In this one is indeed playing one's own active part—so that all the time one is a member, it is what "we" are doing, but one is also sharing in something far bigger than one could oneself accomplish. Here, therefore, is a reassuring contrast to all the forces, within and without the child, that are so apt to draw him into rivalry and strife, and a living model, in which the child himself participates, of the satisfactions which harmonious co-operation can give and the great things which it can accomplish.

IV

These then are the values which the child's exploratory allied activities in the outer world can signify for him. But how far they will in fact do so becomes now the teacher's problem—a problem partly, as we have seen, of restrictive conditions, but partly also of psychological understanding and patience and resource. The problem of understanding has here been our main concern; but even where this and all other needs are met, the Primary School teacher's task is no light one. The resources of young children are still very limited; their attention is quickly fatigued; they are easily distracted and diverted; and they are only very imperfectly masters in their own minds. Their mood may change, or a fit of obstinacy or defiance or quarrelsomeness may come over them suddenly. Thus the way may be blocked to the very kind of activity that might relieve and help them. These are the inevitable hazards of any teaching methods that seek to work *with* the child rather than to stamp a set pattern *on* him.

Yet a teacher who understands what he needs to do can through his steadfast support of the positive, constructive side of the child, make all the difference. He can get his children mostly so eager and absorbed that attention does not flag and is not distracted or blocked. His secret will be always to tempt them on, to keep them engaged, and to make them go on feeling that this is *their* adventure, *their* enterprise, *their* set of discoveries and *their* achievement. He will indeed also know when to stop; that is, when real unavoidable flagging and fatigue sets in. Yet he will throughout enjoy the sense that he is not only aiding children to learn, in the most real and lasting way, but also strengthening the forces of future growth in them. In one direction after another, he will be extending their power of setting their own further goals, finding their own way forward, keeping their own educational process going. For every one of their roads of exploring, ordering, and constructing, imagining and testing in the real world does in fact lead on endlessly. The great number of future non-scientists can thus be borne forward to the appreciation and enjoyment of science, and the smaller number of future scientists straight to its dedicated pursuit.

V

This is obviously still in many ways a simplified picture. It aims at making clear a point of view which seems both important and valid, but there are qualifications which must be recognised along with it. Thus:

(a) As was emphasised from the outset, children differ, in capacity and temperament and personal bent, so that there can be no one rule for them all. Apart from sheer native limitations which nothing can touch, there are variations of need which must be understood and met. The ways that lead broadly into the "scientific" world are for a good many children not their most helpful roads to inward balance or security or happy growth. Their road may be that of music or craftsmanship or modelling or writing or trying to excel in some bodily skill or game, or even the pure abstractions of mathematics. In a number of these children the exploring and allied interests may indeed also be strong, and if so, everything which encourages and enriches them may still have much inward feeling-value over and above its educational one. In other instances, however, there may be little such interest or response, and this fact needs equally to be accepted. Throughout, the teacher can only give his most valuable help by co-operating with whatever marked personal interests there are, as faithfully as he does with the would-be scientific ones.

In general the teacher can only go by what he finds—but can only find by sympathetically and patiently *looking*. In some children the "exploring" motive springs will be found so vigorous that all that needs to be done is to open ways for them. In other cases, though present they may be fitful, hesitant or self-unsure; here the teacher may need to coax them on or to infuse confidence. Even where various soundings have elicited little or no interest, the teacher may need to think of the possibility that it may merely be blocked in those directions. By dint of patient trying he may discover ways through which he *can* unlock new gates for real and fruitful growth in the child. The possible directions of growth are after all as manifold as our world itself. The material in this books shows that these are no impractical counsels of perfection, but roads that may well be open for most teachers with most children and there is usually no lack of response and counter-encouragement from the children themselves as they go along.

(b) It must be recognised that education which seeks to take these forms establishes a new relation between the school and the children's homes. If they are not only to learn by their own active enquiries, but also to derive inward support and help from doing so, the efforts of the school may well be defeated unless the climate of the home marches reasonably with them. Otherwise the child may merely be involved in new emotional difficulties and conflicts. A girl of nine, whose mother held views diametrically opposite to those of her favourite teacher, was cruelly teased by her older brother about this clash. "Whom do you believe," he asked, "mother or teacher?" The little girl replied at once, "I believe teacher." But then, overcome with confusion and a sense of betrayal, she rushed to her mother and added, "But I love mommy." This situation may not always be avoidable, though it need not be thus wantonly brought to a head. However, it illustrates how important it may be for teachers to explain to parents what they are trying to do and why, and to draw them, if at all possible, into active interest and co-operation. This, though increasingly accepted in principle, is still too largely the exception rather than the rule. Yet clearly the kind of education that seeks to get inside the mind of the child and to help him in every way to grow from within will only finally prosper if parents can be induced to play their part no less than teachers. They must somehow come to see their own vital share in this enterprise. Instead of taking "schooling" for granted, rather like other municipal services and thinking of it as just the drilling of some needed gimmicks into their children's minds, parents must view it as an essential part of their children's *lives* and thus in every sense also *their* affair. They must be persuaded into sympathetic and lively participation in what the teacher and school are trying to do; and they must give their own encouragement and best help to their children who are seeking to grow by questioning and inquiry, exploration and experiment. It would be this kind of co-operative and harmonious effort that would bear the fullest fruits.

Notes

Chapter 1. Introduction and Biographical Sketch

1. Dorothy E. M. Gardner, *Susan Isaacs: The First Biography* (London: Methuen Educational Ltd., 1969). Biographical material here is taken, for the most part, from this book. Other details come from interviews with persons who knew and worked with Susan Isaacs.
2. Ibid., p. 19.
3. Loc. cit.
4. Ibid., p. 43, quoted from Nathan Isaacs.

Chapter 2. The Contemporary Setting

1. Lloyd DeMause, ed., *The History of Childhood* (New York: The Psychohistory Press, 1974), p. 1.
2. Susan Isaacs, *Psychological Aspects of Child Development* (London: University of London Press, 1935), p. 9.
3. Joseph Featherstone, "Rousseau and Modernity," *Harvard Educational Review*, 19, no. 2 (1975).
4. Priscilla Robertson, "The Home as a Nest," in DeMause, *The History of Childhood*, p. 422.
5. DeMause, *The History of Childhood*, especially chapter 1, "The Evolution of Childhood."
6. Ibid., pp. 51, 54.
7. Ibid., p. 52.
8. Cf. Jonathan Gathorne-Hardy, *The Rise and Fall of the British Nanny*. (London: Hodder and Stoughton, 1972).
9. Cf. Stephen Kern, "Explosive Intimacy: Psychodynamics of the Victorian Family," *History of Childhood Quarterly* 1, no. 3 (Winter 1974): 437.ff
10. DeMause, *The History of Childhood*, p. 52.
11. Cf. especially Philippe Aries, *Centuries of Childhood: A Social History of Family Life* (New York: Alfred A. Knopf, 1962); Ivy Pinchbeck, and Margaret Hewitt, *Children in English Society* (London: Routledge & Kegan Paul, 1973); Peter Laslett, *The World We Have Lost* (London: Methuen, 1971).
12. Robertson, "The Home as a Nest," pp. 422, 428.
13. Gardner Murphy, and Joseph Kovach, *Historical Introduction to Modern Psychology*, 3rd ed. (1949; reprint ed., New York: Harcourt Brace Jovanovich, 1972), p. 214.
14. Ibid., pp. 105–6.
15. J. C. Flügel, *A Hundred Years of Psychology, 1833–1933*, 3rd ed. (1933: reprint ed., London: Duckworth & Co., 1964), p. 119.
16. Robert Thompson, *The Pelican History of Psychology* (Harmondsworth, Middlesex: Penguin Books, 1968), p. 99.
17. Murphy and Kovach, *Introduction to Modern Psychology*, p. 104.
18. Francis Galton, *Hereditary Genius: An Inquiry into its Laws and Consequences* (London: Macmillan & Co., 1869), p. 45.
19. Ibid., pp. 45, 41.
20. *Eugenics Review* 25 (April 1933–January 1934).
21. G. F. Stout, *A Manual of Psychology*, 5th ed. rev. and enlarged (1899; reprint ed., London: University Tutorial Press, 1938), p. 31.

22. William James, *Talks to Teachers on Psychology* (1892; reprint ed., New York: W. W. Norton, 1958), pp. 34, 35.
23. McDougall, William, *Outline of Psychology* (New York: Charles Scribner & Sons, 1923), pp. 19, 70.
24. Quoted in Thompson, *The Pelican History of Psychology*, p. 178.
25. Flügel, *A Hundred Years of Psychology*, p. 262.
26. Quoted in L. S. Hearnshaw, *Cyril Burt, Psychologist* (Ithaca, N.Y.: Cornell Univ. Press, 1979), p. 47.
27. Susan S. Brierley, Preface to *An Introduction to Psychology* 4th ed. rev. (London: Methuen Co., 1921), p. vi.
28. Ibid., p. 7.
29. Ibid., Appendix to 1928 rev. ed., p. 152.
30. Ibid., p. 153.
31. Ibid.
32. Ibid.
33. Wilhelm Preyer, *The Mind of the Child: Part I—The Senses; Part II—the Will; Part III—The Development of the Intellect* (New York: Appleton & Co., 1888), pp. xii, xv.
34. James Sully, *Studies of Childhood* (London: Longmans Green & Co., 1895), p x.
35. William Stern, *Psychology of Early Education Up to the Sixth Year of Age* (Supplemented by Extracts from the Unpublished Diaries of Clara Stern) (London: Allen & Unwin, 1924). © 1914, p. 57.
36. Ibid., p. 53.
37. Ibid., p. 54.
38. Charlotte Bühler, *The First Year of Life*, Trans. Pearl Greenberg and Rowena Ripin. (1927; English ed., New York: John Day & Co., 1930), p. 3.
39. Susan Isaacs, *Psychological Aspects of Child Development*, p. 23. Italics the author's.
40. Cf. L. S. Hearnshaw, *Cyril Burt*, for a very full and up-to-date account of Cyril Burt's life and work.
41. Cyril Burt, Preface to *Mental and Scholastic Tests*, 2nd ed. (1921; reprint ed., London: Staples Press Ltd., 1947), p. iv.
42. Ibid., p. 34.
43. Robert Blair, *The Distribution and Relation of Educational Abilities* (London: Longmans Green & Co., 1918). Cf. also Robert Blair, Chief Education Officer, London County Council: *Handbook containing general information with reference to the work in connection with the Children's Care (Central) Sub-Committee.* (London: J. Truscott & Son, 1910).
44. Ibid., p. xix.
45. Burt, *Mental and Scholastic Tests*, p. 16.
46. Ibid., p. 1.
47. Cyril Burt, "The Development of Reasoning in School Children," *Journal of Experimental Pedagogy* 5 (1919–20).
48. Ibid., p. 73.
49. Ibid., p. 74.
50. Ibid., p. 76.
51. Ibid., p. 77.
52. Quoted in Hearnshaw, *Cyril Burt*, p. 52.
53. Quoted in Thompson, *Pelican History of Psychology*, p. 326.
54. Cf. N. J. Block and Gerald Dworkin, *The IQ Controversy* (New York: Pantheon Books, 1976).
55. John Rickman, "On 'Unbearable' Ideas and Impulses," in *Selected Contributions of Psycho-Analysis* (London: Hogarth Press, 1957).
56. George Henry Lewes, *Problems of Life and Mind*, 3rd series. Quoted in Hearnshaw, L. S., *A Short History of British Psychology 1840–1940* (London: Methuen & Co., 1964), p. 52.
57. Francis Galton, *Inquiries*. Quoted in Hearnshaw, *A Short History*, p. 60.
58. Hearnshaw, *A Short History*, p. 167.
59. Susan Isaacs, *Psychological Aspects of Child Development*, p. 134.
60. Cf. Sigmund Freud, *Civilization and its Discontents*, trans. James Strachey (1930; reprint ed., New York: W. W. Norton & Co., 1961).
61. Susan Isaacs, *Psychological Aspects of Child Development*, p. 139–40.
62. C. F. Mowat, *Britain Between the Wars, 1918–1940* (London: Methuen, 1955), p. 214.

63. Ernest Jones, *Psycho-Analysis* (1929; reprint ed., London: Ernest Benn, Ltd., 1932), pp. 10–11.
64. W. A. C. Stewart, *The Educational Innovators, vol. 2: Progressive Schools 1881–1967* (London: Macmillan, St. Martin's Press, 1968), p. 113.
65. W. H. Hereford, *The School, an Essay towards Humane Education* (1889), quoted in Evelyn Lawrence, ed., *Friedrich Froebel and English Education* (London: Routledge & Kegan Paul, 1952, 1964), p. 42.
66. Ibid., p. 38.
67. Nanette Whitbread, *The Evolution of the Nursery-Infant School: A History of Infant and Nursery Education in Britain, 1800–1970* (London: Routledge & Kegan Paul, 1972), p. 38.
68. Quoted in Stewart, *The Educational Innovators*, p. 116.
69. Margaret McMillan, *Early Childhood* (London: Swan Sonnenschein & Co., 1901), p. 26.
70. Whitbread, *Evaluation of the Nursery-Infant School*, p. 48ff.
71. Ibid., p. 59.
72. Cf. L. A. H. Smith, *Activity and Experience: Sources of English Informal Education* (New York: Agathon Press, 1976).
73. Cf. William Boyd and Wyatt Rawson, *The Story of the New Education* (London: Heinemann, 1965).
74. R. J. W. Selleck, *English Primary Education and the Progressives, 1914–1939* (London: Routledge & Kegan Paul, 1972), p. 63.
75. Boyd and Rawson, *Story of the New Education*.
76. W. H. G. Armytage, *Four Hundred Years of English Education* (Cambridge: At the University Press, 1964, 1970), p. 228.
77. T. Percy Nunn, *Education: Its Data and First Principles* (London: Edward Arnold & Co., 1920), pp. 17, 276.
78. Quoted in Selleck, *English Primary Education*, p. 123.
79. Ibid.
80. Ibid.
81. From the Prefatory Note, *Handbook of Suggestions for the Consideration of Teachers*, (London: His Majesty's Stationery Office, 1918).
82. *Primary Education: Suggestions for the Consideration of Teachers and Others Concerned With the Work of Primary Schools* (London: Her Majesty's Stationery Office, 1959). The authors of this handbook for teachers, although by tradition not identified in the book itself, were Miss Stella Duncan, Mrs. Ellen Mee, and Mr. Robin Tanner.
83. Ibid., pp. 53–54.
84. L. A. Selby-Bigge, *The Board of Education* (1934), quoted in Armytage, *Four Hundred Years* p. 204ff.
85. *The Education of the Adolescent* (London: His Majesty's Stationery Office, 1927), p. 36.
86. *Report of the Consultative Committee on the Primary School* (London: His Majesty's Stationery Office, 1931), p. 75.
87. Quoted in Willem van der Eyken, *Education, the Child, and Society: A Documentary History 1900–1973* (Harmondsworth, Middlesex: Penguin Books, 1973), p. 356.
88. *Story of a School*, (London: Her Majesty's Stationery Office, 1949), p. 7.
89. Lt. Comdr. J. C. Wedgewood, quoted in van der Eyken, *Education, the Child, and Society*, p. 237, from the Parliamentary Debate about the Fisher Bill, 1917.
90. R. H. Tawney, "Keep the Workers' Children in their Place," quoted in van der Eyken, *Education, the Child, and Society*, p. 253.
91. Eustace Percy, *Some Memories* (London: Eyre & Spottiswood, 1958), pp. 105–6.
92. Quoted in Selleck, *English Primary Education*, p. 100.

Chapter 3. The Malting House School Study

1. Gardner, *Susan Isaacs*, p. 54–55.
2. Ibid., p. 56. Cf. also David Lampe, *Pyke, The Unknown Genius*, (London: Evans Brothers, Ltd., 1959).
3. A full description of the school is given in *Adventures in Education*, by Willem van der Eyken and Barry Turner (London: Allen Lane, The Penguin Press, 1969), p. 15 ff., and in Lampe, *Pyke*, p. 37 ff.

4. Susan Isaacs, *Intellectual Growth in Young Children* (London: Routledge, 1930), p. 45.
5. Ibid., p. 47.
6. Susan Isaacs, *Social Development in Young Children* (London: Routledge, 1933), p. 21.
7. Isaacs, *Intellectual Growth*, p. 17–19.
8. Isaacs, *Social Development*, p. 19.
9. Private correspondence with Mrs. Evelyn Lawrence Isaacs.
10. Isaacs, *Social Development*, p. 19.
11. Susan Isaacs, "The Function of the School for the Young Child," *The Forum of Education*, no. 5 (1927), p. 116n.
12. Isaacs, *Intellectual Growth*, p. 20.
13. Ibid., p. 21.
14. Ibid., pp. 21–22.
15. Ibid., p. 28.
16. Ibid., p. 33.
17. Susan Isaacs, "The Reaction of a Group of Children to Unusual Social Freedom" (Unpublished ms., 1927?), p. 15. This and other unpublished documents about the Malting House School were kindly made available by Dr. Willem van der Eyken.
18. Isaacs, *Intellectual Growth*, p. 35.
19. Ibid., p. 33.
20. Ibid.
21. Isaacs, Unpublished ms., p. 16.
22. Isaacs, *Intellectual Growth*, p. 39.
23. Ibid., pp. 40–41.
24. Isaacs, Unpublished ms.
25. van der Eyken and Turner, *Adventures in Education*, p. 65.
26. Gardner, *Susan Isaacs*, p. 65–66.
27. Isaacs, *Social Development*, p. 10.
28. Ibid., p. 1.
29. Ibid., p. 18.
30. Ibid., p. 19. Both W. H. G. Armytage and Bertrand Russell mistakenly described the school as an application of psychoanalytic theory to education. Cf. Armytage, *Four Hundred Years of English Education* (Cambridge, At the University Press, 1964), p. 228, and Russell, *Autobiography* (Boston: Little, Brown, 1967).
31. Cf. Melanie Klein, *The Psycho-analysis of Children*. (London: Hogarth Press, 1932.)
32. Isaacs, *Social Development*, p. 28.
33. Isaacs, *Intellectual Growth*, p. 49.
34. Ibid., p. 52.
35. Ibid., p. 59.
36. Ibid., p. 65.
37. Ibid., p. 64.
38. Ibid., p. 65.
39. Ibid.
40. Ibid., p. 101.
41. Ibid.
42. Ibid., p. 106.
43. Ibid., p. 109.
44. Ibid., p. 164.
45. Ibid., p. 167.
46. The third book of case studies of individual children was planned but never completed.
47. Isaacs, *Social Development*, p. 12.
48. Ibid.
49. Ibid., p. 13.
50. Ibid.
51. Ibid., p. 345.
52. Ibid., p. 24.
53. Ibid., p. 30.
54. Ibid., p. 93.

55. Ibid., p. 21.
56. Ibid., p. 22.
57. Ibid., p. 280.
58. Ibid., p. 282.
59. Ibid., p. 25.
60. Ibid., pp. 206–7.
61. Ibid., p. 208.
62. Ibid., p. 250.
63. Ibid., p. 251.
64. Ibid., p. 253.
65. Ibid., p. 267.
66. Ibid., p. 269.
67. Ibid., p. 271.
68. Ibid.
69. Ibid.
70. Ibid.
71. Ibid., p. 275.
72. Ibid., p. 404.
73. Ibid., p. 405.
74. Ibid., p. 407.
75. Ibid., p. 408.
76. Ibid., p. 369.
77. Ibid., p. 421.
78. Ibid.
79. Ibid.
80. Ibid., p. 425.
81. Ibid.
82. Ibid., p. 309.
83. Ibid., p. 429.
84. Ibid.
85. Ibid., p. 456.

Chapter 4. Two Books for Lay Audiences

1. Susan Isaacs, *The Nursery Years: The Mind of the Child from Birth to Six Years* (London: Routledge & Sons, Ltd., 1929), p. 3.
2. Ibid., p. 16.
3. Ibid., pp. 23–24.
4. Ibid., p. 31.
5. Ibid., p. 11.
6. Ibid., p. 38.
7. Ibid., p. 83.
8. Ibid., p. 92.
9. Ibid., p. 93.
10. Ibid., p. 95.
11. Ibid., p. 96.
12. Ibid., p. 99.
13. Ibid., p. 100.
14. Ibid., p. 134.
15. Susan Isaacs, *The Children We Teach: Seven to Eleven Years* (London: Univ. of London Press, 1932), pp. 109–10.
16. Ibid., p. 20.
17. Ibid., p. 27.
18. Ibid.
19. Ibid., pp. 41–42.
20. Ibid., pp. 59–60.
21. Ibid., p. 68.

22. Ibid., p. 70.
23. Ibid., p. 73.
24. Ibid.
25. Ibid., p. 74.
26. Ibid., p. 88.
27. Ibid., p. 91.
28. Ibid., p. 109.
29. Ibid., p. 112.
30. Ibid., pp. 129–30.
31. Ibid., p. 133, quoted from Cyril Burt, "The Development of Reasoning in School Children."
32. Ibid., p. 134.
33. Ibid., p. 151.
34. Ibid.
35. Ibid., p. 154.

Chapter 5. Further Practical Work

1. See Bibliography.
2. Quoted in Gardner, *Susan Isaacs*, p. 81–82.
3. Ibid., pp. 92ff.
4. See list of contacts, in Preface.
5. Unpublished letter by B. Irene Grove.
6. Unpublished ms., quoted by permission of Miss May.
7. Gardner, *Susan Isaacs*, pp. 97–98.
8. Ibid., p. 100.
9. *The Educational Guidance of the School Child: Suggestions on Child Study and Guidance Embodying a Scheme of Pupils' Records.* Foreword by Sir Percy Nunn, Introduction by Keith Struckmeyer, M.A. Under the authorship of Dr. Susan Isaacs, Dr. R. A. C. Oliver, and Dr. H. E. Field (London: Evans Bros., 1936).
10. Ibid., p. 7.
11. Ibid., p. 8.
12. Ibid., p. 13.
13. Ibid., p. 16.
14. Ibid., p. 63.
15. Ibid., p. 65.
16. Ibid., pp. 70–72.
17. Ibid.
18. Ibid., p. 74.
19. Ibid., p. 75.
20. Ibid., p. 76.
21. Ibid., p. 79.
22. Ibid., p. 87.
23. Figures quoted from Padley and Cole, *Evacuation Survey* (London: Routledge, 1940). Quoted in Susan Isaacs, ed., *The Cambridge Evacuation Survey: A Wartime Study in Social Welfare and Education* (London: Methuen & Co., 1941).
24. Isaacs, ed., *Cambridge Evacuation Survey*, p. 2.
25. Ibid.
26. Ibid., p. 3.
27. Edited by Sidonie M. Gruenberg (New York and London: Child Study Association of America, 1942). Other contributors included Paul V. McNutt, Anna M. Rosenberg, Gen. Lewis B. Hersey, Pearl S. Buck, Dr. Martha M. Eliot, Dorothy Canfield Fisher, and Eleanor Roosevelt.
28. Isaacs, ed., *Cambridge Evacuation Survey*, p. 12.
29. Isaacs, in Gruenberg, ed., *The Family in a World at War*, pp. 159–60.
30. Isaacs, ed., *Cambridge Evacuation Survey*, pp. 92–94.
31. Ibid., p. 93.

32. Ibid., p. 9.
33. Ibid., note.
34. Isaacs, in Gruenberg, ed., *The Family in a World at War,* p. 174.
35. Isaacs, ed., *Cambridge Evacuation Survey,* p. 4.
36. Ibid., p. 11.

Chapter 6. Susan Isaacs and Others

1. *International Journal of Psycho-Analysis* 12 (1931): 371ff.
2. *British Journal of Educational Psychology* 1 (1931): 106ff.
3. C. W. Valentine, *The Psychology of Early Childhood* (London: Methuen & Co., 1942).
4. *Social Development in Young Children,* p. 164.
5. Valentine, *Psychology of Early Childhood,* p. 363.
6. Cf. also Valentine's earlier, *The New Psychology of the Unconscious* (London: Christopher's, 1921, 1932), and his later *Psychology and Its Bearing on Education* (London: Methuen & Co., Ltd., n.d.). Preface by author dated 1949.
7. *Pedagogical Seminary and Journal of Genetic Psychology* 29 (1931): 417ff.
8. *International Journal of Psycho-Analysis* 12 (1931): 379ff.
9. Susan Isaacs, and Victoria M. Bennett, *Health and Education in the Nursery* (London: Routledge, 1930).
10. *Eugenics Review* 25 (April 1933–January 1934): 280ff.
11. *British Journal of Educational Psychology* 3 (1933): 291ff.
12. *International Journal of Psycho-Analysis* 15 (1934): 86ff.
13. *Journal of Educational Psychology* 25 (1934): 234ff.
14. *International Journal of Psycho-Analysis* 14 (1933): 437ff.
15. P. Woodham-Smith, "The History of the Froebel Movement in England," in *Froebel and English Education,* ed. and with an introduction by Evelyn Lawrence (London: Routledge & Kegan Paul, 1952), p. 90ff.
16. John Dewey, *Psychology,* in *Early Works of John Dewey, 1882–1898* (Carbondale and Edwardsville, Ill.: Southern Illinois Univ. Press, 1967), 2. 7.
17. Ibid., p. 8.
18. Ibid., p. 9.
19. Ibid., pp. 76–77.
20. Ibid., p. 78.
21. Ibid.
22. Ibid., p. 83.
23. Ibid., p. 105.
24. Ibid., p. 108.
25. Ibid.
26. Ibid.
27. Ibid., p. 109.
28. Ibid., p. 113.
29. Ibid., p. 114.
30. Ibid., pp. 117–18.
31. Ibid., pp. 126–27.
32. Ibid., p. 134.
33. John Dewey, *Experience and Nature* (London and Chicago: Open Court Publishing Company, 1925), p. 7.
34. Cf. Martin Dworkin, ed., *John Dewey on Education* (New York: Teachers College Press, 1959), p. 134.
35. John Dewey, *The Influence of Darwin on Philosophy and Other Essays* (1919; reprint ed., New York: Peter Smith, 1951), p. v.
36. Ibid., p. 54.
37. Ibid., pp. 59–60.
38. Ibid., p. 38.
39. Ibid., p. 18.
40. John Dewey, *How We Think* (New York: D. C. Heath, 1910), p. iii.

41. Ibid.
42. Ibid.
43. Ibid., p. 6.
44. Ibid., p. 11.
45. Ibid., p. 13.
46. Ibid., p. 15.
47. Ibid., p. 21.
48. Ibid., pp. 25–26.
49. Ibid., p. 29.
50. Ibid., p. 30.
51. Ibid., pp. 33–34.
52. Ibid., p. 43.
53. Ibid., p. 55.
54. Ibid., pp. 220–21.
55. Dewey, *Experience and Nature*, p. 7.
56. Evelyn Lawrence, "Foreword" to *A Brief Introduction to Piaget* by Nathan Isaacs (New York: Agathon Press, 1960), p. 7.
57. Biographical data drawn from Evelyn Lawrence's "Foreword," Ibid., from the minutes of a memorial meeting held in his honor at the University of London Institute of Education in June 1966, and from Dorothy E. M. Gardner, *Susan Isaacs*.
58. Lawrence, "Foreword," p. 8.
59. Nathan Isaacs, *The Foundations of Common Sense: A Psychological Preface to the Problems of Knowledge*, with a foreword by Sir Cyril Burt (London: Routledge & Kegan Paul, 1949). The dedication reads: "To the memory of Susie, my partner in 26 years' explorations and discussions."
60. Ibid., p. 12.
61. Ibid., p. 13.
62. Ibid.
63. Ibid., p. 42.
64. Ibid., p. 17.
65. Ibid., p. 102.
66. Ibid., p. 41.
67. Ibid., p. 104.
68. Ibid.
69. Nathan Isaacs, "Children's Why Questions" as reprinted in N. Isaacs, *Children's Ways of Knowing*, (New York and London: Teachers College Press, 1974), pp. 16–17.
70. Ibid., p. 21.
71. Nathan Isaacs, *Piaget: Some Answers to Teachers' Questions* (London: National Froebel Foundation, 1965), pp. 9ff.
72. Nathan Isaacs, "Piaget and Progressive Education," *Some Aspects of Piaget's Work* (London: National Froebel Foundation, 1955), p. 35.
73. Ibid.
74. Ibid., p. 18.
75. Ibid., p. 23.
76. Ibid., p. 24.
77. Ibid., pp. 30–31.
78. Ibid., p. 30.
79. Ibid., p. 31.
80. Nathan Isaacs, *The Growth of Understanding in the Young Child* (London: Ward Lock Educational Co., 1961).
81. Nathan Isaacs, *New Light on Children's Ideas of Number*, (London: The Educational Supply Association, Ltd., 1960).
82. Nathan Isaacs, and Evelyn Lawrence Isaacs, *A Brief Introduction to Piaget*, (New York: Agathon Press, 1972).
83. Nathan Isaacs, *Piaget: Some Answers to Teachers' Questions*.
84. Ibid., pp. 7–8.
85. Ibid., p. 10.
86. Ibid., p. 11.

87. Ibid., p. 12.
88. Nathan Isaacs, *What is Required of the Nursery-Infant Teacher in this Country Today?* (1957; reprint ed., London: National Froebel Foundation, 1967 and 1970).
89. Ibid., p. 2.
90. Ibid., pp. 3–4.
91. Ibid., p. 3.
92. Ibid., p. 4.
93. Ibid., p. 5.
94. Ibid., p. 6.
95. Ibid.
96. Ibid., p. 15.
97. Ibid., p. 16.
98. Ibid.
99. Nathan Isaacs, *Early Scientific Trends in Children,* (London: National Froebel Foundation, 1958).
100. Ibid., p. 3.
101. Ibid., p. 4.
102. Ibid., p. 5.
103. Ibid., p. 7.
104. Ibid., p. 8.
105. Ibid., p. 12.
106. Ibid., p. 13.
107. Ibid., p. 17.
108. Nathan Isaacs, *Children Learning Through Scientific Interests* (London: National Froebel Foundation, 1966).
109. Elizabeth Hitchfield, "Early Scientific Trends in Children—a tribute to the work of Nathan Isaacs," *Education 3–13*, 8, no. 2. (Autumn 1980): 24–27.
110. Ibid., p. 27.
111. Nathan Isaacs, "Some Basic Reflections about Language," *National Froebel Foundation Bulletin*, no. 115, December 1958, pp. 2–19 and no. 116, February 1959, pp. 18–27.
112. Nathan Isaacs, "Some Thoughts about Language and Thought," *National Froebel Foundation Bulletin*, no. 128, February 1961, pp. 1–16.
113. Ibid., p. 10.
114. Ibid., p. 11.
115. Ibid.
116. Ibid., p. 12.
117. Ibid., p. 17.
118. Ibid., p. 14.
119. Ibid.
120. Ibid., p. 15.
121. Ibid., pp. 15–16.
122. Susan Isaacs, Review of Piaget's *The Child's Conception of Causality, Mind,* 1931, pp. 91–92, 97.
123. Susan Isaacs, *Intellectual Growth in Young Children* (London: Routledge, 1930), p. 80.
124. The use of this word is interesting. Susan Isaacs, a practicing psychoanalyst, always spelled it with a *ph,* to distinguish this particular aspect of mental life from the ordinary, rather derogatory word *fantasy,* as in "That's mere fantasy." Piaget, for his part, used the French expression, *l'imagination ludique* rather than *fantaisie,* as he might have. His more exact expression comes from the Latin root, *ludere,* "to play." So it seems that both were concerned to convey something other than a merely capricious or trivial meaning.
125. It is important to remember that Susan Isaacs was presenting the view of the psychoanalyst here, whereas, by Piaget's own account, he had turned his back on psychoanalysis at an early stage.
126. Susan Isaacs, *Intellectual Growth in Young Children,* p. 88.
127. Jean Piaget, "An Autobiography," in *Jean Piaget, The Man and His Ideas* ed. Richard I. Evans and trans. Eleanor Duckworth (New York: E. P. Dutton, 1973), p. 122–23.
128. Jean Piaget, "Intellectual Development Among Young Children: A Critical Study,"

being a review of Susan Isaacs's *Intellectual Growth in Young Children, Mind,* April 1931, pp. 5–6. (Trans. A. A. Smith, 1982.)
  129. Ibid., pp. 5, 11.
  130. Ibid., p. 12.
  131. Susan Isaacs, *Intellectual Growth in Young Children,* p. 51.
  132. Ibid., p. 79 and note.
  133. Ibid., pp. 94, 84.
  134. Jean Piaget, "Retrospective and Prospective Analysis in Child Psychology," *British Journal of Educational Psychology,* 1931, p. 130.
  135. *Mind,* 1934, p. 99.
  136. Susan Isaacs, *Intellectual Growth in Young Children,* p. 67.
  137. Jean Piaget, "Intellectual Development Among Young Children," p. 23.
  138. Ibid., p. 24.
  139. Ibid., p. 30.
  140. Ibid., p. 33.
  141. Ibid.
  142. J. C. Flügel, *A Hundred Years of Psychology, 1883–1933* 1933; reprint ed., including a section on work after 1933 (London: Gerald Duckworth & Co., 1951).
  143. Anna Freud, *The Psycho-Analytic Treatment of Children,* Part 1 (1926); Part 2 (1927); Part 3 (1945) (New York: International Universities Press, Ltd., 1946). Parts 1 and 2 translated from the German by Nancy Procter-Gregg. The first four lectures in Part 1 are entitled: "An Introductory Phase in the Analysis of Children," "The Methods of Children's Analysis," "The Role of Transference in the Analysis of Children," and "The Analysis of Children and Their Upbringing."
  144. Anna Freud, *Psychoanalysis for Teachers and Parents,* trans. B. Low. (1935; reprint ed., Boston: Beacon Press paperback, 1960), pp. 86, 89.
  145. Anna Freud, "The Analysis of Children and Their Upbringing," p. 45.
  146. Ibid.
  147. Ibid., p. 49.
  148. Anna Freud, "The Role of Transference in the Analysis of Children," p. 45.
  149. Anna Freud, "The Methods of Children's Analysis," p. 29.
  150. Ibid., p. 30.
  151. "Symposium . . . ," in John Rickman, ed., *Selected Contributions to Psycho-Analysis,* International Psycho-Analytic Library, no. 52, p. 157.
  152. Flügel, *A Hundred Years of Psychology,* pp. 244–245.
  153. Ibid., pp. 243ff.
  154. John Rickman, *Selected Contributions to Psycho-Analysis,* p. xvi.
  155. Ernest Jones, "Preface" to *Developments in Psycho-Analysis,* ed. Melanie Klein, Joan Rivière (London: Hogarth, 1952), pp. v–vi.
  156. Rickman, *Selected Contributions,* p. 55.
  157. D. W. Winnicott, Paper #16, "A Personal View" in *The Maturational Process and the Facilitating Environment: Studies in the Theory of Emotional Development* (London: Hogarth Press, 1965), p. 173.
  158. Cyril L. Burt, "The Mental Differences Between Individuals," in B.A.A.S. *Report of the 91st Meeting, Liverpool, 1923,* p. 228. Quoted in Selleck, p. 143.
  159. Cf. Hearnshaw, *English Primary Education, Cyril Burt;* Cf. also N. J. Block, and Gerald Dworkin, eds., *The IQ Controversy* (New York: Random House, Pantheon Books, 1976), and Leon J. Kamin, *The Science and Politics of I.Q.* (New York: Wiley & Sons, 1974); and Stephen Jay Gould, *The Mismeasure of Man* (New York: W. W. Norton, 1981).
  160. Cyril L. Burt, "General Ability and Special Aptitudes," *Educational Research I,* 1959, p. 3. Quoted in Hearnshaw, *Cyril Burt,* p. 122.
  161. Susan Isaacs, *The Children We Teach,* pp. 74, 63–64.
  162. Cyril L. Burt, *Mental and Scholastic Tests,* 2nd ed. (London: Staples Press, 1947). First published in 1921 as a London County Council Report.
  163. Cyril L. Burt, *The Young Delinquent* (New York: D. Appleton & Co., 1925), p. v.
  164. Ibid., p. 4.
  165. Ibid., p. 9.

166. Hearnshaw, *Cyril Burt*, p. 97.
167. Isaacs, *The Children We Teach*, pp. 44, 47.
168. Hearnshaw, *Cyril Burt*, pp. 73–4.
169. Burt, *The Young Delinquent*, p. 6 n.
170. Burt, *Mental and Scholastic Tests*, p. 202.
171. Ibid., p. 201.
172. Ibid., p. 165.
173. Ibid., p. 219.
174. Cf. Burt's discussion of such measures in *The Young Delinquent*, pp. 57–59.
175. Cyril L. Burt, *How the Mind Works*, 2nd ed. (1933; reprint ed., London: George Allen & Unwin, Ltd., 1945), p. 28.
176. Ibid., p. 41.
177. Cf. Isaacs, *The Children We Teach*, chap. 2, "Individual Differences," p. 23ff.
178. Burt, *How the Mind Works*, p. 237.
179. Hearnshaw, *Cyril Burt*, p. 312.
180. Ibid., p. 286.
181. Ibid., p. 310.
182. Cf. Block and Dworkin, *The IQ Controversy*, pp. 4–44.
183. Selleck, *English Primary Education*, p. 28.
184. Nunn, *Education*, pp. 90ff.
185. Cf. Selleck, *English Primary Education*, pp. 28ff., Whitbread, *The Nursery-Infant School*, pp. 57ff., Boyd and Rawson, *The New Education*, pp. 21ff.
186. Selleck, *English Primary Education*, p. 28.
187. *Dr. Montessori's Own Handbook*, p. 4.
188. Ibid., p. 9.
189. Ibid., p. 21.
190. Ibid., pp. 32–33.
191. Ibid., p. 36.
192. Ibid., p. 87.
193. Ibid., p. 76.
194. Ibid., p. 78.
195. Ibid., p. 93.
196. Quoted in W. H. Kilpatrick, *Montessori Examined* (London: Constable & Co., 1915), p. 42.
197. Nunn, *Education*, p. 79, 99.
198. Kilpatrick, *Montessori Examined*.
199. Ibid., pp. 45, 49.
200. Ibid., p. 20.
201. Susan Isaacs, *Intellectual Growth*, pp. 230–81.
202. Ibid., p. 20.
203. Ibid., p. 21.
204. Ibid., pp. 21–22.
205. Nathan Isaacs, "Critical Notice," *Journal of Child Psychology and Psychiatry* 7 (1966): 155–58. Quoted in van der Eyken, *Education, Child, & Society*, pp. 295ff.
206. Ibid., p. 297.
207. Ibid., p. 301.

Chapter 7: In Conclusion

1. Susan Isaacs, *Social Development*, p. 421.
2. Cf. Basil Bernstein, "Class and Pedagogies: Visible and Invisible," reprinted in *Rethinking Educational Research* ed. W. B. Dochrell and D. Hamilton, (London: Hudder & Stoughton, 1960), pp. 115ff.
3. L. A. H. Smith, *Activity and Experience: Sources of Informal English Education* (New York: Agathon Press, 1973).
4. Cf. C. H. Kempe, and R. E. Helfer, eds., *The Battered Child*, 3rd ed. (Chicago: Univ. of Chicago Press, 1980); Selma Fraiberg, *Every Child's Birthright: In Defense of Mothering* (New

York: Basic Books, 1977); and *The Magic Years: Understanding and Handling The Problems of Early Childhood* (New York: Charles Scribner's Sons, 1959), inter alia.

5. Nathan Isaacs, *Children's Ways of Knowing*, p. 27.
6. J. Klein, *Samples from English Cultures*, vol. 2, as quoted in Harold Entwistle, *Child-Centered Education* (London: Methuen & Co., 1976), p. 191.
7. J. F. Gordon, "The Disadvantaged Pupil" as quoted in Entwistle, Ibid.
8. Ibid.
9. Bernstein, "Class and Pedagogies," p. 124.
10. Philip Jackson, *Life in Classrooms* (New York: Holt, Rinehart & Winston, 1968).
11. David Cohen and Marvin Lazarson, "Education and the Corporate Order," in *Education in American History* ed. Michael Katz (N.Y.: Praeger Publishers, 1973), p. 483.
12. Ibid., p. 326.
13. Bernstein, "Class and Pedagogies," p. 117.
14. George Dennison, *The Lives of Children* (New York: Random House, 1969); Cf also Sarah Lawrence Lightfoot, *Worlds Apart: Relationships Between Families and Schools* (New York: Basic Books, 1978).
15. Basil Bernstein, ed., *Class, Codes, and Control*, 3 vols. (London: Routledge & Kegan Paul, 1973), vol. 1., chapter 9, "Social Class Language and Socialization," pp. 170 ff. See also Walter Brandis and Basil Bernstein, *Selection and Control: Teacher's Ratings of Children in the Infant School* (London: Routledge & Kegan Paul, 1974).
16. Cf. in this regard Freud's brief essay, "Some Reflections on Schoolboy Psychology."
17. Bernstein, *Class, Codes, and Control*, p. 176.
18. Selma Fraiberg, "Magic Years," p. 116.
19. Leon S. Sheleff, *Generations Apart: Adult Hostility to Youth* (New York: McGraw-Hill, 1981), among many others on the "generation gap."
20. Konrad Lorenz, *On Aggression* (Harmondsworth, Middlesex, England: Penguin Books, 1966), and Selma Fraiberg, *Every Child's Birthright,* among others.
21. Fraiberg, Ibid., p. 33.
22. Ibid., pp. 46, 35.
23. Ibid., pp. 45, 47.
24. Ibid., pp. 47–49.
25. Ibid. p. 62.
26. Johan Huizinger, *Homo Ludens: A Study of the Play Element in Culture* (1950; reprint ed., Boston: The Beacon Press, 1955), p. 4.
27. Ibid., p. 5.
28. Cf. Sigmund Freud, *Civilization and Its Discontents* trans. James Strachey (New York: W. Norton, 1961).
29. Susan Isaacs, "Modification of the Ego Through the Work of Psycho-Analysis," written in 1939 and included in *Childhood and After*, pp. 91–92.

Bibliography

This bibliography is in several sections. It is designed to provide not only documentation for the book, but also additional references to works by the key figures of the time, to which an interested reader might wish to turn.
1. Works by Susan Isaacs
2. Works by Nathan Isaacs
3. Other Original Sources
4. Periodicals Consulted
5. Secondary Sources

1. Works by Susan Isaacs

Following is a full listing of Susan Isaacs's published works, in chronological order.* It is taken in large part from D. E. M. Gardner's biography *Susan Isaacs: The First Biography*, but corrected by the author.

1916.	"Authority and Freedom." *Parents' Review*, no. 17.
1918.	"Analysis of the Spelling Process." *Journal of Experimental Pedagogy*, no. 4.
1920.	"The Present Attitude of Employees to Industrial Psychology." *British Journal of Psychology*, no. 10.
1921.	"Science and Human Values in Industry." *The Co-operative Educator*, January 1921.
	An Introduction to Psychology. London: Methuen.
1923.	"A Note on Sex Differences from the Psycho-Analytical Point of View." *British Journal of Medical Psychology*, no. 3.
	"Conflict and Dream." *The Highway*, May 1923.
1927.	"Penis-Faeces-Child." *International Journal of Psycho-Analysis*, no. 8.
	"The Function of the School for the Young Child." *The Forum of Education*, no. 5.
1928.	"The Mental Hygiene of the Pre-School Child." *British Journal of Medical Psychology*, no. 8.
1929–36.	"Ursula Wise" columns in *The Nursery World*.
1929.	"Some Reflections on Corporal Punishment." *The New Era*, July 1929.
	"Privation and Guilt." *International Journal of Psycho-Analysis*, no. 10.

*Additional unpublished documents were made available by Dr. Willem van der Eyken.

"The Infant's Mind in the First Year of Life" (five articles). *The Nursery World* 8.
"The Child's Conception of the World." A review of Piaget's book of that title, *Mind*, no. 38.
"A Critical Review of Piaget." *Journal of Genetic Psychology*, no. 36.
"Biological Interests of Young Children." *The Forum of Education*, no. 7 (1929) and no. 8 (1930).
The Nursery Years: Birth to Six Years. London: Routledge.

1930. *Intellectual Growth in Young Children*. London: Routledge.
"What the Nursery School can do for Young Children." *The Highway*, February 1930.
"The Psychologist in Child Welfare." *Mother and Child 1. Health and Education in the Nursery* (with Dr. Victoria M. Bennett). London: Routledge.

1931. "The Humane Education of Young Children." *Report of the 19th Annual Conference of Educational Associations*. London: University of London Animal Welfare Society.
"Education of Children under Seven Years of Age." Memorandum submitted to Hadow Committee. *British Journal of Educational Psychology* 1.
"The Child's Conception of Causality." A review of Piaget's book of that title, *Mind*, no. 39.
"Contribution a la Psychologie Sociale Des Jeunes Enfants." *Journal de Psychologie* 28.

1932. "Some Notes on the Incidence of Neurotic Difficulties in Young Children." *British Journal of Educational Psychology*, no. 2. *The Children We Teach: Seven to Eleven Years*. London: University of London Press.

1933. *Social Development in Young Children*. London: Routledge.
"The Emotional Development of Children up to the Age of Seven Plus." With Sir Cyril Burt. Board of Education Report of the Consultative Committee on Infant and Nursery Schools (the Hadow Report).
"Original Sin." *Twentieth Century*.
"Intellectual Growth in Young Children." *Report of the Summer Short Course for Teachers of Physical Teaching of the Blind*, July 1933.

1934. "Rebellious Children." *Mother and Child*, no. 3.
"Critical Notice of J. Piaget." A review of his book, *The Moral Judgement of the Child*, *Mind*, January 1934.
"Rebellious and Defiant Children." A public lecture, Institute of Psycho-Analysis. Published in *Childhood and After*.
"Preventive Measures in Childhood." Discussion on Mental Hygiene, *Proceedings of the Royal Society of Medicine* 28.

1935. "Bad Habits." *International Journal of Psycho-Analysis*, no. 16.

1936. "Habit" and "The Nursery as a Community." Chapters in *On the Bringing Up of Children*, edited by John Rickman, London: Routledge & Kegan Paul.
The Educational Guidance of the School Child. Chapter 2, et. seq.
"Property and Possessiveness." Symposium, *British Journal of Medical Psychology*, no. 15.
The Psychological Aspects of Child Development. London: Evans.
"Personal Freedom and Family Life," *The New Era*, September 1936.

1937. "Security for Young Children." *Child Study* (U.S.A.), November 1937.
"The Educational Value of the Nursery School." London: The Nursery School Association of Great Britain. Reprinted in *Childhood and After*.

1938. "Child Psychology and the Accident Problem." *National Froebel Foundation Bulletin* (1960). Reprinted from *Safety Education Session of the National Safety Congress*, May 1938.
"Recent Advances in the Psychology of Young Children." Address to the British Psychology Society at the 26th Annual Conference of Educational Associations.
"'Safety First' Re-Examined." *Home and School*, October 1938.
"Criteria for Interpretation," *International Journal of Psycho-Analysis*, no. 20.
"Temper Tantrums in Early Childhood in their Relation to Internal Objects." *International Journal of Psycho-Analysis*, no. 21.

1939. "Modifications of the Ego through the work of Analysis." Paper read at Symposium of the Joint Meeting of the British and French Psycho-Analytical Societies, Paris, April 1939.
"A Special Mechanism in a Schizoid Boy." *International Journal of Psycho-Analysis*, no. 20.

1940. "The Uprooted Child." *The New Era*, March 1940.

1941. *The Cambridge Evacuation Survey.* London: Methuen.

1942. "Children of Great Britain in Wartime." In *The Family in a World at War*, edited by Sidonie Matsner Gruenberg.

1943. "An Acute Psychotic Anxiety Occurring in a Boy of Four Years." Expanded from 1938 paper, read to British Psycho-Analytical Society, *International Journal of Psycho-Analysis*, no. 24.

1945. "Notes on Metapsychology as Process Theory: Some Comments." *International Journal of Psycho-Analysis*, no. 26.
"Fatherless Children." *New Education Fellowship Monograph*, no. 8.
"Children in Institutions." Memorandum presented to the Home Office Care of Children Committee.

1947. "The Essential Needs of Children." *The New Era* (part of "Children in Institutions," published separately).

1948. *Childhood and After.* London: Routledge & Kegan Paul.
"The Nature and Function of Phantasy." *International Journal of Psycho-Analysis*, no. 29. Included in Joan Rivière, ed. *Developments in Psycho-Analysis*, London: Hogarth Press, 1952.
Troubles of Children and Parents. London: Methuen. Selections from columns of *The Nursery World*.
"Regression," with Paula Heimann. Included in Joan Rivière, ed., *Developments in Psycho-Analysis*.

1948? "Suggestions for a Clinic Playroom," in collaboration with Lucy G. Fildes and Gwen Chesters. Issued by The Child Guidance Council, Woburn House, Upper Woburn Place, London.

2. Works by Nathan Isaacs

Following is a full listing of Nathan Isaacs's published works, in chronological order. It is taken in large part from *Children's Ways of Knowing: Nathan Isaacs on Education, Psychology, and Piaget*, edited by Mildred Hardeman, but corrected by the author.

1927.	"Education and Science." Appendix to *Intellectual Growth in Young Children*, by Susan Isaacs.
1930.	"Children's Why Questions." Appendix to *Intellectual Growth in Young Children*, by Susan Isaacs.
1930–31.	"Psycho-Logic." *Proceedings of the Aristotelian Society*, no. 31.
1932–33.	"The Logic of Language." *Proceedings of the Aristotelian Society*, no. 33.
1949.	*The Foundations of Common Sense: A Psychological Preface to the Problems of Knowledge*. London: Routledge & Kegan Paul.
1950–51.	"The Temporal Correspondence Approach to Truth." *Proceedings of the Aristotelian Society*, no. 51. "Methodology and Research in Psycho-Pathology." *The British Journal of Medical Psychology*, no. 24.
1952.	"Froebel's Educational Philosophy in 1952." In *Froebel and English Education*, edited by E. Lawrence.
1954.	"About *The Child's Conception of Number* by Jean Piaget." *National Froebel Foundation Bulletin*, no. 91.
1955.	"Piaget's Work and Progressive Education." In *Some Aspects of Piaget's Work*, London: National Froebel Foundation. "The Wider Significance of Piaget's Work." In *Some Aspects of Piaget's Work*, with T. R. Theakston.
1957.	"What is Required of the Nursery-Infant Teacher in this Country Today?" *National Froebel Foundation Bulletin*, no. 109.
1958.	*Early Scientific Trends in Children*. London: National Froebel Foundation. "Some Basic Reflections about Language, part 1." *National Froebel Foundation Bulletin*, no. 115.
1959.	"Some Basic Reflections about Language, part 2." *National Froebel Foundation Bulletin*, no. 116. "What do Linguistic Philosophers Assume?" *Proceedings of the Aristotelian Society*, no. 60.
1960.	*Approaches to Science in the Primary School*. With E. Lawrence and W. Rawson. London: The Educational Supply Association.
1960–61.	"On a Gap in the Structure of our General Psychology." *Journal of Child Psychology and Psychiatry and Allied Disciplines*, no. 1.
1961.	*The Growth of Understanding in the Young Child: A Brief Introduction to Piaget's Work*. London: Ward Lock Educational Co. Reprinted in *A Brief Introduction to Piaget*. New York: Agathon Press. "Some Thoughts about Language and Thought," *National Froebel Foundation Bulletin*, no. 128. "Future Education and the Training of Teachers." With Eglantyne Jebb, Evelyn Lawrence, and Molly Brearley. Memorandum submitted to the Robbins Committee on Higher Education, *National Froebel Foundation Bulletin*, no. 133.
1962.	"The Case for Bringing Science into the Primary School." In *The Place of Science in Primary Education*, edited by W. H. Perkins. London: The British Association for the Advancement of Science.
1963.	"Children's Scientific Interests." In *Studies in Education: the First Years in School*. London: University of London Institute of Education, Evans Brothers.

"Critical Notice: 'Intelligence and Experience' by J. McV. Hunt." *National Froebel Foundation Bulletin,* no. 141.

"Critical Notice: 'Fostering Intellectual Development in Young Children' by K. D. Wann, M. S. Dorn, and E. A. Liddle." *National Froebel Foundation Bulletin,* no. 149.

1965. *Piaget: Some Answers to Teachers' Questions.* London: National Froebel Foundation.

"Memorandum for the Plowden Committee." *Froebel Journal,* no. 2.

3. Other Original Sources

Bernstein, Basil.

1973. *Class, Codes, and Control.* 3 vols. London: Routledge & Kegan Paul.

Blatz, William E.; Millichamp, Dorothy; Fletcher, Margaret.

1935. *Nursery Education: Theory and Practice.* London: Wm. Morrow & Co.

Blair, Robert.

1910. *Handbook containing general information with reference to the work in connection with the Children's Care (Central) Sub-Committee of the London County Council.* London: J. Truscott & Son., Ltd.

Brandis, Walter, and Bernstein, Basil.

1974. *Selection and Control: Teachers' Ratings of Children in the Infant School.* London: Routledge & Kegan Paul.

Bridges, Katharine.

1931. *Social and Emotional Development of the Pre-School Child.* London: Kegan-Paul et al.

Bühler, Charlotte.

1930. *The First Year of Life.* Translated by Pearl Greenberg and Rowena Ripin. New York: John Day & Co.

1935. *From Birth to Maturity.* London: Kegan Paul.

Burlingham, Dorothy, and Freud, Anna.

1943. *Infants Without Families: the case for and against residential nurseries.* Reports on the Hampstead Nurseries 1939–1945. London: Allen & Unwin.

Burt, Sir Cyril.

1916. *The Distribution and Relations of Educational Abilities.* Report to the London County Council. Preface by Robert Blair, Chief Education Officer. London: County Council.

1921. *Mental and Scholastic Tests.* Report to London County Council. Reprint. London: Staples Press, Ltd.

1937. *The Backward Child.* 2nd ed. London: University of London Press, 1942.

1940. *The Factors of the Mind: an Introduction to Factor-Analysis in Psychology.* London: University of London Press.

1944. *The Young Delinquent.* London: University of London Press.

1947. *Intelligence and Fertility: the Effect of the Differential Birthrate on Inborn Mental Characteristics.* London: Eugenics Society and Hamish Hamilton Medical Books.

1952.	*The Causes and Treatment of Backwardness.* 4th ed. London: University of London Press, 1957.
1953.	*The Contributions of Psychology to Social Problems.* London: Oxford University Press.
1959.	*A Psychological Study of Typography.* Cambridge: Cambridge University Press.
1968.	*Psychology and Psychical Research.* London: Society for Psychical Research.

Burt, Sir Cyril, ed.

1933.	*How the Mind Works.* London: George Allen & Unwin, Ltd.

Chadwick, M.

1928.	*Difficulties in Child Development.* London: Allen & Unwin.

Cook, H. Caldwell.

1917.	*The Play Way: An Essay in Educational Method.* 4th ed. London: Heinemann, 1922.

Daniel, M. V.

1947.	*Activity in the Primary School.* Oxford; Blackwell.

Davidson, A., and Fay, J.

1952.	*Phantasy in Childhood.* London: Routledge & Kegan Paul.

Dewey, John.

1886.	*Psychology.* New York: Harper & Bros.
1896.	*Interest as Related to Will.* Bloomington, Ill.: The National Herbart Society.
1902.	*The Child and the Curriculum.* Chicago: University of Chicago Press.
1909.	*How We Think.* London: D. C. Heath & Co.
1910.	*The Influence of Darwin on Philosophy, and Other Essays in Contemporary Thought.* New York: P. Smith.
1913.	*Interest and Effort in Education.* Boston: Houghton Mifflin Co.
1917.	*Creative Intelligence.* New York: Henry Holt & Co.
1924.	*Democracy and Education.* New York: Macmillan.
1922.	*Human Nature and Conduct.* New York: Henry Holt & Co.
1925.	*Experience and Nature.* London & Chicago: Open Court Pub. Co.
1929.	*The Sources of a Science of Education.* New York: Liveright.
1943.	*The School and Society.* Chicago: University of Chicago Press.
1976–83.	*The Early Works, 1882–1898. The Middle Works, 1899–1924. The Later Works, 1925–1953.* Edited by JoAnn Boydston. Carbondale, Ill.: Southern Illinois University Press.

English, O. Spurgeon, and Pearson, Gerald H. J.

1937.	*Common Neuroses of Children and Adults.* New York: W. W. Norton & Co.

Flügel, J. C.

1921.	*The Psycho-Analytic Study of the Family.* 10th ed. London: Hogarth Press, 1960.
1924.	*Social Aspects of Psycho-Analysis.* (*See* Jones, Ernest, ed.)
1934.	*Men and Their Motives.* London: K. Paul, Trench, Trubner & Co.

1945.   *Man, Morals, & Society: A Psycho-Analytic Study.* London: Duckworth.

Fraiberg, Selma.

1959.   *The Magic Years.* New York: Charles Scribner's Sons.

1972.   *Every Child's Birthright.* New York: Basic Books.

Freud, Anna.

1928.   *Introduction to the Technique of Child Analysis.* Translated by L. P. Clark. *Nervous and Mental Disorders Monograph Series,* no. 48.

1935.   *Psycho-Analysis for Teachers and Parents: Introductory Lectures.* Translated by Barbara Low. New York: Emerson Books.

1943.   *War and Children.* New York: Medical War Books.

1946.   *The Psycho-Analytic Treatment of Children.* Part 1, 1926. Part 2, 1927. Part 3, 1946. New York: International University Press.

1950.   *The Ego and Mechanisms of Defense.* New York: International University Press.

1965.   *Normality and Pathology in Childhood: Assessments of Development.* New York: International University Press.

1966 ff.   *The Writings of Anna Freud.* New York: International University Press. Reprint. London: International Psycho-Analytic Library and Hogarth Press, 1974.

1974.   *Introduction to Psycho-Analysis: Lectures for Child Analysts and Teachers, 1922–1935.* Volume I of *The Writings of Anna Freud.* London: International Psycho-Analytic Library and Hogarth Press.

Freud, Sigmund.

1910.   *Three Contributions to the Theory of Sex.* Translated by A. A. Brill. New York: *Journal of Nervous and Mental Disorders,* no. 7.

1913.   *The Interpretation of Dreams.* Translated by A. A. Brill. Retranslated by James Strachey. New York: Basic Books, 1956.

1917.   *The Psycho-Pathology of Everyday Life.* Translated by A. A. Brill. Retranslated by James Strachey. London: Ernest Benn, Ltd., 1966.

1920.   *Introductory Lectures on Psycho-Analysis.* New York: Liveright.

1924.   *Beyond the Pleasure Principle.* Translated by C. J. M. Hubback. New York: Boni & Liveright.

1927.   *The Ego and the Id.* Translated by Joan Rivière. Retranslated by James Strachey. New York: W. W. Norton, 1960.

1930.   *Civilization and Its Discontents.* Translated by Joan Rivière. Retranslated by James Strachey. New York: W. W. Norton, 1961.

1933.   *New Introductory Lectures on Psycho-Analysis.* Translated by W. J. H. Sprott. New York: W. W. Norton.

1935.   *A General Introduction to Psycho-Analysis.* Revised edition translated by Joan Rivière. New York: Liveright.

1946.   *Totem and Taboo: Resemblances between the Psychic Lives of Savages and Neurotics.* Translated by A. A. Brill. New York: Vintage Books.

1949.   *Collected Papers.* Authoritative translation under the supervision of Joan Rivière. London: International Psycho-Analytic Library and the Hogarth

	Press. See also *Standard Edition of Complete Psychological Works.* London: Hogarth Press, 1966–74.
1949.	*An Outline of Psycho-Analysis.* Translated by James Strachey. New York: W. W. Norton.

Galton, Sir Francis.

1869.	*Hereditary Genius: an Inquiry into its Laws and Consequences.* 2nd ed. London: Macmillan & Co., Ltd., 1892.
1883.	*Inquiries into the Human Faculty and its Development.* New York: Macmillan & Co.
1889.	*Natural Inheritance.* New York: Macmillan & Co.
1901.	*The Possible Improvement of the Human Breed under the Existing Conditions of Law and Sentiment.* Washington, D.C.: Smithsonian Institution Annual Report.
1905.	*Restrictions in Marriage. Studies in National Eugenics. Eugenics as a Factor in Religion.* London: John Lewis & Co.
1906.	*Noteworthy Families.* London: J. Murray.
1907.	*Probability, the Foundation of Eugenics.* Herbert Spencer Lecture. Oxford: Clarendon Press.

Gesell, Arnold.

1925.	*The Mental Growth of the Pre-School Child.* New York: Macmillan & Co.
1928.	*Infancy and Human Growth.* New York: Macmillan & Co.
1929.	*Learning and Growth in Identical Infant Twins.* Worcester, MA: Clark University Press.

Green, George H.

1921.	*Psychanalysis (sic) in the Classroom.* "New Impression", 1924. London: University of London Press, Ltd.

Griffiths, Ruth.

1935.	*A Study of Imagination in Early Childhood, and its Function in Mental Development.* Preface by J. C. Flügel. London: Kegan Paul, Trench, Trubner & Co., Ltd.

Groos, Karl.

1901.	*The Play of Man.* Translated by Elizabeth L. Baldwin. London: Wm. Heinemann.

Gruenberg, Sidonie Matsner, ed.

1942.	*The Family in a World at War.* New York & London; Harper & Bros.

Hardeman, Mildred, ed.

1974.	*Children's Ways of Knowing: Nathan Isaacs on Education, Psychology, and Piaget.* New York & London, Teachers College Press.

Hazlitt, Victoria.

1933.	*The Psychology of Infancy.* London: Methuen & Co., Ltd.

Hill, J. C.

1927.	*Dreams and Education.* London: Methuen.

Holmes, Edmond.

1911.	*What Is and What Might Be.* Reprint. London: Constable & Co., Ltd., 1928.

Horney, Karen.
1939. *New Ways in Psycho-Analysis.* New York: W. W. Norton & Co.

James, William.
1892. *Talks to Teachers on Psychology.* Reprint. New York: W. W. Norton & Co., 1958.

Jones, Ernest.
1913. *Papers on Psycho-Analysis.* New York: W. Wood & Co.
1929. *Psycho-Analysis.* Reprint. London: Ernest Benn, Ltd., 1932.
1949. *What is Psycho-Analysis?* London: Allen & Unwin.
1951. *Essays in Applied Psycho-Analysis.* London: Hogarth Press.

Jones, Ernest, ed.
1924. *Social Aspects of Psycho-Analysis.* Lectures by Ernest Jones, James Glover, J. C. Flügel, and others. London: William & Norgate.

Klein, Melanie.
1932. *The Psycho-Analysis of Children.* Translated by A. Strachey. Rev. Ed. New York: Delacorte Press, 1975.
1937. *Love, Hate, and Reparation.* Reprint. London: Hogarth Press and Institute of Psycho-Analysis, 1967.
1948. *Contributions to Psycho-Analysis 1921–1945.* Introduction by Ernest Jones. London: Hogarth Press.
1952. *Developments in Psycho-Analysis.* Edited by Joan Rivière. London: Hogarth.
1975. *Envy and Gratitude, and other works, 1946–1963.* London: Hogarth.
1975. *Love, Guilt, and Reparation, and other works 1921–1945.* London: Hogarth Press.
1975–80. *Writings of Melanie Klein.* London: Hogarth Press.

Lorenz, Konrad.
1966. *On Aggression.* Harmondsworth, Middlesex: Penguin Books.

Low, Barbara.
1920. *Psycho-Analysis: A Brief Account of the Freudian Theory.* London: Allen & Unwin. Introduction by Ernest Jones.
1928. *The Unconscious in Action: its Influence upon Education.* London: University of London Press, Ltd.

Lowenfeld, Margaret.
1935. *Play in Childhood.* Reprint. Portway Bath, Cedric Chivers, Ltd., 1969.

Mackinder, J. M.
1924. *Individual Work in Infants' Schools.* Introduction by T. Percy Nunn. 3rd ed. London: Cassell & Co., Ltd., 1927.

May, Dorothy E.
1963. *Children in the Nursery School: Studies of Personal Adjustment in Early Childhood.* London: University of London Press.

McDougall, William.
1923. *An Outline of Psychology.* 11th ed. London: Methuen & Co., Ltd., 1947.
1926. *An Outline of Abnormal Psychology.* London: Methuen & Co., Ltd.

McMillan, Margaret.
1901. *Early Childhood.* London: Swan Sonnenschein & Co.

Malinowski, B.
1927. *Sex and Repression in Savage Society.* New York: Harcourt Brace.

Mead, Margaret.
1928. *Coming of Age in Samoa.* New York: Morrow.
1930. *Growing up in New Guinea.* New York: Morrow.

Mellor, Edna.
1950. *Education Through Experience in the Infant School Years.* Oxford: Blackwell.

Miller, Crichton.
1921. *The New Psychology and the Teacher.* London: Jarrolds.

Montessori, Maria.
1909. *The Montessori Method: Scientific Pedagogy as Applied to Child Education in "The Children's Houses."* 2nd ed. New York: Frederick A. Stokes Co., 1912.
1914. *Dr. Montessori's Own Handbook.* 2nd & 3rd eds. London: William Heinemann, 1915, 1919.
1917. *Spontaneous Activity in Education (The Advanced Montessori Method).* New York: Frederick A. Stokes Co.
1932. *Peace and Education.* Geneva: International Bureau of Education.
1967. *The Absorbent Mind.* New York: Holt, Rinehart, & Winston.

Nunn, Sir Percy.
1920. *Education: Its Data and First Principles.* 24th ed. London: Edward Arnold and Co., 1949.

Parkhurst, Helen.
1922. *Education on the Dalton Plan.* Introduction by Percy Nunn. London: G. Bell.

Piaget, Jean.
1923. *Language and Thought of the Child.* Reprint. New York: Meridian Books, 1955.
1924. *Judgement and Reasoning in the Child.* Reprint. New York: Harcourt Brace, 1928.
1926. *The Child's Conception of the World.* London: K. Paul, Trench, & Trubner.
1930. *The Child's Conception of Physical Causality.* New York: Harcourt Brace & Co.
1932. *The Moral Judgement of the Child.* Reprint. Glencoe, New York: The Free Press, 1960.
1937. *The Construction of Reality in the Child.* Reprint. New York: Basic Books, 1954.
1950. *The Psychology of Intelligence.* New York: Harcourt Brace.
1951. *Play, Dreams, and Imitation in Childhood.* Translated by C. Gattegno and F. M. Hodgson. Melbourne, London, Toronto: Wm. Heinemann, Ltd., in association with The New Education Fellowship.
1953. *Logic and Psychology.* Manchester: Manchester University Press.

1964.   *Early Growth of Logic in the Child: Classification and Seriation.* With Bärbel Inhelder. London: Routledge & Kegan Paul.

1969.   *Mechanisms of Perception.* London: Routledge & Kegan Paul.

1967.   *Six Psychological Studies.* New York: Random House.

1970.   *Genetic Epistemology.* Translated by Eleanor Duckworth. New York: Columbia University Press.

1972.   *Principles of Genetic Epistemology.* London: Routledge & Kegan Paul.

1972.   *Psychology and Epistemology: Towards a Theory of Knowledge.* Harmondsworth, Middlesex: Penguin Books.

1973.   *Memory and Intelligence.* With Bärbel Inhelder. London: Routledge & Kegan Paul.

Preyer, Wilhelm.

1888.   *The Mind of the Child. Part 1: The Senses; Part 2: The Will; Part 3: The Development of the Intellect.* Translated by H. W. Brown. Edited by William Torrey Harris. New York: D. Appleton & Co.

Rickman, John, ed.

1936.   *On the Bringing Up of Children.* Preface to first edition by Dr. John Rickman; preface and postscript to 1952 edition by Melanie Klein. Reprint. London: Routledge & Kegan Paul, 1952.

1937.   *On Unbearable Ideas. Selected Contributions to Psycho-Analysis,* no. 52. Edited by Ernest Jones. London: International Psycho-Analytic Library.

Russell, Bertrand.

1926.   *On Education.* London: Unwin Books.

1967.   *Autobiography.* Boston: Little, Brown Co.

Smith, Henrietta Brown, ed.

1912.   *Education By Life.* 7th ed. London: George Philip & Son, Ltd., 1925.

Spearman, Charles.

1923.   *The Nature of "Intelligence" and the Principles of Cognition.* 2nd ed. London: Macmillan Co., 1927.

1927.   *The Abilities of Man: Their Nature and Measurement.* New York: Macmillan Co.

1930.   *The Creative Mind.* London: Nisbet & Co.

n.d.   *Collected Papers.* London: University of London, University College Psychological Laboratory.

1950.   *Human Ability.* With Ll. Wynn Jones. London: Macmillan.

Stern, William.

1914.   *The Psychology of Early Childhood up to the Sixth Year of Age.* 3rd ed., rev. and enlarged, supplemented by extracts from the unpublished diaries of Clara Stern. Translated by Anna Barwell. London: Allen & Unwin, Ltd., 1924.

Stout, G. F.

1899.   *A Manual of Psychology.* 5th ed. rev. and enlarged, London: University Tutorial Press, Ltd., 1938.

Sully, James.

| 1895. | *Studies of Childhood.* London: Longmans, Green & Co. |

Valentine, C. W.

1921.	*The New Psychology of the Unconscious.* Reprint. London: Christopher, 1932.
1942.	*The Psychology of Early Childhood.* London: Methuen.
n.d.	*Psychology and Its Bearing on Education.* Preface by author dated 1949. London: Methuen & Co., Ltd.

Watts, A. F.

| 1944. | *The Language and Mental Development of Children.* London: Harrap & Co., Ltd. |

Winnicott, D. W.

1944.	*Children's Communities.* Edited by Peggy Volkov. London: New Education Fellowship.
1958.	*Collected Papers: Through Paediatrics to Psychoanalysis.* London: Inst. of Psycho-Analysis and Hogarth Press.
1965.	*The Family and Individual Development.* London: Tavistock Publications.
1965.	*The Maturational Process and the Facilitating Environment.* No. 64 in *Studies in the Theory of Emotional Development.* London: Inst. of Psycho-Analysis and Hogarth Press.
1971.	*Playing and Reality.* London: Tavistock Publications.

4. Periodicals Consulted

The British Journal of Educational Psychology
The British Journal of Medical Psychology
Education
The Eugenics Review
The Forum of Education
The Harvard Educational Review
The History of Childhood Quarterly
Home and School
The International Journal of Psycho-Analysis
The Journal of Educational Psychology
The Journal of Experimental Pedagogy
Mind
The National Froebel Foundation Bulletin
The New Era
The Nursery World
Proceedings of the Aristotelian Society

5. Secondary Sources

The references in this section of the bibliography fall into two categories:
A. Works consulted that are directly related to this book;
B. American books that describe and provide bibliographies about the British informal schools, their teachers, and their work.

A.*

Ariès, Philippe.
1962.   *Centuries of Childhood.* New York: Knopf.
Armytage, W. H. G.
1964.   *Four Hundred Years of English Education.* Cambridge: At the University Press.
Block, N. J., and Dworkin, Gerald.
1976.   *The I.Q. Controversy.* New York: Pantheon Books.
Boyd, William, and Rawon, Wyatt.
1965.   *The Story of the New Education.* London: Heinemann.
Crichton-Miller, Hugh.
1921.   *The New Psychology & the Teacher.* London: Jarrolds.
Clarke, Sir Fred.
1948.   *Freedom in the Educative Society.* London: University of London Press.
DeMause, Lloyd.
1974.   *The History of Childhood.* New York: The Psychohistory Press.
Dennison, George.
1969.   *The Lives of Children.* New York: Random House.
Dochrell, W. B., and Hamilton, D., eds.
1960.   *Rethinking Educational Research.* London: Hudder & Stoughton.
Donaldson, Margaret.
1978.   *Children's Minds.* London: Croom Holm.
Dworkin, Martin, ed.
1959.   *John Dewey on Education.* New York: Teachers College Press.
Entwistle, Harold.
1976.   *Child-Centered Education.* London: Methuen.
Evans, Richard.
1973.   *Jean Piaget: The Man and His Ideas.* New York: E. P. Dutton.
Flügel, J. C.
1933.   *A Hundred Years of Psychology.* Reprint. London: Gerald Duckworth & Co., 1951.
Gardner, Dorothy E. M.
1969.   *Susan Isaacs: The First Biography.* London: Methuen Educational Ltd.
Gathorne-Hardy, Jonathan.
1972.   *The Rise and Fall of the British Nanny.* London: Hodder & Stoughton.
Gould, Stephen Jay.
1981.   *The Mismeasure of Man.* New York: W. W. Norton & Co.
Hearnshaw, L. S.

---

*See also references in Lydia A. H. Smith, *Activity and Experience,* cited in section 5.B.

1964. *A Short History of British Psychology. 1840–1940.* London: Methuen.
1979. *Cyril Burt, Psychologist.* Ithaca, New York: Cornell University Press.

Huizinga, Johan.
1950. *Homo Ludens: A Study of the Play Element in Culture.* Boston: Beacon Press.

Jackson, Philip.
1968. *Life in Classrooms.* New York: Holt, Rinehart & Winston.

Jones, Ernest.
1955. *The Life & Work of Sigmund Freud.* New York: Basic Books.

Kamin, Leon J.
1974. *The Science and Politics of I.Q.* New York: John Wiley & Sons.

Katz, Michael, ed.
1973. *Education in American History.* New York: Praeger Publishers.

Kempe, C. H., and Helfer, R. E., eds.
1980. *The Battered Child.* 3rd ed. Chicago: University of Chicago Press.

Kilpatrick, William Heard.
1915. *Montessori Examined.* London: Constable & Co.

Lampe, David.
1959. *Pyke, the Unknown Genius.* London: Evans Bros. Ltd.

Laslett, Peter.
1971. *The World We Have Lost.* London: Methuen.

Lawrence, Evelyn, ed.
1952. *Friedrich Froebel and English Education.* London: Routledge & Kegan Paul.

Lightfoot, Sarah Lawrence.
1978. *Worlds Apart: Relationships Between Families and Schools.* New York: Basic Books.

Low, Barbara.
1920. *Psychoanalysis: A Brief Outline of Freudian Theory.* London: Allen & Unwin.

Mowat, Charles Loch.
1955. *Britain Between the Wars, 1918–1940.* London: Methuen.

Murchison, Carl, ed.
1935. *A Handbook of Social Psychology.* Worcester, MA: Clark University Press.

Murphy, Gardner.
1968. *Psychological Thought from Pythagoras to Freud.* New York: Harcourt, Brace, & World, Inc.

Murphy, Gardner, and Kovach, Joseph.
1972. *Historical Introduction to Modern Psychology.* 3rd ed. New York: Harcourt, Brace, Jovanovich, Inc.

Murray, E. R.
1914. *Froebel as a Pioneer in Modern Psychology.* London: George Philip & Son, Ltd.

Pinchbeck, Ivy, and Hewitt, Margaret.

1973. *Children in English Society.* 2 vols. London: Routledge & Kegan Paul.

Selleck, R. J. W.
1972. *English Primary Education and the Progressives, 1914–1939.* London: Routledge & Kegan Paul.

Sheleff, Leon.
1981. *Generations Apart: Adult Hostility to Youth.* New York; McGraw-Hill.

Skidelsky, Robert.
1969. *English Progressive Schools.* Harmondsworth, Middlesex: Penguin Books, Ltd.

Spearman, Charles.
1937. *Psychology Down the Ages.* London: Macmillan.

Standing, E. M.
1962. *The Montessori Revolution in Education.* New York: Schocken.

Stewart, W. A. C.
1968. *The Educational Innovators.* 2 vols. London: Macmillan, St. Martin's Press.

Thomson, Robert.
1968. *The Pelican History of Psychology.* Harmondsworth, Middlesex: Penguin Books.

van der Eyken, Willem.
1973. *Education, the Child, and Society: A Documentary History 1900–1973.* Harmondsworth, Middlesex: Penguin Books.

van der Eyken, Willem, and Turner, Barry.
1969. *Adventures in Education.* London: Allen Lane, The Penguin Press.

Whitbread, Nanette.
1972. *The Evolution of the Nursery-Infant School.* London: Routledge & Kegan Paul.

B.

Although American interest in British child-centered, "open" classrooms has died down somewhat, they still remain one of the most interesting chapters in educational history. Susan Isaacs, of course, had much to do with them. The following works should be consulted by readers who wish to learn about them:

Barth, Roland S.
1972. *Open Education and the American School.* New York: Agathon Press.

Barth, Roland S., and Rathbone, Charles H.
1971. *A Bibliography of Open Education.* Cambridge, MA and Newton, MA, jointly published by the Advisory for Open Education and Educational Development Center, Inc.

Smith, Lydia A. H.
1976. *Activity and Experience: Sources of English Informal Education.* New York: Agathon Press.

Weber, Lillian.
1971. *The English Infant School and Informal Education.* Englewood Cliffs, N.J.: Prentice-Hall.

Index

Advice and information for parents and educators, (Part Two), 225–321
    active enquiry, 313–21
    attention span, 250–53
    bad temper, 229–31, 236–38, 245–50
    companions, need for, 238–39
    concentration, 250–53
    consistency, need for, 256–57
    eating, 248–50
    "facts of life", 241–45
    fears, 232–34
    freedom, 291–98
    group behavior, 276–87
    guilt and shame, 287–91
    humaneness, training in, 273–76
    independence, training for, 239–41
    kindness to animals, 273–76
    masturbation, 257–58
    "modern methods", 234–36
    needs, essential, 303–12
    nervous habits, 247–48, 248–50, 257–58
    nervousness, 231–32
    obedience, 226–28
    "original sin", 287–91
    punishment, 228–29, 236–38, 260–62, 266–70
    reading and writing, 252–55
    responsibility, training in, 225–26
    role of parents and nurses, 225–62
    role of teachers, 313–21
    safety, 298–303
    scientific interests, 271–73
    self-control, 258–60
    showing off, 238–39
    sleeping, 231–32
    toys, 252
    "trials of childhood", 263–66

Bennet, Victoria, 157
Bernstein, Basil, 218–19
Binet, Alfred, 39
Bridges, Katharine, 100–101

Bühler, Charlotte, 37, 101, 157
Burt, Cyril, 40–43, 58, 157, 197–203

Cambridge Evacuation Survey, The, 140–53
    characteristics of evacuated children, 150–51
    conduct of study, 140–52
    conclusions, 152–53
    problems in evacuation plan, 140–41
    purpose of, 141, 148
    wartime evacuation, 140–41
Childhood, studies of, 35–38
    Bühler, Charlotte, 37, 101, 157
    Gesell, Arnold, 38, 51
    Preyer, Wilhelm, 35
    Stern, William, 36
    Sully, James, 36
Child-rearing practices
    family bonding, 152–53, 219–20
    social class implications, 215–19
    theory of, 24–28, 214, 220–21
Children We Teach, The, 120–29
    characteristics of Primary School child, 121–29
    curriculum, Infants' School, 121–29
    curriculum, Primary School, 121–29
    differences among children, 122
    mental tests, use of, 122–23
    methods of teaching, 121–29
    teachers' responsibilities, 121–29

Darwin, Charles, 29, 35, 44
Department of Child Development, University of London, 130–34
    Nunn, Sir Percy, 54, 130
    program of study, 131–32
    records of, 132
    student accounts, 133
    teaching method, 133
Dewey, John, 32, 161–69

Educational Guidance of the School Child, The,

134–40
  origin of study, 134
  school records, 134–40
    purpose for, 135–37
    samples, 142–47
    use of, 137–40
Ellis, Havelock, 45

Flügel, J. C., 154–55
Freud, Anna, 190–97, 220
Freud, Sigmund, 44–48
Froebel, Friedrich, 49–51
Froebelians, 51–55

Galton, Francis, 30, 39
Gesell, Arnold, 38, 51

Hall, G. Stanley, 157

Intellectual Growth in Young Children, 76–86. *See also* Malting House School
  biological interests, 85
  children's thinking, 81ff.
  cognitive development, 81–82
  destructive impulses, 86
  fantasies, 83–85
    fantasy and thought, 84–85
  implications for educators, 108–13
  play, imaginative, 38ff.
  psychoanalytic interpretation, 102–8
IQ tests. *See* Testing, mental
Isaacs, Nathan
  active enquiry in children, 177, 313–21
  children's why questions, 83, 172–73
  language of children, 176, 180–82
  Malting House School, 62ff.
  marriage to Susan Isaacs, 20
  on Montessori, 208–9
  on Piaget, 174–77, 185–90
  work, 169–82
Isaacs, Susan
  biography, 17–23
  Department of Child Development, University of London, 21, 130
  Malting House School, 20, 62–113
  marriage to Nathan Isaacs, 20
  on Montessori, 207–9, 253–55
  on Piaget, 124, 185–90
  psychoanalyst, 21
  reviews of works, 154–61
    Creak, M., 158
    Flügel, J. C., 154–55
    Jones, Ernest, 157–59
    Low, Barbara, 160
    McCarthy, Dorothea, 159
    Sturt, Mary, 158
    Valentine, C. W., 155–57
    Willoughby, J., 157

James, William, 32
Jones, Ernest, 157, 159, 190–97

Klein, Melanie, 190–97

McDougall, William, 32
McMillan, Rachel and Margaret, 51
Malting House School, 62–113
  activities, 77ff.
  basic function, 67
  children who attended, 65
    IQ scores, 44, 65
  environment, 66
  equipment and materials, 64, 71
  evaluations of children, 72
  founding, 62
  freedom, 67–69, 71
  laboratory, as a, 74
  language, children's, 71
  mental testing, 44, 65
  method, 66
  observations, 74, 77–81, 86–87, 90–93, 95–99
  parents, 71–72
  Pyke, Geoffrey, 63
  records, 75–76
  response to school, 73–74
  rules and limitations, 68–69
  safety, 68
  school subjects, 65
  staff, 70
Montessori, Maria, 52, 203–9, 253–55

"New Education," The, 48–61
  Froebel, Friedrich, 49–51
  Froebelians, 51–55
  Governmental support, 56–59
    Hadow Committee, 57
    Handbooks for teachers, 56
    Plowden Report, 213
    Publications, 56–59
  McMillan, Rachel and Margaret, 51
  Montessori, Maria, 52, 203–9, 253–55
  New Education Fellowship, 54
  New Era, The, 54, 214
    progressive schools, list of, 63

Nunn, Sir Percy, 54, 130
  opposition to, 59–61
Nunn, Sir Percy, 54, 130
Nursery World, The, 114–20
  character formation, 120
  child's inner world, 115–17
  infantile sexuality, 116–20
  infant's mental life, 115–20
  play, 116–17
  "Some Don'ts for Parents", 120
  superego, formation of, 118

Piaget, Jean, 35, 38, 124, 174–77, 182–90
Preyer, Wilhelm, 35
Psychoanalysis, 44–48
  analysts with children, 108, 113
  Ellis, Havelock, 45
  Freud, Anna, 190, 220
    differences with Melanie Klein, 191–97
  Freud, Sigmund, 44–48
  infantile sexuality, 88–89, 95–98, 116–20
  infant's mental life, 115–20, 291–98, 314–17
  interpretation of Malting House School, 102–8
  Klein, Melanie, 190
    differences with Anna Freud, 191–97
Psychology, systems of, 29–35
  Behaviorists, 35
  Dewey, John, 32, 161–69
  evolutionary perspective, 29, 31, 44
  Galton, Francis, 30, 39
  Gestaltists, 34
  James, William, 32
  McDougall, William, 32
  Spearman, Charles, 33
  Spencer, Herbert, 29
  Stout, G. F., 32
  Sully, James, 32
  Watson, John, 35, 101
Pyke, Geoffrey, 63

Social Development in Young Children, 87–101. See also Malting House School
  friendliness and cooperation, 93–94
  guilt and shame, 98–99
  hostility and aggression, 88, 90–93
  implications for educators, 108–13
  infantile sexuality, 88–89, 95–98
  love and hate, 89–90
  psychoanalytic interpretation, 102–8
  sexual interests, 88–89
"Some Don'ts for Parents", 120
Spearman, Charles, 33
Spencer, Herbert, 29
Stern, William, 36
Stout, G. F., 32
Sully, James, 32, 36

Terman, Lewis, 43
Testing, mental, 38–44
  Binet, Alfred, 39
  Burt, Cyril, 40–43, 58, 157, 197–203
  Galton, Francis, 39
  IQ tests, 43
    at Malting House School, 44, 65
    in Primary Schools, 122–23
    social class implications, 203
    with young children, 136–37
  Terman, Lewis, 43
  U.S. Army tests, 43

Valentine, D. W., 155–57

Watson, John, 35, 101